Mathematics for GCSE

Hundreds of practice questions
and worked examples for GCSE Maths.

Foundation Level – the Basics

Contents

Number and Algebra

Geometry and Measures

Section 14 — Angles and Properties of 2D Shapes

Section 15 — Units, Measuring and Estimating

Section 16 — Speed, Distance and Time

Section 17 — Constructions

Section 18 — Bearings and Scale Drawings

Section 19 — Area and Perimeter

Section 20 — 3D Shapes

Section 21 — Transformations

Statistics and Probability

Section 22 — Collecting Data

Section 23 — Analysing Data

Section 24 — Probability

Throughout the book, the more challenging questions are marked like this: **1**

This symbol means there's a photocopiable answer template on the CD-ROM in the Answer Book:

Contributors:
Jane Appleton, Cath Brown, Katharine Brown, Pamela Chatley, Eva Cowlishaw, Alastair Duncombe,
Helen Greaves, Simon Greaves, Stephen Green, Philip Hale, Phil Harvey, Judy Hornigold, Claire Jackson,
Charlotte O'Brien, Rosemary Rogers, Manpreet Sambhi, Neil Saunders, Jonathan Stevens, Jan Walker,
Kieran Wardell, Jeanette Whiteman

Editors:
Chris Burton, Helena Hayes, Andy Park, David Ryan, Jonathan Wray

Proofreaders:
Sharon Keeley-Holden, Mark Moody, Sam Norman, Glenn Rogers

Published by CGP

ISBN: 978 1 84762 685 1

Groovy Website: www.cgpbooks.co.uk

Printed by Elanders Ltd, Newcastle upon Tyne.
Jolly bits of clipart from CorelDRAW®

Based on the classic CGP style created by Richard Parsons

Photocopying — it's dull, grey and sometimes a bit naughty. Luckily, it's dead cheap, easy and
quick to order more copies of this book from CGP — just call us on 0870 750 1242. Phew!

Section 1 — Non-Calculator Arithmetic

1.1 Negative Numbers — Adding and Subtracting

Negative numbers are numbers that are less than zero.
They're written with a minus sign in front of them.

You can count places on a number line to help with calculations involving negative numbers.

Example 1

Use the number line to work out: a) $1 - 5$ b) $-2 + 6$

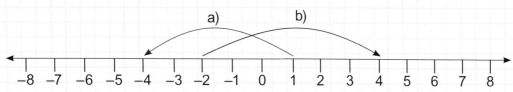

a) 1. Start at 1.

    2. Count 5 places down.

    3. You finish at −4, so $1 - 5 = -4$.

b) 1. Start at −2.

    2. Count 6 places up.

    3. You finish at 4, so $-2 + 6 = 4$.

Exercise 1

1 Use a number line to work out:

   a) $2 - 4$ **b)** $4 - 8$

   c) $3 - 9$ **d)** $0 - 7$

   e) $-1 - 4$ **f)** $-3 - 2$

2 Use a number line to work out:

   a) $-2 + 3$ **b)** $-8 + 10$

   c) $-7 + 13$ **d)** $-5 + 2$

   e) $-8 + 6$ **f)** $-7 + 7$

3 The thermometer on the right shows temperature.
Use it to find the temperature that is:

   a) 2 °C higher than −3 °C   **b)** 3 °C higher than −5 °C

   c) 6°C higher than −6 °C   **d)** 5 °C lower than 3 °C

   e) 3 °C lower than −1 °C   **f)** 4 °C lower than 0 °C.

°C
7
6
5
4
3
2
1
0
−1
−2
−3
−4
−5
−6

4 The temperature at midnight is −4 °C. At midday the temperature is 7 °C higher.

What is the temperature at midday?

5 At 6:00 pm the temperature is 6 °C. At 11:00 pm the temperature is 8 °C lower.

What is the temperature at 11:00 pm?

Rules for Adding and Subtracting Negative Numbers

Adding a negative number is the same as subtracting.

Subtracting a negative number is the same as adding.

Look at the signs next to each other in a calculation to work out what you need to do:

> + next to − means subtract
>
> − next to − means add

Example 2

Negative numbers in calculations are often written in brackets.

Work out:

a) 5 + (−3)

1. There's a + and a − sign next to each other.   5 + (−3)

2. So replace them with one − sign.   5 − 3

3. Work it out.   5 − 3 = 2

b) 3 − (−1)

1. There are two − signs next to each other.   3 − (−1)

2. So replace them with one + sign.   3 + 1

3. Work it out.   3 + 1 = 4

Exercise 2

1 Work these out without using a calculator:

a) 6 + (−3)   b) 5 + (−1)   c) 9 + (−6)

d) 13 + (−10)   e) 8 + (−8)   f) −5 + (−6)

g) −3 + (−7)   h) −6 + (−3)   i) −10 + (−5)

2   Work these out without using a calculator:

a) 4 – (–3)   b) 2 – (–5)   c) 2 – (–2)

d) 0 – (–8)   e) 4 – (–9)   f) –7 – (–2)

g) –5 – (–3)   h) –2 – (–5)   i) –6 – (–10)

3   Work out the following without using a calculator:

a) 1 + (–4)   b) 10 – (–11)   c) 13 + (–15)

d) –5 + (–5)   e) 14 + (–2)   f) 7 + (–10)

g) 12 + (–15)   h) –22 – (–9)   i) –2 + (–3)

j) 5 + (–8)   k) 12 – (–10)   l) –15 + (–3)

Example 3

What is the difference in temperature between 4 °C and –3 °C?

1. 'Difference' means you need to subtract, ⟶ 4 – (–3)
    so write the question out as a calculation.
    Put the biggest number first. ⟶ 4 + 3 = 7 °C

2. Then you can solve it like the ones in Exercise 2.

Exercise 3

1   What is the difference in temperature between –1 °C and 5 °C?

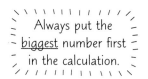

Always put the _biggest_ number first in the calculation.

2   What is the difference in temperature between –2 °C and –5 °C?

3   At 6:00 pm, Carly measures the temperature outside as 3 °C.
    At midnight, the temperature has dropped to –2 °C.

    What is the difference between the temperature at 6:00 pm and midnight?

4   The temperature inside a freezer is –20 °C.
    The temperature in the kitchen is 15 °C.

    What is the difference in temperature between the kitchen and the freezer?

5   A penguin jumps into the water from a rock 1 m above the sea surface.
It dives to 4 m below the sea surface.

How many metres has it moved down?

6   Frank goes shopping. Before he starts, his bank account
has £35 in it. When he has finished shopping,
his account is overdrawn by £17.

How much did Frank spend while shopping?

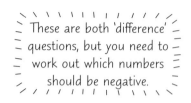

These are both 'difference' questions, but you need to work out which numbers should be negative.

1.2   Negative Numbers — Multiplying and Dividing

A multiplication or division with one positive and one negative number
will have a negative (–ve) answer.

If both numbers are negative, the answer will be positive (+ve).

+ and – means –ve answer

– and – means +ve answer

These rules only apply to multiplication and division questions.

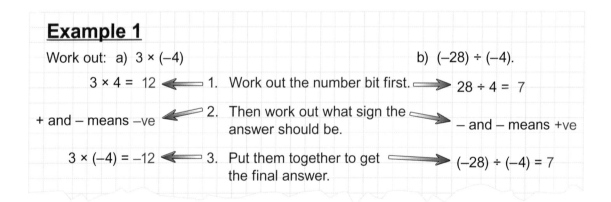

Example 1

Work out: a) 3 × (–4)   b) (–28) ÷ (–4).

3 × 4 = 12   ⟸   1. Work out the number bit first. ⟹   28 ÷ 4 = 7

+ and – means –ve   ⟸   2. Then work out what sign the ⟹   – and – means +ve
answer should be.

3 × (–4) = –12   ⟸   3. Put them together to get ⟹   (–28) ÷ (–4) = 7
the final answer.

Exercise 1

1   Work these out without using a calculator:

a) 2 × (–2)   **b)** 4 × (–5)

c) 3 × (–6)   **d)** 5 × (–8)

e) (–5) × 5   **f)** (–9) × 4

g) (–8) × 3   **h)** (–7) × 5

2 Work these out without using a calculator:

a) $10 \div (-2)$

b) $16 \div (-4)$

c) $15 \div (-5)$

d) $30 \div (-6)$

e) $(-12) \div 2$

f) $(-14) \div 7$

g) $(-22) \div 11$

h) $(-18) \div 3$

3 Work these out without using a calculator:

a) $(-2) \times (-7)$

b) $(-8) \times (-3)$

c) $(-10) \times (-4)$

d) $(-7) \times (-7)$

e) $(-4) \times (-3)$

f) $(-7) \times (-6)$

4 Work these out without using a calculator:

a) $(-20) \div (-4)$

b) $(-16) \div (-8)$

c) $(-27) \div (-3)$

d) $(-36) \div (-6)$

e) $(-24) \div (-6)$

f) $(-27) \div (-9)$

5 Work these out without using a calculator:

a) $9 \times (-2)$

b) $(-5) \times (-3)$

c) $(-4) \times 10$

d) $6 \times (-4)$

e) $(-3) \times (-8)$

f) $(-45) \div (-9)$

g) $(-24) \div 8$

h) $8 \div (-4)$

i) $16 \div (-8)$

j) $(-45) \div 5$

k) $28 \div (-7)$

l) $(-5) \times 10$

m) $(-6) \times (-6)$

n) $(-10) \times 7$

o) $36 \div (-4)$

p) $10 \times (-3)$

q) $8 \times (-4)$

r) $(-32) \div (-8)$

1.3 Ordering Numbers and Place Value

You can split numbers up into columns.

The digit in each column tells you how many of each thing you've got:

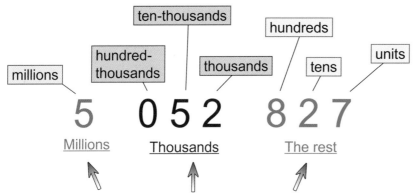

Big numbers are written with their digits in groups of three, where each group shows millions, thousands, etc.

Example 1

Write down the value of each digit in 5 052 827.

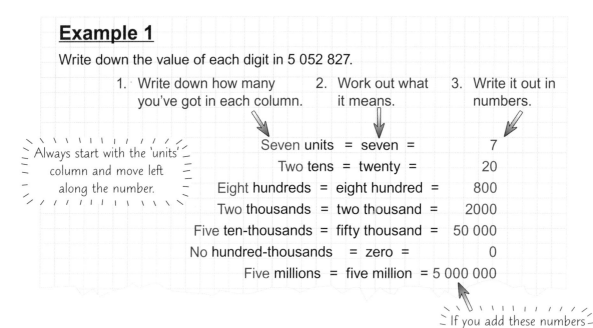

Exercise 1

1   Write down the value of each digit in the following numbers:

    a) 325   **b)** 6022

    c) 46 570   **d)** 429 315

    e) 1 483 215

2 Write down the value of the <u>highlighted</u> digit in the following numbers:

a) 52 43<u>1</u>

b) <u>2</u> 534 899

c) 2<u>9</u>4

d) 6<u>2</u>31

e) 8<u>1</u>6 204

f) <u>5</u>19

g) 2 <u>5</u>51 873

h) 40<u>9</u>6

i) 51 <u>2</u>07

j) 6 00<u>4</u> 439

k) 6<u>3</u> 001

l) 7<u>8</u>00

m) 255 <u>6</u>50

n) 9 1<u>0</u>5 873

o) <u>3</u>00 056

Example 2

Write the number 1281739 in words.

1. First, split the number up into groups of three:

   Start on the right-hand side of the number and move left, putting a space every three numbers. → 1 281 739

2. Then read each group from left to right. → 1 million, 281 thousand, 739

3. Write it fully in words. → One million, two hundred and eighty-one thousand, seven hundred and thirty-nine.

Exercise 2

1 Write each of these numbers in words:

a) 235868

b) 862143

c) 1389

d) 62178

e) 9314577

f) 510489

g) 25304

h) 60025

i) 1068090

2 Write each of these as numbers:

a) One thousand, four hundred and fifty-one.

b) Sixty-six thousand, one hundred and seventeen.

c) Nine hundred and eight thousand, two hundred and fifteen.

d) Seven million, three hundred and forty-seven thousand, seven hundred and eighty-two.

Putting Numbers in Order

Example 3

Put these numbers in order, from smallest to biggest:

87   467   512   32   1256   1304   372   6

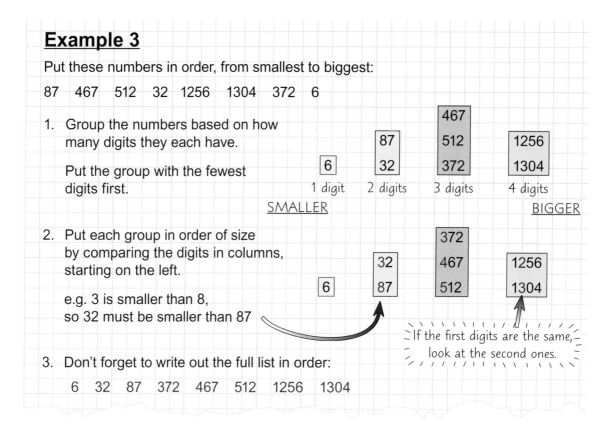

1. Group the numbers based on how many digits they each have.

    Put the group with the fewest digits first.

2. Put each group in order of size by comparing the digits in columns, starting on the left.

    e.g. 3 is smaller than 8, so 32 must be smaller than 87

3. Don't forget to write out the full list in order:

    6   32   87   372   467   512   1256   1304

Exercise 3

1   Put each set of numbers in order, from smallest to biggest.

a) 53, 27, 108, 387, 6591, 2672

b) 8, 7, 98, 35, 647, 132

c) 51, 207, 67, 344, 8641, 1247

d) 63, 32, 769, 821, 674, 6128

e) 6, 4, 69, 24, 62, 559, 471, 547

f) 846, 721, 796, 2197, 1076, 1145

g) 54, 45, 55, 540, 504, 505, 450

h) 320, 230, 323, 3200, 2300, 2030

2   Put each of the following sets of numbers in order, from smallest to biggest.

a) 21, 978, 215, 54, 640, 11

b) 890, 2154, 3961, 564, 642, 1009

c) 394, 8, 7506, 225, 6645, 2, 639

d) 9, 1150, 19, 31, 7422, 32, 6128

e) 12, 564, 9, 5698, 4127, 251, 76, 3

f) 319, 8361, 4, 871, 3649, 62, 7, 54

g) 584, 531, 8534, 95, 42, 580, 3567, 49

h) 5621, 84, 3647, 5608, 630, 81, 542

3 Put these numbers in order, from smallest to biggest:

86, 6, 6086, 8, 8608, 686, 6860, 806

1.4 Whole Number Arithmetic — Addition and Subtraction

Addition

> Stick a line underneath to keep the answer separate.

Example 1

Work out 387 + 675.

1. Write one number above the other, making sure the units columns line up.

```
  3 8 7
+ 6 7 5
```

2. Add up the units column first: 7 + 5 = 12

   Write the '2' at the bottom of the units column and carry the '1' over to the next column.

```
  3 8 7
+ 6 7 5
    ₁2
```

3. Now add up the tens column, including the carried over '1' : 8 + 7 + 1 = 16

```
  3 8 7
+ 6 7 5
  ₁6₁2
```

4. Do the same with the hundreds column: 3 + 6 + 1 = 10

```
  3 8 7
+ 6 7 5
1 0₁6₁2
```

   Read off the final answer: 387 + 675 = 1062

Example 2

Work out 1345 + 178.

1. Again, make sure the units columns line up.

```
  1 3 4 5
+   1 7 8
  5₁2₁3
```

2. Work it out just like in Example 1, adding up the columns from right to left.

3. When you get to the last column, there's no adding to do — so write the number straight into the answer.

```
  1 3 4 5
+   1 7 8
1 5₁2₁3
```

Exercise 1

1 Work out the following without using your calculator.

    a)   38
        + 59

    b)   27
        + 44

    c)   46
        + 57

    d) 164
        + 29

    e) 215
        + 84

    f)   748
        + 179

    g)   915
        + 245

    h) 1195
        + 641

    i)   2095
        + 3546

2 Work out the following without using your calculator.

    a) 68 + 27

    b) 88 + 43

    c) 345 + 218

    d) 178 + 356

    e) 378 + 85

    f) 77 + 256

    g) 1708 + 2913

    h) 6892 + 2619

    i) 768 + 2306

    j) 1886 + 754

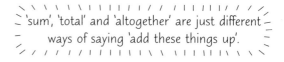

Write the sums in columns first.

3 Find the total of 128 and 343.

'sum', 'total' and 'altogether' are just different ways of saying 'add these things up'.

4 What is the sum of 589 and 1088?

5 There are 219 people on a train.
At the next station, 87 people get on the train.

How many people are now on the train in total?

6 Jessica buys a computer costing £569 and a printer costing £146.

How much has she spent altogether?

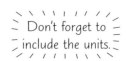

Don't forget to include the units.

7 Kyle drives 284 miles from London to Newcastle,
then he drives 119 miles to Edinburgh.

What is the total distance he has driven?

8 Find the total of 456, 170 and 37.

9 Rachael is clothes shopping. She buys the things shown below.

How much has she spent altogether?

£195 £327 £68

Subtraction

Example 3

Work out 354 − 172.

1. Write the first number above the second with the units columns lined up.

$$\begin{array}{r} 3\,5\,4 \\ -\,1\,7\,2 \\ \hline \end{array}$$

2. Starting with the units column, take the bottom number away from the top number: 4 − 2 = 2

$$\begin{array}{r} 3\,5\,4 \\ -\,1\,7\,2 \\ \hline 2 \end{array}$$

3. The top number in the next column is smaller than the bottom number, so 'borrow ten' from the next column along.

This makes the '5' in the tens column into a '15' and changes the '3' in the hundreds column to a '2'.

$$\begin{array}{r} {}^{2}\cancel{3}\,{}^{1}5\,4 \\ -\,1\,7\,2 \\ \hline 8\,2 \end{array}$$

4. Now do the subtraction in the tens column: 15 − 7 = 8

5. Finally, do the subtraction in the last column, using the '2' as the top number: 2 − 1 = 1

$$\begin{array}{r} {}^{2}\cancel{3}\,{}^{1}5\,4 \\ -\,1\,7\,2 \\ \hline 1\,8\,2 \end{array}$$

Exercise 2

1 Work out the following without using your calculator.

a)
$$\begin{array}{r} 79 \\ -\,36 \\ \hline \end{array}$$

b)
$$\begin{array}{r} 97 \\ -\,48 \\ \hline \end{array}$$

c)
$$\begin{array}{r} 66 \\ -\,27 \\ \hline \end{array}$$

d)
$$\begin{array}{r} 184 \\ -\,58 \\ \hline \end{array}$$

e)
$$\begin{array}{r} 295 \\ -\,76 \\ \hline \end{array}$$

f)
$$\begin{array}{r} 348 \\ -\,173 \\ \hline \end{array}$$

g)
$$\begin{array}{r} 932 \\ -\,217 \\ \hline \end{array}$$

h)
$$\begin{array}{r} 835 \\ -\,647 \\ \hline \end{array}$$

i)
$$\begin{array}{r} 1848 \\ -\,571 \\ \hline \end{array}$$

2 Work out the following without using your calculator.

a) 98 – 28   **b)** 64 – 36

c) 186 – 57   **d)** 125 – 87

e) 347 – 219   **f)** 458 – 272

g) 556 – 188   **h)** 515 – 246

i) 1347 – 809   **j)** 2382 – 754

k) 3547 – 1062   **l)** 2027 – 1618

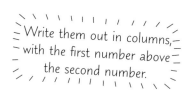
Write them out in columns, with the first number above the second number.

3 Find the difference between 149 and 228.

4 What is 78 less than 241?

5 A bakery bakes 768 loaves of bread one morning. It sells 589 of the loaves.

How many loaves are left?

6 Liam is driving 443 miles from Exeter to Glasgow. At lunchtime, he has driven 259 miles.

How much further does he have to drive?

7 The number of people watching a play was 1163 on Friday night but only 826 came on Thursday night.

How many more people watched the play on Friday?

8 Adel is looking at a mobile phone on the internet.

He sees it for sale on one website with two different prices advertised, as shown on the right.

What is the difference between the online price and the instore price?

Mega-Phone 8000

Features include:
- time travel
- eternal youth
- mysteries of the universe

Instore price: £325
Online price: £279

9   2547 people watched a football match. 359 people left before the final whistle.

How many people were there at the end of the match?

10   In a crowd of 5755 people, 2867 are women.
How many men are in the crowd?

1.5   Whole Number Arithmetic — Multiplication and Division

Multiplication by 10, 100, 1000...

When a number is multiplied by 10, 100, 1000 etc., each digit in the number moves to the left:

× 10   each digit moves one place to the left.

× 100   each digit moves two places to the left.

× 1000   each digit moves three places to the left.

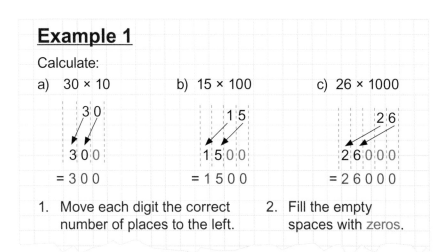

Example 1
Calculate:

a)   30 × 10   b) 15 × 100   c) 26 × 1000

1. Move each digit the correct number of places to the left.

2. Fill the empty spaces with zeros.

Exercise 1

Answer the following questions **without** using your calculator.

1   Work out:

a) 3 × 10   b) 5 × 10   c) 20 × 10

d) 35 × 10   e) 60 × 10   f) 8 × 100

g) 12 × 100   h) 30 × 100   i) 60 × 100

j) 72 × 100   k) 4 × 1000   l) 20 × 1000

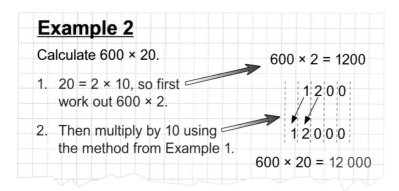

Example 2

Calculate 600 × 20.

1. 20 = 2 × 10, so first work out 600 × 2.

2. Then multiply by 10 using the method from Example 1.

600 × 2 = 1200

1 2 0 0

1 2 0 0 0

600 × 20 = 12 000

2 Work out:

a) 5 × 30   b) 12 × 20   c) 30 × 20

d) 50 × 60   e) 70 × 80   f) 500 × 30

g) 40 × 600   h) 70 × 200   i) 300 × 40

More Multiplication

Use the grid method for multiplying big numbers together.

Example 3

Work out 572 × 43

1. First, split each number up into units, tens, hundreds, etc.

    572 = 500 + 70 + 2

    43 = 40 + 3

2. Then put these 'bits' of numbers around the outside of a grid.

3. Multiply together the bits on the edge of each box.

4. Add up all the results inside the boxes.

5. The answer is your final total:

    572 × 43 = 24 596

	500	70	2
40	500 × 40 = 20 000	70 × 40 = 2800	2 × 40 = 80
3	500 × 3 = 1500	70 × 3 = 210	2 × 3 = 6

```
    2 0 0 0 0
      2 8 0 0
      1 5 0 0
        2 1 0
          8 0
+          6
  ─────────────
    2 4,5 9 6
```

It looks like you've got to add loads of things together, but lots of these digits are zero.

Exercise 2

1 Copy and complete the grid to work out 64 × 5.

	60	4
5	60 × 5 = ...	4 × 5 = ...

2 Copy and complete the grid to work out 83 × 4.

	80	3
4	80 × ...... = ...	3 × ...... = ...

3 Copy and complete the grid to work out 76 × 13.

	70	......
10	70 × 10 = ...	6 × 10 = ...
......	...... × 3 = ...	6 × ...... = ...

4 Use the grid method to work out each of the following:

    a) 58 × 4   **b)** 72 × 3   **c)** 84 × 5

    d) 69 × 4   **e)** 41 × 6   **f)** 34 × 7

    g) 82 × 8   **h)** 59 × 9

5 Use the grid method to work out each of the following:

    a) 15 × 13   **b)** 19 × 16   **c)** 31 × 17

    d) 53 × 41   **e)** 34 × 22   **f)** 49 × 23

    g) 86 × 24   **h)** 91 × 25

6 Copy and complete the grid to work out 226 × 7.

	......	20	6
7	...... × 7 = 1400	20 × 7 = ...	6 × 7 = 42

7 Copy and complete the grid below to work out 465 × 23.

	400	......	5
......	400 × ...... = ...	...... × ...... = ...	5 × 20 = 100
3	400 × 3 = ...	...... × 3 = ...	5 × 3 = ...

8 Use the grid method to work out each of the following:

a) 121 × 3   **b)** 142 × 4   **c)** 162 × 5

d) 224 × 3   **e)** 316 × 5   **f)** 408 × 4

9 Use the grid method to work out each of the following:

a) 180 × 12   **b)** 256 × 27   **c)** 235 × 19

d) 334 × 48   **e)** 567 × 69   **f)** 224 × 83

Answer the following questions without using your calculator:

10 What number is 5 times 82?

11 A computer game costs £42.
How much do four computer games cost?

12 Eggs are packed in boxes of 6.
How many eggs are there in 78 boxes?

13 7 coaches of chess fans travel to a match.
Each coach carries 57 people.
How many fans are on the coaches in total?

14 Multiply 52 by 39.

15 Zak earns £68 a day.
How much does he earn in 12 days?

16 What is the answer when 6 is multiplied by 212?

17 Find the product of 346 and 5.

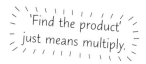

'Find the product' just means multiply.

18 A tin of beans weighs 437 grams.
What is the weight of 12 tins of beans?

19 Use the grid method to work out 1240 × 3.

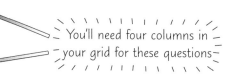

You'll need four columns in your grid for these questions

20 Jordan earns £2312 a month.
How much does he earn in 4 months?

Division

Use short division to divide a big number by a smaller number.

Example 4

Work out 624 ÷ 8

1. Set out the division with the first number inside
   a 'box' and the second number outside.

   $8\overline{)624}$

2. Start by working out how many times the number outside
   the box (8) will go into the first number in the box (6).

   $\begin{array}{r} 0 \\ 8\overline{)624} \end{array}$

   The answer is 0, because 8 is bigger than 6.
   So write a 0 above the box, over the 6.

3. 8 didn't go into 6, so now look at the first <u>two</u> numbers
   in the box and work out how many times 8 will go into 62.

   $\begin{array}{r} 07 \\ 8\overline{)6\,2^64} \end{array}$

   The answer is 7 times (7 × 8 = 56) with 6 (62 – 56) left over.
   Write a 7 above the box and carry the 6 over to the next column.

4. Look at the last number, including the 6 carried over:
   8 goes into 64 8 times. So write an 8 above the box.

   $\begin{array}{r} 078 \\ 8\overline{)6\,2^64} \end{array}$

5. The number on top of the box is the answer to the division: 624 ÷ 8 = 78.

Example 5

Work out 2750 ÷ 11

1. 11 is bigger than 2 so work out how many times 11 goes into 27.

   The answer is 2 with 27 − 22 = 5 left over.
   So write a 2 above the box, and carry 5 to the next number.

$$\begin{array}{r} 0\,2 \\ 11\,\overline{)\,2\,7^5 5\,0} \end{array}$$

2. 11 goes into 55 exactly 5 times, with nothing left over. ⟹

$$\begin{array}{r} 0\,2\,5 \\ 11\,\overline{)\,2\,7^5 5\,0} \end{array}$$

3. 11 doesn't go into 0.
   So write a 0 above the box. ⟹

$$\begin{array}{r} 0\,2\,5\,0 \\ 11\,\overline{)\,2\,7^5 5\,0} \end{array}$$

4. Read off your final answer from above the box: 2750 ÷ 11 = 250

Exercise 3

1 Use the short division method to work out the following:

a) $4\,\overline{)\,64}$

b) $6\,\overline{)\,84}$

c) $5\,\overline{)\,95}$

d) $4\,\overline{)\,112}$

e) $3\,\overline{)\,105}$

f) $5\,\overline{)\,125}$

2 Use the short division method to work out the following:

a) 48 ÷ 3

b) 56 ÷ 4

c) 72 ÷ 3

d) 96 ÷ 8

e) 84 ÷ 7

f) 96 ÷ 6

g) 92 ÷ 4

h) 80 ÷ 5

i) 162 ÷ 6

j) 156 ÷ 4

k) 147 ÷ 7

l) 136 ÷ 8

m) 135 ÷ 9

n) 234 ÷ 3

o) 224 ÷ 4

3 Use the short division method to work out the following:

a) 165 ÷ 15

b) 276 ÷ 12

c) 363 ÷ 11

d) 492 ÷ 12

Try writing out the times table of the smaller number first to help.

4 Use the short division method to work out the following:

a) 1044 ÷ 4

b) 1110 ÷ 5

c) 1341 ÷ 3

d) 1068 ÷ 6

e) 2104 ÷ 4

f) 2534 ÷ 7

g) 2760 ÷ 12

h) 1905 ÷ 15

Do questions **5–13** without using your calculator.

5 Divide 87 by 3

6 How many sixes are there in 84?

7 72 students are divided into 4 teams.
How many students are in each team?

8 £85 is shared equally amongst 5 people.
How much does each person get?

9 How many sevens are there in 161?

10 A shopkeeper divides 175 apples into bags of 5.
How many bags are filled with apples?

11 Kerry has 128 photographs to stick into an album.
Each page holds 8 photographs.

How many pages will she need to display all of the photographs?

12 A set of four tyres for a sports car costs £316. How much does it cost for one tyre?

13 A group of six friends is going on holiday.
The total cost of the holiday is £1524.

How much does it cost each person if they split the cost equally?

1.6 Order of Operations — BODMAS

Operations in a calculation are things like addition, subtraction, multiplication and division.

The order you do these things in is really important.

BODMAS tells you the order you should do things in a calculation:

BRACKETS ← Work out things in brackets first.

OTHER ← Then do other things like squaring and powers.

DIVISION ← Divide/Multiply groups of numbers
MULTIPLICATION working from left to right.

You'll come across these later.

ADDITION ← Add/Subtract groups of numbers
SUBTRACTION working from left to right.

Example 1

Calculate: $10 - 2 + 3 \times 4$

1. The calculation involves subtraction, addition and multiplication.

2. Use BODMAS to see that the multiplication ────────→ $10 - 2 + 3 \times 4$
   needs to be done first: $3 \times 4 = 12$

3. Working from left to right, the subtraction needs ────────→ $10 - 2 + 12$
   to be done before the addition: $10 - 2 = 8$

4. Finally, do the addition. $8 + 12 = 20$

Exercise 1

1   Calculate:

a) $4 + 2 \times 5$

b) $5 \times 3 + 2$

c) $7 \times 2 + 3$

d) $6 + 4 \times 4$

e) $10 - 3 \times 3$

f) $4 \times 4 - 2$

g) $6 \times 3 - 1$

h) $9 - 2 \times 2$

i) $8 + 4 \div 2$

j) $10 \div 2 + 3$

k) $7 + 6 \div 3$

l) $12 \div 4 + 8$

m) $9 + 5 - 4$

n) $10 \div 5 \times 3$

o) $10 - 7 + 9$

2 Calculate:

a) $3 \times 2 + 4 \times 1$

b) $5 \times 3 + 2 \times 6$

c) $6 \div 2 + 3 \times 6$

d) $8 \times 2 - 9 \div 3$

e) $5 \times 3 - 15 \div 5$

f) $8 + 5 \times 2 - 7$

g) $5 + 10 \div 2 + 3$

h) $10 - 4 \times 2 - 1$

i) $8 + 10 - 3 \times 5$

j) $9 - 3 + 10 \div 2$

k) $4 \times 2 - 20 \div 2$

l) $100 \div 5 - 9 \times 7$

Example 2

Calculate $48 \div (14 - 2)$

1. Use BODMAS to see that you need to work out the bit in the brackets first: $14 - 2 = 12$

$48 \div (14 - 2)$

2. Now do the division:

$48 \div 12 = 4$

Example 3

Add brackets to the following calculation to make it correct: $8 - 3 \times 2 = 10$

1. There are two possibilities for where the brackets can go:

$8 - (3 \times 2)$ or $(8 - 3) \times 2$

2. Work each possibility out using BODMAS to see which is equal to 10.

$8 - (3 \times 2) = 8 - 6 = 2$ ✗

$(8 - 3) \times 2 = 5 \times 2 = 10$ ✓

3. So the answer must be $(8 - 3) \times 2 = 10$.

Exercise 2

1 Calculate:

a) $(4 + 2) \times 3$

b) $(8 - 5) \times 2$

c) $5 \times (5 + 1)$

d) $7 \times (9 - 4)$

e) $(4 + 8) \div 6$

f) $(15 - 5) \div 5$

g) $(17 - 8) \div 3$

h) $(15 + 6) \div 7$

i) $20 \div (8 + 2)$

j) $36 \div (9 - 3)$

k) $(5 + 3) - (1 + 4)$

l) $(2 + 3) - (4 - 2)$

m) $(2 + 1) \times (5 - 3)$

n) $(8 - 5) \times (6 - 2)$

o) $(5 + 7) \div (3 \times 2)$

2 Copy each of these calculations and add brackets to make them correct:

a) 4 + 3 × 5 = 35

b) 5 + 2 × 4 = 28

c) 10 − 3 × 2 = 14

d) 8 × 5 − 2 = 24

e) 6 + 8 ÷ 2 = 7

f) 9 − 6 ÷ 3 = 1

g) 16 ÷ 4 − 2 = 8

h) 10 − 2 + 3 = 5

i) 12 − 6 + 4 = 2

j) 30 − 10 − 6 = 26

k) 24 − 13 − 8 = 19

3 Calculate:

a) 15 − 5 × 2

b) 9 + 12 ÷ 3

c) 22 − 40 ÷ 8

d) (6 + 7) × 2

e) (35 − 11) ÷ 6

f) 5 × 6 + 3 × 2

g) (8 + 3) − (5 + 4)

h) 15 − 8 + 21 ÷ 7

i) 20 ÷ 2 × (5 − 3)

1.7 Ordering Decimals

Decimal numbers can be split up into columns just like whole numbers.
The columns after the decimal point are called decimal places.

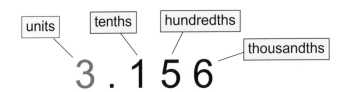

$$3 \, . \, 1 \, 5 \, 6$$

Example 1

Write down the value of
each digit in 3.156 as:

a) words

b) a number

Three units = 3.000

One tenth = 0.100

Five hundredths = 0.050

Six thousandths = 0.006

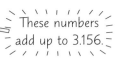

These numbers add up to 3.156.

Exercise 1

1 For each of the following decimal numbers, write down in **words** the value of the digit in:

(i) the tenths column

(ii) the hundredths column

a) 3.43

b) 0.14

c) 6.42

d) 4.26

e) 10.87

f) 0.74

2 Write down the value of each digit in the following decimal numbers as:

(i) words   (ii) a number

a) 1.8   b) 9.34   c) 3.208

3 Write down the value of the <u>highlighted</u> digit in the following decimal numbers, as a **number**.

a) 0.0<u>7</u>   b) 0.<u>7</u>9

c) 14.16<u>9</u>   d) 0.2<u>9</u>3

e) 22.<u>9</u>52   f) 0.0<u>9</u>7

Example 2

Put the following numbers in order, from smallest to biggest:

0.05   3.5   0.5   5   0.0035   0.045   0.55   0.0034

1. 3.5 and 5 both have a whole number part, so these must be bigger than the rest.

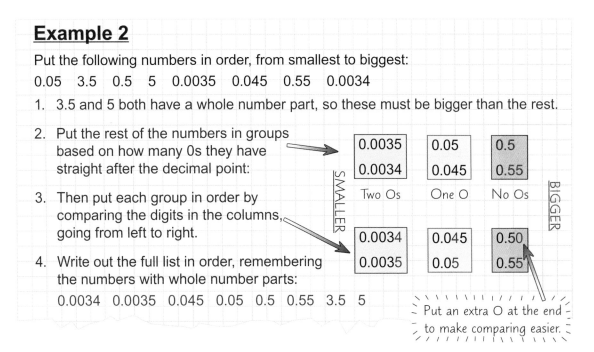

2. Put the rest of the numbers in groups based on how many 0s they have straight after the decimal point:

3. Then put each group in order by comparing the digits in the columns, going from left to right.

4. Write out the full list in order, remembering the numbers with whole number parts:

0.0034 0.0035 0.045 0.05 0.5 0.55 3.5 5

Put an extra O at the end to make comparing easier.

Exercise 2

1 Put each of the following sets of numbers in order, from smallest to biggest.

a) 0.45, 0.04, 0.07   b) 0.39, 0.69, 0.063

c) 0.023, 0.001, 0.032   d) 0.123, 2.31, 0.021

e) 0.9 0.09 0.89 0.08   f) 8.8, 0.98, 0.99, 0.087

g) 0.033, 0.0038, 0.31, 0.037   h) 0.069, 0.067, 0.73, 0.7

i) 0.788, 0.869, 0.659, 0.576   j) 0.233, 0.322, 0.202, 0.302

k) 1.09, 1.98, 0.84, 0.75   l) 2.87, 2.67, 2.74, 2.73

m) 1.3, 1.23, 1.2, 1.35   n) 8.37, 8.3, 8.6, 8.03

1.8   Multiplying and Dividing Decimals by 10, 100, 1000

Multiplication

Just like with whole numbers, when you're multiplying a decimal number by 10, 100, 1000, etc., you move each digit to the left:

× 10   each digit moves one place to the left.

× 100   each digit moves two places to the left.

× 1000   each digit moves three places to the left.

Example 1

Calculate:

a)   3.56 × 10   b) 0.125 × 100   c) 4.2 × 1000

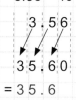

= 3 5 . 6

= 1 2 . 5

= 4 2 0 0

1. Keep the decimal point fixed and move each digit the correct number of places to the left.

2. Fill all the empty spaces with zeros. Sometimes you can get rid of them — i.e. 012.500 = 12.5.

3. But if they're between the decimal point and other digits, then you can't get rid of them.

Exercise 1

1   Work out the following without using your calculator:

    a) 4.25 × 10   **b)** 7.51 × 10   **c)** 8.64 × 10

    d) 12.68 × 10   **e)** 0.42 × 10   **f)** 26.23 × 10

    g) 133.55 × 10   **h)** 1.256 × 10   **i)** 3.889 × 10

    j) 13.4 × 10   **k)** 42.6 × 10   **l)** 0.65 × 10

2   Work out the following without using your calculator:

    a) 4.245 × 100   **b)** 6.381 × 100   **c)** 12.059 × 100

    d) 4.67× 100   **e)** 0.32 × 100   **f)** 9.08 × 100

    g) 1.2 × 100   **h)** 3.5 × 100   **i)** 56.3 × 100

    j) 0.7 × 100   **k)** 3.581 × 100

3 Work out the following without using your calculator:

a) 9.438 × 1000

b) 1.045 × 1000

c) 0.254 × 1000

d) 1.23 × 1000

e) 0.55 × 1000

f) 8.9 × 1000

Division

When a number is divided by 10, 100, 1000, etc., each digit in the number moves to the right:

÷ 10   each digit moves one place to the right.

÷ 100   each digit moves two places to the right.

÷ 1000   each digit moves three places to the right.

Example 2

Calculate: a) 156.2 ÷ 10   b) 13.7 ÷ 100   c) 0.8 ÷ 1000

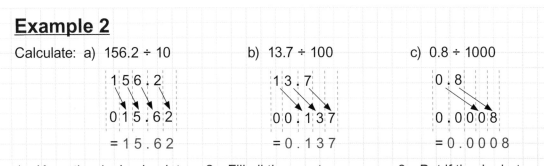

a) = 15.62   b) = 0.137   c) = 0.0008

1. Keep the decimal point fixed and move each digit the correct number of places to the right.

2. Fill all the empty spaces with zeros. Sometimes you can get rid of a few — i.e. 00.137 = 0.137

3. But if they're between the decimal point and other digits, then you can't get rid of them — i.e. 0.0008 ≠ 0.8

Exercise 2

1 Work these out without using your calculator.

a) 34.2 ÷ 10

b) 68.8 ÷ 10

c) 108.6 ÷ 10

d) 655.4 ÷ 10

e) 43.38 ÷ 10

f) 0.21 ÷ 10

g) 126.4 ÷ 10

h) 0.298 ÷ 10

i) 1.2 ÷ 10

2 Work these out without using your calculator.

a) 415.8 ÷ 100

b) 654.3 ÷ 100

c) 105.3 ÷ 100

d) 4589.1 ÷ 100

e) 57.2 ÷ 100

f) 10.9 ÷ 100

g) 0.433 ÷ 100

h) 1.45 ÷ 100

i) 0.7 ÷ 100

3 Work these out without using your calculator.

a) 4258.1 ÷ 1000   b) 1225.9 ÷ 1000   c) 5688.2 ÷ 1000

d) 458.3 ÷ 1000   e) 789.9 ÷ 1000   f) 99.5 ÷ 1000

g) 0.85 ÷ 1000   h) 4.2 ÷ 1000   i) 2.3 ÷ 1000

4 Work these out without using your calculator.

a) 93.4 ÷ 10   b) 56.3 ÷ 100

c) 2.356 × 1000   d) 5.127 × 100

e) 5.5 ÷ 10   f) 6.01 × 10

g) 0.4 ÷ 1000   h) 25.7 × 1000

i) 45.9 × 1000   j) 0.3 ÷ 10

k) 0.04 ÷ 100   l) 0.06 × 1000

1.9   Decimal Arithmetic

Addition

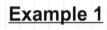

Example 1

Calculate 0.572 + 8.48

> *Write a O here so both numbers have the same number of decimal places — it makes them much easier to add together.*

1. First write one number above the other, making sure the decimal points line up.

```
  0.572
+ 8.480
```

2. Then add up each column moving from right to left, just like when adding whole numbers:

3. Remember to carry numbers to the next column when the answer has two digits.

```
  0.572
+ 8.480
───────
  9.052
```

4. Read off the final answer: 0.572 + 8.48 = 9.052

> *The decimal point in the answer __must__ line up with the others.*

Exercise 1

1 Work out the following without using your calculator.

    a)   0.25   **b)**   1.64   **c)**   4.57
        + 0.37   + 2.38   + 3.06

    d)   17.88   **e)**   0.8   **f)**   3.45
        + 13.72   + 0.25   + 5.8

    g)   19.3   **h)** 23.95
        + 13.72   + 47.6

2 Work out the following without using your calculator.

    a) 0.66 + 0.18   **b)** 3.67 + 5.16   **c)** 13.06 + 22.25

    d) 78.54 + 23.91   **e)** 0.29 + 0.9   **f)** 1.66 + 2.5

    g) 22.4 + 7.68   **h)** 15.54 + 31.7   **i)** 7.8 + 15.94

    j) 0.69 + 12.6   **k)** 13.74 + 1.063   **l)** 2.82 + 1.145

3 Find the total of £3.78 and £2.64.

4 Robbie buys a calculator for £7.95 and a sports bag for £19.29.

    How much does he spend altogether?

5 A cup costs £4.55 and a saucer costs £2.89.

    What is the cost of a cup and a saucer?

6 A long jumper jumps a distance of 7.65 m on his first jump.
He jumps 0.72 m further on his second jump.

    How long was his second jump?

7 Find the total of 45.5 km and 13.26 km.

8 A cafe sells sandwiches and hot drinks. Their menu is shown below:

Sandwiches		Hot drinks	
Egg	£1.89	Tea	£0.87
Chicken	£2.25	Coffee	£1.15
Bacon	£3.54		

a) What is the cost of a chicken sandwich and a cup of coffee?

b) Ben buys a bacon sandwich and a cup of tea.
What is the total cost?

c) How much does it cost to buy an egg sandwich and a chicken sandwich?

d) Hattie buys a cup of coffee, a cup of tea and a bacon sandwich.
How much does this cost altogether?

Subtraction

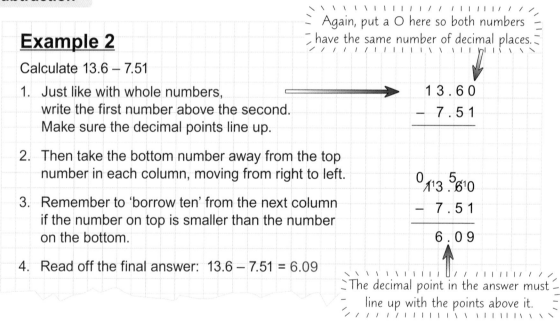

Example 2

Calculate 13.6 − 7.51

1. Just like with whole numbers,
write the first number above the second.
Make sure the decimal points line up.

Again, put a O here so both numbers have the same number of decimal places.

```
  1 3 . 6 0
−    7 . 5 1
```

2. Then take the bottom number away from the top
number in each column, moving from right to left.

3. Remember to 'borrow ten' from the next column
if the number on top is smaller than the number
on the bottom.

```
  0  5
 ₁13 .₆10
−   7 . 5 1
───────────
    6 . 0 9
```

4. Read off the final answer: 13.6 − 7.51 = 6.09

The decimal point in the answer must line up with the points above it.

Exercise 2

1 Work out the following without using your calculator.

a) 0.75
    − 0.34

b) 5.69
    − 3.27

c) 4.83
    − 2.16

2 Work out the following without using your calculator.

a) 14.55
   − 11.86
   ‾‾‾‾‾‾

b) 0.9
   − 0.28
   ‾‾‾‾‾‾

c) 3.57
   − 1.8
   ‾‾‾‾‾

d) 29.8
   − 6.45
   ‾‾‾‾‾‾

e) 34.75
   − 28.9
   ‾‾‾‾‾‾

3 Work out the following without using your calculator.

a) 0.78 − 0.26

b) 1.56 − 0.37

c) 22.77 − 13.49

d) 56.04 − 32.87

e) 0.66 − 0.5

f) 2.34 − 1.7

g) 18.9 − 5.88

h) 44.09 − 13.8

i) 9.8 − 4.56

j) 24.89 − 18.9

k) 8.97 − 3.698

l) 11.9 − 4.614

4 Find the difference between £4.56 and £2.38.

5 What is the difference between 9.72 km and 3.45 km?

6 A CD costs £14.65 in a high street shop.
The same CD costs £9.72 online.

How much more does the CD cost in the shop?

Shop — £14.65
Online — £9.72

7 Suresh runs 5.65 miles on Sunday. He runs 4.08 miles on Tuesday.

How much further did he run on Sunday?

8 A full bag of flour weighs 3.5 kg.
A baker uses 0.76 kg of flour to make some bread.

How much does the bag of flour weigh now?

9 A newsagent sells a selection of magazines:

Magazine Prices

Carpet Mad   £3.22

Wig Digest   £2.79

Tea Monthly £4.20

What Scarf? £2.55

a) How much more expensive is Tea Monthly than Wig Digest?

b) Mia buys a copy of Carpet Mad magazine with a £5 note.
How much change will she get?

c) Will uses a voucher to get 75 p off the cost of What Scarf? magazine.
How much does he pay for it?

d) Georgia buys Tea Monthly using a £20 note.
How much change does she get?

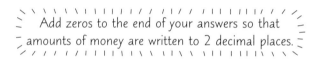

Add zeros to the end of your answers so that amounts of money are written to 2 decimal places.

Multiplication and Division

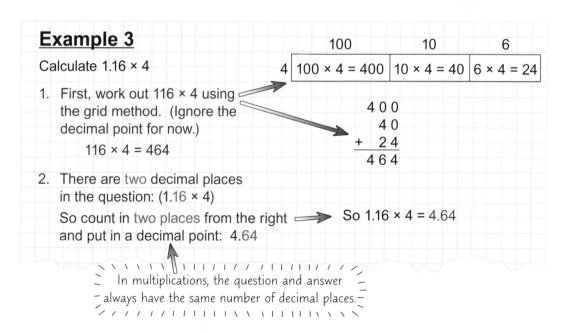

Example 3

Calculate 1.16 × 4

	100	10	6
4	100 × 4 = 400	10 × 4 = 40	6 × 4 = 24

1. First, work out 116 × 4 using the grid method. (Ignore the decimal point for now.)

   116 × 4 = 464

```
  400
   40
+  24
  464
```

2. There are two decimal places in the question: (1.16 × 4)

   So count in two places from the right and put in a decimal point: 4.64

   So 1.16 × 4 = 4.64

In multiplications, the question and answer always have the same number of decimal places.

Example 4

Calculate 1.16 × 40

1. 40 = 4 × 10, so first just multiply by 4, ⟶ 1.16 × 4 = 4.64
   using the method above.

2. Then multiply by 10 by moving each digit one ⟶ 4 . 6 4
   place to the left, like you've done before.   4 6 . 4 0

   You can leave off the final 0, so, 1.16 × 40 = 46.4

Exercise 3

1 Work out the following without using your calculator.

    a) 5.6 × 3   **b)** 3.7 × 5   **c)** 12.7 × 4

    d) 21.3 × 7   **e)** 0.56 × 2   **f)** 1.34 × 3

    g) 2.78 × 6   **h)** 1.98 × 7   **i)** 3.55 × 8

    j) 0.98 × 9   **k)** 0.76 × 8   **l)** 6.87 × 9

2 Work out the following without using your calculator.

    a) 5.6 × 30   **b)** 3.7 × 50   **c)** 12.7 × 400

    d) 21.3 × 70   **e)** 0.56 × 200   **f)** 1.34 × 300

    g) 2.78 × 600   **h)** 1.98 × 700   **i)** 3.55 × 800

    j) 0.98 × 9000   **k)** 0.76 × 8000   **l)** 6.87 × 9000

Example 5

Calculate 86.4 ÷ 4

1. Set out the division like this — with the decimal
   inside the 'box' and the second number outside.

2. Work out the division exactly like you would a whole
   number division, using the short division method.

3. Make sure you put a decimal point in your answer.
   Put it above the box, directly above the decimal
   point in the question.

$$4\overline{)86.4}$$

$$\begin{array}{r} 2 \\ 4\overline{)86.4} \end{array}$$

$$\begin{array}{r} 2\,1 \\ 4\overline{)86.{}^{2}4} \end{array}$$

$$\begin{array}{r} 2\,1.6 \\ 4\overline{)86.{}^{2}4} \end{array}$$

Example 6

Calculate 86.4 ÷ 400

1. 400 = 4 × 100, so first just divide by 4, ──────▶ 86.4 ÷ 4 = 21.6
    using the method above.

2. Then divide by 100 by moving each digit two ──────▶ 2 1 . 6
    places to the right, like you've done before.

    Fill any spaces with 0s, but only keep   0 0 . 2 1 6
    those that you need: 86.4 ÷ 400 = 0.216

Exercise 4

1 Work out the following without using your calculator.

    a) 6.8 ÷ 4   **b)** 8.5 ÷ 5   **c)** 8.7 ÷ 3

    d) 0.72 ÷ 3   **e)** 1.56 ÷ 4   **f)** 8.61 ÷ 7

    g) 32.8 ÷ 2   **h)** 22.2 ÷ 6   **i)** 96.3 ÷ 9

2 Work out the following without using your calculator.

    a) 6.8 ÷ 40   **b)** 8.5 ÷ 50   **c)** 8.7 ÷ 30

    d) 0.72 ÷ 30   **e)** 1.56 ÷ 400   **f)** 8.61 ÷ 700

    g) 32.8 ÷ 200   **h)** 22.2 ÷ 600   **i)** 96.3 ÷ 9000

1.10 Non-Calculator Arithmetic Problems

Exercise 1

Answer each of these questions **without using a calculator**.

1 A pair of shoes costing £42.50 is reduced by £8.25 in a sale.

    What is the sale price of the shoes?

2 267 people start to watch a film in the cinema.
    The film is so bad that 85 people leave after the first 15 minutes.

    How many people are left in the cinema?

3 Anna, Beth, Clare and Danni all took part in a shot put competition.
Here are the distances thrown by each person:

> Distance Thrown:
>
> Anna   4.87 m
>
> Beth   4.78 m
>
> Clare 5.04 m
>
> Danni 4.7 m

a) Write the distances in order, starting with the smallest.

b) Who threw the furthest?

4 Jake drives to work every day.
The return journey is 17.82 miles.

How far does he drive in 10 days?

5 Work out the following:

a) −6 × −4

b) −2 × 7

c) 9 × −5

d) −8 × −3

6 A school canteen buys a 9.5 kg bag of chips.
Each bag contains 100 portions of chips.

How much does each portion weigh?

7 A train leaves Liverpool with 156 passengers on board.
During the journey, 39 people get off the train and 88 people join the train.

How many passengers are on the train when it arrives at its destination?

8 The lowest temperature ever recorded in Scotland is −27 °C.
The lowest temperature ever recorded in Northern Ireland is −18 °C.

What is the difference between the two temperatures?

9 Jasmine records the time it takes her to run 100 metres.
   Here are her last four times.

   | 13.6 s | 13.05 s | 13.55 s | 13.4 s |

   a) What is her fastest time?

   b) What is the difference between her fastest and slowest times?

10 Randeep buys a cupcake for £1.76 and a hot chocolate for £2.58.

   a) What is the total cost?

   b) She pays with a £5 note. How much change will she get?

11 Jamal works 7 hours a day for 5 days a week.

   a) How many hours does he work each week?

   b) How many hours does he work in four weeks?

12 One lap of a track is 0.4 km.
   Paul runs 90 laps of the track in one week.

   How far has he run altogether?

Paul

13 A crate of milk holds 24 bottles.

   How many bottles are there in 8 crates?

14 The temperature in a freezer is –10 °C.
   The door is left open and the temperature rises by 7 °C.

   What is the temperature in the freezer now?

15 A hotel manager is working out the seating for a wedding.
   He needs one table of 8 chairs and 9 tables of 6 chairs.

   Which one of these calculations does **not** give the total number of chairs needed?

   | 8 + 6 × 9 | | (8 + 6) × 9 | | 9 × 6 + 8 |

16 30 friends share a prize of £210.60.

How much does each friend get?

17 Write down the value of the <u>highlighted</u> digit in the following numbers:

    a) 3<u>2</u>8

    b) <u>2</u>351

    c) 2<u>5</u>

    d) 32<u>5</u>4

    e) <u>5</u>20.4

    f) 5.<u>3</u>67

    g) 64.2<u>8</u>7

    h) 0.<u>2</u>1

    i) <u>6</u> 253 697

    j) 2<u>3</u>1 546

    k) 18 2<u>4</u>2.34

    l) 507.35<u>1</u>

18 Ollie works in a restaurant.
He gets paid £6.35 for each hour he works.

How much does he get paid if he works for 6 hours?

19 Which one of these calculations has the answer −10?

    $(-5) \times (-2)$ $5 - (-5)$ $(-5) \times 2$

20 1000 raffle tickets are sold to raise money for charity.
Each ticket costs £1.25.

What is the total amount of money raised?

21 Freddie and Cheryl are both working out the answer to this calculation:

    $30 - 15 \div 3$

Freddie says the answer is 25 but Cheryl thinks the answer is 5. Who is correct?

22 A group of five friends win a lottery prize of £2350.
They decide to give £875 to charity and equally share what is left.

How much does each friend get?

Section 2 — Approximations

2.1 Rounding — Whole Numbers

Numbers are sometimes approximated (or rounded) to make them easier to work with.

For example, a number like 5468 could be rounded:

- to the nearest ten (= 5470)
- to the nearest hundred (= 5500)
- to the nearest thousand (= 5000)

Example 1

a) Round 34 to the nearest ten.
   34 is between 30 and 40.
   Look at the digit in the units column.
   It's less than 5, so round down.

   a) 34 — round down to 30

b) Round 160 to the nearest hundred.
   160 is between 100 and 200.
   Look at the digit in the tens column.
   It's more than 5, so round up.

   b) 160 — round up to 200

c) Round 2500 to the nearest thousand.
   2500 is between 2000 and 3000.
   Look at the digit in the hundreds column.
   It's equal to 5, so round up.

   c) 2500 — round up to 3000

Exercise 1

1   Round each of these numbers to the nearest 10.

   a) 28   b) 72

   c) 14   d) 67

   e) 45   f) 92

   g) 99   h) 95

   i) 123   j) 248

   k) 751   l) 875

Look at the digit in the units column when rounding to the nearest 10.

2 Round each of these numbers to the nearest 100.

a) 140

b) 170

c) 275

d) 388

e) 650

f) 446

g) 1230

h) 3460

i) 889

j) 6273

k) 2449

l) 8951

Don't worry about the units, just look at the tens column.

3 Round each of these numbers to the nearest 1000.

a) 2400

b) 6800

c) 3500

d) 3920

e) 2050

f) 6192

g) 7499

h) 870

i) 9580

4 Round each of these numbers to the nearest 1000.

a) 23 100

b) 11 900

c) 81 420

d) 54 900

e) 76 500

f) 19 620

Remember to look at the hundreds column when rounding to the nearest thousand.

5 Round 1481 to the nearest:

a) ten

b) hundred

c) thousand

6 Round 2645 to the nearest:

a) ten

b) hundred

c) thousand

7 Round 2528 to the nearest:

a) ten

b) hundred

c) thousand

8 A whole number rounds to 150 to the nearest ten and 200 to the nearest hundred. List all the numbers this could be.

9 A whole number rounds to 450 to the nearest ten and 400 to the nearest hundred. List all the numbers this could be.

Rounding to the Nearest Whole Number

Numbers with decimal places can also be rounded.

Example 2

a) Round 3.2 to the nearest whole number.

   3.2 is between 3 and 4. Look at the digit in the tenths column. It's less than 5, so round down.

   a) 3.2 — round down to 3

b) Round 14.8 to the nearest whole number.

   14.8 is between 14 and 15. Look at the digit in the tenths column. It's more than 5, so round up.

   b) 14.8 — round up to 15

c) Round 8.5 to the nearest whole number.

   8.5 is between 8 and 9. Look at the digit in the tenths column. It's equal to 5, so round up.

   c) 8.5 — round up to 9

Exercise 2

1 Round each of these numbers to the nearest whole number.

a) 2.6
b) 8.1
c) 7.3

d) 7.5
e) 18.4
f) 19.6

g) 29.4
h) 39.5
i) 99.8

j) 0.7
k) 349.1
l) 125.5

2 Choose numbers from this list which round to 8 to the nearest whole number.

| 8.1 | 9.1 | 8.8 | 7.6 | 8.5 | 7.5 | 8.3 | 7.8 |

3 Choose numbers from this list which round to 25 to the nearest whole number.

| 24.8 | 25.5 | 26.1 | 25.8 | 25.3 | 24.5 | 24.3 | 25.1 |

4 Write down a number between 8 and 9 that rounds to 9 to the nearest whole number.

5 Write down five numbers that round to 18 to the nearest whole number.

Exercise 3 — Mixed Exercise

1 Round 4382 to the nearest:

   a) ten   **b)** hundred   **c)** thousand

2 Round 294.8 to the nearest:

   a) whole number   **b)** ten   **c)** hundred

3 Round the numbers on these calculator displays to the nearest:

   (i) whole number   **(ii)** ten   **(iii)** hundred

   a) 618.2   **b)** 164.7   **c)** 50.15

4 Flora picked 417 blackberries.
How many is this to the nearest 10?

5 321 people enter a competition.
How many is this to the nearest 100?

6 A website gets 4863 visitors in one week.
Round this number to the nearest 1000.

7 A car's speed is measured to be 43.8 mph.
Round this number to the nearest whole number.

2.2 Rounding — Decimal Places

You can also round to different numbers of decimal places.

For example, a number like 8.947 could be rounded:

> • to one decimal place (= 8.9)
> • to two decimal places (= 8.95)

Example 1

a) Round 4.762 to one decimal place.

4.762 is between 4.7 and 4.8.
Look at the digit in the second decimal place.
It's greater than 5, so round up.

a) 4.762 — round up to 4.8

b) Round 4.762 to two decimal places.

4.762 is between 4.76 and 4.77.
Look at the digit in the third decimal place.
It's less than 5, so round down.

b) 4.762 — round down to 4.76

Exercise 1

1 Round each of these numbers to one decimal place:

a) 1.21   b) 2.82   c) 1.39

d) 0.32   e) 0.78   f) 3.45

g) 5.67   h) 21.35   i) 2.147

j) 3.108   k) 8.552   l) 0.063

2 Write down all the numbers in the box that round to 0.4 to one decimal place.

0.4	0.45	0.347	0.335	0.405
0.35	0.4124	0.39	0.4671	0.307

3 Write down five numbers that round to 1.8 to one decimal place.

4 Round the following numbers to two decimal places:

    a) 4.567   **b)** 8.131   **c)** 1.011

    d) 2.435   **e)** 0.017   **f)** 0.049

    g) 1.065   **h)** 11.766   **i)** 21.941

    j) 5.005   **k)** 0.0424   **l)** 6.2571

5 Round the following numbers to the number of decimal places stated.

    a) 0.134 — to 2 d.p.   **b)** 0.68 — to 1 d.p.

    c) 21.353 — to 2 d.p.   **d)** 0.25 — to 1 d.p.

    e) 0.396 — to 2 d.p.   **f)** 3.308 — to 2 d.p.

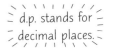

d.p. stands for decimal places.

    g) 0.005 — to 2 d.p.   **h)** 18.19 — to 1 d.p.

    i) 29.505 — to 2 d.p.   **j)** 5.949 — to 1 d.p.

6 The length of a pencil is 15.75 cm.
    Round this length to one decimal place.

7 The length of a snake is 1.245 metres.
    Round this length to one decimal place.

8 The mass of the field vole on the right is 0.038 kilograms.
    Round this mass to two decimal places.

Not shown actual size.

9 The average distance that a group of students live from a school is 2.457 km.
    Round this figure to two decimal places.

10 Round the following numbers to three decimal places:

    a) 0.9673   **b)** 0.2547

    c) 2.4365   **d)** 6.53267

Look at the digit in the fourth decimal place when you're rounding to 3 d.p.

    e) 3.63825   **f)** 0.03056

    g) 5.68414   **h)** 0.008723

2.3 Estimating Answers

You can estimate the answer to a calculation by rounding numbers in the calculation to numbers that are easier to use.

Even though the answer isn't exactly right, it can still be useful.

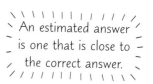

An estimated answer is one that is close to the correct answer.

Example 1

Use rounding to estimate the answers to: a) 21 × 9   b) 444 ÷ 12

1. Round both numbers in the calculation to numbers that are easier to use.

    a) To the nearest 10:

    21 rounds to 20 and 9 rounds to 10

2. Rewrite the calculation using the rounded numbers.

    So estimate 21 × 9 using

    20 × 10 = 200

3. Estimate the answer using the rounded numbers.

    b) To the nearest 100: 444 rounds to 400

    To the nearest 10:   9 rounds to 10

    So estimate 444 ÷ 12 using

    400 ÷ 10 = 40

The actual answers are:
21 × 9 = 189 and 444 ÷ 12 = 37
so these estimates are pretty close.

Example 2

Use rounding to estimate the answer to 46 ÷ 1.8.

1. Again, rewrite the calculation using rounded numbers.

    To the nearest 10: 46 rounds to 50

    To the nearest whole number: 1.8 rounds to 2

2. Estimate the answer using the rounded numbers.

    So estimate 46 ÷ 1.8 using

    50 ÷ 2 = 25

Exercise 1

Answer questions **1-17 without using your calculator**.

1   a) Round 137 and 170 to the nearest hundred.

    b) Use your answer to part a) to estimate 137 + 170.

So, work out 137 to the nearest hundred. Then work out 170 to the nearest hundred. Then add them.

2 **a)** Round 204 and 89 to the nearest hundred.

   b) Use your answer to part **a)** to estimate 204 − 89.

3 **a)** Round 511 and 118 to the nearest hundred.

   b) Use your answer to part **a)** to estimate 511 − 118.

4 **a)** Round 33 and 12 to the nearest ten.

   b) Use your answer to part **a)** to estimate 33 ÷ 12.

5 **a)** Round 26 and 12 to the nearest ten.

   b) Use your answer to part **a)** to estimate 26 × 12.

6 By rounding to the nearest 100, estimate 210 + 376.

7 By rounding to the nearest 100, estimate 237 − 128.

8 By rounding to the nearest 10, estimate 19 × 11.

9 By rounding to the nearest 10, estimate 38 ÷ 9.

10 By rounding to the nearest 100, estimate 398 ÷ 97.

11 Use rounding to estimate the answer to each of these calculations.

   a) 289 + 308   **b)** 395 + 96   **c)** 711 − 213

   d) 675 − 83   **e)** 14 × 7   **f)** 24 × 8

   g) 27 × 12   **h)** 55 × 11   **i)** 250 × 13

   j) 21 ÷ 9   **k)** 42 ÷ 11   **l)** 35 ÷ 15

   m) 235 ÷ 24   **n)** 950 ÷ 96

12 a) Round 43 to the nearest 10 and 8.2 to the nearest whole number.

   b) Use your answer to part **a)** to estimate 43 ÷ 8.2

13 a) Round 612 to the nearest hundred and 5.3 to the nearest whole number.

   b) Use your answer to part **a)** to estimate 612 × 5.3.

14 Use rounding to estimate the answer to each of these calculations.

   a) 31 × 1.9   **b)** 22 × 2.8

   c) 101 × 2.5   **d)** 81 ÷ 2.2

   e) 54 ÷ 4.8   **f)** 40.4 ÷ 4.9

15 A packet of 8 pens costs 95p.
Use rounding to estimate the cost in pence of one pen.

16 Richard is cooking pasta.
The instructions on the bag suggest 75 g of pasta per person.

Use rounding to estimate how much pasta Richard needs to cook for eleven people.

17 A piece of toy rail track has a length of 9.8 cm.
Estimate the length in cm of 18 pieces of track joined together.

18 It costs Tom £14.80 to buy five tickets for a bus journey.
Estimate the cost of one ticket in pounds (£).

19 Use rounding to estimate the answer to the following calculations.

   a) 832 ÷ (52.6 + 47.3)   **b)** (1020 ÷ 215) × 29

   c) 38 × (306 ÷ 62)   **d)** (1998 ÷ 10.4) − (4.7 × 20.2)

Remember to do the calculations in the brackets first.

2.4 Rounding Problems

Exercise 1

1 For each situation below, round the numbers to the nearest whole number.

> Remember to include units in your answer.

   a) James cycled to school in 18.8 minutes.

   b) The length of a piece of rope was measured to be 204.5 cm.

   c) The volume of a bucket was found to be 6.45 litres.

2 Round 2.638 to:

   a) two decimal places

   b) one decimal place

3 Round 8.932 to:

   a) two decimal places

   b) one decimal place

   c) the nearest whole number

4 The area of a circular pond is calculated to be 12.568 m². Round the area of the pond to:

   a) the nearest whole number

   b) 1 decimal place

5 Round these values to 1 decimal place.

   a) The perimeter of a circular pond was calculated to be 15.71 m.

   b) The volume of concrete needed to make a path was calculated to be 2.85 m³.

   c) The area of a room was calculated to be 30.175 m².

6 For each situation below, round the numbers to two decimal places.

   a) A bag of tomatoes was found to weigh 0.836 kg.

   b) A runner ran 1.381 miles.

   c) The average height in a class was found to be 1.435 metres.

7 The average speed of a car is calculated to be 74.667 km/h.
   Round the speed of the car to:

   a) two decimal places

   b) one decimal place

   c) the nearest whole number

8 The volume of a jug is calculated to be 311.058 cm³.
   Round the volume of the jug to:

   a) the nearest ten

   b) the nearest whole number

   c) 1 decimal place

9 8 people share a £10 343 lottery win equally between them.

   a) Use a calculator to find the exact amount each person wins.

   b) How much does each person win to the nearest £100?

10 A pack of 6 tins of dog food costs £2.55.

   a) Use a calculator to find the average cost of each tin.

   b) What is the cost of each tin to the nearest 10p?

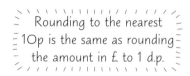
Rounding to the nearest 10p is the same as rounding the amount in £ to 1 d.p.

11 6 grandchildren spend £188 on a present for their grandma and share the cost equally.
   Find how much each grandchild spends on the present to the nearest £1.

12 7 friends split a taxi fare of £18.
   How much should they each pay, to the nearest 10p, if they all pay the same amount?

Exercise 2

1   Use rounding to estimate the answer to these calculations.

   a) 271 + 198   **b)** 750 + 121

   c) 1081 − 259   **d)** 17 ÷ 8

   e) 42 × 9   **f)** 35 ÷ 19

   g) 8.4 ÷ 1.9   **h)** 21 × 1.8

   i) 7.5 × 2.2   **j)** 284 × 50.2

2   At a local football match, there are 784 home fans and 137 away fans.
    Estimate the total number of people at the match.

3   A college has 1986 pupils.
    332 of the pupils study history.

    Use rounding to estimate the total number of people who don't study history.

4   A box of 16 cupcakes weighs 432 g.
    Estimate the weight of one cupcake in grams.

5   Use rounding to help you choose the correct answer (**A**, **B** or **C**)
    to each of the following calculations. Do not use your calculator.

   a) 582 × 2.1   **A**: 119.52   **B**: 1222.2   **C**: 4545.2

   b) 1.76 × 6.3   **A**: 1.328   **B**: 5.788   **C**: 11.088

   c) 440.32 ÷ 51.2   **A**: 1.85   **B**: 8.6   **C**: 78.125

6   It costs £4.70 to buy the toys needed for one childrens 'party bag'.
    If 21 children attend a party, estimate how much it would cost to
    buy all the toys for the party bags.

7   Karen works 10.25 hours one week, and earns £6.85 per hour.
    Estimate the amount of money she earns for the week.

Section 3 — Powers

3.1 Squares, Cubes and Roots

Squares and Cubes

Squares and cubes show that a number is multiplied by itself.

For example, the square of 4 is 4×4 and is written as 4^2. ← The little ^{2} means that 2 lots of 4 are multiplied together.
The square of a number is always positive.

The cube of 4 is $4 \times 4 \times 4$ and is written as 4^3.
The cube of a positive number is positive, but the cube of a negative number is negative.

Example 1

Find:
a) 4^2 $4^2 = 4 \times 4 = 16$

b) $(-4)^2$ $(-4)^2 = (-4) \times (-4) = 16$

c) 4^3 $4^3 = 4 \times 4 \times 4 = 64$

d) $(-4)^3$ $(-4)^3 = (-4) \times (-4) \times (-4) = -64$

Exercise 1

1 Copy and complete these calculations:

   a) $5^2 = \ldots \times \ldots = 25$ b) $2^2 = 2 \times \ldots = \ldots$

   c) $3^2 = \ldots\ldots\ldots = \ldots$ d) $5^3 = \ldots \times \ldots \times \ldots = 125$

   e) $2^3 = \ldots \times 2 \times \ldots = \ldots$ f) $3^3 = \ldots\ldots\ldots = \ldots$

2 Copy and complete the table below **without using a calculator**.

x	6	7	8	9	10
x^2	36				

3   Work out the following.
     You **may use a calculator** if you need to.

   a) 11^2 **b)** 12^2 **c)** 15^2

   d) 18^2 **e)** 20^2 **f)** 25^2

   g) 30^2 **h)** 50^2 **i)** 100^2

4   For each of the following:

   (i) write the square as a multiplication.

   (ii) work out the multiplication, using a calculator if you need to.

   a) $(-1)^2$ **b)** 0.1^2 **c)** $(-10)^2$

   d) 0.3^2 **e)** 0.8^2 **f)** $(-3)^2$

   g) $(-5)^2$ **h)** $(-0.2)^2$ **i)** $(-0.4)^2$

   j) $(-15)^2$ **k)** 1.1^2 **l)** $(-2.5)^2$

5   Work out the following.
     You **may use a calculator** if you need to.

   a) 6^3 **b)** 9^3 **c)** 10^3

   d) 11^3 **e)** 15^3 **f)** 18^3

   g) 20^3 **h)** 25^3 **i)** 30^3

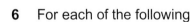

6   For each of the following

   (i) write the cube as a multiplication.

   (ii) work out the multiplication, using a calculator if you need to.

   a) $(-3)^3$ **b)** $(-5)^3$ **c)** $(-10)^3$

   d) 0.4^3 **e)** 0.5^3 **f)** 1.5^3

   g) $(-6)^3$ **h)** $(-0.3)^3$ **i)** $(-0.8)^3$

   j) $(-12)^3$ **k)** $(-0.2)^3$ **l)** $(-2.5)^3$

Square Roots

Finding the square root of a number is the opposite of squaring it.

Every positive number has two square roots — one positive ($\sqrt{x}$) and one negative ($-\sqrt{x}$).
For example, the positive square root of 2 is $\sqrt{2}$.
The negative square root of 2 is $-\sqrt{2}$.

Negative numbers don't have square roots.

Example 2

Find both square roots of 16.

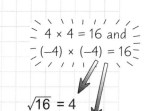

4 × 4 = 16 and
(−4) × (−4) = 16

1. You need to find the number that when multiplied by itself gives 16.

$\sqrt{16} = 4$

2. 16 = 4 × 4, so the positive square root is 4.

3. Don't forget the negative square root. ⟹ $-\sqrt{16} = -4$

Exercise 2

1 Copy and complete each of the following:

a) 4 = 2 × ......
   So $\sqrt{4}$ = ... and $-\sqrt{4}$ = ...

b) 9 = 3 × ......
   So $\sqrt{9}$ = ... and $-\sqrt{9}$ = ...

2 Copy and complete the table below **without using a calculator**.

x	16	25	36	100
$\sqrt{x}$	4			
$-\sqrt{x}$	−4			

3 **Without using a calculator**, find:

a) $\sqrt{49}$　　　　　　　**b)** $-\sqrt{49}$　　　　　　　**c)** $\sqrt{81}$

d) $-\sqrt{81}$　　　　　　　**e)** $\sqrt{121}$　　　　　　　**f)** $-\sqrt{121}$

4 Find **both** square roots of these numbers. You **may use a calculator** if you need to.

a) 64　　　　　　　　**b)** 144

c) 169　　　　　　　　**d)** 10 000

e) 196　　　　　　　　**f)** 225

g) 324　　　　　　　　**h)** 625

Watch out – the $\sqrt{}$ button on your calculator will only give you the <u>positive</u> square root.

5 Use your calculator to find **both** square roots of these decimals.

a) 0.25   b) 2.25   c) 0.36

d) 0.64   e) 1.44   f) 18.49

Cube Roots

Finding the cube root of a number is the opposite of cubing it.
Every number has exactly one cube root.
The symbol $\sqrt[3]{}$ is used for cube roots.

Example 3

Find the cube root of:

> You need to know cube numbers to easily find cube roots without a calculator.

a) 64

   1. You need to find the number that gives 64 when three lots of the number are multiplied together.

   2. $64 = 4 \times 4 \times 4$, so the cube root is 4. $\sqrt[3]{64} = 4$

b) −64

   $-64 = -4 \times -4 \times -4$, so the cube root is −4. $\sqrt[3]{-64} = -4$

Exercise 3

1 Copy and complete the table below.

x	8	27	64	1000
$\sqrt[3]{x}$			4	

2 **Use your calculator** to find these cube roots.

a) $\sqrt[3]{64}$ b) $\sqrt[3]{125}$ c) $\sqrt[3]{-8}$

d) $\sqrt[3]{-1}$ e) $\sqrt[3]{1728}$ f) $\sqrt[3]{-125}$

g) $\sqrt[3]{216}$ h) $\sqrt[3]{512}$ i) $\sqrt[3]{-1000}$

> Your calculator should have a cube root button which looks a little like this: $\sqrt[3]{\square}$

Exercise 4 — Mixed Exercise

1   Find each of the following.
    You **may use a calculator** if you need to.

a) 13^2

b) 14^3

c) $\sqrt{256}$

d) $-\sqrt{324}$

e) 200^2

f) $\sqrt[3]{343}$

g) $6^2 + 6^3$

h) $\sqrt[3]{-27}$

i) 0.6^3

j) $12^3 - 12^2$

k) $\sqrt{8100}$

l) $-\sqrt{8100}$

m) $(-19)^2$

n) $(-11)^3$

o) $\sqrt{0.49}$

3.2   Index Notation

Squares and cubes are examples of powers.

Powers show something that is being multiplied by itself.
They are usually written using 'index notation'
— the index tells you how many lots of the base to multiply together.

For example, $2^4 = 2 \times 2 \times 2 \times 2$ — this is four 2's multiplied together.
It is read as "2 to the power 4".

Example 1

Write $3 \times 3 \times 3 \times 3 \times 3$ using index notation.

The base is 3. There are 5 lots of the base multiplied together, so the index is 5.

5 lots of the base.

$3 \times 3 \times 3 \times 3 \times 3 = 3^5$

Example 2

Find the value of 2^6.

You might have a button on your calculator for working out powers, but it's best to write out the multiplication.

1. The base is 2. The index is 6.
    So rewrite the power as 6 lots of 2 multiplied together.

$2^6 = 2 \times 2 \times 2 \times 2 \times 2 \times 2$

2. Use a calculator to find the answer.

$2^6 = 64$

Exercise 1

1 Which number is **(i)** the base and **(ii)** the index in each of these?

    a) 6^4

    b) 3^7

    c) 4^2

    d) 2^4

    e) 5^{11}

    f) 100^{15}

    g) $3 \times 3 \times 3 \times 3$

    h) $6 \times 6 \times 6$

    i) 5×5

    j) $8 \times 8 \times 8 \times 8 \times 8$

    k) $11 \times 11 \times 11 \times 11 \times 11 \times 11$

2 Write each of these using index notation.

    a) 3×3

    b) 8×8

    c) $2 \times 2 \times 2$

    d) $5 \times 5 \times 5 \times 5$

    e) $7 \times 7 \times 7 \times 7 \times 7$

    f) $9 \times 9 \times 9 \times 9 \times 9 \times 9$

    g) $12 \times 12 \times 12 \times 12$

    h) $17 \times 17 \times 17$

    i) $25 \times 25 \times 25 \times 25$

    j) $100 \times 100 \times 100$

3 For each of the following:

    (i) write the power as a multiplication.

    (ii) use a calculator to find the answer.

    a) 2^4

    b) 2^5

    c) 3^4

    d) 4^6

    e) 6^3

    f) 6^4

4 Use a calculator to find the value of each of these powers.

    a) 3^5

    b) 5^5

    c) 7^4

    d) 8^5

    e) 11^4

    f) 12^6

5 Use a calculator to work out the following.

    a) $3^2 + 2^3$

    b) $2^3 + 3^3$

    c) $3^4 - 4^2$

    d) $5^2 + 6^2$

    e) $3^5 - 5^3$

    f) $3^4 - 9^2$

Powers of 10

Numbers that have 10 as the base are called powers of 10.

Exercise 2

1 Find the value of these powers of 10.
Use a calculator if you need to.

a) 10^2 **b)** 10^3 **c)** 10^4

d) 10^5 **e)** 10^6 **f)** 10^7

g) 10^8 **h)** 10^9 **i)** 10^1

2 Copy and complete the following sentences.
Use your answers to Question **1** to help you.
The first one has been done before you.

a) "10^2 can be written as a '1' followed by ....2......... zeros."

b) "10^3 can be written as a '1' followed by .... zeros."

c) "10^5 can be written as a '1' followed by .... zeros."

d) "10^7 can be written as a '1' followed by .... zeros."

3 Rewrite each of these numbers using index notation with 10 as the base.

a) 100 **b)** 1000

c) 10 000 **d)** 100 000

e) 1 000 000 **f)** 10 000 000

g) 1 000 000 000 **h)** 1 000 000 000 000

4 Use a calculator to work out the following.

a) $10^3 - 6^2$ **b)** $2^4 + 10^3$

c) $10^4 - 7^3$ **d)** $2^7 + 10^5$

Powers with Letters

Powers with letters work exactly the same way as they do with numbers.

Example 3

Write $a \times a \times a \times a \times a \times a$ using index notation.

The base is a. There are 6 lots of the base multiplied together, so the index is 6.

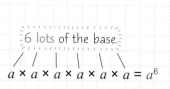

6 lots of the base.

$$a \times a \times a \times a \times a \times a = a^6$$

Exercise 3

1   Write each of these using index notation.

a) $b \times b$

b) $c \times c \times c$

c) $h \times h \times h \times h$

d) $t \times t \times t \times t \times t$

e) $s \times s \times s \times s \times s \times s \times s$

f) $k \times k \times k \times k \times k \times k$

g) $y \times y \times y \times y$

h) $m \times m \times m \times m \times m$

2   Write each of these powers as a multiplication.

a) a^3

b) y^2

c) d^4

d) m^6

e) x^5

f) p^8

Exercise 4 — Mixed Exercise

1   Copy and complete these sentences:

a) 1 million (10^6) can be written as 1 followed by .... zeros.

b) 1 billion (10^9) can be written as 1 followed by .... zeros.

2   Write each of the following using index notation

a) $7 \times 7 \times 7 \times 7$

b) $9 \times 9 \times 9 \times 9 \times 9$

c) 12

d) $e \times e \times e$

e) $x \times x \times x \times x$

f) $z \times z \times z \times z \times z \times z$

3 Write each of the following as a multiplication.

a) 6^6

b) 11^5

c) 5^7

d) a^4

e) d^7

f) y^6

4 Use your calculator to find the value of each of these powers.

a) 7^5

b) 12^5

c) 8^7

d) 10^{10}

e) 10^{12}

f) 10^{15}

5 Which number is bigger, 4^3 or 3^4?

3.3 Index Laws

Remember:

Use the index laws to multiply and divide powers with the same base.

- To multiply two powers with the same base, add the indexes: $a^m \times a^n = a^{m+n}$

- To divide two powers with the same base, subtract the indexes: $a^m \div a^n = a^{m-n}$

There are two other important index facts you need to know.

- Anything to the power 1 is equal to itself: $a^1 = a$

- Anything to the power 0 is equal to 1: $a^0 = 1$

Example 1

Simplify the following. Leave your answers in index form.

a) $3^4 \times 3^5$

This is a multiplication, so add the indexes. $3^4 \times 3^5 = 3^{4+5} = 3^9$

b) $10^8 \div 10^5$

This is a division, so subtract the indexes. $10^8 \div 10^5 = 10^{8-5} = 10^3$

Exercise 1

1 Copy and complete the following calculations.

a) $3^2 \times 3^4 = 3^{\cdots + \cdots} = 3^{\cdots}$

b) $5^2 \times 5^4 = 5^{\cdots + \cdots} = 5^{\cdots}$

c) $3^4 \div 3^2 = 3^{\cdots - \cdots} = 3^{\cdots}$

d) $4^5 \div 4^3 = 4^{\cdots - \cdots} = 4^{\cdots}$

2 Simplify the following. Leave your answers in index form.

a) $6^3 \times 6^5$ **b)** $4^3 \times 4^3$

c) $4^7 \times 4^4$ **d)** $6^5 \times 6^7$

e) $2^3 \times 2^{10}$ **f)** $12^2 \times 12^4$

g) $10^7 \times 10^3$ **h)** $7^1 \times 7^6$

3 Simplify the following. Leave your answers in index form.

a) $5^6 \div 5^2$ **b)** $6^7 \div 6^4$

c) $8^6 \div 8^3$ **d)** $5^7 \div 5^2$

e) $6^8 \div 6^6$ **f)** $12^7 \div 12^3$

g) $2^{18} \div 2^{11}$ **h)** $10^{19} \div 10^8$

4 Simplify these powers.

    a) 5^1 **b)** 3^1

    c) 6^0 **d)** 1^1

    e) 14^0 **f)** 1^0

5 Simplify the following.
Leave your answers in index form.

    a) $4^5 \times 4^{11}$ **b)** $12^{13} \div 12^7$

    c) $8^2 \times 8^9$ **d)** $7^{11} \div 7^6$

    e) $4^{15} \div 4^7$ **f)** $8^8 \div 8^4$

    g) $15^{12} \times 15^{14}$ **h)** $129^5 \times 129^2$

    i) $72^{13} \div 72^7$ **j)** $188^8 \times 188^4$

6 Simplify the following.
Give your answers as numbers.

    a) $3^5 \div 3^4$

    b) $5^4 \div 5^4$

    c) $8^3 \div 8^2$

    d) $10^6 \div 10^6$

7 For each of the following, find the number that should replace the square.

    a) $3^3 \times 3^6 = 3^\blacksquare$

    b) $8^\blacksquare \times 8^4 = 8^6$

    c) $6^5 \times 6^\blacksquare = 6^{12}$

    d) $9^6 \div 9^4 = 9^\blacksquare$

    e) $5^\blacksquare \div 5^5 = 5^7$

    f) $10^6 \div 10^\blacksquare = 10^4$

8 Simplify the following.

a) $a^6 \times a^4$

b) $e^8 \div e^3$

c) $b^8 \div b^5$

d) $y^8 \div y^2$

> Remember — powers work just the same with letters as they do with numbers.

Example 2

Simplify the following without using a calculator. Leave your answers in index form.

a) $3^2 \times 3^4 \times 3^5$

The index of the result will be 2 + 4 + 5.

$3^2 \times 3^4 \times 3^5 = 3^{2+4+5} = 3^{11}$

b) $(2^6 \times 2^8) \div 2^2$

1. The index of the result will be (6 + 8) – 2.

2. Remember BODMAS — work out the bit in the brackets first, then do the subtraction.

$(2^6 \times 2^8) \div 2^2 = 2^{(6+8)-2}$

$= 2^{14-2} = 2^{12}$

Exercise 2

1 Simplify the following **without using a calculator**. Leave your answers in index form.

a) $3^2 \times 3^5 \times 3^7$

b) $5^2 \times 5^3 \times 5^8$

c) $(7^3 \times 7^5) \div 7^6$

d) $(8^4 \times 8^7) \div 8^9$

e) $7^8 \div (7^4 \times 7^2)$

f) $6^2 \times 6 \times 6^5$

2 Simplify the following.

a) $a^2 \times a^3 \times a^4$

b) $e^2 \times e^5 \times e^7$

c) $(a^6 \times a^5) \div a^4$

d) $(z^8 \div z^2) \times z^4$

Section 4 — Factors, Multiples & Primes

4.1 Multiples

The multiples of a number are just the numbers that are in its times table.

So the multiples of 2 are 2, 4, 6, 8, 10, 12... and the multiples of 5 are 5, 10, 15, 20, 25, 30...

Example 1

a) List the multiples of 5 between 23 and 43.

Starting at 20, the times table of 5 is: 20, 25, 30, 35, 40, 45...
— so the multiples between 23 and 43 are: 25, 30, 35, 40

b) Which of the numbers in the box below are:

(i) multiples of 3?

(ii) multiples of 5?

| 24 | 7 | 28 | 35 | 39 |

1. 3 divides into 24 and 39 exactly
 — so 24 and 39 are multiples of 3.

     (i) 24 and 39

   But 3 doesn't divide exactly into 7, 28 or 35
 — these aren't multiples of 3.

2. The only number in the box that 5 divides into exactly is 35.

     (ii) 35

Exercise 1

1 List the first five multiples of:

  a) 4   **b)** 10   **c)** 3

  d) 6   **e)** 7   **f)** 9

2 Write down the numbers from the box that are:

  a) multiples of 3

  b) multiples of 4

  c) multiples of 5

| 2 | 5 | 8 | 9 | 11 | 12 |
| 14 | 15 | 16 | 18 | 20 | 21 |

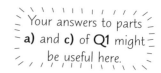

Your answers to parts **a)** and **c)** of **Q1** might be useful here.

3 Write down all the multiples of 5 that are less than 30.

4 Write down all the multiples of 7 that are less than 60.

5 **a)** Find the only multiple of 8 between 10 and 20.

b) List the multiples of 9 between 20 and 50.

c) Find the only multiple of 6 between 25 and 35.

6 Write down the numbers from the box that are:

a) multiples of 10

b) multiples of 15

5	10	15	20	25	30	35
40	45	50	55	60	65	70
75	80	85	90	95	100	105

7 **a)** List the multiples of 3 between 19 and 35.

b) List the multiples of 4 between 19 and 35.

8 Write down the numbers from the box that **aren't** multiples of 11.

22	36	55	71	77
99	101	111	121	132

4.2   Least Common Multiple

Common Multiples

A common multiple is a number that is in the times table of two different numbers.

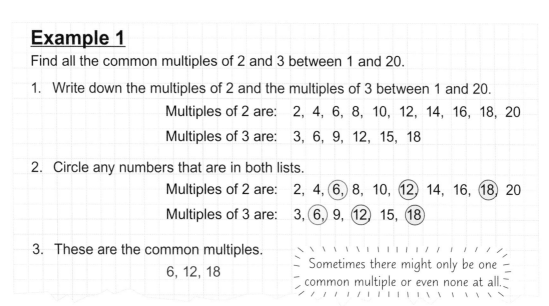

Example 1
Find all the common multiples of 2 and 3 between 1 and 20.

1. Write down the multiples of 2 and the multiples of 3 between 1 and 20.

Multiples of 2 are: 2, 4, 6, 8, 10, 12, 14, 16, 18, 20

Multiples of 3 are: 3, 6, 9, 12, 15, 18

2. Circle any numbers that are in both lists.

Multiples of 2 are: 2, 4, ⑥ 8, 10, ⑫ 14, 16, ⑱ 20

Multiples of 3 are: 3, ⑥ 9, ⑫ 15, ⑱

3. These are the common multiples.

6, 12, 18

Sometimes there might only be one common multiple or even none at all.

Exercise 1

1 **a)** Write down the first eight multiples of 3.

   b) Write down the first eight multiples of 4.

   c) Circle any numbers that are in both lists. 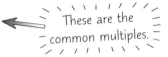 These are the common multiples.

2 For each pair of numbers below:

   (i) Write down the first eight multiples of each number.

   (ii) Circle the common multiples — any numbers that are in both lists.

   a) 2 and 6   **b)** 4 and 7

   c) 6 and 9   **d)** 5 and 7

   e) 6 and 8   **f)** 4 and 5

3 Write down the numbers from the box that are:

   a) multiples of 5

   b) multiples of 8

   c) common multiples of 5 and 8.

15	18	24	32	35	40
44	47	50	56	62	74
80	88	95	108	110	120

4 **a)** List the multiples of 3 between 19 and 37.

   b) List the multiples of 7 between 19 and 37.

   c) Find the only common multiple of 3 and 7 between 19 and 37.

5 Find the only common multiple of 5 and 6 between 1 and 40.

6 List all the common multiples of 8 and 10 between 1 and 100.

Least Common Multiple (LCM)

The least common multiple (LCM) of a group of numbers
is the smallest common multiple of those numbers.

Example 2

Find the least common multiple (LCM) of 2 and 3.

1. Write down the multiples of 2 and 3.

    Multiples of 2 are: 2, 4, 6, 8, 10, 12...

    Multiples of 3 are: 3, 6, 9, 12, 15, 18...

2. The least common multiple is the smallest number that is in both lists.

    Multiples of 2 are: 2, 4, (6,) 8, 10, 12...

    Multiples of 3 are: 3, (6,) 9, 12, 15, 18...

    So the LCM of 2 and 3 is 6.

Exercise 2

1   a) Write down the first five multiples of 3.

    b) Write down the first five multiples of 5.

    c) Circle the least common multiple — the smallest number that is in both lists.

2   a) Write down the first five multiples of 2.

    b) Write down the first five multiples of 6.

    c) Find the least common multiple of 2 and 6.

3   a) Write down the first five multiples of 4.

    b) Write down the first five multiples of 10.

    c) Find the least common multiple of 4 and 10.

4   Find the least common multiple of each of these pairs of numbers.

a) 3 and 4	b) 6 and 5	c) 2 and 7
d) 3 and 8	e) 5 and 9	f) 3 and 9

5 Find the least common multiple of each of these pairs of numbers.

 a) 2 and 8   b) 4 and 12   c) 5 and 10

 d) 4 and 20   e) 6 and 9   f) 9 and 12

 g) 6 and 10   h) 10 and 15   i) 8 and 20

6 a) Write down the first six multiples of 2, 3 and 4.

    b) Circle the smallest number that is in all three lists.

7 a) Write down the first six multiples of 3, 6 and 9.

    b) Find the least common multiple of 3, 6 and 9.

8 Find the least common multiple of 2, 4 and 5.

The LCM of three numbers is the smallest number that is a multiple of all three.

4.3 Factors

The factors of a number are all the numbers that divide into it ('go into it') exactly.

For example, the factors of 8 are 1, 2, 4 and 8 — all these numbers divide into 8 exactly.

Example 1

Find all the factors of 24.

1. Start by writing 1 × 24.

2. Then try 2 × something to make 24.
    2 × 12 = 24. So write this on the next row.

3. Carry on trying to make 24 by
    multiplying pairs of numbers: 3 × something,
    4 × something etc...

4. Write each pair of numbers in a new row.
    Put a dash if a number doesn't divide exactly.

5. Stop when you get a repeated number.

6. Write down all the numbers in the
    multiplications.

Increasing by 1 each time

1 × 24
2 × 12
3 × 8
4 × 6
5 × –
------
6 × 4

You've already had 4 × 6.

So, the factors of 24 are:
1, 2, 3, 4, 6, 8, 12, 24

Exercise 1

1 **a)** Copy and complete the list below to find all the factors of 12.

```
1 × 12
2 × ....
3 × ....
4 × 3
```

b) Copy and complete the list on the right to find all the factors of 18.

```
1 × 18
2 × ....
3 × ....
4 × —
5 × ....
6 × 3
```

2 Write down the numbers in the box that are factors of:

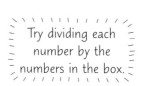

a) 21   **b)** 40

c) 8   **d)** 28

e) 7   **f)** 25

Try dividing each number by the numbers in the box.

3 The number 4 has three factors. Find them all.

4 The number 15 has four factors. Find them all.

5 Find all the factors of each number below.

a) 8   **b)** 16   **c)** 9

d) 10   **e)** 20   **f)** 25

g) 35   **h)** 32   **i)** 40

6 Write down the numbers from the box below that are factors of 150.

```
1   5   8   12   15   18   25   30   32
40  44  50  60   68   75   100  120  150
```

4.4 Highest Common Factor

A common factor is a number that divides exactly into two different numbers.

Common Factors

Example 1

Find the common factors of 6 and 20.

1. Find the factors of 6 and 20.

   Factors of 6 are: 1, 2, 3, 6

   Factors of 20 are: 1, 2, 4, 5, 10, 20

2. Circle any number that is in both lists.

   Factors of 6 are: ① ② 3, 6

   Factors of 20 are: ① ② 4, 5, 10, 20

3. These are the common factors.

   1 and 2

Exercise 1

1 **a)** List all the factors of 4.

   b) List all the factors of 10.

   c) Circle any numbers that are in both lists. 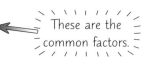 These are the common factors.

2 **a)** List all the factors of 8.

   b) List all the factors of 12.

   c) Circle any numbers that are in both lists.

3 **a)** List all the factors of 9.

   b) List all the factors of 15.

   c) Find the common factors of 9 and 15.

4 Find the common factors of 12 and 14.

5 Find the common factors of the following pairs of numbers.

   a) 15 and 20   **b)** 12 and 15   **c)** 30 and 45

   d) 25 and 55   **e)** 25 and 50   **f)** 18 and 27

Highest Common Factor (HCF)

The highest common factor (HCF) of a group of numbers is the largest common factor of those numbers. It's the biggest number that divides into all of them exactly.

Example 2

Find the highest common factor (HCF) of 16 and 24.

1. Write down the factors of 16 and the factors of 24.

   Factors of 16 are: 1, 2, 4, 8, 16

   Factors of 24 are: 1, 2, 3, 4, 6, 8, 12, 24

2. The highest common factor is the biggest number that is in both lists.

   Factors of 16 are: 1, 2, 4, ⑧, 16

   Factors of 24 are: 1, 2, 3, 4, 6, ⑧, 12, 24

   So the HCF of 16 and 24 is 8.

Exercise 2

1   **a)** Write down all the factors of 5.

   b) Write down all the factors of 20.

   c) Circle the highest common factor — the biggest number that is in both lists.

2   **a)** Write down all the factors of 9.

   b) Write down all the factors of 16.

   c) Find the highest common factor of 9 and 16.

3   **a)** Write down all the factors of 20.

   b) Write down all the factors of 30.

   c) Use your list to find the highest common factor of 20 and 30.

4   Find the highest common factor of each of these pairs of numbers.

   a) 8 and 16   **b)** 6 and 12

   c) 7 and 14   **d)** 4 and 24

   e) 9 and 18   **f)** 10 and 30

5 Find the highest common factor of each of these pairs of numbers.

   a) 5 and 7   **b)** 8 and 15   **c)** 4 and 9

   d) 8 and 11   **e)** 9 and 14   **f)** 12 and 17

6 Find the highest common factor of each of these pairs of numbers.

   a) 6 and 10   **b)** 8 and 20   **c)** 10 and 15

   d) 6 and 9   **e)** 9 and 21   **f)** 12 and 20

   g) 18 and 25   **h)** 14 and 15   **i)** 21 and 36

   j) 12 and 36   **k)** 35 and 42   **l)** 56 and 63

7 **a)** List all the factors of 4, 8 and 12.

   b) Circle the biggest number that is in all three lists.

8 **a)** List all the factors of 3, 6 and 9.

   b) Find the highest common factor of 3, 6 and 9.

> The HCF of three numbers is the biggest number that divides exactly into all three.

9 Find the highest common factor of 8, 12 and 16.

4.5 Factors and Multiples Problems

Exercise 1

1 Find the first five multiples of:

   a) 8   **b)** 11   **c)** 20

   d) 14   **e)** 12   **f)** 25

2 From the numbers in the box below, write down:

   a) any number that is a factor of 56

   b) all numbers that are not multiples of 2

   c) all the factors of 12

   d) any number that is a multiple of 9

1	2	3	6	7	11
12	15	27	28	36	39
48	60	63	75	81	96

3   For each pair of numbers below, find:

(i) the highest common factor of the numbers

(ii) the least common multiple of the numbers

a) 7 and 9   **b)** 8 and 12

c) 15 and 25   **d)** 16 and 20

4 Anna has 36 identical sweets, and wants to arrange them into equal piles.

a) First she makes piles of 2 sweets.
How many piles can she make?

b) Could she make 5 equal piles of sweets? Explain your answer.

c) List the different ways Anna can divide the 36 sweets into equal piles.

5 A baker has 12 identical cakes. List all the different ways he
can divide them up into packets of equal numbers of cakes.

4.6   Prime Numbers

A prime number is a number that has no factors except itself and 1.

In other words, the only numbers that 'go' exactly into a prime number are itself and 1.

But remember... 1 is **not** a prime number.

Example 1

Which of the numbers in the box on the right are prime? | 16 17 18 19 20 |

1. Look for factors of each of the numbers.   16 = 2 × 8, so 16 isn't prime

2. If you can find factors, then   18 = 3 × 6, so 18 isn't prime
    the number isn't prime.   20 = 4 × 5, so 20 isn't prime

                                                   17 has no factors other than 1 and 17.
3. If there are no factors other than itself   19 has no factors other than 1 and 19.
    and 1, then the number is prime.
                                                   So the prime numbers are 17 and 19.

Exercise 1

1 **a)** Find <u>all</u> the factors of the three numbers in the box. ➡️ 6 7 9

    b) Which of the three numbers is a prime number?
        Explain your answer.

2 Look at this list of numbers:

    11 13 15 17 19

    a) Which number in the list is <u>not</u> prime?

    b) Explain how you know that this number is not prime.

3 **a)** Which three numbers in the box are <u>not</u> prime?

    b) Explain how you know that these
        numbers are not prime.   31 33 35 37 39

4 Write down the prime numbers from this list: 5, 15, 22, 34, 47, 51, 59

5 **a)** Write down the four prime numbers less than 10.

    b) Find the two prime numbers between 20 and 30.

6 **a)** Find the largest prime number that is less than 60.

    b) Find all the prime numbers between 40 and 50.

7 Explain why 36 is not a prime number.

8 Without doing any calculations, explain how you can
tell that none of the numbers in the list below are prime.

    20 30 40 50 70 90 110 130

Section 5 — Fractions

5.1 Equivalent Fractions

Fractions Basics

Fractions tell you how many parts of a total you have.

The bottom number of a fraction tells you how many equal parts something is split into. It is called the denominator.

$$\frac{5}{7}$$

The top number tells you how many parts you have. It is called the numerator.

Example 1

What fraction of this shape is shaded?

1. The shape is divided into 12 equal parts so the denominator is 12.

2. 5 parts are shaded so the numerator is 5.

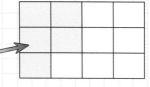

The fraction shaded is $\frac{5}{12}$.

Exercise 1

1 Write down the fraction of each shape below that is shaded.

a)

b)

c)

d)

e)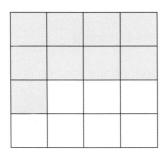

f)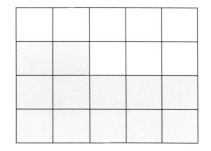

2 Explain why the diagram to the right does **not** show a shaded fraction of $\frac{1}{4}$.

3 Copy each grid below and shade to show the given fraction.

a) $\frac{5}{8}$

b) $\frac{9}{10}$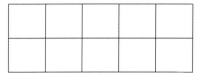

c) $\frac{8}{15}$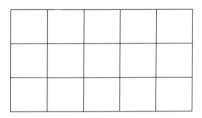

d) $\frac{9}{14}$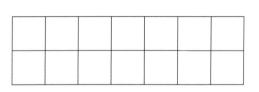

Equivalent Fractions

Equivalent fractions are fractions that are equal in size.

The two shapes below are the same size and have an equal area shaded.

This means the fractions of the two shapes that are shaded are equivalent.

$\frac{2}{4}$ is equivalent to $\frac{1}{2}$

Example 2

Write down the equivalent fractions shown in the diagram on the right.

1. In the first diagram, 1 part out of 4 is shaded, so the fraction is $\frac{1}{4}$.

2. In the second diagram, 4 parts out of 16 are shaded, so the fraction is $\frac{4}{16}$.

3. The same area of the two shapes is shaded, so: $\frac{1}{4}$ is equivalent to $\frac{4}{16}$

Exercise 2

1 Write down the equivalent fractions shown in each pair of diagrams below.

a)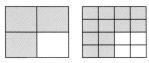

b)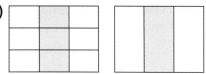

c)

d)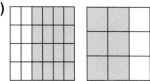

2 a) Copy the diagram below and shade the shapes to make the fractions equivalent.

T **b)** Write down the values of a, b and c.

 = = =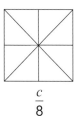

$$\frac{1}{2} \quad = \quad \frac{a}{4} \quad = \quad \frac{b}{6} \quad = \quad \frac{c}{8}$$

Make sure an equal area is shaded in each square.

3 For the pairs of shapes below, write down **(i)** the fraction of each shape that is shaded and **(ii)** whether the pair of fractions is equivalent.

a)

b)

c)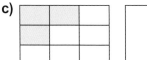

d)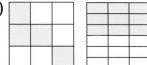

4 Gary and Robert each have a cake of the same size. Gary cuts his cake into 12 slices and eats 4 slices. Robert cuts his cake into 6 slices. How many slices should Robert eat so that he has eaten the same amount as Gary?

Use these to help you.

More Equivalent Fractions

To find an equivalent fraction, you multiply or divide
the numerator and denominator by the same number.

Example 3

Find the value that replaces the square: $\dfrac{1}{5} = \dfrac{\blacksquare}{20}$.

1. Find what you need to multiply by to get
   from one denominator to the other.

2. To get from 5 to 20, multiply by 4.

3. Multiply the numerator by the same
   number to find the missing value.

$$\dfrac{1}{5} = \dfrac{\blacksquare}{20} \quad \times 4$$

$$\times 4 \quad \dfrac{1}{5} = \dfrac{4}{20}$$

Example 4

Find the value of b if $\dfrac{12}{30} = \dfrac{4}{b}$.

1. Find what you need to divide by to get
   from one numerator to the other.

2. To get from 12 to 4, divide by 3.

3. Divide the denominator by the same
   number to find b.

$$\div 3 \quad \dfrac{12}{30} = \dfrac{4}{b}$$

$$\dfrac{12}{30} = \dfrac{4}{b} \qquad b = 30 \div 3 = 10$$

$$\div 3$$

Exercise 3

1   Copy and complete these sentences to find the value that replaces the star: $\dfrac{4}{5} = \dfrac{\bigstar}{10}$

a) To get from 5 to 10, multiply by ....

b) To find the value that replaces the star, multiply .... by ....

c) The value that replaces the star is ....

2 The fractions $\frac{8}{14}$ and $\frac{a}{7}$ are equivalent. Copy and complete these sentences.

a) To get from 14 to 7, divide by ....

b) To find the value of a, divide .... by ....

c) The value of a is ....

3 The fractions $\frac{2}{3}$ and $\frac{4}{b}$ are equivalent. Copy and complete these sentences.

a) To get from 2 to 4, ... 2 by ....

b) To find the value of b, ... 3 by ....

c) The value of b is ....

Hi Mum

4 Find the value of a in each of these fractions.

a) $\frac{1}{2} = \frac{a}{4}$

b) $\frac{3}{4} = \frac{a}{8}$

c) $\frac{1}{2} = \frac{a}{10}$

d) $\frac{2}{3} = \frac{a}{9}$

e) $\frac{6}{18} = \frac{a}{6}$

f) $\frac{15}{35} = \frac{a}{7}$

g) $\frac{4}{12} = \frac{a}{6}$

h) $\frac{9}{15} = \frac{a}{5}$

i) $\frac{9}{21} = \frac{a}{7}$

5 Find the value of a in each of these fractions.

a) $\frac{1}{2} = \frac{3}{a}$

b) $\frac{2}{5} = \frac{8}{a}$

c) $\frac{4}{7} = \frac{16}{a}$

d) $\frac{3}{8} = \frac{15}{a}$

e) $\frac{6}{8} = \frac{18}{a}$

f) $\frac{8}{18} = \frac{4}{a}$

g) $\frac{10}{14} = \frac{5}{a}$

h) $\frac{9}{12} = \frac{3}{a}$

i) $\frac{12}{30} = \frac{4}{a}$

6 Find the value of a and b in each of these equivalent fractions.

a) $\frac{1}{3} = \frac{a}{6} = \frac{b}{12}$

b) $\frac{1}{4} = \frac{3}{a} = \frac{b}{24}$

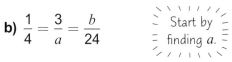

Start by finding a.

c) $\frac{6}{21} = \frac{2}{a} = \frac{b}{14}$

d) $\frac{10}{12} = \frac{5}{a} = \frac{b}{18}$

e) $\frac{8}{20} = \frac{a}{5} = \frac{6}{b}$

f) $\frac{16}{36} = \frac{4}{a} = \frac{b}{27}$

75

Example 5

Are the fractions $\frac{1}{5}$ and $\frac{3}{20}$ equivalent?

1. Find a multiplier for the numerators:
   To get from 1 to 3, multiply by 3.

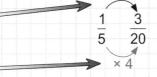

2. Find a multiplier for the denominators:
   To get from 5 to 20, multiply by 4.

3. If these two multipliers are the same, then the fractions are equivalent.

The multipliers are different, so the fractions are not equivalent.

Exercise 4

1 Copy and complete these sentences to work out if the fractions $\frac{3}{7}$ and $\frac{9}{21}$ are equivalent.

a) To get from 3 to 9, multiply by ....

b) To get from 7 to 21, multiply by ....

Write "are" or "are not" in this space.

c) The multipliers are ...., so $\frac{3}{7}$ and $\frac{9}{21}$ .... equivalent.

Write "the same" or "different" in this space.

2 Copy and complete these sentences to work out if the fractions $\frac{4}{11}$ and $\frac{12}{44}$ are equivalent.

a) To get from 4 to 12, multiply by ....

b) To get from 11 to 44, multiply by ....

c) The multipliers are ...., so $\frac{4}{11}$ and $\frac{12}{44}$ .... equivalent.

3 Are each of these pairs of fractions equivalent?

a) $\frac{3}{4}, \frac{15}{20}$

b) $\frac{2}{3}, \frac{4}{9}$

c) $\frac{1}{3}, \frac{3}{15}$

d) $\frac{6}{8}, \frac{2}{4}$

e) $\frac{10}{25}, \frac{2}{5}$

f) $\frac{15}{35}, \frac{3}{7}$

Simplifying a fraction means writing an equivalent fraction using the smallest possible numbers.

Simplifying a fraction is also called cancelling down or 'writing a fraction in its simplest terms'.

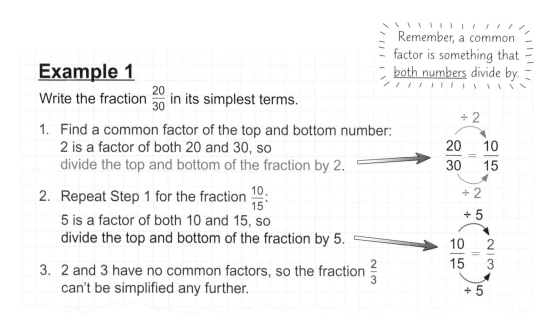

Example 1

Write the fraction $\frac{20}{30}$ in its simplest terms.

1. Find a common factor of the top and bottom number:
   2 is a factor of both 20 and 30, so
   divide the top and bottom of the fraction by 2.

2. Repeat Step 1 for the fraction $\frac{10}{15}$:
   5 is a factor of both 10 and 15, so
   divide the top and bottom of the fraction by 5.

3. 2 and 3 have no common factors, so the fraction $\frac{2}{3}$ can't be simplified any further.

Remember, a common factor is something that both numbers divide by.

$$\frac{20}{30} = \frac{10}{15} \qquad (\div 2)$$

$$\frac{10}{15} = \frac{2}{3} \qquad (\div 5)$$

Exercise 1

Answer these questions **without using a calculator**.

1 Find the numbers that replace each shape to write these fractions in their simplest terms.

a)

b)

c)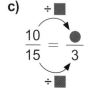

2 a) Find a number greater than 1 which is a common factor of 2 and 10.

b) Divide 2 and 10 by your answer to part a) to write the fraction $\frac{2}{10}$ in its simplest terms.

3 Find the numbers that replace each shape to write these fractions in their simplest terms.

a) $\dfrac{12}{18} = \dfrac{6}{\bigstar} = \dfrac{2}{\newmoon}$

b) $\dfrac{14}{42} = \dfrac{7}{\bigstar} = \dfrac{\blacktriangle}{\newmoon}$

c) $\dfrac{16}{20} = \dfrac{\bigstar}{10} = \dfrac{\blacktriangle}{\newmoon}$

d) $\dfrac{24}{30} = \dfrac{\bigstar}{15} = \dfrac{\blacktriangle}{\newmoon}$

4 Write each fraction in its simplest terms.

a) $\dfrac{2}{4}$

b) $\dfrac{2}{8}$

c) $\dfrac{5}{20}$

d) $\dfrac{3}{12}$

e) $\dfrac{2}{30}$

f) $\dfrac{7}{14}$

g) $\dfrac{6}{12}$

h) $\dfrac{12}{24}$

i) $\dfrac{15}{30}$

j) $\dfrac{4}{6}$

k) $\dfrac{10}{25}$

l) $\dfrac{15}{20}$

m) $\dfrac{9}{15}$

n) $\dfrac{9}{30}$

o) $\dfrac{16}{28}$

p) $\dfrac{24}{36}$

q) $\dfrac{30}{50}$

r) $\dfrac{32}{40}$

Simplifying Fractions Using a Calculator

Fractions can be put into a calculator using the fraction button — $\boxed{a^b_c}$ or $\boxed{\tfrac{\blacksquare}{\square}}$.

For example, you can enter the fraction $\dfrac{2}{4}$ by pressing:

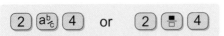

Which button you have depends on your calculator — but both do the same thing.

To simplify a fraction using your calculator, enter the fraction and then press the equals button.

Example 2

Simplify the fraction $\frac{32}{48}$ using your calculator.

(3)(2)(a^b_c)(4)(8)(=)   [2⌐3]   So $\frac{32}{48}$ in its simplest terms is $\frac{2}{3}$.

Exercise 2

1   Simplify these fractions using your calculator.

a) $\frac{36}{54}$

b) $\frac{75}{375}$

c) $\frac{162}{243}$

d) $\frac{138}{483}$

e) $\frac{375}{1000}$

f) $\frac{336}{432}$

g) $\frac{252}{693}$

h) $\frac{112}{252}$

i) $\frac{144}{468}$

j) $\frac{289}{867}$

k) $\frac{249}{830}$

l) $\frac{671}{793}$

Example 3

Simplify the fraction $\frac{2.4 + 3.4}{9.3 - 0.6}$ using your calculator.

1. Type in the numerator
    inside brackets. $\longrightarrow$ (( )(2)(•)(4)(+)(3)(•)(4)( ))

2. Press the fraction button. $\longrightarrow$ (a^b_c)

3. Type in the denominator
    inside brackets and then $\longrightarrow$ (( )(9)(•)(3)(−)(0)(•)(6)( ))(=)
    press the equals button.
                                                          [2⌐3]

So $\frac{2.4 + 3.4}{9.3 - 0.6}$ in its simplest terms is $\frac{2}{3}$.

Exercise 3

1 Simplify the following fractions using your calculator.

a) $\dfrac{2.4 + 4}{8}$

b) $\dfrac{7.2}{9.4 + 0.2}$

c) $\dfrac{23.4}{19.6 + 15.5}$

d) $\dfrac{11.7 - 2.1}{10.3 + 1.7}$

e) $\dfrac{2.9 - 1.4}{8.1 - 0.6}$

f) $\dfrac{24 - 4.8}{23.8 + 14.6}$

g) $\dfrac{8.9 + 5.5}{31.2 - 9.6}$

h) $\dfrac{9.6 + 3.6}{17 - 1.16}$

i) $\dfrac{4.1 - 0.14}{11.12 - 5.84}$

j) $\dfrac{2.48 + 4.15}{19.72 - 5.134}$

Hooray for calculators.

5.3   Ordering Fractions

Ordering fractions means putting them in order of size. If fractions have the same denominator then you can use their numerators to put them in order.

Example 1

Write these fractions in order, from smallest to largest: $\dfrac{4}{9}, \dfrac{7}{9}, \dfrac{2}{9}$

1. All three fractions have the same denominator, 9.

2. So use the numerators to order the fractions.

smallest to largest

$\dfrac{2}{9}, \dfrac{4}{9}, \dfrac{7}{9}$

Exercise 1

1 For each pair of fractions, write down which is the **smallest**.

a) $\dfrac{1}{6}, \dfrac{5}{6}$

b) $\dfrac{4}{5}, \dfrac{2}{5}$

c) $\dfrac{3}{10}, \dfrac{7}{10}$

d) $\dfrac{7}{12}, \dfrac{5}{12}$

e) $\dfrac{2}{7}, \dfrac{4}{7}$

f) $\dfrac{5}{8}, \dfrac{3}{8}$

2 For each group of fractions, write down which is the **largest**.

a) $\dfrac{3}{10}, \dfrac{7}{10}, \dfrac{9}{10}$

b) $\dfrac{5}{16}, \dfrac{13}{16}, \dfrac{7}{16}$

c) $\dfrac{7}{12}, \dfrac{1}{12}, \dfrac{5}{12}$

d) $\dfrac{13}{15}, \dfrac{11}{15}, \dfrac{7}{15}$

e) $\dfrac{8}{17}, \dfrac{5}{17}, \dfrac{11}{17}, \dfrac{9}{17}$

f) $\dfrac{7}{25}, \dfrac{12}{25}, \dfrac{9}{25}, \dfrac{14}{25}, \dfrac{13}{25}$

3 Write each set of fractions below in order, from smallest to largest.

a) $\dfrac{4}{9}, \dfrac{7}{9}, \dfrac{5}{9}$

b) $\dfrac{5}{12}, \dfrac{1}{12}, \dfrac{7}{12}$

c) $\dfrac{7}{15}, \dfrac{4}{15}, \dfrac{2}{15}$

d) $\dfrac{3}{16}, \dfrac{11}{16}, \dfrac{9}{16}$

e) $\dfrac{8}{20}, \dfrac{7}{20}, \dfrac{11}{20}, \dfrac{9}{20}$

f) $\dfrac{21}{31}, \dfrac{8}{31}, \dfrac{4}{31}, \dfrac{11}{31}$

g) $\dfrac{18}{42}, \dfrac{14}{42}, \dfrac{11}{42}, \dfrac{32}{42}$

h) $\dfrac{4}{22}, \dfrac{14}{22}, \dfrac{2}{22}, \dfrac{21}{22}, \dfrac{9}{22}$

i) $\dfrac{7}{25}, \dfrac{12}{25}, \dfrac{9}{25}, \dfrac{14}{25}, \dfrac{13}{25}$

j) $\dfrac{67}{98}, \dfrac{33}{98}, \dfrac{71}{98}, \dfrac{68}{98}, \dfrac{58}{98}$

Finding a Common Denominator

Putting fractions over a common denominator means rewriting them so they both have the same denominator.

Example 2

Rewrite the fractions $\dfrac{1}{2}$ and $\dfrac{1}{8}$ so they have a common denominator.

1. For the common denominator, look for a number that both 2 and 8 divide into (go into) exactly.

2. You can use 8 — because 2 and 8 both go into 8.

3. Rewrite $\dfrac{1}{2}$ as an equivalent fraction with 8 as the denominator by multiplying both the top and bottom by 4.

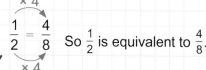

So $\dfrac{1}{2}$ is equivalent to $\dfrac{4}{8}$.

Putting the fractions over a common denominator gives $\dfrac{4}{8}$ and $\dfrac{1}{8}$.

Exercise 2

1 Rewrite the fractions $\frac{1}{4}$ and $\frac{1}{8}$ so they have a common denominator of 8.

2 Rewrite the fractions $\frac{2}{3}$ and $\frac{7}{9}$ so they have a common denominator of 9.

3 Rewrite these pairs of fractions so they have a common denominator.

a) $\frac{1}{2}, \frac{1}{4}$ b) $\frac{1}{3}, \frac{1}{9}$ c) $\frac{3}{5}, \frac{7}{10}$

d) $\frac{1}{3}, \frac{5}{12}$ e) $\frac{3}{8}, \frac{3}{4}$ f) $\frac{3}{4}, \frac{7}{12}$

g) $\frac{3}{5}, \frac{13}{20}$ h) $\frac{2}{5}, \frac{8}{25}$ i) $\frac{3}{7}, \frac{5}{14}$

j) $\frac{11}{12}, \frac{5}{6}$ k) $\frac{13}{18}, \frac{7}{9}$ l) $\frac{5}{8}, \frac{11}{24}$

4 a) Find a fraction equivalent to $\frac{3}{4}$ which has a denominator of 16.

b) Find a fraction equivalent to $\frac{5}{8}$ which has a denominator of 16.

c) Use your answers to rewrite the fractions $\frac{3}{4}, \frac{5}{8}$ and $\frac{3}{16}$
so they have a common denominator.

5 Rewrite these sets of fractions so they have a
common denominator.

a) $\frac{1}{2}, \frac{1}{4}, \frac{3}{8}$ b) $\frac{1}{3}, \frac{5}{6}, \frac{11}{12}$

c) $\frac{4}{5}, \frac{3}{10}, \frac{1}{20}$

Example 3

Rewrite the fractions $\frac{5}{6}$ and $\frac{3}{8}$ so they have a common denominator.

1. 6 and 8 both divide into 24, so use 24 as the common denominator.

$$\overset{\times 4}{\frac{5}{6}} = \frac{20}{24} \quad \text{So } \frac{5}{6} \text{ is equivalent to } \frac{20}{24}.$$
$$\times 4$$

2. Rewrite $\frac{5}{6}$ as an equivalent fraction with 24 as the denominator by multiplying both the top and bottom by 4.

$$\overset{\times 3}{\frac{3}{8}} = \frac{9}{24} \quad \text{So } \frac{3}{8} \text{ is equivalent to } \frac{9}{24}.$$
$$\times 3$$

3. Rewrite $\frac{3}{8}$ as an equivalent fraction with 24 as the denominator by multiplying both the top and bottom by 3.

Putting the fractions over a common denominator gives $\frac{20}{24}$ and $\frac{9}{24}$.

Exercise 3

1 Rewrite the fractions $\frac{1}{2}$ and $\frac{1}{3}$ so they have a common denominator of 6.

2 Rewrite the fractions $\frac{1}{4}$ and $\frac{5}{6}$ so they have a common denominator of 12.

3 **a)** Find a number which is a multiple of both 3 and 4. ← *That means that 3 and 4 both 'go into' this number exactly.*

b) Use your answer to rewrite the fractions $\frac{1}{3}$ and $\frac{1}{4}$ so they have a common denominator.

4 **a)** Find a number which is a multiple of both 8 and 12.

b) Use your answer to rewrite the fractions $\frac{3}{8}$ and $\frac{7}{12}$ so they have a common denominator.

5 Rewrite these pairs of fractions so they have a common denominator.

a) $\frac{1}{2}, \frac{1}{5}$ **b)** $\frac{1}{3}, \frac{1}{5}$ **c)** $\frac{1}{7}, \frac{1}{10}$

d) $\frac{1}{6}, \frac{2}{9}$ **e)** $\frac{2}{3}, \frac{3}{4}$ **f)** $\frac{1}{7}, \frac{5}{6}$

g) $\frac{2}{9}, \frac{1}{2}$ **h)** $\frac{3}{8}, \frac{4}{5}$ **i)** $\frac{7}{8}, \frac{3}{10}$

Ordering Fractions With Different Denominators

Fractions with different denominators can still be ordered.

First you need to rewrite them with a common denominator.

Example 4

Write the fractions $\frac{1}{2}$, $\frac{3}{8}$ and $\frac{3}{4}$ in order, from smallest to largest.

1. 8 is a multiple of 2, 4 and 8, so rewrite $\frac{1}{2}$ and $\frac{3}{4}$ with a common denominator of 8.

$$\frac{1}{2} \overset{\times 4}{=} \frac{4}{8} \qquad \frac{3}{4} \overset{\times 2}{=} \frac{6}{8}$$

2. Use the numerators to put the fractions in order, as before.

So the fractions are equivalent to $\frac{4}{8}$, $\frac{3}{8}$ and $\frac{6}{8}$.

Putting these in order: $\frac{3}{8}$, $\frac{4}{8}$ and $\frac{6}{8}$.

3. Write the ordered fractions in their original form.

So the order is $\frac{3}{8}$, $\frac{1}{2}$, $\frac{3}{4}$.

Exercise 4

1 a) Find a fraction equivalent to $\frac{3}{5}$ which has a denominator of 15.

   b) Use your answer to write down which fraction is bigger: $\frac{3}{5}$ or $\frac{11}{15}$.

2 a) Rewrite the fractions $\frac{5}{8}$ and $\frac{11}{24}$ so they have a common denominator of 24.

   b) Use your answer to write down which fraction is bigger: $\frac{5}{8}$ or $\frac{11}{24}$.

3 a) Rewrite the fractions $\frac{1}{2}$ and $\frac{2}{3}$ so they have a common denominator of 6.

   b) Use your answer to write the fractions $\frac{2}{3}$, $\frac{5}{6}$ and $\frac{1}{2}$ in order, from smallest to largest.

4 By rewriting the fractions so they have a common denominator of 12, put these groups of fractions in order, from smallest to largest.

   a) $\frac{2}{3}$, $\frac{3}{4}$, $\frac{7}{12}$

   b) $\frac{1}{6}$, $\frac{1}{2}$, $\frac{5}{12}$

   c) $\frac{5}{6}$, $\frac{2}{4}$, $\frac{7}{12}$

   d) $\frac{5}{12}$, $\frac{1}{3}$, $\frac{1}{4}$, $\frac{1}{6}$

5 By rewriting the fractions so they have a common denominator of 20, put these groups of fractions in order, from smallest to largest.

a) $\dfrac{1}{2}$, $\dfrac{3}{10}$, $\dfrac{7}{20}$

b) $\dfrac{1}{4}$, $\dfrac{9}{20}$, $\dfrac{2}{5}$

c) $\dfrac{3}{5}$, $\dfrac{7}{20}$, $\dfrac{1}{4}$

d) $\dfrac{3}{4}$, $\dfrac{17}{20}$, $\dfrac{4}{5}$, $\dfrac{7}{10}$

6 Put these groups of fractions in order, from smallest to largest.

a) $\dfrac{3}{4}$, $\dfrac{3}{8}$, $\dfrac{7}{16}$

b) $\dfrac{9}{16}$, $\dfrac{1}{2}$, $\dfrac{5}{8}$

c) $\dfrac{3}{4}$, $\dfrac{17}{24}$, $\dfrac{7}{12}$

d) $\dfrac{1}{3}$, $\dfrac{7}{15}$, $\dfrac{2}{5}$

e) $\dfrac{3}{14}$, $\dfrac{2}{7}$, $\dfrac{1}{2}$

f) $\dfrac{5}{6}$, $\dfrac{2}{3}$, $\dfrac{11}{18}$, $\dfrac{4}{9}$

5.4 Adding and Subtracting Fractions

Fractions with a common denominator can be added or subtracted by adding or subtracting the numerators.

Example 1

Work out $\dfrac{2}{11} + \dfrac{5}{11}$.

The denominators are the same, so add the numerators.

$$\frac{2}{11} + \frac{5}{11} = \frac{2+5}{11} = \frac{7}{11}$$

Example 2

Work out $\dfrac{9}{10} - \dfrac{3}{10}$. Give your answer in its simplest terms.

1. The denominators are the same, so subtract the numerators.

$$\frac{9}{10} - \frac{3}{10} = \frac{9-3}{10} = \frac{6}{10}$$

2. Simplify the fraction by dividing the top and bottom number by 2.

$$\frac{6}{10} \overset{\div 2}{\underset{\div 2}{=}} \frac{3}{5}$$

Exercise 1

Answer these questions **without using a calculator**.

1 Copy and complete these calculations.

a) $\dfrac{1}{5} + \dfrac{2}{5} = \dfrac{1+2}{} = \dfrac{}{5}$

b) $\dfrac{1}{8} + \dfrac{2}{8} = \dfrac{1+}{8} = \dfrac{}{8}$

c) $\dfrac{4}{7} - \dfrac{1}{7} = \dfrac{-1}{7} = \dfrac{}{7}$

d) $\dfrac{4}{5} - \dfrac{2}{5} = \dfrac{-}{5} = \dfrac{}{}$

2 Add these pairs of fractions.

a) $\dfrac{1}{7} + \dfrac{4}{7}$

b) $\dfrac{1}{5} + \dfrac{3}{5}$

c) $\dfrac{2}{9} + \dfrac{5}{9}$

d) $\dfrac{3}{11} + \dfrac{4}{11}$

e) $\dfrac{1}{3} + \dfrac{1}{3}$

f) $\dfrac{2}{5} + \dfrac{1}{5}$

g) $\dfrac{4}{9} + \dfrac{1}{9}$

h) $\dfrac{4}{13} + \dfrac{8}{13}$

i) $\dfrac{4}{15} + \dfrac{7}{15}$

3 Subtract these pairs of fractions.

a) $\dfrac{5}{9} - \dfrac{3}{9}$

b) $\dfrac{5}{11} - \dfrac{3}{11}$

c) $\dfrac{2}{3} - \dfrac{1}{3}$

d) $\dfrac{4}{5} - \dfrac{1}{5}$

e) $\dfrac{7}{9} - \dfrac{2}{9}$

f) $\dfrac{9}{13} - \dfrac{3}{13}$

g) $\dfrac{11}{15} - \dfrac{7}{15}$

h) $\dfrac{11}{13} - \dfrac{4}{13}$

i) $\dfrac{12}{17} - \dfrac{4}{17}$

4 Work out these calculations.

a) $\dfrac{5}{13} + \dfrac{6}{13}$

b) $\dfrac{10}{12} - \dfrac{9}{12}$

c) $\dfrac{17}{21} - \dfrac{13}{21}$

d) $\dfrac{8}{17} + \dfrac{4}{17}$

e) $\dfrac{14}{19} - \dfrac{12}{19}$

f) $\dfrac{9}{17} + \dfrac{6}{17}$

5 Work out these calculations. Give your answers in their simplest terms.

a) $\dfrac{1}{4} + \dfrac{1}{4}$

b) $\dfrac{5}{6} - \dfrac{1}{6}$

c) $\dfrac{2}{10} + \dfrac{3}{10}$

d) $\dfrac{1}{8} + \dfrac{3}{8}$

e) $\dfrac{8}{9} - \dfrac{2}{9}$

f) $\dfrac{7}{10} - \dfrac{3}{10}$

g) $\dfrac{5}{9} - \dfrac{2}{9}$

h) $\dfrac{3}{14} + \dfrac{9}{14}$

i) $\dfrac{9}{20} + \dfrac{3}{20}$

j) $\dfrac{8}{21} + \dfrac{10}{21}$

k) $\dfrac{15}{16} - \dfrac{3}{16}$

l) $\dfrac{17}{18} - \dfrac{5}{18}$

6 Owen eats $\dfrac{3}{7}$ of a pizza. Barry eats $\dfrac{2}{7}$ of the pizza.

What fraction of the pizza has been eaten?

7 A box contains mini doughnuts. Luke eats $\dfrac{4}{12}$ of the doughnuts.

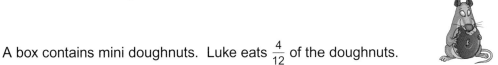

Lexie eats $\dfrac{2}{12}$ of the doughnuts. What fraction of the doughnuts have been eaten?

Give your answer in its simplest terms.

Fractions With Different Denominators

Fractions with different denominators can also be added and subtracted.

You need to rewrite them with a common denominator first.

Example 3

Work out $\dfrac{1}{3} + \dfrac{2}{9}$.

1. 9 is a multiple of 3 and 9, so rewrite $\dfrac{1}{3}$ with a denominator of 9 by multiplying top and bottom by 3.

2. Now the fractions have a common denominator, add the numerators as before.

$$\overset{\times 3}{\dfrac{1}{3}} = \dfrac{3}{9}\underset{\times 3}{}$$

$$\dfrac{3}{9} + \dfrac{2}{9} = \dfrac{3+2}{9} = \dfrac{5}{9}$$

Example 4

Work out $\frac{3}{4} - \frac{1}{6}$.

1. Rewrite the fractions with a common denominator of 12.

2. Now the fractions have a common denominator, subtract the numerators as before.

$$\overset{\times 3}{\frac{3}{4} = \frac{9}{12}} \quad \overset{\times 2}{\frac{1}{6} = \frac{2}{12}}$$
$$\underset{\times 3}{} \quad \underset{\times 2}{}$$

$$\frac{9}{12} - \frac{2}{12} = \frac{9 - 2}{12} = \frac{7}{12}$$

Exercise 2

Answer these questions **without using a calculator**.

1 Copy and complete these calculations.

a) $\dfrac{3}{8} + \dfrac{1}{4} = \dfrac{3}{8} + \dfrac{}{8} = \dfrac{}{8}$

b) $\dfrac{7}{12} + \dfrac{1}{3} = \dfrac{7}{12} + \dfrac{}{12} = \dfrac{}{12}$

c) $\dfrac{2}{3} - \dfrac{2}{9} = \dfrac{}{9} - \dfrac{2}{9} = \dfrac{}{9}$

d) $\dfrac{9}{10} - \dfrac{3}{5} = \dfrac{9}{10} - \dfrac{}{10} = \dfrac{}{10}$

e) $\dfrac{1}{2} + \dfrac{1}{3} = \dfrac{3}{6} + \dfrac{}{6} = \dfrac{}{6}$

f) $\dfrac{1}{3} + \dfrac{1}{4} = \dfrac{}{12} + \dfrac{3}{12} = \dfrac{}{12}$

g) $\dfrac{3}{4} - \dfrac{1}{5} = \dfrac{15}{20} - \dfrac{}{20} = \dfrac{}{20}$

h) $\dfrac{5}{8} - \dfrac{1}{3} = \dfrac{}{24} - \dfrac{}{24} = \dfrac{}{24}$

2 a) Rewrite the fractions $\frac{4}{9}$ and $\frac{5}{18}$ so they have a common denominator.

   b) Use your answer to work out $\frac{4}{9} + \frac{5}{18}$.

3 a) Rewrite the fractions $\frac{2}{3}$ and $\frac{1}{5}$ so they have a common denominator.

   b) Use your answer to work out $\frac{2}{3} - \frac{1}{5}$.

4 By first rewriting the fractions so they have a common denominator, add or subtract these fractions. Give your answers in their simplest terms.

a) $\dfrac{3}{5} + \dfrac{3}{10}$

b) $\dfrac{3}{4} + \dfrac{1}{8}$

c) $\dfrac{1}{3} - \dfrac{5}{18}$

d) $\dfrac{19}{20} - \dfrac{3}{10}$

e) $\dfrac{3}{5} + \dfrac{1}{20}$

f) $\dfrac{11}{20} - \dfrac{2}{5}$

g) $\dfrac{1}{4} + \dfrac{11}{20}$

h) $\dfrac{11}{24} + \dfrac{3}{8}$

i) $\dfrac{5}{6} + \dfrac{1}{24}$

j) $\dfrac{11}{16} - \dfrac{1}{4}$

k) $\dfrac{23}{24} - \dfrac{3}{4}$

l) $\dfrac{5}{6} - \dfrac{5}{18}$

5 By first rewriting the fractions so they have a common denominator, add or subtract these fractions. Give your answers in their simplest terms.

a) $\dfrac{1}{2} + \dfrac{2}{5}$

b) $\dfrac{1}{2} - \dfrac{2}{7}$

c) $\dfrac{1}{2} + \dfrac{3}{7}$

d) $\dfrac{2}{3} - \dfrac{1}{4}$

e) $\dfrac{3}{4} + \dfrac{1}{5}$

f) $\dfrac{2}{5} - \dfrac{1}{6}$

g) $\dfrac{3}{5} - \dfrac{3}{7}$

h) $\dfrac{7}{8} - \dfrac{2}{3}$

i) $\dfrac{5}{8} - \dfrac{2}{5}$

6 At a bowling alley, $\dfrac{3}{12}$ of the bowling balls are pink and $\dfrac{4}{6}$ are blue.

What is the total fraction of bowling balls that are either pink or blue?

7 Ellie's hair is $\dfrac{7}{8}$ m long. As a practical joke, Ellie's sister cuts off $\dfrac{1}{3}$ m of Ellie's hair. How long is Ellie's hair now?

8 Ellie's sister is making a cake. She puts $\dfrac{11}{12}$ kg of sugar in a bowl. Ellie removes $\dfrac{1}{8}$ kg of the sugar and replaces it with salt.

How much sugar is left in the bowl?

Adding and Subtracting Fractions with a Calculator

Example 5

Use a calculator to work out $\frac{9}{21} + \frac{3}{7}$.

Type the sum into the calculator using the fraction button ($a\frac{b}{c}$ or $\frac{\blacksquare}{\square}$).

⑨ $a\frac{b}{c}$ ② ① ＋ ③ $a\frac{b}{c}$ ⑦ ＝ ⎧ $6,7$ ⎫   So $\frac{9}{21} + \frac{3}{7} = \frac{6}{7}$.

Exercise 3

Use a calculator for this exercise.

1 Work out these calculations using your calculator.

a) $\frac{1}{2} + \frac{1}{3}$ b) $\frac{2}{5} + \frac{3}{7}$ c) $\frac{3}{12} - \frac{2}{14}$

d) $\frac{5}{28} - \frac{1}{7}$ e) $\frac{8}{15} + \frac{3}{12}$ f) $\frac{11}{32} + \frac{2}{9}$

g) $\frac{2}{13} + \frac{4}{11}$ h) $\frac{4}{54} - \frac{8}{108}$ i) $\frac{12}{111} + \frac{8}{185}$

2 A plank of wood is $\frac{9}{13}$ m long. Jim cuts a $\frac{2}{17}$ m piece of wood off the plank.

Find the length of wood that is left.

3 On a train, $\frac{11}{18}$ of passengers have single tickets
and $\frac{1}{4}$ have return tickets. The rest don't have tickets.

What fraction of passengers have a ticket?

4 At a "Giant Vegetable Competition" at a country fair, $\frac{11}{21}$ of the vegetables
are leeks and $\frac{5}{28}$ are pumpkins. Find the fraction of all vegetables in the
competition that are either leeks or pumpkins.

5.5 Multiplying Fractions

Multiplying by Unit Fractions

A unit fraction has 1 as its numerator — for example: $\frac{1}{2}$, $\frac{1}{3}$, $\frac{1}{5}$, $\frac{1}{10}$

Multiplying a number by a unit fraction is the same as dividing that number by the denominator.

Example 1

Work out $12 \times \frac{1}{3}$

Multiplying by $\frac{1}{3}$ is the same as dividing by 3.

$$12 \times \frac{1}{3} = 12 \div 3$$
$$= 4$$

Exercise 1

1   Work out these multiplications **without using a calculator**.

a) $8 \times \frac{1}{4}$

b) $10 \times \frac{1}{5}$

c) $15 \times \frac{1}{5}$

d) $45 \times \frac{1}{3}$

e) $27 \times \frac{1}{9}$

f) $40 \times \frac{1}{8}$

g) $16 \times \frac{1}{4}$

h) $35 \times \frac{1}{5}$

i) $39 \times \frac{1}{3}$

Multiplying Whole Numbers by Fractions

To multiply a whole number by a fraction:
- multiply by the numerator
- divide by the denominator

You can do these steps in any order.

Example 2

Work out $8 \times \frac{3}{4}$

1. Multiply by the numerator
    — so multiply 8 by 3.

2. Divide by the denominator
    — so divide the result by 4.

$$8 \times \frac{3}{4} = \frac{8 \times 3}{4} = \frac{24}{4}$$
$$= 24 \div 4 = 6$$

Or divide 8 by 4 first, then multiply the result by 3. You'll get the same answer.

Example 3

Find $\frac{3}{5}$ of 20.

1. 'Of' means '×', so multiply as before.

2. Multiply by 3, then divide the result by 5.

$$\frac{3}{5} \times 20 = \frac{3 \times 20}{5} = \frac{60}{5}$$

$$= 60 \div 5 = 12$$

Exercise 2

Answer these questions **without using a calculator**.

1 Copy and complete these calculations.

a) $12 \times \frac{2}{3} = \frac{12 \times 2}{3} = \frac{}{3} = \text{.......}$

b) $15 \times \frac{3}{5} = \frac{15 \times}{5} = \frac{}{5} = \text{.......}$

c) $14 \times \frac{2}{7} = \frac{\times}{7} = \frac{}{} = \text{.......}$

d) $9 \times \frac{4}{12} = \frac{\times}{} = \frac{}{} = \text{.......}$

2 Work out these multiplications. Give your answers in their simplest terms.

a) $8 \times \frac{3}{4}$

b) $5 \times \frac{8}{10}$

c) $7 \times \frac{4}{14}$

d) $6 \times \frac{8}{12}$

e) $9 \times \frac{5}{15}$

f) $10 \times \frac{6}{12}$

g) $18 \times \frac{2}{9}$

h) $11 \times \frac{4}{22}$

i) $12 \times \frac{5}{20}$

j) $15 \times \frac{2}{6}$

k) $16 \times \frac{2}{8}$

l) $15 \times \frac{3}{9}$

3 Find:

a) $\frac{1}{3}$ of 18

b) $\frac{1}{4}$ of 12

c) $\frac{2}{5}$ of 15

d) $\frac{3}{5}$ of 10

e) $\frac{4}{5}$ of 15

f) $\frac{2}{6}$ of 9

g) $\frac{5}{6}$ of 12

h) $\frac{6}{8}$ of 4

i) $\frac{2}{7}$ of 21

Multiplying Fractions

To multiply one fraction by another fraction, multiply the numerators and the denominators separately.

Example 4

Work out $\frac{3}{4} \times \frac{2}{5}$

1. Multiply the numerators.

2. Multiply the denominators.

$$\frac{3}{4} \times \frac{2}{5} = \frac{3 \times 2}{4 \times 5} = \frac{6}{20}$$

3. Simplify the fraction by dividing the top and bottom number by 2.

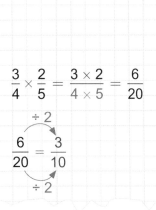

$$\frac{6}{20} = \frac{3}{10}$$

Exercise 3

Answer these questions **without using a calculator**.

1 Copy and complete these calculations.

a) $\frac{1}{2} \times \frac{1}{3} = \frac{1 \times 1}{2 \times 3} = \underline{\quad}$

b) $\frac{1}{2} \times \frac{1}{4} = \frac{1 \times 1}{2 \times 4} = \underline{\quad}$

c) $\frac{1}{2} \times \frac{3}{7} = \frac{1 \times}{2 \times} = \underline{\quad}$

d) $\frac{1}{4} \times \frac{3}{4} = \frac{\times 3}{\times 4} = \underline{\quad}$

e) $\frac{1}{3} \times \frac{2}{5} = \frac{\times 2}{3 \times} = \underline{\quad}$

f) $\frac{1}{2} \times \frac{3}{5} = \frac{1 \times}{\times} = \underline{\quad}$

g) $\frac{3}{4} \times \frac{3}{5} = \frac{3 \times}{\times} = \underline{\quad}$

h) $\frac{4}{5} \times \frac{2}{3} = \frac{\times}{\times} = \underline{\quad}$

2 Work out these multiplications.

a) $\frac{1}{2} \times \frac{3}{4}$

b) $\frac{1}{3} \times \frac{1}{3}$

c) $\frac{1}{2} \times \frac{3}{8}$

d) $\frac{1}{2} \times \frac{1}{7}$

e) $\frac{3}{4} \times \frac{1}{2}$

f) $\frac{1}{2} \times \frac{5}{7}$

g) $\frac{3}{5} \times \frac{3}{5}$

h) $\frac{2}{3} \times \frac{2}{5}$

i) $\frac{3}{4} \times \frac{3}{7}$

3 Work out these multiplications.

a) $\dfrac{2}{5} \times \dfrac{4}{7}$

b) $\dfrac{4}{5} \times \dfrac{3}{7}$

c) $\dfrac{5}{6} \times \dfrac{5}{8}$

d) $\dfrac{5}{7} \times \dfrac{3}{4}$

e) $\dfrac{2}{5} \times \dfrac{7}{9}$

f) $\dfrac{2}{9} \times \dfrac{5}{7}$

4 Work out these multiplications. Give your answers in their simplest terms.

a) $\dfrac{1}{2} \times \dfrac{2}{3}$

b) $\dfrac{1}{3} \times \dfrac{3}{4}$

c) $\dfrac{1}{2} \times \dfrac{2}{6}$

d) $\dfrac{1}{2} \times \dfrac{4}{7}$

e) $\dfrac{3}{4} \times \dfrac{2}{3}$

f) $\dfrac{2}{7} \times \dfrac{3}{4}$

g) $\dfrac{2}{3} \times \dfrac{6}{7}$

h) $\dfrac{3}{4} \times \dfrac{8}{9}$

i) $\dfrac{6}{8} \times \dfrac{4}{5}$

Multiplying Fractions Using a Calculator

Example 5

Use a calculator to work out $\dfrac{4}{7} \times \dfrac{5}{12}$.

Type the multiplication into the calculator using the fraction button (a^b_c or $\blacksquare$).

$\boxed{4}\ \boxed{a^b_c}\ \boxed{7}\ \boxed{\times}\ \boxed{5}\ \boxed{a^b_c}\ \boxed{1}\ \boxed{2}\ \boxed{=}$ $\boxed{5{\scriptstyle\rfloor}21}$ So $\dfrac{4}{7} \times \dfrac{5}{12} = \dfrac{5}{21}$.

Exercise 4

1 Work out these multiplications using a calculator.

a) $\dfrac{5}{6} \times \dfrac{8}{15}$

b) $\dfrac{7}{15} \times \dfrac{3}{14}$

c) $\dfrac{9}{16} \times \dfrac{5}{12}$

d) $\dfrac{9}{10} \times \dfrac{5}{21}$

e) $\dfrac{7}{8} \times \dfrac{12}{17}$

f) $\dfrac{17}{20} \times \dfrac{4}{17}$

g) $\dfrac{7}{15} \times \dfrac{5}{21}$

h) $\dfrac{15}{16} \times \dfrac{8}{13}$

i) $\dfrac{11}{14} \times \dfrac{7}{22}$

Finding the Reciprocal

Swapping the numerator and denominator of a fraction gives the reciprocal of the fraction.

Example 1

Find the reciprocal of: a) $\frac{3}{5}$ b) $\frac{1}{6}$ c) 3

1. Swap the numerator and denominator. $\longrightarrow$ a) The reciprocal of $\frac{3}{5}$ is $\frac{5}{3}$.

2. If the numerator of the fraction is 1, the reciprocal is a whole number. $\longrightarrow$ b) The reciprocal of $\frac{1}{6}$ is $\frac{6}{1}$ = 6.

3. The reciprocal of a whole number is a fraction with numerator 1. $\longrightarrow$ c) $3 = \frac{3}{1}$, so the reciprocal of 3 is $\frac{1}{3}$.

Exercise 1

1 Find the reciprocal of these fractions.

a) $\frac{2}{3}$ b) $\frac{1}{3}$ c) $\frac{3}{4}$

d) $\frac{1}{5}$ e) $\frac{3}{8}$ f) $\frac{2}{5}$

g) $\frac{1}{7}$ h) $\frac{7}{10}$ i) $\frac{1}{9}$

2 Find the reciprocal of these numbers.

a) 5   b) 2   c) 8

d) 9   e) 4   f) 7

g) 6   h) 10   i) 12

Dividing by Fractions

To divide by a fraction, you multiply by its reciprocal.

> Remember to multiply the top and bottom of the fraction separately.

Example 2

Work out:

a) $\dfrac{2}{3} \div \dfrac{3}{4}$ Multiply $\dfrac{2}{3}$ by the reciprocal of $\dfrac{3}{4}$ $\dfrac{2}{3} \times \dfrac{4}{3} = \dfrac{2 \times 4}{3 \times 3} = \dfrac{8}{9}$

b) $\dfrac{3}{5} \div 2$ Multiply $\dfrac{3}{5}$ by the reciprocal of 2 $\dfrac{3}{5} \times \dfrac{1}{2} = \dfrac{3 \times 1}{5 \times 2} = \dfrac{3}{10}$

Exercise 2

Answer these questions **without using a calculator**.

1 Copy and complete these calculations.

a) $\dfrac{1}{2} \div \dfrac{2}{3} = \dfrac{1}{2} \times \dfrac{3}{2} = \dfrac{1 \times 3}{2 \times 2} = \underline{\quad}$

b) $\dfrac{1}{3} \div \dfrac{3}{4} = \dfrac{1}{3} \times \dfrac{4}{3} = \dfrac{1 \times 4}{3 \times 3} = \underline{\quad}$

c) $\dfrac{1}{3} \div \dfrac{3}{5} = \dfrac{1}{3} \times \dfrac{}{3} = \dfrac{1 \times }{3 \times 3} = \underline{\quad}$

d) $\dfrac{3}{4} \div \dfrac{4}{5} = \dfrac{3}{4} \times \dfrac{5}{} = \dfrac{3 \times 5}{4 \times } = \underline{\quad}$

e) $\dfrac{1}{7} \div \dfrac{1}{2} = \dfrac{1}{7} \times ...... = \dfrac{1 \times }{7} = \underline{\quad}$

f) $\dfrac{1}{5} \div \dfrac{2}{7} = \dfrac{1}{5} \times \dfrac{}{} = \dfrac{1 \times }{5 \times } = \underline{\quad}$

2 Work out these calculations. Give your answers in their simplest terms.

a) $\dfrac{1}{2} \div \dfrac{4}{5}$

b) $\dfrac{1}{3} \div \dfrac{1}{2}$

c) $\dfrac{1}{5} \div \dfrac{1}{3}$

d) $\dfrac{2}{5} \div \dfrac{1}{2}$

e) $\dfrac{3}{8} \div \dfrac{1}{2}$

f) $\dfrac{2}{3} \div \dfrac{3}{4}$

g) $\dfrac{5}{8} \div \dfrac{3}{4}$

h) $\dfrac{8}{15} \div \dfrac{4}{5}$

i) $\dfrac{3}{8} \div \dfrac{2}{3}$

j) $\dfrac{2}{5} \div \dfrac{7}{10}$

k) $\dfrac{5}{12} \div \dfrac{2}{3}$

l) $\dfrac{9}{20} \div \dfrac{3}{4}$

3 Copy and complete these calculations.

a) $2 \div \dfrac{2}{3} = 2 \times \dfrac{3}{2} = \dfrac{2 \times 3}{2} = \dfrac{}{2} = \ldots\ldots$

b) $4 \div \dfrac{2}{5} = 4 \times \dfrac{5}{} = \dfrac{4 \times 5}{} = \dfrac{}{} = \ldots\ldots$

c) $6 \div \dfrac{3}{4} = 6 \times \dfrac{}{} = \dfrac{6 \times }{} = \dfrac{}{} = \ldots\ldots$

> Remember that $\dfrac{a}{b}$ means $a \div b$.

4 Work out these calculations. Give your answers in their simplest terms.

a) $5 \div \dfrac{1}{3}$

b) $6 \div \dfrac{2}{5}$

c) $9 \div \dfrac{3}{4}$

d) $9 \div \dfrac{3}{2}$

e) $10 \div \dfrac{5}{6}$

f) $12 \div \dfrac{4}{5}$

5 Copy and complete these calculations.

a) $\dfrac{1}{4} \div 2 = \dfrac{1}{4} \times \dfrac{1}{2} = \dfrac{1 \times }{4 \times } = \dfrac{}{}$

b) $\dfrac{3}{4} \div 2 = \dfrac{3}{4} \times \dfrac{1}{} = \dfrac{3 \times 1}{4 \times } = \dfrac{}{}$

c) $\dfrac{3}{4} \div 4 = \dfrac{3}{4} \times \dfrac{}{} = \dfrac{3 \times }{4 \times } = \dfrac{}{}$

d) $\dfrac{4}{5} \div 5 = \dfrac{4}{5} \times \dfrac{}{} = \dfrac{4 \times }{5 \times } = \dfrac{}{}$

6 Work out these calculations. Give your answers in their simplest terms.

a) $\dfrac{2}{3} \div 2$

b) $\dfrac{3}{5} \div 3$

c) $\dfrac{5}{7} \div 5$

d) $\dfrac{4}{7} \div 2$

e) $\dfrac{6}{7} \div 2$

f) $\dfrac{6}{8} \div 3$

g) $\dfrac{8}{9} \div 4$

h) $\dfrac{10}{11} \div 5$

i) $\dfrac{12}{13} \div 3$

> The reciprocal of a whole number is 'one over' that number.

7 Alek buys a piece of ribbon which is $\dfrac{3}{4}$ m long. He cuts the ribbon into 6 equal parts.

Work out the length of each piece of ribbon. Give your answer as fraction.

8 A gang of 4 squirrels work together to collect some nuts.

$\frac{3}{4}$ of the nuts are divided out equally between the 4 squirrels.

Work out what fraction of the nuts each squirrel gets.

9 Bernard makes a trifle for his dinner party.
He decides to eat most of the trifle himself.

He shares out $\frac{2}{5}$ of the trifle equally between his 4 guests.

Work out what fraction of the trifle each of his guests gets.

Dividing Fractions Using a Calculator

Example 3

Use a calculator to work out $\frac{2}{3} \div \frac{11}{12}$.

Type the division into the calculator using the fraction buttons (a^b_c or $\frac{\blacksquare}{\square}$).

(2) (a^b_c) (3) (÷) (1) (1) (a^b_c) (1) (2) (=) ⎡ 8╷11 ⎤ So $\frac{2}{3} \div \frac{11}{12} = \frac{8}{11}$.

Exercise 3

1 Use your calculator to work out:

a) $\frac{11}{20} \div \frac{4}{5}$

b) $\frac{5}{16} \div \frac{5}{12}$

c) $\frac{9}{25} \div \frac{11}{20}$

d) $\frac{15}{32} \div \frac{5}{8}$

e) $\frac{9}{16} \div \frac{7}{12}$

f) $\frac{3}{10} \div \frac{16}{25}$

g) $\frac{13}{18} \div \frac{17}{20}$

h) $\frac{12}{19} \div \frac{10}{11}$

i) $\frac{8}{15} \div \frac{18}{25}$

Writing Fractions as Decimals Using a Calculator

All fractions can be written as a decimal. You can write fractions as decimals using a calculator by dividing the numerator by the denominator.

Example 1

Write $\frac{46}{125}$ as a decimal using a calculator.

Divide the numerator by the denominator.

$\boxed{4}\ \boxed{6}\ \boxed{\div}\ \boxed{1}\ \boxed{2}\ \boxed{5}\ \boxed{=}\ \boxed{0.368}$ So $\frac{46}{125} = 0.368$.

Exercise 1

1 Use your calculator to write these fractions as decimals.

a) $\frac{1}{8}$

b) $\frac{3}{8}$

c) $\frac{5}{16}$

d) $\frac{7}{8}$

e) $\frac{3}{40}$

f) $\frac{9}{40}$

g) $\frac{5}{8}$

h) $\frac{7}{20}$

i) $\frac{7}{16}$

j) $\frac{5}{32}$

k) $\frac{7}{40}$

l) $\frac{23}{50}$

m) $\frac{13}{40}$

n) $\frac{26}{50}$

o) $\frac{31}{80}$

p) $\frac{176}{200}$

q) $\frac{329}{500}$

r) $\frac{97}{128}$

Writing Fractions as Decimals Without a Calculator

Remember:

$$\frac{1}{10} = 0.1 \qquad \frac{1}{100} = 0.01 \qquad \frac{1}{1000} = 0.001$$

Example 2

a) Write $\frac{9}{10}$ as a decimal.

  1. Write the fraction as a multiple of $\frac{1}{10}$. $\dfrac{9}{10} = 9 \times \dfrac{1}{10}$

  2. Then rewrite the fraction as a decimal. $= 9 \times 0.1 = 0.9$

b) Write $\frac{7}{100}$ as a decimal.

  1. Write the fraction as a multiple of $\frac{1}{100}$. $\dfrac{7}{100} = 7 \times \dfrac{1}{100}$

  2. Then rewrite the fraction as a decimal. $= 7 \times 0.01 = 0.07$

Example 3

Write $\frac{33}{1000}$ as a decimal.

1. Write the fraction as a multiple of $\frac{1}{1000}$. $\dfrac{33}{1000} = 33 \times \dfrac{1}{1000}$

2. Then rewrite as a decimal:
   There are three decimal places in 33 × 0.001, so $= 33 \times 0.001 = 0.033$
   there should be three decimal places in the answer.

Exercise 2

Answer these questions **without using a calculator**.

1   **a)** Write the fraction $\frac{6}{10}$ as a multiple of $\frac{1}{10}$.

     b) Use your answer to write $\frac{6}{10}$ as a decimal.

2 a) Write the fraction $\frac{9}{100}$ as a multiple of $\frac{1}{100}$.

b) Use your answer to write $\frac{9}{100}$ as a decimal.

3 a) Write the fraction $\frac{95}{1000}$ as a multiple of $\frac{1}{1000}$.

b) Use your answer to write $\frac{95}{1000}$ as a decimal.

4 Write these fractions as decimals.

a) $\frac{3}{10}$

b) $\frac{7}{10}$

c) $\frac{9}{10}$

d) $\frac{1}{10}$

e) $\frac{3}{100}$

f) $\frac{9}{100}$

g) $\frac{57}{100}$

h) $\frac{93}{100}$

i) $\frac{33}{100}$

j) $\frac{9}{1000}$

k) $\frac{5}{1000}$

l) $\frac{45}{1000}$

m) $\frac{81}{1000}$

n) $\frac{421}{1000}$

o) $\frac{873}{1000}$

Example 4

Write $\frac{4}{5}$ as a decimal.

1. First, find a fraction which is equivalent to $\frac{4}{5}$ which has 10, 100 or 1000 as the denominator.

2. Multiply the numerator and denominator by 2 to rewrite the fraction with denominator 10.

3. Change the fraction to a decimal as before.

$$\frac{4}{5} = \frac{8}{10}$$

$$\frac{8}{10} = 8 \times \frac{1}{10} = 8 \times 0.1 = 0.8$$

Exercise 3

Answer these questions **without using a calculator**.

1 **a)** Find the value of a if $\frac{1}{5} = \frac{a}{10}$.

   b) Use your answer to write the fraction $\frac{1}{5}$ as a decimal.

2 **a)** Find a fraction which is equivalent to $\frac{1}{50}$ and which has a denominator of 100.

   b) Use your answer to write $\frac{1}{50}$ as a decimal.

3 For each of these fractions: **(i)** rewrite the fraction so that its has a denominator of 10,
   (ii) write the fraction as a decimal.

   a) $\frac{1}{2}$

   b) $\frac{3}{5}$

   c) $\frac{2}{5}$

4 For each of these fractions: **(i)** rewrite the fraction so that its has a denominator of 100,
   (ii) write the fraction as a decimal.

   a) $\frac{1}{20}$

   b) $\frac{2}{25}$

   c) $\frac{7}{20}$

   d) $\frac{3}{20}$

   e) $\frac{11}{50}$

   f) $\frac{29}{50}$

5 For each of these fractions: **(i)** rewrite the fraction so that it has a denominator of 1000,
   (ii) write the fraction as a decimal.

   a) $\frac{4}{500}$

   b) $\frac{45}{500}$

   c) $\frac{60}{500}$

   d) $\frac{11}{200}$

   e) $\frac{50}{200}$

   f) $\frac{10}{250}$

6 Write these fractions as decimals.

   a) $\frac{9}{50}$

   b) $\frac{7}{25}$

   c) $\frac{9}{20}$

   d) $\frac{31}{50}$

   e) $\frac{11}{20}$

   f) $\frac{16}{25}$

Writing Decimals as Fractions

You can change a decimal to a fraction by writing it as a fraction with a denominator of 10, 100 or 1000, then simplifying.

Example 5

Write these decimals as fractions. Give your answers in their simplest terms.

a) 0.8
   1. The final digit is in the tenths column, so write a fraction using 10 as the denominator.
   2. Simplify the fraction.

$$0.8 = \frac{8}{10} = \frac{4}{5}$$

b) 0.32
   1. The final digit is in the hundredths column, so write a fraction using 100 as the denominator.
   2. Simplify the fraction.

$$0.32 = \frac{32}{100} = \frac{8}{25}$$

c) 0.222
   1. The final digit is in the thousandths column, so write a fraction using 1000 as the denominator.
   2. Simplify the fraction.

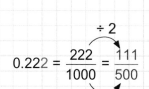

$$0.222 = \frac{222}{1000} = \frac{111}{500}$$

Exercise 4

1 Write these decimals as fractions **without using a calculator**.
   Give your answers in their simplest terms.

a) 0.3   b) 0.9   c) 0.5

d) 0.2   e) 0.4   f) 0.6

g) 0.37   h) 0.73   i) 0.25

j) 0.35   k) 0.15   l) 0.75

m) 0.44   n) 0.06   o) 0.08

p) 0.125   q) 0.025   r) 0.004

5.8 Fraction Problems

Exercise 1

Answer these questions **without using a calculator**.

1 Write down the fraction of each of the shapes below that is shaded.

a) 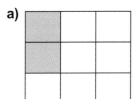   b) 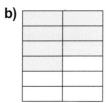   c)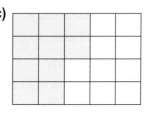

2 Find the value that replaces the circle in each of these fractions.

a) $\dfrac{4}{5} = \dfrac{\bigcirc}{15}$

b) $\dfrac{3}{4} = \dfrac{9}{\bigcirc}$

c) $\dfrac{\bigcirc}{9} = \dfrac{20}{36}$

3 Write these fractions in their simplest terms.

a) $\dfrac{3}{15}$

b) $\dfrac{12}{21}$

c) $\dfrac{24}{40}$

4 Write each of these groups of fractions in order from smallest to largest.

a) $\dfrac{6}{11}, \dfrac{2}{11}, \dfrac{7}{11}$

b) $\dfrac{13}{20}, \dfrac{11}{20}, \dfrac{19}{20}, \dfrac{9}{20}$

c) $\dfrac{3}{4}, \dfrac{9}{16}, \dfrac{1}{2}$

d) $\dfrac{13}{24}, \dfrac{3}{4}, \dfrac{5}{8}, \dfrac{7}{12}$

5 Work out these calculations. Give your answers in their simplest terms.

a) $\dfrac{3}{9} + \dfrac{2}{9}$

b) $\dfrac{2}{3} + \dfrac{1}{4}$

c) $\dfrac{7}{8} - \dfrac{1}{3}$

d) $\dfrac{1}{4} \times \dfrac{2}{5}$

e) $\dfrac{2}{5} \div \dfrac{3}{4}$

f) $\dfrac{1}{4} \div 3$

6 Find $64 \times \frac{1}{8}$.

7 Find $\frac{3}{4}$ of 36.

8 Zaf and Mandy share a box of 35 chocolates. Zaf eats $\frac{11}{35}$ of the chocolates and Mandy eats $\frac{7}{35}$. Who eats the largest fraction of the chocolates?

9 Alan drinks $\frac{2}{5}$ of a can of cola. Frank drinks $\frac{1}{3}$ of a can of cola. Who drinks the most?

10 Dec eats $\frac{3}{8}$ of a bar of chocolate. Dom eats $\frac{1}{3}$ of the same bar. What fraction of the chocolate bar do they eat in total?

11 A block of wood is $\frac{7}{12}$ m long. Pieces of length $\frac{1}{4}$ m and $\frac{1}{6}$ m are cut from the block.

a) What is the total length that has been cut from the block?

b) What length of wood is left over? Give your answer in its simplest terms.

12 Amy, Ben and Carl are sharing a banana. They each eat $\frac{1}{5}$ of the banana. What fraction of the banana do they eat in total?

13 Pat's cat eats $\frac{2}{3}$ of a tin of cat food every day. How many tins of cat food will Pat need to buy to feed the cat for 30 days?

14 A grandad divides $\frac{3}{4}$ kg of sweets equally between his five grandchildren.

Find the amount of sweets, in kg, that each child gets.

15 Write these fractions as decimals.

a) $\frac{8}{10}$ **b)** $\frac{87}{100}$ **c)** $\frac{721}{1000}$

d) $\frac{23}{50}$ **e)** $\frac{3}{25}$ **f)** $\frac{20}{500}$

16 Write these decimals as fractions. Give your answers in their simplest terms.

a) 0.2   **b)** 0.8

c) 0.34   **d)** 0.56

e) 0.606   **f)** 0.07

g) 0.102   **h)** 0.555

i) 0.002

17 Kunal spends £0.28 in a newsagents.
Work out what fraction of a pound (£) he spent.

Give your answer in its simplest terms.

18 A recipe for fruit cocktail uses $\frac{1}{8}$ litre of apple juice, $\frac{1}{4}$ litre of pineapple juice and $\frac{1}{2}$ litre of orange juice.

Will the cocktail fit in a 1 litre jug? Explain your answer.

Section 6 — Ratio and Proportion

6.1 Ratios

Meaning of Ratios

Ratios are used to compare amounts of things.

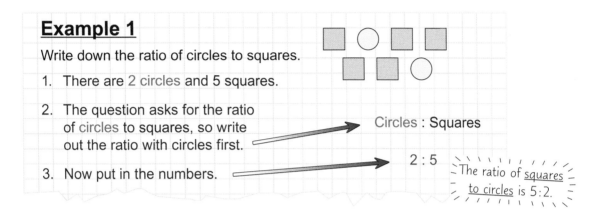

Example 1

Write down the ratio of circles to squares.

1. There are 2 circles and 5 squares.

2. The question asks for the ratio
    of circles to squares, so write
    out the ratio with circles first. ⟶ Circles : Squares

3. Now put in the numbers. ⟶ 2 : 5

The ratio of squares to circles is 5 : 2.

Exercise 1

1 For the shapes below, write down:

   a) the ratio of squares to circles   **b)** the ratio of circles to squares

2 For each of the following, write down the ratio of stars to triangles.

   a)    **b)**

3 Write down the ratio of jet planes to ice creams.

4 In this tiling pattern, what is the ratio of
   green squares to orange squares?

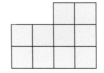

5 There are 17 boys and 14 girls in a class.

    a) Write down the ratio of boys to girls.   **b)** Write down the ratio of girls to boys.

6 On a farm there are 15 pigs and 23 cows. Write down the ratio of cows to pigs.

7 Last season, Wirral Whites football team won 17 matches and lost 19 matches. Write down the ratio of matches won to matches lost.

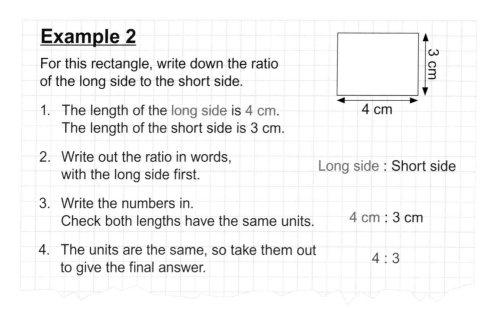

Example 2

For this rectangle, write down the ratio of the long side to the short side.

1. The length of the long side is 4 cm. The length of the short side is 3 cm.

2. Write out the ratio in words, with the long side first.

    Long side : Short side

3. Write the numbers in. Check both lengths have the same units.

    4 cm : 3 cm

4. The units are the same, so take them out to give the final answer.

    4 : 3

Exercise 2

1 For this rectangle, write down the ratio of the long side to the short side.

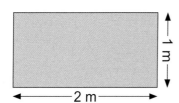

2 For this triangle, write down the ratio of the longest side to the shortest side.

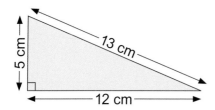

3   The car shown below has a length of 5 m and a width of 2 m.

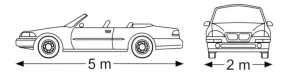

Write down the ratio of:

a) the car's length to its width   **b)** the car's width to its length.

4   Eric and Amy both run a marathon.
Eric takes 4 hours to finish and Amy takes 5 hours.
Write down the ratio of Eric's time to Amy's time.

5   Phil makes some orange juice by mixing 1 litre of orange cordial with 5 litres of water.
What is the ratio of cordial to water in the juice?

6   In a sweet shop, a bag of toffee costs 73p
and a bag of fudge costs 56p.

Write down the ratio of the cost of a
bag of toffee to the cost of a bag of fudge.

Simplifying Ratios

Just like with fractions, you can simplify ratios by dividing the numbers by common factors.

Example 3

Write the ratio 15 : 10 in its simplest form.

1. Look for a number that divides into both 15 and 10.	5 divides into both 15 and 10.
2. Divide both sides of the ratio by this number and rewrite the ratio.	15 ÷ 5 = 3 and 10 ÷ 5 = 2
3. When no other numbers divide into both sides of the ratio, the ratio is in its simplest form.	So the ratio can be written as 3 : 2, and this is the ratio's simplest form.

Exercise 3

1 Write each of the following ratios in its simplest form.

a) 4:2 **b)** 5:10 **c)** 2:6

d) 5:15 **e)** 15:6 **f)** 40:10

g) 4:6 **h)** 24:6 **i)** 20:8

j) 7:28 **k)** 15:9 **l)** 16:12

m) 18:4 **n)** 6:14 **o)** 35:15

p) 55:5 **q)** 16:40 **r)** 18:27

For questions **2** and **3**, write down the given ratio, then simplify your answer.

2 Squares to circles.

3 Circles to triangles.

4 A bag contains 12 green discs, 20 blue discs and 30 orange discs.

a) What is the ratio of blue discs to orange discs?

b) What is the ratio of blue discs to green discs?

Give each of your answers in their simplest form.

5 A floor is made up of 24 black tiles and 8 white tiles.
Find the ratio of black tiles to white tiles in its simplest form.

6 At a party there are 36 girls and 27 boys.
What is the ratio of girls to boys? Give your answer in its simplest form.

7 For this rectangle, find the ratio of the long side length to the short side length.

Give your answer in its simplest form.

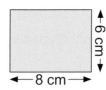

6 cm
8 cm

8 Pink paint is made by mixing 10 litres of red paint with 8 litres of white paint.
Find the ratio of red paint to white paint in its simplest form.

9 There are 16 girls in a school class of 30.

a) How many boys are in the class?

b) Write the ratio of boys to girls in its simplest form.

Example 4

Write the ratio 1 m : 40 cm in its simplest form.

Always change the larger units into the smaller units, e.g. m to cm.

1. Rewrite the ratio so that the units are the same on both sides. ⟹ Then remove the units altogether.

   1 m = 100 cm so

   1 m : 40 cm is the same as 100 cm : 40 cm.

   So the ratio is 100 : 40.

2. 20 divides into both 100 and 40. Use this to simplify the ratio. ⟹

   $\div 20$ 100 : 40 $\div 20$

   5 : 2

   So the simplest form of the ratio is 5 : 2

Some handy conversions

1 m = 100 cm	1 hour = 60 minutes
1 cm = 10 mm	£1 = 100p
1 km = 1000 m	1 kg = 1000 g

Exercise 4

1 Write these ratios in their simplest form.

a) 10 cm : 1 m

b) 1 cm : 2 mm

c) 40 g : 1 kg

d) 15 minutes : 1 hour

e) 20 mm : 4 cm

f) 40p : £1

g) 2 km : 300 m

h) 30 cm : 2 m

i) 8 mm : 4 cm

j) 3 m : 90 cm

k) £5 : 50p

l) 20 minutes : 3 hours

m) 90p : £6

n) 2 hours : 15 minutes

2 The taxi fare to the train station is £5. The bus fare to the station is 75p.
Find the ratio of the taxi fare to the bus fare in its simplest form.

3 A small bag of crisps costs 80p and a king-size bag costs £2.

Find the ratio of the cost of the small bag to the cost of the king-size bag.
Give your answer in its simplest form.

4   For this triangle, find the ratio of the longest side
to the shortest side in its simplest form.

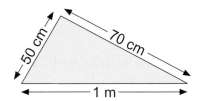

5   A rectangular flower bed measures 4 m by 120 cm.
Find the ratio of the longer side to the shorter side in its simplest form.

Writing Ratios in the Form 1 : n

Another way to simplify ratios is to write them in the form 1 : n, where n is a number.

When you make the left-hand side equal to 1, you might end up with a
fraction or a decimal on the right-hand side.

Example 5

Write the ratio 16 : 24 in the form 1 : n.

1. To get '1' on the left-hand side,
    divide both sides by 16.

2. Now the ratio is in the form 1 : n,
    where n = 1.5

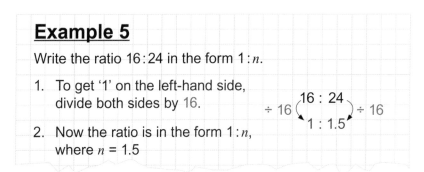

Exercise 5

1   Write each of these ratios in the form 1 : n, where n is a whole number.

a) 4 : 8	**b)** 2 : 6	**c)** 5 : 30
d) 2 : 14	**e)** 6 : 18	**f)** 7 : 35
g) 6 : 24	**h)** 30 : 120	**i)** 24 : 72

2   Write each of these ratios in the form 1 : n, where n is a decimal.

a) 2 : 1	**b)** 2 : 3	**c)** 5 : 7
d) 2 : 7	**e)** 4 : 26	**f)** 8 : 26
g) 4 : 11	**h)** 24 : 6	**i)** 8 : 3

3 Write each of these ratios in the form $1:n$.

a) 10 cm : 5 cm   b) 3 cm : 60 cm

c) 60 g : 15 g   d) £40 : £60

e) 12 ml : 9 ml   f) £60 : £3000

g) 70 m : 210 m   h) 64 g : 80 g

i) 500 kg : 200 kg

4 In a pond there are 5 frogs and 36 fish.

a) Find the ratio of frogs to fish.

b) Write this ratio in the form $1:n$.

5 A model of the Eiffel Tower with height 6 m is built.
The height of the real tower is 300 m.

Find the ratio of the model height to the actual height in the form $1:n$.

6 A farm has 120 animals, 40 of which are donkeys.

a) How many of the animals are not donkeys?

b) Find the ratio of donkeys to other animals in the form $1:n$.

7 On the plans of a building, a rectangle of width 8 cm
represents a room of actual width 1.8 m.

a) Find the ratio of the plan width to the actual width.

b) Write this ratio in the form $1:n$.

6.2 Using Ratios

You can use ratios to solve problems.

Example 1

The ratio of men to women in an office is 3:4.
If there are 9 men in the office, how many women are there?

1. Write down what you know and what you need to find out.

    men : women
    3:4
    = 9:?

2. Work out what you have to multiply the left-hand side by to get from 3 to 9.

    $9 \div 3 = 3$

3. Multiply the right-hand side by the same number.

    3:4
    9:12   × 3

So there are 12 women.

Example 2

A cereal contains raisins and oats in the ratio 2:5. A box of the cereal contains 250 g of oats. Find how many grams of raisins it contains.

1. Work out what you have to multiply the right-hand side by to get from 5 to 250.

    raisins : oats
    2:5
    = ?:250

    $250 \div 5 = 50$

2. Multiply the left-hand side by the same number.

    × 50   2:5
    100:250

3. Remember to put the units in the answer.

So there are 100 g of raisins.

Exercise 1

1 For a class of pupils, the ratio of blue eyes to brown eyes is 2:3.
   8 pupils have blue eyes.

   How many pupils have brown eyes?

2 The ratio of red to yellow sweets in a bag is 3:4.
   The bag contains 12 yellow sweets.

   How many red sweets are in the bag?

3 In a wood there are oak trees and beech trees in the ratio 2:9.
There are 42 oak trees. How many beech trees are there?

4 The ages of a father and son are in the ratio 8:3.
If the father is 48, how old is the son?

5 In a supermarket the ratio of apples to bananas is 5:3.
If there are 450 bananas, how many apples are there?

6 Ben feeds his horses carrots.
For every 11 carrots the horses eat, Ben eats 3 carrots.

If the horses eat 55 carrots, how many does Ben eat?

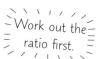
Work out the ratio first.

For questions **7-11**, remember to give the correct units in your answer.

7 A drink is made by mixing squash and water in the ratio 1:4.
How much water would be needed with 2 litres of squash?

8 A recipe uses sugar and butter in the ratio 2:1.
How much butter would be needed with 100 g of sugar?

9 A photo of width 10 cm is enlarged so that the ratio of the widths of the two pictures is 2:7.

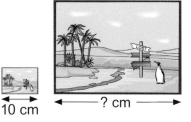

10 cm   ? cm

How wide is the enlarged picture?

10 Meera and Sabrina sell some things at a car boot sale.
They split the money they make in the ratio 7:6.

If Sabrina gets £48, how much does Meera get?

11 Tim has a cardboard cut-out of his favourite ninja.
The height of the cut-out and the ninja's actual height are in the ratio 5:6.

If the cut-out is 165 cm high, find the ninja's actual height in cm.

Using Ratios to Find Fractions

You can use a ratio to write something as a fraction of a total.

Or you can start with a fraction and use it to write a ratio.

Example 3

A box of doughnuts contains jam doughnuts and chocolate doughnuts in the ratio 3:5.
What fraction of the doughnuts are chocolate flavoured?

1. Add the two numbers in the ratio to find the total number of parts. $\longrightarrow$ 3 + 5 = 8 parts altogether.

2. The total number of parts is the denominator of your fraction.

   5 of the parts are chocolate.

   Fraction that are chocolate is $\frac{5}{8}$.

Exercise 2

1 A tiled floor has blue and white tiles in the ratio 1:3.
What fraction of the tiles are blue?

2 A necklace has yellow beads and red beads in the ratio 3:2.
What fraction of the beads are yellow?

3 The ratio of girls to boys in a class is 4:3.
What fraction of the class is girls?

4 A recipe uses white flour and brown flour in the ratio 9:4.
What fraction of the flour is brown?

5 A zoo has good penguins and evil penguins in the ratio 2:1.
What fraction of the penguins are evil?

6 The ratio of women to men in a tennis club is 13:7.
What fraction of the players are men?

Example 4

All of Hannah's DVDs are either horror films or comedies.
If $\frac{2}{7}$ of her DVDs are horror films, find the ratio of comedies to horror films.

1. Use the fraction you know to find the ⟶ number of parts for each type of film.

$\frac{2}{7}$ means that 2 parts out of 7 are horror films.

So 7 − 2 = 5 parts are comedies.

2. Write it as a ratio, making sure you put the numbers the right way round.

Ratio of comedies to horror films is 5 : 2.

Exercise 3

1   Aiden has a bag of red sweets and green sweets. $\frac{1}{3}$ of the sweets are red.
Find the ratio of red to green sweets.

2 $\frac{1}{8}$ of the items made in a factory are faulty.
What is the ratio of faulty items to non-faulty items?

3   Jack has watched $\frac{3}{10}$ of the episodes in a DVD box set.
Write down the ratio of episodes he's watched to episodes he hasn't watched.

4 $\frac{5}{12}$ of the children at a school eat school dinners and the rest bring a packed lunch.
What is the ratio of children who bring a packed lunch to those who eat school dinners?

5 $\frac{3}{19}$ of the members of a chess club are left handed.
Find the ratio of right-handed club members to left-handed club members.

Exercise 4 — Mixed Exercise

1   In Amy's sock drawer there are stripy and plain socks in the ratio 5 : 1.
    What fraction of Amy's socks are stripy?

2   $\frac{1}{6}$ of the balls in a bag are red and the rest are blue.
    What is the ratio of red to blue balls in the bag?

3   The ratio of males to females at a music festival is 13 : 17.
    What fraction of the people are male?

4   At a birthday party there are purple balloons and red balloons in the ratio 3 : 8.
    What fraction of the balloons are purple?

5   During one hour at a pizza restaurant, $\frac{3}{8}$ of the pizzas ordered had a squirrel topping.
    The rest had a potato topping. Write down the ratio of squirrel to potato pizzas ordered.

6   A rugby team won half of their matches by more than 10 points, won a quarter
    of their matches by less than 10 points, and lost the rest of their matches.

    Write the ratio of games they won to games they lost.

6.3   Dividing in a Given Ratio

Ratios can be used to divide an amount into two or more shares.
The numbers in the ratio show how big each share is.

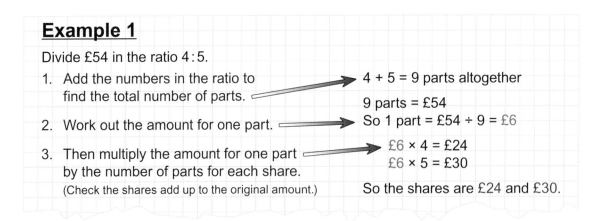

Example 1

Divide £54 in the ratio 4 : 5.

1. Add the numbers in the ratio to   → 4 + 5 = 9 parts altogether
    find the total number of parts.

                                             9 parts = £54
2. Work out the amount for one part. → So 1 part = £54 ÷ 9 = £6

3. Then multiply the amount for one part → £6 × 4 = £24
    by the number of parts for each share.   £6 × 5 = £30
    (Check the shares add up to the original amount.)   So the shares are £24 and £30.

Exercise 1

1 Divide 30 in the ratio 1:2.

Remember — start by adding the numbers in the ratio.

2 Divide 50 in the ratio 2:3.

3 Divide 27 in the ratio 5:4.

4 Divide 35 in the ratio 3:4.

5 Divide £48 in the following ratios.

   a) 1:3   **b)** 5:1   **c)** 7:5

6 Share 90 kg in these ratios.

   a) 7:2   **b)** 12:18   **c)** 4:1

Don't forget the units.

7 Share 56 m in these ratios.

   a) 1:7   **b)** 10:4   **c)** 22:6

8 Divide 1000 ml in these ratios.

   a) 1:9   **b)** 15:35   **c)** 3:17

9 Find the smallest share when each amount below is divided in the given ratio.

   a) £22 in the ratio 5:6   **b)** 450 g in the ratio 22:28

   c) 45 kg in the ratio 2:3   **d)** 180 ml in the ratio 5:7

   e) 72 cm in the ratio 5:13   **f)** £150 in the ratio 7:23

10 Find the largest share when each amount below is divided in the given ratio.

   a) 56p in the ratio 5:3   **b)** £30 in the ratio 1:3

   c) 36 g in the ratio 3:2   **e)** 150 kg in the ratio 7:3

   e) 240 ml in the ratio 5:7   **f)** 52 m in the ratio 3:10

Example 2

A drink is made using apple juice and lemonade in the ratio 3:7.
How much lemonade is needed to make 5 litres of the drink?

1. Add the numbers to find the total number of parts. ⟶ 3 + 7 = 10 parts altogether

2. Work out the amount for one part. ⟶ 10 parts = 5 litres
So 1 part = 0.5 litres

3. Then multiply the amount for one part by the number of parts for lemonade. ⟶ 0.5 litres × 7
= 3.5 litres of lemonade

Exercise 2

1   Share 32 sandwiches in the ratio 3:5.

2   Kat and Lindsay share 30 cupcakes in the ratio 3:2.
How many do they each get?

3   There are 56 people in an office. The ratio of men to women is 9:5.
How many men and how many women are there?

4   Orange paint is made by mixing yellow and red paint in the ratio 4:3.
How much of each colour is needed to make 42 litres of orange paint?

5   There are 28 passengers on a bus. The ratio of passengers talking on the phone to
those not talking on the phone is 5:2. How many passengers are on the phone?

6   In a school of 600 pupils, the ratio of right-handed pupils to left-handed pupils is 7:1.
How many right-handed pupils are there?

7   Elsa and Daniel share the profits of their business in the ratio 2:3.
How much of a £5700 profit would Daniel get?

8   Lauren is 16 and Cara is 14. Their grandad gives them £1200 to
share in the ratio of their ages. How much money do they each get?

9   A 180° angle is split into two smaller angles in the ratio 2:4.
Find the size of the smaller angle.

10 Nicky and Charlie share a bag of 36 sweets in the ratio 4:5.

   a) How many sweets do they each get?

   b) How many more sweets than Nicky gets does Charlie get?

11 Gemma and Omar have a combined height of 330 cm.
    Their heights are in the ratio 5:6.

    How much taller than Gemma is Omar?

12 A box of 48 chocolates contains dark, milk and white chocolates in the ratio 2:3:1.
    How many of each type of chocolate are in the box?

13 Claire owns 20 handbags, which are black, brown and purple in the ratio 5:3:2.
    She is choosing a bag and doesn't want it to be brown.

    How many bags does she have to choose from?

6.4 Proportion

If two things are in direct proportion, then the ratio between them is always the same.
For example, if 1 item costs £2, then 2 items will cost £4, 3 items will cost £6, etc.
The ratio is always 1 item:£2.

Example 1

8 chocolate bars cost £6. Find the cost of 10 chocolate bars.

1. Find the cost of one bar by dividing ⟶ 8 bars cost £6
    the total cost by the number of bars.   so 1 bar costs £6 ÷ 8 = £0.75

2. Then multiply by the new number of bars. ⟶ 10 bars cost £0.75 × 10 = £7.50

Example 2

A box of 10 biscuits costs £2.50. A box of 15 of the same biscuits costs £3.00.
Which box of biscuits is the best value?

1. Find the cost of one   ⟶ 10 biscuits cost £2.50
    biscuit for each box.   so 1 biscuit costs £2.50 ÷ 10 = £0.25

                                  ⟶ 15 biscuits cost £3.00
                                    so 1 biscuit costs £3.00 ÷ 15 = £0.20

2. The box with the lowest cost
    per biscuit is the best value.   The box of 15 biscuits is the best value.

Exercise 1

1 1 pair of jeans costs £35. Find the cost of:

   a) 2 pairs of jeans   **b)** 5 pairs of jeans   **c)** 20 pairs of jeans

2 3 pencils cost 42p. Find the cost of:

   a) 1 pencil   **b)** 5 pencils   **c)** 10 pencils

3 10 litres of paint costs £45. Find the cost of:

   a) 1 litre   **b)** 6 litres   **c)** 14 litres

4 The cost of 6 books is £36. What is the cost of 8 books?

5 The cost of 5 concert tickets is £210. How much would 9 of these tickets cost?

6 6 jackets cost £480. Find the cost of 11 of these jackets.

7 6 kg of carrots costs £5.40. Find the cost of 5 kg of carrots.

8 It takes 1.8 kg of flour to make 3 loaves of bread.
How much flour is needed to make 5 loaves?

9 To make 4 jugs of squash you need 5 litres of water.
How much water is needed to make 3 jugs of squash?

10 A small box of tea costs £1.20 and contains 20 tea bags.
A large box costs £1.60 and contains 40 tea bags.

   a) What is the cost of one tea bag in the small box?

   b) What is the cost of one tea bag in the large box?

   c) Which box is the best value?

11 A small tube of Caraminty Hair Gunk weighs 50 g and costs £4.00.
A large tube weighs 125 g and costs £12.50.

   a) What is the cost of 1 g of gunk from the small tube?

   b) What is the cost of 1 g of gunk from the large tube?

   c) Which tube of gunk is the best value?

12 A pack of 8 cereal bars costs £2.00.
A pack of 10 of the same cereal bars costs £3.00.

Which pack is better value?

13 A 2 kg bag of pasta costs £2.50 and a 5 kg bag of the same pasta costs £7.50.
Which bag is the best value?

14 Mike's sunflower has grown 31.5 cm in 9 days.
Shelley's sunflower has grown 45 cm in 12 days.

Whose sunflower has been growing faster?

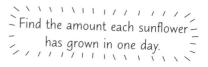
Find the amount each sunflower has grown in one day.

Example 3

13 oranges cost £3.25. How many oranges can I buy for £4.00?

1. Find how many oranges you can
    buy for £1 by dividing the number
    of oranges by the total cost.   →

    £3.25 buys 13 oranges, so £1 buys:
      13 ÷ £3.25 = 4 oranges

2. Then multiply by the new   →
    amount of money.

    £4.00 buys:
      4 × £4.00 = 16 oranges.

Exercise 2

1 12 gobstoppers cost £2.40.

   a) How many gobstoppers can be bought for £1?

   b) How many gobstoppers can be bought for £1.60?

2 Sarah can drive 336 miles on £42 worth of petrol.
How far can she drive on £10 worth of petrol?

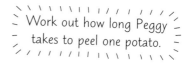
Work out how long Asif needs to work to get paid £1.

3 Asif works 30 hours this week and gets paid £240.
How many hours does he need to work next week to get paid £280?

4 It takes Peggy 12 minutes to peel 30 potatoes.
How long will it take her to peel 85 potatoes?

Work out how long Peggy takes to peel one potato.

5 Jack exercises on the treadmill for 20 minutes
and burns 128 calories. His target is to burn 160 calories.

How long should he spend on the treadmill?

Exchange Rates

Example 4

If £100 is worth $160, convert £40 into dollars ($).

1. Work out how much £1 is worth. ⟶ £100 is worth $160
    so £1 is worth $160 ÷ 100 = $1.60

2. Then multiply by the new amount. ⟶ £40 is worth 40 × $1.60 = $64

Example 5

Oliver has 30 euros (€) left over from his holiday. How many pounds can he exchange his euros for?

Exchange Rate
£1 = €1.14

1. Using the exchange rate, work out how ⟶ €1.14 = £1
    many pounds €1 is worth. Divide the so €1 = £1 ÷ 1.14 = £0.877...
    amount in pounds by the amount in euros.

    €30 = 30 × £0.877

2. Then multiply by the number of euros ⟶ = £26.32 (to the nearest penny)
    Oliver has.

Remember to give answers to the nearest penny.

Exercise 3

1 £1 is worth $1.60. Convert the following amounts into dollars ($).

    a) £10   **b)** £20   **c)** £100

    d) £61   **e)** £4000   **f)** £14.50

2 £20 is worth 2620 Japanese yen. Convert the following amounts into Japanese yen.

    a) £1   **b)** £5   **c)** £12

    d) £7   **e)** £35   **f)** £500

3 £5 is worth 375 Indian rupees. Convert each of these amounts into Indian rupees.

    a) £1   **b)** £11   **c)** £6.50

    d) £108   **e)** £1020   **f)** £66.98

4 Convert £65.50 into South African rand, given that £11 is worth 121 South African rand.

5 At the end of her holiday Poppy had 45 euros left. She changed the money back into pounds using the exchange rate £1 = €1.14. How many pounds did she get back?

6 Using an exchange rate of £1 = $1.60, convert $200 into pounds.

7 Philip changed £50 into Swiss francs before going on holiday to Switzerland.
The exchange rate was £1 = 1.47 Swiss francs.

a) How many Swiss francs did he get?

At the end of his holiday, Philip changed his remaining 30 Swiss francs back into pounds.

b) Given that the exchange rate was now £1 = 1.50 Swiss francs, how much money did he get back in pounds?

8 Using an exchange rate of £100 = 1055 Chinese yuan, convert 65 Chinese yuan into pounds.

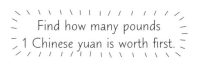
Find how many pounds 1 Chinese yuan is worth first.

6.5 Ratio and Proportion Problems

Exercise 1

1 A builder mixes 10 bags of cement with 25 bags of sand. Write down the ratio of cement to sand:

a) in its simplest form

b) in the form $1:n$

c) in the form $n:1$

2 A field of sheep contains white sheep and black sheep in the ratio $8:1$.

a) What fraction of the sheep are white?

b) If there are 7 black sheep in the field, how many white sheep are there?

3 30 m of material costs £21. How much would 18 m of this material cost?

4   A jar of peanut butter gives this nutritional information:

Typical Values per 100 g	
Energy	600 calories
Protein	25 g
Carbohydrate	16 g
Fat	48 g

   a) Find the ratio of fat to carbohydrate in its simplest form.

   b) Find the ratio of protein to fat in the form $1:n$.

   c) Each jar contains 650 g of peanut butter.
   How many calories of energy would this provide?

5   During one day, a shop has 63 customers. 18 of them are men.

   a) Find the ratio of male to female customers.
   Give your answer in its simplest form.

   b) What fraction of the customers are men?

6   Ryan earns £192 for cleaning 12 cars.
   How much would he earn if he cleaned 16 cars?

7   A cycling challenge has two routes — A and B.
   $\frac{3}{5}$ of the competitors choose route A, and the rest choose route B.

   What is the ratio of competitors choosing route A to those choosing route B?

8   Convert £56 into Turkish lira given that £100 is worth 260 Turkish lira.

9   Two pirates share 360 gold doubloons in the ratio $7:2$.
   What be the amount each pirate receives?

10 A recipe for four people uses 75 g of cheese.
   Raksha is making the recipe for 5 people.

   How much cheese does she need? Give your answer to the nearest gram.

11 If 7 copies of the same DVD costs £84,
   how many copies of the DVD can be bought for £48?

12 Meatybix breakfast cereal comes in two sizes:

The large box weighs 750 g and costs £12.
The small box weighs 250 g and costs £5.

Which box of the delicious meat-based cereal is the best value?

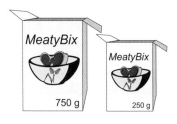

13 A car uses 35 litres of petrol to travel 250 km.

a) How far, to the nearest km, can the car travel on 50 litres of petrol?

b) How many litres of petrol would the car use to travel 400 km?

14 Every Christmas, Catie and Joe's grandmother gives them a total of £99.
The £99 is always shared between them in the ratio of their ages.

a) This year Catie is 6 years old and Joe is 5 years old.
How much do they each receive?

b) How much did they each receive last year?

15 Part of this recipe for Fruit Punch is missing.

Fruit Punch Recipe

400 ml orange juice

300 ml lemonade

    ml pineapple juice

Paul knows that the ratio of orange juice to pineapple juice is 1 : 2.

a) What is the missing amount of pineapple juice?

b) Find the ratio of orange juice to lemonade in its simplest form.

c) Paul only has 240 ml of orange juice to make the punch with.
How much lemonade and pineapple juice should he use?

16 Grace buys 11 pens for £12.32 and 6 note pads for £5.88.
How much would she pay altogether for 8 pens and 5 note pads?

17 Helen is on holiday in Croatia. The exchange rate for Croatian currency is £1 = 8 kuna
On one day, this is what she spends.

What is the total amount she
has spent that day in pounds?

Coffee	9.20 kuna
Bicycle hire	80 kuna
Pizza	32 kuna
Ice cream	4 kuna
Lemonade	6 kuna

Section 7 — Percentages

7.1 Percentages

'Per cent' means 'out of 100'. A percentage is used to write an amount as a number out of 100.

Example 1

The grid on the right is made from 100 small squares.

What percentage of the grid is shaded?

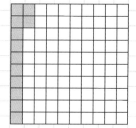

1. Count the number of shaded squares.

12 squares are shaded.

2. Write this amount as a fraction of the whole grid.

There are 100 squares, so $\frac{12}{100}$ are shaded.

3. Now write it as a percentage.

12% of the grid is shaded.

If the bottom number in the fraction is 100, the top number is the percentage.

Example 2

A bag contains 100 sweets. 40 of the sweets are toffees and the rest are chocolates. What percentage of the sweets are chocolates?

1. Find the number of chocolates.

$100 - 40 = 60$ of the sweets are chocolates.

2. Write this amount as a fraction of the total number of sweets.

There are 100 sweets, so $\frac{60}{100}$ are chocolates.

3. Now write it as a percentage.

60% of the sweets are chocolates.

Exercise 1

Answer these questions **without using a calculator**.

1 Each grid is made from 100 squares. Find the percentage of each grid that is shaded.

a)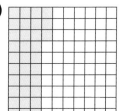

b)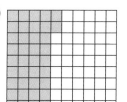

c)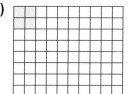

d)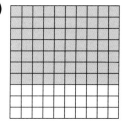

2 Write each of these as a percentage:

   a) 27 out of 100   **b)** 79 out of 100   **c)** 50 out of 100

   d) 4 out of 100   **e)** 90 out of 100   **f)** 45 out of 100

3 A club has 100 members. 45 of the members are women.
   What percentage of the members are women?

4 A bag contains 100 coins. 23 of the coins are 50p pieces.
   What percentage of the coins are 50p pieces?

5 A bakery sells 100 loaves of bread.
   45 of the loaves are brown and the rest are white.

   a) What percentage of the loaves are brown?

   b) What percentage of the loaves are white?

6 Out of 100 students on a course, 75 are male.
   What percentage of students on the course are female?

7 85 students out of a class of 100 pass an exam.
   What percentage of the class failed the exam?

Example 3

Write each of these amounts as a percentage:

a) 7 out of 10   b) 58 out of 200   c) 12 out of 25

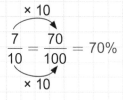

$$\frac{7}{10} = \frac{70}{100} = 70\%$$

$$\frac{58}{200} = \frac{29}{100} = 29\%$$

$$\frac{12}{25} = \frac{48}{100} = 48\%$$

1. Write the amount as a fraction with the bigger number on the bottom.

2. Now write this as an equivalent fraction with 100 on the bottom and find the percentage as usual.

Exercise 2

Answer these questions **without using a calculator**.

1 Write each of the following as a percentage:

a) 3 out of 10

b) 9 out of 10

c) 6 out of 10

d) 4 out of 50

e) 32 out of 50

f) 17 out of 50

g) 60 out of 200

h) 12 out of 200

i) 140 out of 200

j) 3 out of 20

k) 8 out of 20

l) 11 out of 20

m) 2 out of 25

n) 10 out of 25

o) 22 out of 25

p) 500 out of 1000

q) 300 out of 1000

r) 420 out of 1000

2 Ellie scored 15 out of 20 in a test. What is her mark as a percentage?

3 11 out of 25 students in a class are boys. What percentage of the class is boys?

4 A 50 g bar of chocolate contains 10 g of fat. What percentage of the chocolate is fat?

5 Rich buys 200 stamps. 120 of the stamps are first class.
What percentage of the stamps are first class?

6 Paul flipped a coin 20 times. The coin landed showing 'heads' 11 times.
What percentage of flips landed with 'tails' showing?

Example 4

A football team won 12 out of their last 15 games.
What percentage of games did they win?

Remember — the bigger number goes on the bottom.

1. Write the amount as a fraction. $\longrightarrow$ $\dfrac{12}{15}$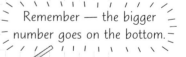

2. Divide the top number by the bottom number. $\quad 12 \div 15 = 0.8$

3. Then multiply by 100 to give the percentage. $\quad 0.8 \times 100 = 80\%$

Exercise 3

You may use a calculator for this exercise.

1 Write each of the following as a percentage:

a) 9 out of 12   **b)** 3 out of 12   **c)** 6 out of 12

d) 32 out of 40   **e)** 16 out of 40   **f)** 26 out of 40

g) 36 out of 120   **h)** 78 out of 120   **i)** 6 out of 120

j) 84 out of 240   **k)** 180 out of 240   **l)** 216 out of 240

m) 240 out of 800   **n)** 176 out of 800   **o)** 528 out of 800

p) 140 out of 560   **q)** 532 out of 560   **r)** 196 out of 560

2 There are 18 girls in a class of 30 students. What percentage of the class is girls?

3 Ravi scored 52 out of 80 in a maths exam. What is his mark as a percentage?

4 A school raised £450 in a raffle. They donated £414 to charity.
What percentage of the money was given to charity?

5 There are 1250 students in a school. On one day, 75 students were absent.
What percentage of students were absent that day?

6 The winner of a hot dog eating contest ate 55 hot dogs in 10 minutes.
22 of the hot dogs he ate had mustard on, and the rest had ketchup.

What percentage of the hot dogs had ketchup on?

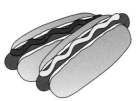

Percentages, fractions and decimals are different ways of writing part of something.

Use these flowcharts to switch between the three types:

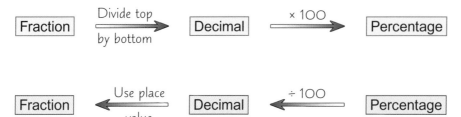

Example 1

Write $\frac{7}{10}$ as: a) a decimal;   b) a percentage

a) Divide the top of the fraction by the bottom. $7 \div 10 = 0.7$

Move each digit one place to the right.

b) Multiply the decimal by 100. $0.7 \times 100 = 70\%$

You could also write the fraction as $\frac{70}{100}$ and use that to find the percentage.

Example 2

Write 35% as: a) a decimal;   b) a fraction in its simplest form

a) Divide the percentage by 100. $35 \div 100 = 0.35$

b) 1. The final digit of 0.35 is in the hundredths column, so write 0.35 as 35 hundredths. $0.35 = \frac{35}{100}$

   2. Divide the top and bottom by 5 to simplify the fraction. $\frac{35}{100} \overset{\div 5}{\underset{\div 5}{=}} \frac{7}{20}$

% means "out of 100". So 35% is 35 out of a 100, which is $\frac{35}{100}$.

Exercise 1

Answer these questions **without using a calculator.**

1 The grid on the right is made from 100 small squares.

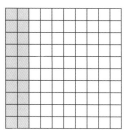

    a) How many of the squares are shaded?

    b) What **fraction** of the grid is shaded?

    c) Write the amount of the grid that is shaded as a **decimal**.

    d) What **percentage** of the grid is shaded?

    e) What **percentage** of the grid is not shaded?

    f) Write the amount of the grid that is not shaded as
    a **fraction** in its simplest form.

2 Write these percentages as **(i)** decimals **(ii)** fractions in their simplest form:

    a) 39%   **b)** 48%   **c)** 50%

    d) 13%   **e)** 9%   **f)** 60%

    g) 25%   **h)** 30%   **i)** 55%

    j) 75%   **k)** 5%   **l)** 22%

3 Write these decimals as **(i)** percentages **(ii)** fractions in their simplest form:

    a) 0.67   **b)** 0.77   **c)** 0.01

    d) 0.84   **e)** 0.43   **f)** 0.9

    g) 0.7   **h)** 0.5   **i)** 0.25

    j) 0.12   **k)** 0.45   **l)** 0.05

4 Write these fractions as **(i)** decimals **(ii)** percentages:

    a) $\dfrac{49}{100}$ **b)** $\dfrac{33}{100}$ **c)** $\dfrac{16}{100}$

    d) $\dfrac{3}{10}$ **e)** $\dfrac{4}{10}$ **f)** $\dfrac{9}{10}$ Write this as an equivalent fraction with 10 on the bottom first.

    g) $\dfrac{1}{2}$ **h)** $\dfrac{1}{4}$ **i)** $\dfrac{3}{5}$

5 70% of a class of students take a packed lunch to school.
Write this percentage as a fraction in its simplest form.

6 $\frac{4}{5}$ of the audience at a play are children. What percentage of the audience is children?

7 To pass an exam a student needed to get 0.6 of the questions correct.
What was the percentage pass mark?

Exercise 2

Remember — divide the top of a fraction by the bottom to get a decimal.

You may use a calculator to answer these questions.

1 Write these fractions as **(i)** decimals **(ii)** percentages:

a) $\frac{9}{20}$

b) $\frac{21}{25}$

c) $\frac{13}{50}$

d) $\frac{24}{30}$

e) $\frac{18}{40}$

f) $\frac{27}{45}$

g) $\frac{6}{40}$

h) $\frac{9}{15}$

i) $\frac{21}{60}$

2 9 out of 20 apples in a bag are red and the rest are green.
What percentage of the apples are red?

3 Amy sits an exam and gets a mark of $\frac{18}{25}$. What is her percentage mark?

4 A company employs 250 people. 165 employees are women.
Give the proportion of women in the company as a decimal.

Proportion is another way of saying "part of something".

Example 3

Which is bigger, 42% or $\frac{2}{5}$?

1. Write both amounts as decimals.

Write this as 0.40 so both decimals have 2 d.p.

42% ⟶ 42 ÷ 100 = 0.42

$\frac{2}{5}$ ⟶ 2 ÷ 5 = 0.40

2. Compare the sizes of the decimals.

0.42 is bigger than 0.40, so 42% is bigger than $\frac{2}{5}$.

Example 4

Write these in order of size, starting with the smallest: $\frac{6}{8}$, 77%, 0.7

1. Write $\frac{6}{8}$ and 77% as decimals.

$\frac{6}{8}$ ⟶ 6 ÷ 8 = 0.75

77% ⟶ 77 ÷ 100 = 0.77

2. Write each decimal with two decimal places and put the decimals in order.

0.75   0.77   0.70

0.70   0.75   0.77

3. Finally, put the original amounts in order.   0.7, $\frac{6}{8}$, 77%

Exercise 3

Answer questions **1** and **2 without using a calculator**.

1   Which is bigger:

a) 52% or $\frac{1}{2}$?

b) $\frac{3}{4}$ or 73%?

c) 0.62 or $\frac{3}{5}$?

d) 0.77 or 70%?

2   Write each set of numbers in order, starting with the smallest:

a) 40%, $\frac{39}{100}$, 0.38

b) 0.76, $\frac{3}{4}$, 78%

c) $\frac{1}{4}$, 0.22, 23%

d) $\frac{83}{100}$, 0.8, 85%

e) $\frac{3}{10}$, 0.33, 35%

f) $\frac{2}{5}$, 0.04, 45%

You may use a calculator to answer questions **3** and **4**.

3 Which is bigger:

a) 65% or $\frac{17}{25}$?
b) $\frac{22}{40}$ or 0.56?
c) 0.4 or $\frac{9}{20}$?

4 Write each set of numbers in order, starting with the smallest:

a) $\frac{3}{20}$, 0.16, 14%
b) 78%, 0.72, $\frac{19}{25}$
c) 0.2, $\frac{7}{28}$, 22%

7.3 Finding Percentages

Finding Percentages Without a Calculator

Example 1

Find 50% of 18.

1. 50% is the same as $\frac{1}{2}$. $50\% = \frac{50}{100} = \frac{1}{2}$

2. So find 50% of 18
    by dividing by 2. $\longrightarrow$ $18 \div 2 = 9$

Example 2

Find:

a) 25% of £80

1. 25% is the same as $\frac{1}{4}$. $25\% = \frac{25}{100} = \frac{1}{4}$

2. So find 25% of 80 $80 \div 4 = £20$ *Don't forget to include the units in the answer.*
    by dividing by 4.

b) 75% of £80.

75% is 25% × 3 and $\longrightarrow$ So 75% is £20 × 3 = £60
25% of £80 is £20.

Exercise 1

Answer these questions **without using a calculator**.

1 Find each of these percentages:

   a) 50% of 4   **b)** 25% of 20   **c)** 50% of 30 kg

   d) 25% of £16   **e)** 50% of £3   **f)** 25% of 40

2   **a)** Find 25% of £24.

     b) Find 75% of £24.

3   **a)** Find 25% of 200.

     b) Find 75% of 200.

4 50% of a class of 28 students are girls. How many girls are in the class?

5 Jack gets paid £800 each month. He saves 25% of everything he gets paid. How much does he save each month?

6 4000 tickets went on sale for a concert. 75% of the tickets were sold in the first hour. How many tickets were sold in the first hour?

7 25% of the 120 cars in a car park are black. How many black cars are in the car park?

8 Of the 56 passengers on a bus, 75% were adults. How many adults were on the bus?

Example 3

Find 10% of 120.

1. 10% is the same as $\frac{1}{10}$.

2. So find 10% of 120 by dividing by 10. ⟹ $120 \div 10 = 12$

$$10\% = \frac{10}{100} = \frac{1}{10}$$

Example 4

Find 35% of 40.

1. First find 10% of 40. ⟹ $40 \div 10 = 4$

2. Next, find 30% and 5% of 40:

    30% is 10% × 3. ⟹ $4 \times 3 = 12$

    5% is 10% ÷ 2. ⟹ $4 \div 2 = 2$

This is the best method to use to find percentages that end in a 0 or a 5 (apart from 25, 50 and 75).

3. Add these two values ⟹ 35% of 40 is $12 + 2 = 14$
    together to find 35%

Exercise 2

Answer these questions **without using a calculator**.

1 a) Find 10% of 50.   b) Find 20% of 50.

2 a) Find 10% of 80.   b) Find 20% of 80.

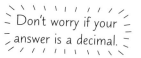

Don't worry if your answer is a decimal.

3 a) Find 10% of 60.   b) Find 30% of 60.

4 a) Find 10% of £25.   b) Find 40% of £25.

5 Find each of these percentages:

    a) 20% of £150   b) 30% of 70

    c) 40% of £20   d) 70% of 40 km

6 a) Find 10% of 20.   b) Find 5% of 20.

7 a) Find 10% of £140.   b) Find 5% of £140.

8 **a)** Find 10% of 80. **b)** Find 5% of 80. **c)** Find 15% of 80.

9 **a)** Find 10% of £200. **b)** Find 5% of £200. **c)** Find 45% of £200.

10 Find each of these percentages:

   a) 10% of 30 **b)** 20% of 140 **c)** 60% of £70

   d) 5% of 120 **e)** 5% of 50 **f)** 35% of £400

   g) 15% of £30 **h)** 90% of 40 **i)** 5% of 180

   j) 35% of 60 **k)** 65% of £60 **l)** 40% of 350

11 Lily buys a pack of charity Christmas cards for £4. 10% of the cost is donated to charity.

   How much is the donation?

12 Dan gets paid £850 a month. He pays 20% tax on this amount. How much tax does he pay a month?

13 240 students sat an exam. 10% of the students got a grade C and 15% got a grade D.

   a) How many students got a grade C?

   b) How many students got a grade D?

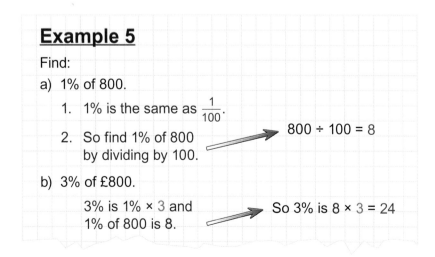

Example 5

Find:

a) 1% of 800.

   1. 1% is the same as $\frac{1}{100}$.

   2. So find 1% of 800 by dividing by 100. → $800 \div 100 = 8$

b) 3% of £800.

   3% is 1% × 3 and 1% of 800 is 8. → So 3% is 8 × 3 = 24

Exercise 3

Answer these questions **without using a calculator**.

1 Find each of these percentages:

a) 1% of £300

b) 1% of 7000

c) 1% of £450

d) 1% of 600

e) 2% of 600

f) 4% of 600

g) 1% of 400

h) 3% of 400

i) 7% of 400

j) 3% of £900

k) 4% of 1100

l) 11% of £300

2 In a batch of 5000 light bulbs, 3% were faulty. How many bulbs were faulty?

3 Adam gets paid £12 000 each year. He spends 2% of this on his phone bill. How much does he spend on his phone bill each year?

Exercise 4

Answer these questions **without using a calculator**.

1 Find each of these percentages:

a) 10% of 75

b) 25% of 24

c) 60% of $20

d) 1% of 500

e) 50% of 720 kg

f) 5% of £12

g) 30% of 80

h) 75% of 16 cm

i) 50% of 1024

j) 15% of £80

k) 25% of 48

l) 7% of 2000

m) 80% of £110

n) 3% of 300 m

o) 25% of 8000

p) 13% of £200

q) 65% of 20

r) 95% of 120

Finding Percentages Using a Calculator

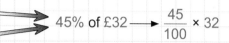

Example 6

Calculate 45% of £32.

1. Rewrite the problem using maths:
   - 45% is the same as $\frac{45}{100}$.
   - 'of' means 'multiply'.

   45% of £32 $\longrightarrow$ $\frac{45}{100} \times 32$

2. Use a calculator to work this out. $\longrightarrow$ $45 \div 100 \times 32 = 14.4$

3. Give your answer with the correct
   units and number of decimal places.   So, 45% of £32 is £14.40

Exercise 5

Use a calculator for this exercise. Hooray.

1   Copy and complete each line below to find the percentages.
    The first one has been done for you.

   a) 55% of 20 $\longrightarrow$ $\frac{55}{100} \times 20$ $\longrightarrow$ $55 \div 100 \times 20 = 11$

   b) 28% of 150 $\longrightarrow$ $\frac{....}{100} \times 150$ $\longrightarrow$ $.... \div 100 \times .... = ...$

   c) 79% of 400 $\longrightarrow$ $\frac{....}{100} \times ....$ $\longrightarrow$ $.... \div 100 \times .... = ...$

2   Find each of these percentages:

a) 15% of 320	b) 23% of 900	c) 19% of 600
d) 78% of 800	e) 36% of £150	f) 8% of £650
g) 22% of 4500	h) 35% of 168	i) 90% of 64
j) 27% of 520	k) 37% of 15	l) 83% of 56
m) 89% of £6	n) 13% of £14	o) 36% of £65

3 Find 58% of £360.

4 780 people work in factory. 45% of the workers are men.
How many men work at the factory?

5 Fatima spent £56 on her weekly shopping. She spent 21% on fruit and vegetables.
How much did she spend on fruit and vegetables?

6 A 350g box of muesli contains 35% oats. What is the weight of oats in the box?

7 A cyclist completes 24% of a 55 km journey on the first day of her journey.
What distance did she cycle on the first day?

7.4 Percentage Increase and Decrease

To increase (or decrease) an amount by a percentage:

- first calculate the percentage
- then add this to (or subtract it from) the original amount.

Example 1

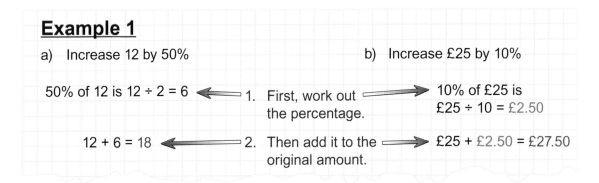

a) Increase 12 by 50%

50% of 12 is 12 ÷ 2 = 6 ←— 1. First, work out the percentage. —→ 10% of £25 is £25 ÷ 10 = £2.50

12 + 6 = 18 ←— 2. Then add it to the original amount. —→ £25 + £2.50 = £27.50

b) Increase £25 by 10%

Example 2

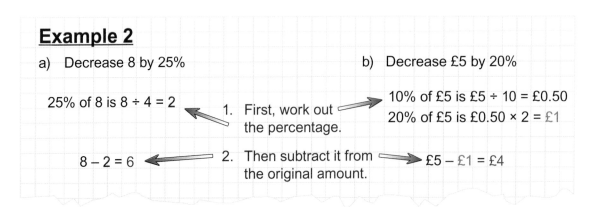

a) Decrease 8 by 25%

25% of 8 is 8 ÷ 4 = 2 ←— 1. First, work out the percentage. —→ 10% of £5 is £5 ÷ 10 = £0.50
20% of £5 is £0.50 × 2 = £1

8 – 2 = 6 ←— 2. Then subtract it from the original amount. —→ £5 – £1 = £4

b) Decrease £5 by 20%

Exercise 1

Answer these questions **without using a calculator**.

1 Work out each of the following.

    a) Increase 8 by 50%

    b) Increase 40 by 50%

    c) Increase 70 by 10%

    d) Increase 12 by 25%

    e) Increase £60 by 10%

    f) Decrease 14 by 50%

    g) Decrease 20 by 25%

    h) Decrease 90 by 10%

    i) Decrease £40 by 25%

    j) Decrease 200 by 1%

2 Work out each of the following.

    a) Increase 100 by 20%

    b) Increase 80 by 75%

    c) Increase 120 kg by 30%

    d) Increase 260 by 20%

    e) Decrease £420 by 20%

    f) Decrease 300 by 30%

    g) Decrease 400 kg by 2%

    h) Decrease 360 by 20%

    i) Increase 40 km by 15%

    j) Decrease 36 by 75%

3 Work out each of the following.

    a) Increase £60 by 15%

    b) Decrease 14 cm by 25%

    c) Increase £20 by 35%

    d) Decrease 8 by 10%

    e) Increase 20 by 15%

    f) Increase 30 by 30%

    g) Decrease £6 by 25%

    h) Decrease 740 kg by 10%

    i) Increase £2.80 by 10%

    j) Increase 300 by 40%

Example 3

Use a calculator to work out these percentage changes:

a) Increase 420 by 35%

b) Decrease £80 by 17%

1. First, work out the percentage.

35% of 420 is
$35 \div 100 \times 420 = 147$

17% of £80 is
$17 \div 100 \times £80 = £13.60$

2. Then add it to/ subtract it from the original amount.

$420 + 147 = 567$

$£80 - £13.60 = £66.40$

Exercise 2

Use a calculator for this exercise.

1 Work out these percentage **increases**.

a) Increase 160 by 35%

b) Increase 45 by 40%

c) Increase 750 by 20%

d) Increase £300 by 12%

e) Increase 68 kg by 75%

f) Increase 340 by 91%

g) Increase 30 by 7%

h) Increase 120 mm by 12%

i) Increase 580 by 24%

j) Increase 1200 by 15%

2 Work out these percentage **decreases**.

a) Decrease 900 by 38%

b) Decrease 420 by 25%

c) Decrease £800 by 56%

d) Decrease £160 by 95%

e) Decrease 270 by 30%

f) Decrease 560 by 37%

g) Decrease 440 by 16%

h) Decrease £360 by 11%

i) Decrease £42 by 55%

j) Decrease 480 by 99%

3 Work out these percentage changes.

a) Increase £9 by 15%

b) Decrease 30 kg by 45%

c) Increase 90 by 9%

d) Decrease 5 by 6%

e) Increase 1340 g by 86%

f) Increase £12 500 by 12%

g) Decrease 750 g by 6%

h) Increase 144 by 12%

i) Increase £56 by 7%

j) Decrease 0.8 kg by 35%

Example 4

20% VAT is added to the product price of a TV to give the selling price.
Without using a calculator, find the selling price of a TV with a product price of £600.

1. First, find the amount of
   VAT that needs to be added. → 10% of £600 is £600 ÷ 10 = £60
   20% of £600 is £60 × 2 = £120

2. Add this to the product price
   to find the selling price. → £600 + £120 = £720

Example 5

A shop is offering a 35% discount on all furniture.
What is the discounted price of a sofa that normally sells for £480?

1. First, find 35% of the
   normal selling price. → 35 ÷ 100 × £480 = £168

2. Subtract this from the normal → £480 − £168 = £312
   selling price to find the sale price.

Exercise 3

Answer questions **1-12 without using a calculator**.

1 20% VAT is added to the product price of a cooker.
If the product price of the cooker is £200, what is the selling price?

2 A packet of cereal normally contains 500 g. A special offer means an extra 50%
is included in each packet. How much cereal is in the special offer packet?

3 A restaurant adds a 10% service charge to a customer's bill.
How much does the customer pay in total when the bill is £50?

4 It costs £80 for a second-class train ticket. A first-class ticket costs 25% more
than a second-class ticket. How much does a first-class ticket cost?

5 The number of students studying at a college last year was 620.
This year the number of students has increased by 20%.

How many students are studying at the college this year?

6 Sam put £500 in a bank account. Each year, 10% of the amount in the account is added as interest. How much money is in Sam's account after one year?

7 A sports shop is offering a discount of 50% on all cycles.
How much would you pay for a cycle that normally costs £120?

8 A pair of shoes costing £40 is reduced in a sale by 15%.
What is the sale price of the shoes?

9 The population of a village is 3500. The population is predicted to decrease by 10% over the next five years. What will the population be in five years time?

10 A family normally spends £900 on electricity each year.
After reducing their usage, their electricity bill was 30% cheaper than normal this year.

How much did they spend on electricity this year?

11 In a furniture sale there is 20% off the cost of all beds.
What is the sale price of a bed normally costing £300?

12 A coat costing £64 is reduced in a sale by 25%. What is the sale price of the coat?

Use a calculator to answer questions **13-23**.

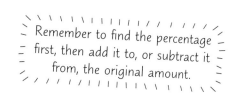

Remember to find the percentage first, then add it to, or subtract it from, the original amount.

13 The price of a small loaf of bread was 60p.
The price is increased by 15%.

What is the new cost of a small loaf?

14 Last year, the price of renting an apartment in Florida was £950.
This year the price has increased by 8%.

What is the cost of renting the apartment this year?

15 20% VAT is added to the product price of a kettle to give the selling price.
If the product price of the kettle is £16.55, what is the selling price?

16 The population of a town last year was 12 400.
This year, the population is 6% higher than last year. What is the population this year?

17 Ellie gets paid £780 a month. She gets a pay rise of 3%.
How much does she now get paid each month?

18 A group of friends have a meal in a café. The bill is £36.
The café adds a 12% service charge to the bill.

How much does the group pay in total?

19 A handbag costing £39 is reduced in a sale by 25%.
What is the sale price of the handbag?

20 Kira gets paid £1300 a month. She pays 20% of this amount as tax.
How much money does she have left each month after tax has been taken off?

21 Rob usually eats 2800 calories a day.
As part of a healthy eating plan he reduces this by 12%.

How many calories a day does he now eat?

22 It costs £6.50 for an adult cinema ticket.
A child ticket costs 30% less than an adult ticket. How much does a child ticket cost?

23 A book shop is offering a discount of 20% on all books.
How much would you pay for a book normally costing £9.95?

7.5   Percentage Problems

Exercise 1

Answer these questions **without using a calculator.**

1 Each grid below is made from 100 small squares.
Write the amount of each grid that is shaded as:

(i) a percentage   **(ii)** a simplified fraction   **(iii)** a decimal

a) 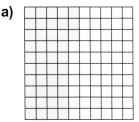   **b)** 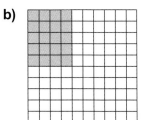   **c)**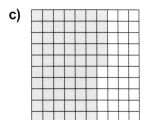

2 A large tin contains 100 biscuits. 39 of the biscuits are creams and the rest are cookies. What percentage of the biscuits are creams?

3 **a)** Find 10% of £600 **b)** Find 20% of £600

c) Find 5% of £600 **d)** Find 35% of £600

4 A 40 g chocolate bar contains 10 g of sugar. What percentage of the chocolate bar is sugar?

5 **a)** Increase 12 kg by 25%. **b)** Decrease 12 kg by 50%.

6 Out of 100 workers in a small business, 64 are women. What percentage of the workers are men?

7 At the start of a journey there were 140 people on a train. 25% of the people got off at the first stop.

How many people got off at the first stop?

8 A jacket costing £60 is reduced in a sale by 15%. What is the sale price of the jacket?

9 Last year, the cost of a holiday to Spain was £1200. This year the cost has increased by 10%.

What is the cost of the same holiday this year?

10 Write 70% as: **a)** a decimal   **b)** a simplified fraction

11 Lewis puts £240 in a savings account. Each year 5% of the amount in the account is added as interest.

How much is in his account after one year?

12 Write 0.04 as: **a)** a simplified fraction   **b)** a percentage

13 Nikki and Mo share a pizza. Nikki eats 35% of the pizza, and Mo eats $\frac{2}{5}$ of the pizza. Who has eaten the most?

14 Wesley used to get paid £800 a month. He receives a pay rise of 3%. How much will he now get each month?

Exercise 2

You may use a calculator to answer these questions.

1 Write each of the following as percentages:

    a) 4 out of 16   **b)** 72 out of 80

    c) 24 out of 120   **d)** 140 out of 400

    e) 5 out of 8   **f)** 28 out of 40

2 Work out 46% of £250.

3 Change these fractions to decimals:

    a) $\frac{21}{30}$ **b)** $\frac{16}{40}$ **c)** $\frac{6}{15}$

4 Izzy got $\frac{68}{80}$ of the questions right in an exam. What is her mark as a percentage?

5 Write these in order, starting with the smallest: $\frac{7}{20}$,   0.3,   34%

6 Isaac gets paid £980 a month. He has to pay 20% of this amount as tax. How much tax does he pay each month?

7 Decrease 640 by 35%.

8 Increase £7 by 15%.

9 The audience for the first night of a show is 1340.
By the last night of the show the audience has increased by 35%.

How many people are in the audience on the last night?

10 Calculate 73% of 56 kg.

11 A suitcase costing £29 is reduced in a sale by 25%.
What is the sale price of the suitcase?

12 Decrease 19 by 24%.

13 In a batch of 4500 eggs, 4% were found to be cracked.
How many eggs in the batch were not cracked?

14 Molly gets paid £16 500 a year. She spends £9570 a year on living expenses.
What percentage of her pay does she spend on living expenses each year?

15 Which is the smallest: $\frac{7}{30}$, 0.33 or 29%?

16 A holiday firm offers a discount of 15% if a holiday is booked online.
What is the online price of a holiday that would normally cost £760?

17 A medium cake costs £4.50 to make. A small cake costs **20% less** to make,
and a large cake costs **36% more** to make.

Work out the cost of making:

a) a small cake

b) a large cake

Section 8 — Algebraic Expressions

8.1 Simplifying Expressions

An algebraic expression uses letters to represent numbers.
Expressions do not contain an equals sign (=).

These are all examples of algebraic expressions:

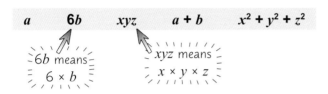

The terms of an expression are separated by + or – signs.

Each term has a + or – sign attached to the front of it.

Terms can be letters, numbers or a mixture of both.

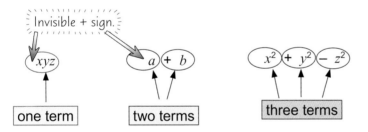

Exercise 1

1 How many terms do each of these expressions have?

a) $3a + 5b - c$

b) $5b$

c) $2x - 6$

d) $5t + s - 24$

e) $3x - 2y + 1$

f) $7 - x$

g) $4m + 3n - x + y$

h) $3x$

i) $24 - y$

j) $2b + c - x + 3y$

k) $2x^3 + 3y$

l) $5x^2$

m) $9 - 6x^4 + y$

n) $3n^2 - 2m + 2x^3 - 4y$

o) $3g - 6h + 1$

Collecting Like Terms

Expressions can sometimes be simplified by collecting like terms.
'Like terms' contain exactly the same letters, but may contain different numbers.

Example 1

By collecting like terms, simplify this expression: $5p + 2p - 4p$

1. This expression contains three terms.
   The only letter in each term is p,
   so they are three like terms.

2. So start with $5p$ and add $2p$ — this gives $7p$.
   Then subtract $4p$ to give the final answer.

$$5p + 2p - 4p = 7p - 4p$$
$$= 3p$$

Example 2

By collecting like terms, simplify the expression $4a + 3b - a - 7b$

> The + or − sign in front of a term actually belongs to that term.

1. '$4a$' and '$-a$' are like terms, and '$+ 3b$' and '$-7b$' are like terms.

2. Rewrite the expression with the like terms collected together.

$$4a + 3b - a - 7b = 4a - a + 3b - 7b$$

3. Combine the like terms:
   $4a - a = 3a$ $3b - 7b = -4b$

$$= 3a \qquad -4b$$

4. Write out the simplified expression.

$$= 3a - 4b$$

Exercise 2

1 Simplify these expressions.

a) $4x + 3x$

b) $5y - 3y$

c) $6b - 3b$

d) $6a + 5a$

e) $2n - n$

f) $4m + m + 2m$

g) $3x + 2x - x$

h) $7y - 3y + 2y$

i) $5b + 2b - 3b$

j) $8g + 5g - 4g$

k) $4v + 9v$

l) $4x - 6x$

m) $7y + 3y - 2y$

n) $3e - 4e + 6e$

o) $8m + 3m - 2m - 5m$

p) $7x + x - 4x$

q) $2h - 5h + h$

r) $7p + p - 5p - 2p$

2 Simplify these expressions.

a) $2x + x + 3y + y$

b) $5a - a + 2b + 5b$

c) $5m - 3m + n + 4n$

d) $2p + 5p + 3q - 2q$

e) $5f + 2f - 2g + 6g$

f) $3a - a + 4c$

g) $5x - 2x - 3y - y$

h) $5p + p + q - 2q$

i) $4f - 3f + 2g - 4g$

j) $5s - 2t - 4s + 5t$

k) $2x + 3y - x - y$

l) $2m + 5n + 4m - n$

m) $7d + 6e - 5d - e$

n) $9p - 3q - 5p - 7q$

o) $5i + 6j + 2i - 8j$

p) $f + g + 8f - 5g$

q) $9x + 6y + 4x + 8y$

r) $4y - 3z - 2y - z$

3 Add together the following pairs of expressions and simplify your answer.

a) $2a + 5b$ and $3a - 2b$

b) $5c$ and $6c - d$

c) $3x - 2y$ and $5x + 7y$

d) $8y + 2x$ and $4x - 3y$

e) $4p - 3q$ and $2p - 5q$

f) $3g + 7h$ and $4g - h$

g) $4x + 2y$ and $2x - z$

h) $a + b$ and $2b + c$

i) $5m - n$ and $8m + n$

j) $7p + 5q - r$ and $3p + q + 4r$

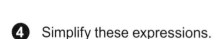
Replace the 'and' with a + sign to add the expressions together.

4 Simplify these expressions.

a) $3x^2 + x^2 + 9y + 2y$

b) $4xy - 2xy + 2b + 5b$

c) $2a^2 - a^2 + b^2 + 4b^2$

d) $9st + 6p + 2st - 3p$

e) $6xy^2 + 2 - 2xy^2 + 3$

f) $12z^3 + 8 - 7z^3 - 3$

Terms with no letters in are 'like terms'.

8.2 Expanding Brackets

You can 'expand' (or remove) brackets by multiplying everything inside the brackets by the letter or number in front.

$$a(b + c) = ab + ac$$
$$a(b - c) = ab - ac$$

Remember — you can write $a \times b$ as ab

And remember, powers work with letters in exactly the same way as they work with numbers.

$$a^2 = a \times a$$
$$a^3 = a \times a \times a$$

Example 1

Expand the brackets in these expressions: a) $3(a + 2)$ b) $8(n - 3)$

a) Multiply both a and 2 by 3. $\Longrightarrow$ $3(a + 2) = (3 \times a) + (3 \times 2) = 3a + 6$

b) Multiply both n and 3 by 8. $\Longrightarrow$ $8(n - 3) = (8 \times n) - (8 \times 3) = 8n - 24$

Example 2

Expand the brackets in these expressions: a) $m(n + 7)$ b) $a(a - 4)$

a) Multiply both n and 7 by m. $m(n + 7) = (m \times n) + (m \times 7)$
$$= mn + 7m$$

b) Multiply both a and 4 by a. $a(a - 4) = (a \times a) - (a \times 4)$
$$= a^2 - 4a$$

Exercise 1

1   Expand the brackets in the following expressions.

a) $2(a + 5)$

b) $4(b + 3)$

c) $3(p + 4)$

d) $2(7 + y)$

e) $8(h - 2)$

f) $9(q - 3)$

g) $2(t + 5)$

h) $4(b - 4)$

i) $3(k + 6)$

j) $3(5 + p)$

k) $7(6 + g)$

l) $5(3 - y)$

m) $5(d + 7)$

n) $4(x + 8)$

o) $6(5 - r)$

2 Expand the brackets in the following expressions.

a) $x(y + 5)$ **b)** $p(q + 2)$ **c)** $a(b + 4)$

d) $m(p + 8)$ **e)** $q(p - 4)$ **f)** $s(5 - t)$

g) $y(5 + x)$ **h)** $n(n - 7)$ **i)** $x(x - 2)$

j) $y(11 - x)$ **k)** $x(8 - x)$ **l)** $n(m - 7)$

Example 3

Simplify these expressions: a) $b \times b \times b \times b$ b) $4a \times 5b$ c) $3a \times 6a$

1. If the same letter is multiplied by itself, write it as a power.

2. Multiply numbers and letters separately.

a) $b \times b \times b \times b = b^4$

b) $4a \times 5b = 4 \times 5 \times a \times b = 20ab$

c) $3a \times 6a = 3 \times 6 \times a \times a = 18a^2$

Example 4

Expand the brackets in the following expressions.
a) $4(5a + 3)$

    1. Multiply both $5a$ and 3 by 4.

    2. Multiply numbers and letters separately in the first term.

$4(5a + 3) = (4 \times 5a) + (4 \times 3)$
$= (4 \times 5 \times a) + (4 \times 3)$
$= 20a + 12$

b) $6x(2x + 4)$

    1. Multiply both $2x$ and 4 by $6x$.

    2. Multiply numbers and letters separately in each term.

$6x(2x + 4) = (6x \times 2x) + (6x \times 4)$
$= (6 \times 2 \times x \times x) + (6 \times 4 \times x)$
$= 12x^2 + 24x$

Exercise 2

1 Simplify the following expressions.

a) $6a \times 4b$ **b)** $2a \times 3a$ **c)** $8p \times 2q$

d) $3a \times 7a$ **e)** $5x \times 3y$ **f)** $9m \times 2m$

g) $12a \times 4b$ **h)** $6p \times 8p$ **i)** $d \times d \times d$

2   Expand the brackets in the following expressions.

a) $3(2p + 4)$

b) $5(4t - 8)$

c) $7(3h + 9)$

d) $2(5d + 4)$

e) $8(7k - 5)$

f) $4(7 + 4p)$

g) $4(5 + 7b)$

h) $3(4 - 2z)$

i) $2(8 - 6m)$

3   Expand the brackets in the following expressions.

a) $3n(2n - 6)$

b) $5u(4u + 8)$

c) $7n(5n - 6)$

d) $3u(u + 8)$

e) $4y(4 + 7y)$

f) $3q(2 - 11q)$

g) $8s(2s - 12)$

h) $6x(4x + 5)$

i) $9v(2 + 8v)$

4   Expand the brackets in the following expressions.

a) $2(3x - y)$

b) $5(u - 2v)$

c) $9(s + 3t)$

d) $4(7a + b)$

e) $3x(4x + 2y)$

f) $2a(3a + 2b)$

g) $3s(2t - 5s)$

h) $4u(v + 3u)$

i) $5y(6y + 2z)$

Example 5

Expand the brackets in the following expressions.   a) $-(q + 4)$ b) $-3(4 - 2a)$

a) $-(q + 4)$ means you need to multiply everything inside the brackets by -1.

Take care with the sign of each term when you're multiplying by a negative number.

$$-(q + 4) = (-1 \times q) + (-1 \times 4)$$
$$= -q + (-4)$$
$$= -q - 4$$

b) Multiply everything in the brackets by -3 this time.

$$-3(4 - 2a) = (-3 \times 4) - (-3 \times 2a)$$
$$= (-3 \times 4) - (-3 \times 2 \times a)$$
$$= (-12) - (-6a)$$
$$= -12 + 6a$$

Remember, subtracting a negative number is the same as adding a positive number.

Exercise 3

1 Expand the brackets in the following expressions.

    a) $-(q + 2)$ **b)** $-(x + 7)$ **c)** $-(h + 3)$

    d) $-(g + 3)$ **e)** $-4(n + 2)$ **f)** $-2(7 + r)$

    g) $-8(3 + a)$ **h)** $-5(4 + z)$ **i)** $-6(a + 4)$

2 Expand the brackets in the following expressions.

    a) $-(p - 3)$ **b)** $-(q - 5)$ **c)** $-(r - 6)$

    d) $-(s - 2)$ **e)** $-4(u - 7)$ **f)** $-2(12 - v)$

    g) $-8(7 - w)$ **h)** $-5(5 - x)$ **i)** $-2(11 - c)$

3 Expand the brackets in the following expressions.

    a) $-2(5 + m)$ **b)** $-5(2 + 3n)$ **c)** $-2(6b - 3)$

    d) $-6(5g - 3)$ **e)** $-7(4v + 8)$ **f)** $-5(10 - 8v)$

    g) $-4(8 - 2z)$ **h)** $-4(2y + 6)$ **i)** $-7(3b + 2)$

4 Expand the brackets in the following expressions.

    a) $-x(2x + 4)$ **b)** $-a(3 - 4a)$ **c)** $-v(v - 8)$

    d) $-y(x + 3y)$ **e)** $-2p(4 - 3p)$ **f)** $-3a(6a - 4b)$

Example 6

Expand the brackets in the expression $2(a + 5) + 3(a + 2)$.

1. Multiply out both sets of brackets: $2(a + 5) + 3(a + 2) = (2a + 10) + (3a + 6)$
    $2(a + 5) = 2a + 10$
    $3(a + 2) = 3a + 6$ $= 2a + 10 + 3a + 6$

2. Then collect like terms. $= 2a + 3a + 10 + 6$

                                              $= 5a + 16$

Exercise 4

1 Simplify the following expressions.

a) $2(z + 3) + 4(z + 2)$ b) $3(c + 1) + 5(c + 7)$ c) $3(w + 4) + 5(w + 2)$

d) $2(4c + 2) + 3(c + 5)$ e) $3(2v + 5) + 6(v + 7)$ f) $4(u + 6) + 8(u + 5)$

g) $5(b - 6) + 7(b + 4)$ h) $7(t - 3) + 2(t + 12)$ i) $8(m - 2) + 9(m + 5)$

2 Simplify the following expressions.

a) $5(p - 3) - (p + 6)$ b) $2(c - 6) - (c + 5)$ c) $5(q - 3) - (q + 1)$

d) $2(j - 5) - (j - 3)$ e) $5(y - 4) - (y - 2)$ f) $5(c - 6) - (c - 3)$

g) $5(2q + 5) - 2(q - 2)$ h) $2(3c - 8) - 8(c + 4)$ i) $4(5q - 1) - 2(q + 2)$

8.3 Factorising

Factorising is the opposite of expanding brackets. It's putting brackets into an expression.

You look for the highest common factor (HCF) of all the terms in an expression, and 'take it outside' a pair of brackets.

Example 1

Factorise these expressions:

a) $6p + 8$

> The expression has a + sign between the two terms, so put a + sign in here.

1. 2 is the HCF of $6p$ and 8.
   So write a pair of brackets with a 2 outside.

$$6p + 8 = 2(\quad + \quad)$$

2. Divide each term in the expression by the common factor, and write the results inside the brackets:
   $$6p \div 2 = 3p \text{ and } 8 \div 2 = 4$$

$$= 2(3p + \quad)$$
$$= 2(3p + 4)$$

So, $6p + 8 = 2(3p + 4)$

b) $12x - 18y$

1. 6 is the HCF of $12x$ and $18y$.
   So 6 goes outside the brackets.

$$12x - 18y = 6(\quad - \quad)$$
$$= 6(2x - \quad)$$

2. Divide each term by the common factor:
   $$12x \div 6 = 2x \text{ and } 18y \div 6 = 3y$$

$$= 6(2x - 3y)$$

So, $12x - 18y = 6(2x - 3y)$

Exercise 1

1 **a)** Find the highest common factor of $2a$ and 10.

   b) Divide both $2a$ and 10 by your answer to **a)**.

   c) Using your answers to **a)** and **b)**, factorise the expression $2a$ + 10.

2 **a)** Find the highest common factor of $5x$ and $15y$.

   b) Factorise the expression $5x - 15y$.

3 Factorise these expressions:

   a) $2a + 4$ **b)** $3b + 12$ **c)** $5c + 15$

   d) $4 + 12x$ **e)** $10d + 35$ **f)** $9x + 12$

   g) $15 + 3y$ **h)** $28 + 7v$ **i)** $15c - 20$

   j) $11p - 22$ **k)** $14 - 7x$ **l)** $24x + 12$

4 Factorise these expressions:

   a) $3a + 6c$ **b)** $9c + 12d$ **c)** $8c + 12f$

   d) $3x + 12y$ **e)** $25d - 35e$ **f)** $12x - 16y$

   g) $3x - 9y$ **h)** $21u - 7v$ **i)** $6s - 42t$

5 Factorise these expressions:

   a) $4a^2 + 12b$ **b)** $3c + 15d^2$ **c)** $5c^2 + 25f$

   d) $6x^2 - 18y$ **e)** $21s - 14t^2$ **f)** $9u^2 - 18v^2$

Example 2

Factorise $3x^2 + 2x$.

1. x is the HCF of $3x^2$ and $2x$.
   So x goes outside the brackets.

2. Divide each term by the common factor, and write the results inside the brackets:
   $3x^2 \div x = 3x$ and $2x \div x = 2$

$3x^2 + 2x \quad = x(\quad + \quad)$

$= x(3x + \quad)$

$= x(3x + 2)$

So, $3x^2 + 2x = x(3x + 2)$

Exercise 2

1 a) Find the highest common factor of x^2 and x.

b) Divide both x^2 and x by your answer to **a)**.

c) Using your answers to **a)** and **b)**, factorise the expression $x^2 + x$.

2 a) Find the highest common factor of $5x^2$ and $16x$.

b) Factorise the expression $5x^2 - 16x$.

3 Factorise these expressions:

a) $3a^2 + 8a$

b) $4b^2 + 19b$

c) $2x^2 + 9x$

d) $7y + 15y^2$

e) $10d^2 + 27d$

f) $4y^2 + 13y$

g) $11y + 3y^2$

h) $22w + 5w^2$

i) $4x^2 - 9x$

j) $21q^2 - 16q$

k) $15y - 7y^2$

l) $27z^2 + 11z$

4 a) Find the highest common factor of $5a^2$ and $10a$.

b) Divide both $5a^2$ and $10a$ by your answer to **a)**.

c) Using your answers to **a)** and **b)**, factorise the expression $5a^2 + 10a$.

Section 9 — Equations and Inequalities

9.1 Solving Equations

Solving an equation means finding the value of an unknown letter that makes both sides equal.

For example, the solution of $2x + 3 = 11$ is $x = 4$ (because if $x = 4$, both sides equal 11).

Example 1

Solve the equation $x + 8 = 15$.

1. You need to get x on its own on one side of the equation so subtract 8 from the left–hand side.

   Always do the same to both sides of an equation. So subtract 8 from the right–hand side too.

2. Now find the solution to the equation.

$$x + 8 = 15$$
$$x + 8 - 8 = 15 - 8$$
$$x = 15 - 8$$
$$x = 7$$

Example 2

Solve the equation $15 - y = 7$.

1. Add y to both sides of the equation — this gets rid of the minus sign in front of y.

2. Now you can solve the equation as before: subtract 7 from both sides of the equation.

3. And find the solution.

$$15 - y = 7$$
$$15 - y + y = 7 + y$$
$$15 = y + 7$$
$$15 - 7 = y + 7 - 7$$
$$8 = y, \text{ or } y = 8$$

Exercise 1

1 Solve these equations to find a value for x.

a) $x + 9 = 12$

b) $x + 5 = 16$

c) $x - 2 = 14$

d) $x - 7 = 19$

e) $x - 3 = 12$

f) $x + 8 = 14$

g) $x - 5 = -3$

h) $x - 12 = -1$

i) $10 = x + 6$

j) $18 = x - 8$

k) $-2 = x - 7$

l) $40 = x - 12$

m) $24 = x - 11$

n) $32 = x - 17$

o) $x - 22 = 27$

2 Solve these equations.

a) $4 - x = 2$

b) $12 - x = 9$

c) $15 - x = 14$

d) $4 - x = 12$

e) $8 - x = 14$

f) $14 - x = 19$

g) $2 - x = 7$

h) $5 - x = 7$

i) $12 - x = 23$

3 Solve the following equations.

a) $z + 4 = 6$

b) $x + 7 = 12$

c) $x - 5 = 0$

d) $t - 1 = 4$

e) $x + 8 = 26$

f) $5 - x = 21$

g) $28 = 20 - x$

h) $m + 16 = 20$

i) $16 = x + 10$

j) $18 - x = 9$

k) $y + 12 = 12$

l) $10 = 3 - p$

m) $28 = 7 + x$

n) $x - 3 = 12$

o) $b + 2 = 1$

p) $x - 8 = 14$

q) $35 = 31 - x$

r) $32 - x = 17$

s) $p - 10 = -6$

t) $x + 4 = 1$

u) $y - 15 = -5$

Example 3

Solve the equation $5z = 15$.

1. Get x on its own by dividing both sides of the equation by 5. ⟶

2. Remember: $5z \div 5 = z$

$5z = 15$

$5z \div 5 = 15 \div 5$

$z = 3$

Example 4

Solve the equation $-6x = 9$.

1. This time, divide both sides by -6.

2. Remember: $-6x \div (-6) = x$

$-6x = 9$

$-6x \div (-6) = 9 \div (-6)$

$x = -1.5$

Dividing a positive number by a negative number gives a negative answer.

Exercise 2

1 Solve the following equations to find a value for x.

a) $2x = 10$ **b)** $3x = 6$ **c)** $6x = 24$

d) $4x = 12$ **e)** $7x = 35$ **f)** $9x = 54$

g) $10x = 110$ **h)** $11x = 143$ **i)** $7x = 63$

j) $3x = 60$ **k)** $8x = 104$ **l)** $20x = 100$

2 Use a calculator to solve the equations below. Write your answers as decimals.

a) $12t = 18$ **b)** $8x = 10$

c) $16x = 56$ **d)** $4x = 26$

e) $5z = 2$ **f)** $14v = 91$

3 Solve these equations **without using a calculator**.
Write your answers as simplified fractions.

a) $10x = 5$ **b)** $3x = 1$

c) $16z = 4$ **d)** $6x = 4$

e) $8y = 3$ **f)** $12x = 9$

4 Solve the following equations. Where necessary, give your answers as decimals.
You **may use a calculator** if you need to.

a) $6x = -18$ **b)** $5z = -20$ **c)** $7x = -14$

d) $15x = -150$ **e)** $6y = -30$ **f)** $4g = -40$

g) $-5t = 50$ **h)** $-8x = 24$ **i)** $-3v = 27$

j) $-7x = 35$ **k)** $-4y = -16$ **l)** $-7x = -56$

m) $-9z = 108$ **n)** $-13x = 195$ **o)** $-3m = -12$

p) $40b = -32$ **q)** $75x = -45$ **r)** $-80x = -56$

Two–Step Equations

"Two–step equations" need to be solved in two stages — and you need to do the stages in the right order.

Example 5

Solve the equation $2x + 3 = 11$.

1. $2x + 3$ means "take your value of x and then: (i) multiply it by 2,   (ii) add 3".

   To get x on its own, "undo" these steps, but in the opposite order.

2. First, subtract 3 from both sides. $\longrightarrow$ $2x + 3 - 3 = 11 - 3$

3. Then divide both sides by 2. $\longrightarrow$ $2x = 8$

                                                      $2x \div 2 = 8 \div 2$

4. Check your answer:
   $(2 \times 4) + 3 = 8 + 3 = 11$ $x = 4$

Exercise 3

1 Solve these equations to find a value for x.

   a) $2x + 6 = 12$ **b)** $3x + 2 = 20$ **c)** $4x + 8 = 24$

   d) $5x + 4 = 29$ **e)** $2x + 8 = 4$ **f)** $3x + 36 = 12$

   g) $8x + 10 = 66$ **h)** $10x + 15 = 115$ **i)** $12x + 9 = 105$

2 Solve the following equations.

   a) $2x - 4 = 6$ **b)** $4y - 6 = 10$ **c)** $3v - 6 = 3$

   d) $5t - 8 = 22$ **e)** $3z - 7 = 11$ **f)** $4q - 9 = 3$

   g) $16x - 6 = 10$ **h)** $15m - 8 = 22$ **i)** $10x - 7 = 73$

3 Solve the following equations.

   a) $12 - 4x = 8$ **b)** $47 - 9x = 11$

   c) $8 - 7x = 22$ **d)** $17 - 10x = 107$

Equations With Brackets

When you've got an equation containing brackets, you need to expand the brackets to get rid of them before you can solve the equation.

Example 6

Solve the equation $3(x + 5) = 21$.

1. First, multiply out the brackets and rewrite the equation.

   $3(x + 5) = (3 \times x) + (3 \times 5) = 3x + 15$

   $3x + 15 = 21$

2. Now solve the equation as normal:
   Subtract 15 from both sides.

   $3x + 15 - 15 = 21 - 15$

   $3x = 6$

   Then divide both sides by 3.

   $3x \div 3 = 6 \div 3$

3. Check your answer:

   $3(2 + 5) = 3(7) = 21$

   $x = 2$

Exercise 4

1 Solve these equations.

a) $3(z + 1) = 18$

b) $2(y + 6) = 18$

c) $4(v + 5) = 44$

d) $5(p + 9) = 50$

e) $6(m + 5) = 48$

f) $2(x + 7) = 20$

g) $3(y - 5) = 6$

h) $8(r - 4) = 24$

i) $10(t - 1) = 20$

j) $4(q - 6) = 40$

k) $3(r - 6) = 9$

l) $5(y - 5) = 10$

2 Solve these equations.

a) $4(p + 8) = 24$

b) $6(x + 3) = 12$

c) $8(b + 4) = 24$

d) $5(u + 2) = 5$

e) $9(r + 10) = 45$

f) $3(x + 5) = 6$

g) $2(p - 8) = -12$

h) $7(y - 4) = -21$

i) $2(z - 6) = -8$

j) $3(y + 5) = -6$

k) $8(x + 3) = -16$

l) $6(r + 7) = -6$

Exercise 5 — Mixed Exercise

1 Solve the following equations. Where necessary, give your answers as decimals.

a) $y + 6 = 11$

b) $v - 5 = 9$

c) $p + 9 = 12$

d) $r + 6 = 3$

e) $2x + 5 = 7$

f) $-5 = r - 12$

g) $4(v + 2) = 20$

h) $12t = -36$

i) $8p - 4 = 60$

j) $4 - x = 3$

k) $8y = 6$

l) $6x + 10 = 40$

m) $y - 3 = -1$

n) $10(y - 12) = 80$

o) $9t - 6 = -60$

p) $15x = 60$

q) $4z - 7 = 2$

r) $12w - 10 = -70$

s) $13u = 169$

t) $5z - 12 = 13$

u) $3(p - 6) = -12$

9.2   Solving Harder Equations

Sometimes equations have an 'unknown' — x or y or some other letter — on both sides.

Example 1

Solve the equation $5x + 6 = 2x + 18$.

1. So that all the x terms are on one side of the equation only, subtract $2x$ from both sides.

$$5x - 2x + 6 = 2x - 2x + 18$$
$$3x + 6 = 18$$

2. Now you can solve the equation as before. Subtract 6 from both sides...
    ...and then divide both sides by 3.

$$3x + 6 - 6 = 18 - 6$$
$$3x = 12$$
$$3x \div 3 = 12 \div 3$$
$$x = 4$$

3. Remember to check your answer:
    $(5 \times 4) + 6 = 26$ and $(2 \times 4) + 18 = 26$

Example 2

Solve the equation $9x - 5 = 3 - x$.

1. All the x terms need to be on one side of the equation, so add x to both sides.

$$9x + x - 5 = 3 - x + x$$
$$10x - 5 = 3$$

2. Now solve the equation as before. Add 5 to both sides...
    ...and then divide both sides by 10.

$$10x - 5 + 5 = 3 + 5$$
$$10x = 8$$
$$10x \div 10 = 8 \div 10$$
$$x = 0.8$$

3. Remember to check your answer:
    $(9 \times 0.8) - 5 = 2.2$ and $3 - 0.8 = 2.2$

Exercise 1

1 Solve the following equations to find a value for x.

    a) $4x = x + 15$ **b)** $11x = x + 20$

    c) $9x = x - 16$ **d)** $10x + 5 = 3x + 19$

    e) $14x + 3 = 5x + 21$ **f)** $15x - 13 = 5x + 27$

    g) $8x - 4 = 2x + 44$ **h)** $15x + 8 = 4x - 47$

    i) $21x - 5 = 5x + 11$

2 Solve the following equations.

    a) $3x - 3 = 5 - x$ **b)** $5x - 8 = 10 - x$

    c) $8x - 3 = 27 - 2x$ **d)** $5x + 9 = 20 - 6x$

    e) $4x + 2 = 51 - 3x$ **f)** $5x - 13 = 87 - 5x$

    g) $8x + 2 = 30 - 6x$ **h)** $7x - 7 = 70 - 4x$

    i) $4x + 3 = 147 - 8x$

3 Solve the following equations. Give your answers as decimals.

    a) $4x - 3 = 1 - 4x$ **b)** $4x + 3 = 6 - 2x$

    c) $13x - 1 = 2 + x$ **d)** $8x + 2 = 10 - 12x$

    e) $15x + 2 = 3x + 11$ **f)** $11x - 5 = 3 + x$

Example 3

Solve the equation $3(x + 2) = x + 8$

1. First multiply out the brackets. $3(x + 2) = (3 \times x) + (3 \times 2) = 3x + 6$

                                           $3x + 6 = x + 8$

2. Now you can solve the equation as before:

    Subtract x from both sides... $3x - x + 6 = x - x + 8$

    ...then subtract 6 from both sides $2x + 6 - 6 = 8 - 6$

    ...and finally divide both sides by 2. $2x \div 2 = 2 \div 2$

3. Remember to check your answer: $x = 1$

    $3(1 + 2) = 9$ and $1 + 8 = 9$

Exercise 2

1 Solve these equations.

a) $2(x + 5) = x + 13$

b) $5(x + 3) = x + 31$

c) $6(x + 8) = x + 53$

d) $7(x - 6) = x - 6$

e) $3(x + 4) = x - 20$

f) $9(x - 6) = x + 10$

g) $10(x - 4) = x - 4$

h) $4(x + 6) = x + 51$

i) $2(x + 12) = x - 13$

j) $3(p - 5) = p - 5$

k) $5(t + 4) = t - 8$

l) $11(v - 2) = v + 8$

m) $4(m - 6) = m$

n) $6(m - 4) = m + 6$

o) $4(z + 2) = z + 11$

2 Solve these equations. Where necessary, give your answers as decimals.

a) $5(y + 2) = 2y + 16$

b) $6(x + 2) = 3x + 48$

c) $6(p + 7) = 4p + 50$

d) $7(t - 5) = 2t - 5$

e) $3(m + 6) = 2m - 20$

f) $10(x + 2) = 5x + 90$

g) $7(u - 2) = 2u + 36$

h) $5(y - 3) = 2y + 33$

i) $5(x + 3) = 2x + 57$

j) $3(v + 2) = 2v + 1$

k) $8(v + 3) = 5v + 3$

l) $7(k - 3) = 4k - 9$

m) $5(y + 12) = 3y - 13$

n) $6(m - 7) = 4m + 5$

o) $4(z - 7) = 2z + 11$

3 Solve these equations.

a) $8(x - 8) = 2(x - 2)$

b) $20(x - 2) = 5(x + 1)$

c) $6(x - 3) = 3(x + 8)$

d) $3(x + 6) = 2(x + 10)$

e) $12(x - 2) = 4(x - 2)$

f) $6(x - 8) = 3(x - 3)$

Exercise 3

1 Solve the following equations.

a) $5(x + 7) = x - 5$

b) $3x + 5 = x + 9$

c) $4(x + 11) = 3x + 51$

d) $7x - 4 = 4x + 5$

e) $5(b + 4) = 3b - 2$

f) $2(g - 4) = g + 1$

g) $6x + 5 = 12 - x$

h) $3(x - 2) = x + 4$

i) $8(k - 4) = 5k + 13$

j) $4(m - 3) = m + 9$

k) $5y - 4 = 12 - 3y$

l) $10(v - 6) = 3v - 4$

m) $9(t - 6) = 8t + 10$

n) $5(a - 2) = a + 2$

o) $6u + 37 = 5 - 2u$

p) $5(p + 6) = 2p + 9$

q) $12p + 8 = 53 - 3p$

r) $5(w + 5) = w + 25$

Sometimes you'll need to write your own equation based on a description of a situation.

Always read the question carefully. And always simplify your equations as much as possible.

Example 1

I think of a number and add 3 to it. The result equals 7.
What is the number I thought of?

1. You don't know what the number is yet.   Call the number x.

2. Adding 3 to x gives $x + 3$.   Then: $x + 3 = 7$
   The result is 7.

   So: $x + 3 - 3 = 7 - 3$
3. Solve the equation in the normal way.

   $x = 4$

Example 2

I think of a number and multiply it by 4. The result equals 28.
What is the number I thought of?

1. You don't know what the number is yet.   Call the number x.

2. Multiplying x by 4 gives $4x$.   Then: $4x = 28$
   The result is 28.

   So: $4x \div 4 = 28 \div 4$
3. Solve the equation in the normal way.

   $x = 7$

Exercise 1

1   Which number did I think of in each situation below? *"I think of a number, and then..."*

   a) ...I add 5 to it. The result equals 12.

   b) ...I add 8 to it. The result equals 23.

   c) ...I subtract 12 from it. The result equals 7.

   d) ...I subtract 14 from it. The result equals 15.

   e) ...I multiply it by 2. The result equals 22.

   f) ...I multiply it by 6. The result equals 54.

2 For each of the following, write an equation and solve it to find x.

a) 3 is added to x and the result is 7.　　**b)** x is multiplied by 6 to give 54.

c) 25 less than x is 4.　　**d)** x multiplied by 8 is 56.

e) x added to 11 is 23.　　**f)** 5 is multiplied by x and it equals 35.

g) 13 is subtracted from x to give 4.　　**h)** 12 times x is 60.

Example 3

I think of a number, double it, and add 3. The result is 15.
What is the number I thought of?

1. You don't know what the number is yet.　　Call the number x.

2. Doubling x gives $2x$.
    Then adding 3 gives $2x + 3$.
    The result is 15.

   Then:　　$2x + 3 = 15$

   So:　　$2x + 3 - 3 = 15 - 3$

       $2x \div 2 = 12 \div 2$

         $x = 6$

3. Solve the equation in the normal way.
    Then check your answer.

Exercise 2

1 Which number did I think of in each situation below?
"I think of a number, and then..."

a) ...multiply it by 3 and then subtract 2. The result is 19.

b) ...double it and then add 3. The result is 13.

c) ...multiply it by 2 and then add 40. The result is 64.

d) ...multiply it by 5 and then subtract 3. The result is 17.

e) ...multiply it by 4 and then add 200 to it. The answer is 240.

f) ...multiply it by 4 and then subtract 10. The answer is 10.

g) ...multiply it by 6 and then add 43. The answer is 61.

h) ...multiply it by 12 and then subtract 8. The answer is 40.

i) ...multiply it by 7 and then add 27. My answer is 90.

j) ...multiply it by 8 and then subtract 5. My answer is 83.

Example 4

The angles in a triangle always add up to 180°.

Use this fact and the diagram on the right to write an equation involving x.

Solve your equation to find x.

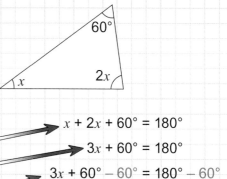

1. Add up the three angles. The result is 180°.

2. Collect like terms to simplify the expression on the left-hand side of the equation.

3. Now solve the equation as normal.

$x + 2x + 60° = 180°$

$3x + 60° = 180°$

$3x + 60° - 60° = 180° - 60°$

$3x \div 3 = 120° \div 3$

$x = 40°$

Exercise 3

1 For each triangle below:

(i) Write an equation involving x.

(ii) Solve your equation to find x.

Remember — the angles in a triangle add up to 180°.

a)

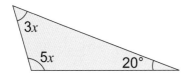

b)

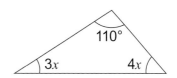

c)

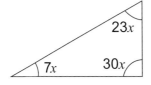

d)

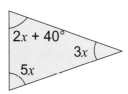

e)

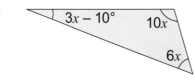

f)

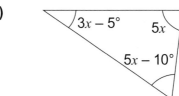

9.4 Solving Inequalities

Inequalities Basics

Write inequalities using these symbols:

> **> greater than**

> **≥ greater than or equal to**

> **< less than**

> **≤ less than or equal to**

You can write inequality symbols between pairs of numbers,
  e.g. 12 > 5 means "12 is greater than 5"

or between a number and an unknown,
  e.g. $x \leq 0$ means "x is less than or equal to zero".

Exercise 1

1 Put the correct sign, **>** or **<**, between each of these pairs of numbers.

a) 5 ☐ 12   b) 13 ☐ 8   c) 15 ☐ 20

d) 1 ☐ 6   e) −1 ☐ 5   f) 8 ☐ −3

g) −1 ☐ 0   h) −1 ☐ −5   i) −6 ☐ −10

j) −10 ☐ −3   k) −4 ☐ −1   l) −8 ☐ −12

m) 6 ☐ −5   n) 7 ☐ 3   o) 3 ☐ −5

p) 4 ☐ −4   q) −6 ☐ 6   r) −3 ☐ −10

2 Describe in words what is meant by the following inequalities.

a) $x \geq 1$ b) $x < 7$ c) $x > -4$

d) $x \leq 9$ e) $x < 8$ f) $x \leq -5$

g) $x \geq 3$ h) $x > 15$ i) $x < -2$

3 Write each of the following as an inequality.

a) x is greater than 4   b) x is less than or equal to 12

c) x is greater than or equal to 8   d) x is less than 3

e) 9 is greater than x f) 7 is less than or equal to x

Example 1

Show the following inequalities on a number line: a) $x > 1$ b) $x \leq 1$

a) "$x > 1$" means x can be any number greater than 1, but not 1 itself.

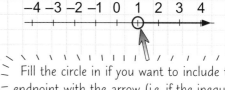

So draw a circle on the number line at 1 and draw an arrow in the increasing direction.

Fill the circle in if you want to include the endpoint with the arrow (i.e. if the inequality is a $\geq$ or $\leq$). Otherwise, leave it blank.

b) "$x \leq 1$" means x can be any number less than or equal to 1.

So draw a circle on the number line at 1 and draw an arrow in the decreasing direction.

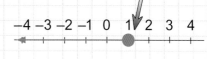

Exercise 2

1   Show the following inequalities on a number line.

a) $x > 3$

b) $x < 7$

c) $x > -2$

d) $x < -6$

e) $x \leq 5$

f) $x \geq 9$

g) $x \geq 12$

h) $x < 22$

i) $x > -6$

j) $x \leq -3$

k) $x < 18$

l) $x > -25$

m) $x \leq 34$

n) $x < 45$

o) $x \geq 57$

p) $x < 65$

q) $x \geq -7$

r) $x \leq -4$

s) $x \geq -3$

t) $x \leq -1$

u) $x < 0$

Solving Inequalities

Solving inequalities is very similar to solving equations. Your answer will also be an inequality.

Example 2

Solve the inequality $x + 4 < 8$.

1. Solve inequalities just like you solve equations — by doing the same thing to both sides.

2. So, subtract 4 from both sides.

$$x + 4 < 8$$
$$x + 4 - 4 < 8 - 4$$

3. If the question uses $<$ or $>$, so will your answer.

$$x < 4$$

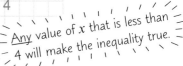

Any value of x that is less than 4 will make the inequality true.

Example 3

Solve the inequality $x - 7 \geq 2$. Show your solution on a number line.

1. Solve the inequality by adding 7 to both sides.

$$x - 7 \geq 2$$

2. If the question uses $\leq$ or $\geq$, so will your answer.

$$x - 7 + 7 \geq 2 + 7$$
$$x \geq 9$$

3. The inequality uses $\geq$, so fill in the circle on your number line.

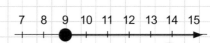

Exercise 3

1 Solve the following inequalities. Show each of your solutions on a number line.

a) $x + 9 > 14$ **b)** $x + 5 < 7$ **c)** $x + 3 \leq 12$

d) $x - 2 \geq 14$ **e)** $x + 3 > 10$ **f)** $x + 6 \leq 9$

g) $x - 7 < 19$ **h)** $x - 1 \geq 2$ **i)** $x - 13 \geq 17$

j) $x + 5 > 2$ **k)** $x - 5 < -3$ **l)** $x + 1 \leq -1$

2 Solve the following inequalities.

a) $x - 9 > 14$ **b)** $x + 3 < 12$ **c)** $x + 2 \geq 14$

d) $x - 8 \leq 22$ **e)** $x + 13 \geq 17$ **f)** $x - 5 > 2$

g) $x - 7 < -6$ **h)** $x + 4 \leq -1$ **i)** $x + 12 > -1$

j) $x - 4 \leq -7$ **k)** $x - 2 \leq 4$ **l)** $x - 2 < -10$

Example 4

Solve the inequality $4x < 12$.

1. Divide both sides of the inequality by 4.

$$4x < 12$$
$$4x \div 4 < 12 \div 4$$

2. Multiplying or dividing by a positive number doesn't change the direction of the inequality sign.

$$x < 3$$

Example 5

Solve the inequality $3x - 2 < 13$.

1. Again, solve the inequality just like an equation:
   First add 2 to both sides...
   ...then divide both sides by 3.

2. Make sure you use the correct inequality symbol in the answer.

$$3x - 2 < 13$$
$$3x - 2 + 2 < 13 + 2$$
$$3x < 15$$
$$3x \div 3 < 15 \div 3$$
$$x < 5$$

Exercise 4

1 Solve the following inequalities.
Where necessary, give your answers as decimals.

a) $3x \geq 9$ b) $5x < 25$ c) $2x > 8$

d) $7x \leq 21$ e) $4x < -16$ f) $9x > -72$

g) $11x \leq 33$ h) $2x < 48$ i) $6x \geq 54$

j) $2x < 15$ k) $4x \geq -35$ l) $2x \leq -1.5$

2 Solve the following inequalities.
Show each of your solutions on a number line.

a) $3x + 2 < 5$ b) $6x - 7 \leq 5$ c) $4x - 8 > 20$

d) $4x + 6 < 18$ e) $5x - 8 \geq 7$ f) $6x + 6 > 30$

g) $5x - 6 < 29$ h) $7x - 2 > 19$ i) $4x - 8 < 12$

j) $2x - 4 \geq 20$ k) $12x - 6 \leq 90$ l) $3x - 9 > 30$

3 Solve the following inequalities.

a) $4x + 8 < 36$ b) $8x + 9 \geq 57$ c) $5x - 3 < 52$

d) $2x + 9 > 27$ e) $4x + 8 < 48$ f) $5x + 7 \leq 27$

g) $9x + 7 \geq 43$ h) $5x - 3 \leq 67$ i) $3x - 1 < 5$

j) $3x + 4 > 1$ k) $7x + 10 > -4$ l) $6x + 7 < -5$

Exercise 5 — Mixed Exercise

1 Put the correct sign, **>** or **<**, between each of these pairs of numbers.

a) 8 ☐ 11   **b)** 4 ☐ 2   **c)** 0 ☐ −6

d) −5 ☐ 1   **e)** −4 ☐ −2   **f)** −3 ☐ −8

2 Describe in words what is meant by the following inequalities.

a) $y < 4$ **b)** $y \geq 11$ **c)** $y > -2$

d) $y > 8$ **e)** $y \leq 6$ **f)** $y \geq 5$

3 Write each of the following as an inequality.

a) y is greater than or equal to 12   **b)** y is greater than −4

c) y is less than 6   **d)** y is less than or equal to −1

4 Solve the following inequalities. Where necessary, give your answers as decimals.

a) $x - 2 < -5$ **b)** $x + 6 \leq -2$ **c)** $2x - 6 < 3$

d) $x + 12 \geq 1$ **e)** $6x < 36$ **f)** $5x < -15$

g) $2x + 7 < -3$ **h)** $x + 5 \geq 5$ **i)** $16x - 13 < -5$

j) $x + 4 \leq 1$ **k)** $x - 5 > 3$ **l)** $15x \geq 75$

m) $4x + 5 \geq 2$ **n)** $x + 6 < 2$ **o)** $8x - 2 \leq -6$

9.5   Equations and Inequalities Problems

Exercise 1

1 Solve the following equations.

a) $x + 3 = 7$ **b)** $2z + 5 = 3$ **c)** $4(x - 2) = 4$

d) $4m + 3 = 15$ **e)** $y + 5 = 12$ **f)** $t - 4 = 9$

g) $4(p + 4) = -28$ **h)** $3u + 4 = 7$ **i)** $a - 7 = 4$

j) $5(x + 7) = 10$ **k)** $7b = 49$ **l)** $5(d - 3) = -10$

m) $v + 1 = 0$ **n)** $4x - 3 = -15$ **o)** $z + 6 = 2$

2 Which number did I think of in each situation below? *"I think of a number, and then..."*

    a) ...multiply it by 7 and then add 13. The answer is 34.

    b) ...multiply it by 2 and then subtract 6. The answer is 194.

    c) ...multiply it by 9 and then add 10. The answer is 55.

    d) ...multiply it by 12 and then subtract 8. The answer is 112.

    e) ...multiply it by 4 and then add 7. The answer is 25.

    f) ...multiply it by 8 and then subtract 9. The answer is −3.

3 Solve the following inequalities and show each solution on a number line.

    a) $v + 3 > 6$ **b)** $a - 5 \leq 1$ **c)** $p + 4 \geq 5$

    d) $s + 3 < 1$ **e)** $x + 4 > 1$ **f)** $z - 3 \leq 2$

    g) $x - 4 \geq -3$ **h)** $v - 6 < -10$ **i)** $3y + 2 \geq 5$

    j) $3x \leq 42$ **k)** $10x + 5 \geq 65$ **l)** $8x - 7 \geq 33$

    m) $15x < 45$ **n)** $9x - 6 < 75$ **o)** $12x + 7 < -5$

4 The angles in a triangle add up to 180°.

    a) Use the triangle below to write an equation involving x.

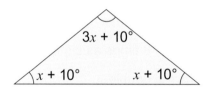

    b) Solve your equation to find the value of x.

    c) Use your value of x to find the size of each angle in the triangle.

5 The angles in a triangle add up to 180°.

    a) Use this fact and the triangle on the right to write an equation involving x.

    b) Solve your equation and so find the size of each angle in the triangle.

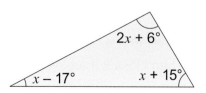

Section 10 — Formulas

10.1 Writing Formulas

A formula is like a set of instructions for working something out.

For example, $s = 4t + 3$ is a formula for s. It tells you how to find s, if you know the value of t.

The part after the equals sign is an algebraic expression.

Example 1

Write a formula for y involving x if:

a) y is 3 more than x.

You need to add 3 to x to get y. $y = x + 3$

b) y is 5 times as big as x.

You need to multiply x by 5 to get y. $y = x \times 5$, so $y = 5x$

Exercise 1

1   Write a formula for y involving x if:

a) y is 5 more than x

b) y is 11 more than x

c) y is 2 less than x

d) y is 3.5 less than x

e) y is 4 times as big as x

f) y is 8 times as big as x

g) y is half of x

h) y is double x

i) y is $\frac{1}{4}$ of x

j) y is the same as x

Example 2

I start with a bag containing m marbles. Then I lose 8 marbles.
Write an expression for the number of marbles I have now.

1. "I start with m marbles." m

2. "Then I lose 8 marbles." — so you need to subtract 8. $\Longrightarrow m - 8$

> An expression is just the bit after the '=' in a formula.

Example 3

My brother has n marbles. I have twice as many marbles as him.
Write an expression for the number of marbles I have.

1. "My brother has n marbles." n

2. "I have twice as many..." — so you need to $2n$
   multiply the amount my brother has by 2.

Exercise 2

1 Luka has a box containing n chocolates. He eats 2 of the chocolates.

Write an expression for the number of chocolates he has left.

2 Zainab has n stamps. A friend gives her 5 more stamps for her collection.

Write an expression for the number of stamps she now has.

3 A dog has n bones. The dog loses 5 bones.

Write an expression for the number of bones he has left.

4 Phil orders n pizzas for his party. He eats 1 of the pizzas before his guests arrive.

Write an expression for how many pizzas he has left.

5 Abigail drives 2.5 miles to the shops. She then drives n miles further.

Write an expression for how many miles Abigail drives in total.

6 Calvin has n CDs. David has 5 times as many CDs.

Write an expression for the number of CDs David has.

7 Harry has s sugar cubes. Zurab has 8 times as many sugar cubes as Harry.

Write an expression for the number of sugar cubes Zurab has.

8 George spends m minutes on his Maths homework,
Chris spends half as long on the homework.

Write an expression for how many minutes
Chris spends on this homework.

Hint: Chris takes half the
time George did, so divide
George's time by 2.

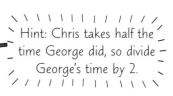

9   Emily has c chairs, which is 3 times as many as Sara.

Write an expression for the number of chairs Sara has.

10 I have c carrots. Su has two and a half times as many carrots as me.

Write an expression for the number of carrots Su has.

11 Jess has 6 shirts, which is s more than Becky.

Write an expression for how many shirts Becky has.

12 Liam has d daffodils, which is 8 more than Zane has. Ron has 4 more daffodils than Zane.

a) Write an expression for how many daffodils Zane has.

b) Write an expression for how many daffodils Ron has.

Example 4

To find y, multiply x by 3, then add 7. Write a formula for y involving x.

1. First multiply x by 3. $3x$

2. Then add 7. $3x + 7$

3. You're asked to write a formula,   So $y = 3x + 7$
      so don't forget the '$y = $ '.

Example 5

I have m marbles. I lose half of those marbles, but then someone gives me 6 of their marbles. Write an expression for how many marbles I have now.

1. "I have m marbles." m

2. "I lose half of those marbles," — so divide m by 2. $\longrightarrow$ $\dfrac{m}{2}$

3. "Someone gives me 6 marbles" — so add 6. $\longrightarrow$ $\dfrac{m}{2} + 6$

Exercise 3

1 Write a formula for y involving x for each of the following.

  a) To find y, multiply x by 5, then add 4.

  b) To find y, multiply x by 2, then subtract 6.

  c) To find y, multiply x by −1, then add 2.

  d) To find y, divide x by 3, then add 11.

  e) To find y, divide x by 2, then subtract 11.

  f) To find y, multiply x by 1.5, then subtract 2.5.

2 I have b flower bulbs. To find the number of flowers that should grow from them, multiply the number of bulbs by 3 and then add 5.

Write an expression for the number of flowers I can expect to grow.

3 Sam has s stickers. He loses half his stickers and then buys himself 5 more.

Write an expression for how many stickers Sam now has.

4 Lara has n friends on a social networking site.
She decides to get rid of half of her friends. She then adds 11 new friends.

Write an expression for how many friends Lara now has.

5 Jeff has p pounds in cash. He doubles his money at a casino.
Then he spends 20 pounds.

Write an expression for the number of pounds he now has.

Example 6

Write a formula for P, the perimeter of a square with sides of length x.

1. The perimeter is the distance around the outside of the shape.

   $P = x + x + x + x$

2. Find an expression for the perimeter by adding up the side lengths.

   $x + x + x + x = 4x$

3. The formula should start with '$P =$ '

   $P = 4x$

Example 7

The total cost of hiring a boat is made up of: i) a cost of £5 for each hour

plus: ii) a fixed cost of £25

Write a formula for C, the total cost of hiring a boat for h hours.

1. Multiply h by 5 to find an expression
    for the total hourly cost.   Cost (in pounds) for h hours = $h \times 5 = 5h$

2. Then add on the fixed cost of £25. $5h + 25$

3. The formula should start with '$C =$ '.   So $C = 5h + 25$

Exercise 4

1 Write a formula for P, the perimeter of an equilateral triangle with sides of length x.

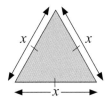

2 Write a formula for P, the perimeter of a regular pentagon with sides of length l.

All sides of a regular shape are the same length.

3 Write down a formula for P, the perimeter of each field shown below.

a)

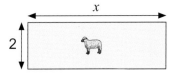

b)

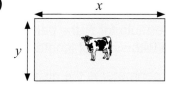

4 At an Internet cafe, it costs 5p per minute to use the Internet.

Complete the formula below to show the cost (C) of using the Internet for m minutes.

$$C = 5..........$$

5 It costs £3 per hour to park a car.

Write a formula for the cost (C) of parking for h hours.

6 It takes 2 minutes to drive 1 km.

Write a formula for the time taken (T) to drive k km.

7 Tom gets paid w pounds for each hour he works in his local shop.

Write a formula for the total amount he gets paid (P) if he works for 8 hours.

8 Katie always eats 2 more apples per week than Laura does.

Write a formula for the number of apples (N)
that Katie eats if Laura eats a apples.

9 Ashkan walks m more miles than Teri.

Write a formula for A, the number of miles Ashkan walks, if Teri walks 3.5 miles.

10 Maddie gets paid w pounds for each hour she works in a restaurant.

a) Write a formula for P, the total amount she gets paid, if she works for 6 hours.

b) After working for 6 hours, she also gets a bonus of £15.
Write a formula for T, the total amount she gets paid including the bonus.

11 Write a formula for the cost (C) of hiring a minibus for n hours
if it costs £5 for each hour plus a fixed charge of £20.

12 To hire a bouncy castle costs a £125 fixed fee plus £50 per hour it is used.

Write a formula for the cost in pounds (C) of hiring a bouncy castle for n hours.

13 Write a formula for the cost (C) of having t trees cut down
if it costs p pounds per tree plus a fixed amount of f pounds.

10.2 Substituting into a Formula

Substituting numbers into a formula means replacing letters with numbers.

Example 1

$P = 3 + q$. Find the value of P when $q = 5$.

1. Write down the formula.

2. Replace q with 5 and do the calculation.

$P = 3 + q$
$= 3 + 5$
$= 8$

So $P = 8$.

Exercise 1

1 $S = 3 + t$. Find the value of S when $t = 2$.

2 $E = 2 + f$. Find the value of E when:

   a) $f = 1$ **b)** $f = 2$ **c)** $f = 3$

3 $Y = x + 3$. Find the value of Y when:

   a) $x = 1$ **b)** $x = 3$ **c)** $x = 5$

4 $M = n - 2$. Find the value of M when $n = 6$.

5   Find the value of y in each of the following when $x = 5$.

   a) $y = x + 2$ **b)** $y = 5 + x$ **c)** $y = 10 - x$

6   Find the value of y in each of the following when $x = 7$.

   a) $y = x + 1$ **b)** $y = x + 4$ **c)** $y = 5 + x$

   d) $y = x - 3$ **e)** $y = x - 7$ **f)** $y = 12 - x$

   g) $y = x - 8$ **h)** $y = x - 11$ **i)** $y = -4 + x$

7   Find the value of y in each of the following when $x = -2$.

   a) $y = 4 + x$ **b)** $y = 2 + x$ **c)** $y = -1 + x$

8   If $x = 4$ and $y = 3$, find the value of z in each of the following.

   a) $z = x + 2$ **b)** $z = y - 1$ **c)** $z = x + y$

   d) $z = x - y$ **e)** $z = y - x$ **f)** $z = x$

9   If $p = -4.8$ and $q = 3.2$, find the value of r in each of the following.

   a) $r = p + 6.7$ **b)** $r = 8 - q$ **c)** $r = 0.2 - p$

   d) $r = p + q$ **e)** $r = p - q$ **f)** $r = q - p$

10   The number of cups of coffee, C, Adam drinks in a day can be worked out using the formula $C = n + 2$, where n is the number of biscuits he eats.

   How many cups of coffee does he drink if he eats:

   a) 2 biscuits   **b)** 8 biscuits   **c)** no biscuits?

11   Bev spends at least 3 hours a week at football training.
The number of goals, G, she scores in a match can be worked out using the formula $G = t - 3$, where t is the number of hours she spends training during the week.

   How many goals does she score if she spends:

   a) 4 hours training   **b)** 6 hours training   **c)** 3 hours training?

Example 2

The area (A) of a rectangle is given by the formula $A = bh$.
Find the value of A when $b = 5$ and $h = 6$.

1. Write down the formula.

2. Replace b and h with the numbers you're given, and do the calculation.

$A = bh = b \times h$
$\qquad\quad = 5 \times 6$
$\qquad\quad = 30$
So $A = 30$.

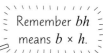

Remember bh means $b \times h$.

Exercise 2

1 $F = 3 \times g$. Find the value of F when $g = 2$.

2 $Y = 4 \times z$. Find the value of Y when:

   a) $z = 2$ **b)** $z = 3$ **c)** $z = 5$

3 $H = 5d$. Find the value of H when:

a) $d = 2$ **b)** $d = 3$ **c)** $d = 10$

4 $A = 6b$. Find the value of A when:

a) $b = 1$ **b)** $b = 4$ **c)** $b = 6$

5 $L = 1.5M$. Find the value of L when:

a) $M = 2$ **b)** $M = 4$ **c)** $M = 3$

6   Find the value of y in each of the following when $x = 3$.

a) $y = \dfrac{6}{x}$ **b)** $y = \dfrac{9}{x}$ **c)** $y = \dfrac{15}{x}$

Divide by x in this question.

7   If $x = 4$ and $y = 2$, find the value of z in each of the following.

a) $z = xy$ **b)** $z = x^2$ **c)** $z = \dfrac{x}{y}$

8   The area in cm², A, of this rectangle is given by the formula $A = 3l$.
Find A for the values of l below.

a) $l = 4$ **b)** $l = 5$

c) $l = 6$ **d)** $l = 8$

e) $l = 14$ **f)** $l = 23$

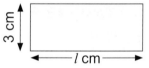

3 cm

l cm

9   The number of burgers, B, needed for a barbeque is worked out using
the formula $B = 2.5n$, where n is the number of people attending.

How many burgers are needed if there are:

a) 4 people   **b)** 10 people   **c)** 16 people?

10 Carla is dividing 20 sweets between her friends. The number of sweets, S,
each friend gets can be worked out using the formula $S = \dfrac{20}{f}$, where f is
the number of friends she is dividing the sweets between.

How many sweets will each friend get if she is dividing between:

a) 4 friends   **b)** 5 friends   **c)** 10 friends?

Example 3

Use the formula $F = 1.8C + 32$ to find the temperatures in degrees Fahrenheit (F) equal to the following temperatures in degrees Celsius (C).

a) $C = 30$ b) $C = -4$

1. Write down the formula.

2. Replace C with the number you're given, and do the calculation.

a) $F = 1.8C + 32$
$= 1.8 \times 30 + 32$
$= 54 + 32$
$= 86$

b) $F = 1.8C + 32$
$= 1.8 \times (-4) + 32$
$= -7.2 + 32$
$= 24.8$

Use BODMAS to work out the order in which to do the calculation.

Exercise 3

1   If $x = 5$, find the value of Y when $Y = 2x + 3$.

2   $F = 4g - 3$. Find the value of F when:

a) $g = 2$ b) $g = 7$ c) $g = -1$

3   Find the value of P in each of the following if $q = 6$.

a) $P = 3q - 1$ b) $P = 20 - 3q$ c) $P = 4 - 2q$

4   $G = h + 2f$. Find the value of G when $h = 5$ and $f = 4$.

5   If $x = 3$ and $y = 8$, find the value of z in each of the following.

a) $z = 3x - y$ b) $z = 4x + y$ c) $z = x + 0.5y$

6   If $x = 4$ and $y = -1$, find the value of z in each of the following.

a) $z = \dfrac{8}{x} + y$ b) $z = x^2 - y$ c) $z = xy + 5$

7   The cost of hiring a taxi is worked out using $C = 0.5m + 3$, where C is the cost in pounds and m is the number of minutes the taxi is in use.

Work out how much it would cost to use the taxi for:

a) 2 minutes   b) 10 minutes

c) 5 minutes   d) 3 minutes

8   The time taken in minutes, T, to cook a joint of beef can be worked out from the formula $T = 35w + 25$, where w is the weight of the beef in kg.

How many minutes will it take to cook a joint of beef that weighs:

a) 1 kg   b) 3 kg   c) 5 kg?

9 If $x = -2$ and $y = 7$, find the value of z in each of the following.

a) $z = -x + 2y$

b) $z = 4x - 3y$

c) $z = -3x - 2y$

d) $z = 1.5x + 0.5y$

e) $z = x^2 + 2y$

f) $z = xy + \dfrac{14}{y}$

10 Use the formula $C = \dfrac{5}{9}(F - 32)$ to convert the following temperatures in degrees Fahrenheit (F) to degrees Celsius (C).

a) 212 °F

b) −40 °F

c) 98.6 °F

Example 4

Use the formula $v = u + at$ to find v if $u = 6$, $a = 4$ and $t = 3$.

1. Write down the formula.

2. Replace u, a and t with the numbers you're given, and do the calculation.

$$v = u + at$$
$$= 6 + 4 \times 3$$
$$= 6 + 12$$
$$= 18$$

Exercise 4

1 a) Use the formula $a = bc$ to find a if $b = 2$ and $c = 3$.

b) Use the formula $a = bc + d$ to find a if $b = 2$, $c = 3$ and $d = 1$.

2 a) Use the formula $P = nt$ to find P if $n = 4$ and $t = 3$.

b) Use the formula $P = nt + c$ to find P if $n = 4$, $t = 3$ and $c = 10$.

3 If $a = 1$, $b = 3$ and $c = 4$, find the value of d in each of the following.

a) $d = ab + 1$

b) $d = 2ab$

c) $d = 2ab + c$

d) $d = ac + b$

e) $d = bc - 10$

f) $d = bc - 2a$

4 $A = bcd$. Find the value of A if $b = 1$, $c = 2$ and $d = 3$.

5 Use the formula $v = u + at$ to find v if:

a) $u = 3$, $a = 7$ and $t = 5$

b) $u = 12$, $a = 17$ and $t = 15$

c) $u = 11$, $a = -2$ and $t = 5$

d) $u = 0$, $a = 5$ and $t = 3$

10.3 Formula Problems

Exercise 1

1 If $x = 2$ and $y = 5$, find the value of z in each of the following.

a) $z = x - 7$ **b)** $z = 2y$ **c)** $z = 5x - 4$

d) $z = 3y - 10$ **e)** $z = 4x - y$ **f)** $z = 10x - 2y$

2 Dean owns T pairs of trainers. Jack owns 7 more pairs than Dean.

Write an expression for the number of pairs of trainers Jack owns.

3 Huw uses the formula $B = n + 5$ to work out how many balloons he needs for a party, where n is the number of guests.

How many balloons does he need if he has:

a) 5 guests? **b)** 8 guests? **c)** 30 guests?

4 Jo earns n pounds per hour.

Write an expression for the amount she earns in 8 hours.

5 The area in cm^2, A, of a rectangular room is given by the formula $A = 6w$.

Find A for the values of w below.

a) $w = 2$ **b)** $w = 1$

c) $w = 0.5$ **d)** $w = 1.5$

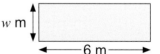

6 Sue runs r km. Ellie runs 5 km less than Sue.

Write an expression for the distance in km that Ellie runs.

7 Ali gets 45 fewer free minutes on his mobile phone each month than Chloe.

    a) If Chloe gets c free minutes, write a formula for a, the number of free minutes Ali gets.

    b) Find a when $c = 95$.

8 **a)** Write a formula for P, the perimeter of the shape shown below.

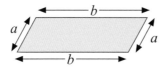

    b) Work out the perimeter of the shape if $a = 2$ and $b = 5$.

9 Mo uses the formula $P = 2n + 1$ to work out how much pocket money, £P, he will get each week. n is the number of times he does the washing up. How much pocket money will he get this week if he washes up:

    a) 2 times   **b)** 7 times   **c)** no times?

10 To book a swimming pool for a party, there is a fixed charge of £30 plus a fee of £1.25 for each person who attends.

    a) Write a formula to calculate the hire cost (C) for n people.

    b) Find C when $n = 32$.

11 Sacha is saving up to buy a new mobile phone. His parents give him £25 to start and he adds £30 each month.

    a) Write a formula for working out S, his total savings after m months.

    b) Find the value of S after 5 months.

Section 11 — Sequences

11.1 Sequences — Explaining the Rule

A sequence is an ordered list of terms.

The rule for extending (continuing) the sequence tells you how to find the next term.

Example 1

Find the rule for extending each of the following sequences:

a) 3, 6, 9, 12, 15...

b) 55, 45, 35, 25, 15...

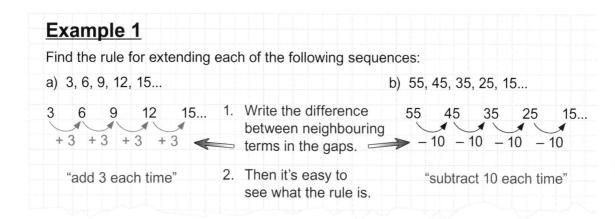

1. Write the difference between neighbouring terms in the gaps.

2. Then it's easy to see what the rule is.

Exercise 1

1 Find the rule for extending the sequence of odd numbers: 1, 3, 5, 7, 9...

2 Find the rule for extending the sequence of even numbers: 2, 4, 6, 8, 10...

3 Find the rule for extending each of the following sequences:

    a) 1, 4, 7, 10, 13...   **b)** 4, 8, 12, 16, 20...

    c) 5, 8, 11, 14, 17...   **d)** 9, 17, 25, 33, 41, 49...

    e) 14, 25, 36, 47, 58...   **f)** 12, 19, 26, 33, 40...

4 Find the rule for extending each of the following sequences:

    a) 10, 8, 6, 4, 2...   **b)** 18, 15, 12, 9, 6...

    c) 36, 31, 26, 21, 16...   **d)** 43, 37, 31, 25, 19...

    e) 240, 228, 216, 204, 192...   **f)** 146, 123, 100, 77, 54...

5 Find the rule for extending each of the following sequences:

a) 16, 12, 8, 4, 0...

b) 6, 11, 16, 21, 26...

c) 54, 66, 78, 90, 102...

d) 29, 44, 59, 74, 89...

e) 328, 286, 244, 202, 160...

f) 115, 99, 83, 67, 51...

g) 17, 10, 3, −4, −11...

h) 12, 37, 62, 87, 112...

i) −8, −2, 4, 10, 16...

j) 140, 113, 86, 59, 32...

> Don't worry about the negative numbers
> — just work out the differences as normal.

Example 2

Find the rule for extending each of the following sequences:

a) 2, 4, 8, 16, 32...

   1. First, try writing the difference between neighbouring terms in the gaps.

   2. This doesn't give an obvious 'addition' rule, so see if each term is being multiplied by some number.

   3. This works. The rule is "multiply by 2 each time".

b) 1536, 384, 96, 24, 6...

   1. You can't find a 'subtraction' rule, so try looking for a 'division' rule.

   2. It works. The rule is "divide by 4 each time".

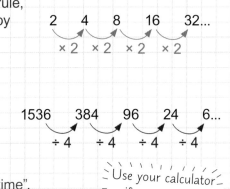

> Use your calculator
> if you need to.

Exercise 2

1 Find the rule for extending each of the following sequences.

a) 1, 3, 9, 27, 81...

b) 3, 6, 12, 24, 48...

c) 5, 15, 45, 135, 405...

d) 3, 12, 48, 192, 768...

e) 7, 21, 63, 189, 567...

f) 5, 25, 125, 625, 3125...

g) 9, 18, 36, 72, 144...

h) 2, 14, 98, 686, 4802...

2 Find the rule for extending each of the following sequences.

a) 32, 16, 8, 4, 2...

b) 324, 108, 36, 12, 4...

c) 112, 56, 28, 14, 7...

d) 3888, 648, 108, 18, 3...

e) 40, 20, 10, 5, 2.5...

f) 243, 81, 27, 9, 3...

g) 1792, 448, 112, 28, 7...

h) 1024, 128, 16, 2, 0.25...

3 Find the rule for extending each of the following sequences:

There's a mix of addition, subtraction, multiplication and division types here.

a) 12, 18, 24, 30, 36...

b) 72, 56, 40, 24, 8...

c) 10 000, 1000, 100, 10, 1...

d) 2, 21, 40, 59, 78...

e) 8, 40, 200, 1000, 5000...

f) 21, 13, 5, −3, −11...

g) 405, 135, 45, 15, 5...

h) −9, −4, 1, 6, 11...

i) 18, 54, 162, 486, 1458...

j) 17, 28, 39, 50, 61...

k) 3200, 800, 200, 50, 12.5...

l) −12, −10, −8, −6, −4...

m) 1.25, 2.5, 5, 10, 20...

n) 500, 50, 5, 0.5, 0.05...

11.2   Sequences — Finding Terms

To write down a sequence you need to know two things:

> 1.   The **first term** of the sequence.
>
> 2.   The **rule** for extending the sequence.

Example 1

The first term of a sequence is 8 and the rule is "add 4 each time".
Write down the first five terms.

1.   Add four to the first term to find the second term. → 8 + 4 = 12

2.   Now add four to the second term to find the third term. → 12 + 4 = 16
     Carry on until you have all five terms.
     16 + 4 = 20
     20 + 4 = 24

3.   Write out the first five terms of the sequence. → 8, 12, 16, 20, 24

Exercise 1

1 Write down the first **five** terms of each sequence below:

    a) The first term is 4 and the rule is "add 3 each time".

    b) The first term is 12 and the rule is "subtract 2 each time".

    c) The first term is 2 and the rule is "multiply by 3 each time".

    d) The first term is 80 and the rule is "divide by 2 each time".

2 Write down the first **six** terms of each sequence below:

    a) Start at 24 and add 16 each time.

    b) Start at 70 and take away 11 each time.

    c) Start at 20 and multiply by 7 each time.

    d) Start at 8000 and divide by 20 each time.

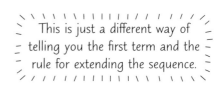

This is just a different way of telling you the first term and the rule for extending the sequence.

3 The rule for extending a sequence is "add 15 each time".

    Find the first five terms of the sequence if the first term is:

    a) 3   **b)** 124   **c)** 316

4 The rule for extending a sequence is "subtract 8 each time".

    Find the first five terms of the sequence if the first term is:

    a) 37   **b)** 129   **c)** 303

5 The rule for extending a sequence is "multiply by 4 each time".

    Find the first five terms of the sequence if the first term is:

    a) 3   **b)** 50   **c)** 11

6 The rule for extending a sequence is "divide by 3 each time".

    Find the first five terms of the sequence if the first term is:

    a) 810   **b)** 486   **c)** 1296

7 For each of the sequences below, find:

(i) the rule for extending the sequence
(ii) the next two terms in the sequence.

a) 2, 9, 16...

b) 12, 17, 22...

c) 14, 11, 8...

d) 17, 13, 9...

e) 18, 25, 32...

f) 67, 55, 43...

g) 84, 64, 44...

h) 53, 55, 57...

8 For each of the sequences below, find:

(i) the rule for extending the sequence
(ii) the next two terms in the sequence.

a) 9, 18, 36...

b) 3, 30, 300...

c) 48, 24, 12...

d) 20 000, 2000, 200...

e) 1, 6, 36...

f) 162, 54, 18...

g) 20, 80, 320...

h) 128, 32, 8...

More Sequences

Example 2

The shapes made from matchsticks below form a sequence.
How many matchsticks are needed to make the next shape in the sequence?

1. Make a sequence of numbers by writing the number of matchsticks in each shape underneath.

    4   7   10

2. Use these numbers to work out the rule for extending the sequence. 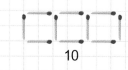   The rule is "add 3 each time".

3. Find the next term in the sequence. 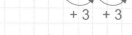   10 + 3 = 13

So 13 matchsticks are needed to make the next shape in the sequence.

Example 3

Find the next three terms in the sequence 4, 5, 7, 10...

1. First, find the rule for extending the sequence by finding the differences between neighbouring terms.

2. The difference is increasing by 1 each time.

3. Use this to find the next three terms in the sequence. Start with 10. Then add 4. Then add 5. Then add 6.

Exercise 2

1 Work out how many matchsticks are needed to make the next shape in each of these sequences.

a)

b)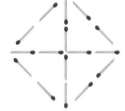

c)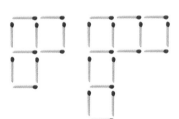

d)

2 For each of the sequences below:

(i) Draw the next three patterns in the sequence.

(ii) Explain the rule for finding the number of circles in the next pattern.

(iii) Work out how many circles will be in the 7th pattern.

a)

b)

3 For each of the sequences below, find:

(i) the rule for extending the sequence

(ii) the next two terms in the sequence.

a) 1, 2, 4, 7, 11...

b) 12, 15, 19, 24, 30...

c) 16, 15, 13, 10...

d) 21, 19, 16, 12...

4 Below is a sequence of triangles made up of different numbers of circles.
The numbers of circles in each triangle form a sequence called the 'triangle numbers'.
For example, the first three triangle numbers are 1, 3 and 6.

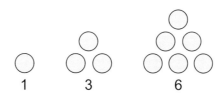

a) Draw the next three triangles in the sequence,
and write down the triangle numbers they show.

b) Explain the rule for finding the next triangle number in the sequence.

c) Find the 7th triangle number.

5 Write down the first **five** terms of each sequence below:

a) The first term is 2 and the rule is "multiply by −2 each time".

b) The first term is 20 and the rule is "multiply by 0.5 each time".

c) The first term is 11 and the rule is "subtract 1.5 each time".

d) The first term is 2 and the rule is "multiply by 2 then add one each time".

6 The first four terms of a sequence are 1, 1, 2, 3...
The rule for extending the sequence is "add together the previous two terms each time".

Find the next four terms.

Section 12 — Graphs and Equations

12.1 Coordinates

Coordinates tell you the position of a point on a grid. The grid is made by the x-axis (which goes across) and the y-axis (which goes up and down).

Coordinates are written in pairs inside brackets, with the x-coordinate (across) first and the y-coordinate (up and down) second.

The place where the x- and y-axes cross is called the origin. It has coordinates (0, 0).

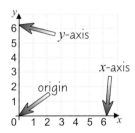

Example 1

Write down the coordinates of points A, B and C shown below.

1. Follow the grid line down from each point and read off the x-coordinate.

2. Follow the grid line across from each point and read off the y-coordinate.

3. Write the coordinates in brackets with the x-coordinate first.

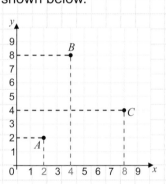

The coordinates are: $A(2, 2)$, $B(4, 8)$, $C(8, 4)$

Exercise 1

1 Find the <u>x-coordinate</u> of each point below.

a)

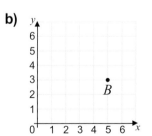

b)

c)

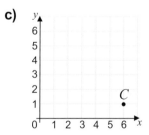

2 Find the _y_-coordinate of each point below.

a)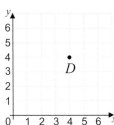

b)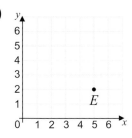

c)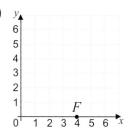

3 Find the coordinates of each point shown on the grid on the right.

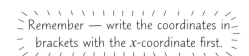

Remember — write the coordinates in brackets with the _x_-coordinate first.

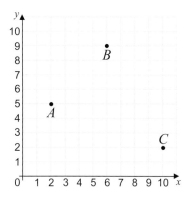

Example 2

Draw the triangle _PQR_ with vertices _P_(5, 8), _Q_(7, 0) and _R_(1, 3).

1. Start by plotting point _P_:
    Read along the horizontal axis until you get to the correct _x_-coordinate: 5

    Read along the vertical axis until you get to the correct _y_-coordinate: 8

2. Repeat for points _Q_ and _R_ and connect the points to draw the triangle.

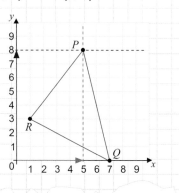

4 On separate copies of the grid below, draw the shapes
T whose vertices are given by the following sets of coordinates.

a) _A_(2, 1), _B_(2, 4), _C_(5, 4), _D_(5, 1)

b) _E_(1, 1), _F_(6, 3), _G_(3, 5)

c) _H_(1, 3), _I_(3, 5), _J_(6, 3), _K_(3, 1)

d) _L_(2, 6), _M_(5, 5), _N_(5, 3), _O_(2, 1)

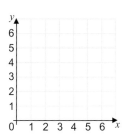

5

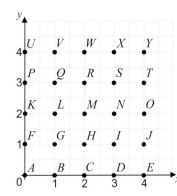

a) Write down the coordinates of the following points:

   (i) A **(ii)** M **(iii)** Q **(iv)** U **(v)** Y

b) Write down the sentence given by the letters with the following coordinates.

   (3, 4)

   (2, 0) (4, 2) (4, 2) (2, 3) (3, 0) (3, 1) (3, 2) (0, 0) (4, 3) (4, 0)

   (2, 0) (4, 2) (2, 2) (4, 0) (3, 3)

   (0, 1) (3, 1) (2, 3) (3, 3) (4, 3)

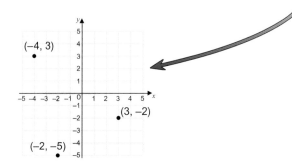

Make sure you find the x-coordinate first, then the y-coordinate.

Coordinates in Four Quadrants

Coordinates can be negative as well as positive.

To show negative coordinates, you need axes in a 'cross', like this.

You can plot and read off coordinates in the same way as with the positive grid.

Example 3

Draw the shape $WXYZ$ with vertices $W(-4, 5)$, $X(3, 2)$, $Y(4, -3)$ and $Z(-5, -2)$.

1. Here, some of the coordinates are negative, so your axes need to go below zero.

2. Read across the horizontal axis for the x-coordinates.

3. Read up and down the vertical axis for the y-coordinates.

4. Plot the points and connect them to draw the shape.

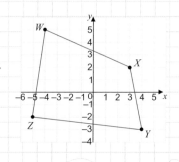

Exercise 2

1 **a)** Find the *x*-coordinate of points *A*-*D*.

b) Find the *y*-coordinate of points *A*-*D*.

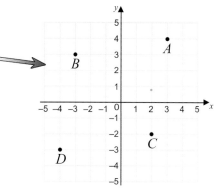

2 Find the coordinates of points *E*-*L* shown on the grid.

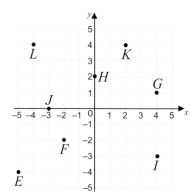

3 Draw a coordinate grid with *x*-values from −5 to 5 and *y*-values from −5 to 5.
Plot the following points on your grid. Join the points you have plotted.

A(0, 5) *B*(5, 1) *C*(3, −4)

D(−3, −4) *E*(−5, 1)

4 Match the coordinates below to letters on the grid.

This should spell out the names of three shapes.

(a) (2, −4) (−4, −4) (−5, −6) (−4, 5) (−2, −4) (−5, 3)

(b) (2, 5) (−4, 1) (−2, −4) (2, 5) (4, 1) (−5, 3)

(c) (2, 5) (−5, −6) (−2, 5) (3, −2) (−4, 1) (4, 5)

Coordinates of a Midpoint

The midpoint of a line is the point exactly halfway between each end.

You can find the coordinates of the midpoint using the coordinates of the end points.

'The line AB' just means the line drawn between point A and point B.

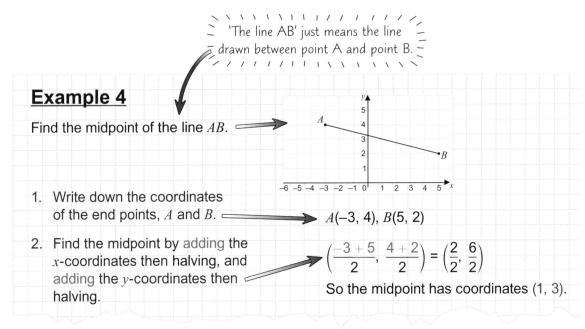

Example 4

Find the midpoint of the line AB.

1. Write down the coordinates of the end points, A and B.

   $A(-3, 4), B(5, 2)$

2. Find the midpoint by adding the x-coordinates then halving, and adding the y-coordinates then halving.

   $$\left(\frac{-3 + 5}{2}, \frac{4 + 2}{2}\right) = \left(\frac{2}{2}, \frac{6}{2}\right)$$

   So the midpoint has coordinates $(1, 3)$.

Exercise 3

1 The line CD has end points $C(1, 1)$ and $D(5, 3)$.
Find the coordinates of the midpoint of CD.

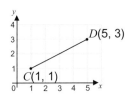

2 The line XY has end points $X(-5, 1)$ and $Y(3, 4)$.
Find the coordinates of the midpoint of XY.

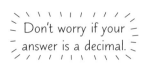

Don't worry if your answer is a decimal.

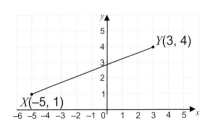

3 **a)** Plot the points $P(1, 0)$ and $Q(3, 6)$ on a square grid.
Join the points to form the line PQ.

b) Find the coordinates of M, the midpoint of PQ.

c) Plot this point on your diagram.

4 **a)** Plot and join the points $U(2, 8)$ and $V(6, 4)$ on a grid.

b) Find the coordinates of the midpoint of the line UV.

5 **a)** Plot and join the points $S(-2, 1)$ and $T(0, 3)$ on a grid.

b) Find the coordinates of the midpoint of the line ST.

6 **a)** Plot and join the points $X(-3, -4)$ and $Y(3, 4)$ on a grid.

b) Find the coordinates of the midpoint of the line XY.

7 Find the coordinates of the midpoint of the line AB,
where the points A and B have these coordinates:

a) $A(1, 1),\ B(3, 5)$ **b)** $A(0, 1),\ B(6, 3)$ **c)** $A(0, 0),\ B(4, 4)$

d) $A(2, 7),\ B(6, 7)$ **e)** $A(-1, 2),\ B(1, 2)$ **f)** $A(-2, 3),\ B(-4, 5)$

g) $A(-1, -6),\ B(5, 8)$ **h)** $A(3, -2),\ B(-1, 4)$ **i)** $A(-1, -9),\ B(-3, -4)$

j) $A(2, 5),\ B(-7, -8)$ **k)** $A(0, -4),\ B(-5, 1)$ **l)** $A(-2, 0),\ B(1, -8)$

8 Find the midpoints of the following line segments:

a) AF **b)** AC **c)** DF

d) BE **e)** BF **f)** CE

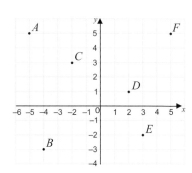

All horizontal lines have an equation of the form y = a number.
For example, $y = 1$, $y = 2$ and $y = 3$ are all horizontal lines.

All vertical lines have an equation of the form x = a number.
For example, $x = 2$, $x = -2$ and $x = -10$ are all vertical lines.

Example 1

Write down the equations of the lines
marked A and B in the diagram.

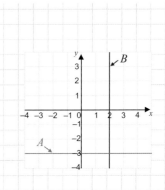

1. The line marked A crosses the y axis at $y = -3$.
   Every point on the line has y-coordinate -3.
   So, A is the line $y = -3$.

2. The line marked B crosses the x axis at $x = 2$.
   Every point on the line has x-coordinate 2.
   So, B is the line $x = 2$.

Example 2

Draw the graphs of the lines $x = -1$ and $y = 3$.

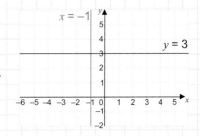

1. The line $x = -1$ is a vertical line through -1 on the
   x-axis. Every point on this line has x-coordinate -1.

2. The line $y = 3$ is a horizontal line through 3 on the
   y-axis. Every point on this line has y-coordinate 3.

Exercise 1

1   Write down the equations of each of the lines
    labelled A to E on the diagram on the right.

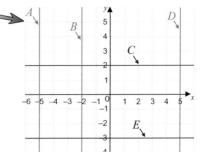

2   Draw a coordinate grid and draw the
    graphs of the lines with these equations:

   a) $y = 3$ **b)** $y = -6$ **c)** $y = -1$

   d) $x = 2$ **e)** $x = 4$ **f)** $x = -5$

3 Draw a coordinate grid.

☐T **a)** Draw the graph of the line which is parallel to the x-axis and which passes through the point (0, −2).

b) Copy and complete the equation of this line:

$y = $ ☐

The line is parallel to the x-axis, so it is horizontal. It goes through (0, −2), so it goes through −2 on the y-axis.

4 Draw a coordinate grid.

☐T **a)** Draw the graph of the line which is parallel to the y-axis and which passes through the point (1, 0).

b) What is the equation of this line?

5 Write down the equation of the line which is parallel to the x-axis and passes through the point (0, 8).

6 Write down the equation of the line which is parallel to the y-axis and passes through the point (−2, 0).

7 Write down the equation of the line which is parallel to the y-axis and passes through the point (1, 1).

8 Write down the equation of the line which is parallel to the x-axis and passes through the point (−8, 6).

9 **a)** What is the y-coordinate of every point on the x-axis?

b) Write down the equation of the x-axis.

10 Write down the equation of the y-axis.

11 **a)** Draw the graphs of the lines with the equations $x = -2$ and $y = 4$.

☐T **b)** Write down the coordinates of the point where the two lines cross.

12 Write down the coordinates of the points where the following pairs of lines cross.

a) $x = 2$ and $y = 4$ **b)** $x = -3$ and $y = 7$

c) $x = 8$ and $y = -11$ **d)** $x = -5$ and $y = -13$

e) $x = -2$ and $y = 12$ **f)** $x = 2.5$ and $y = 5.5$

12.3 Other Straight-Line Graphs

If the equation of a graph contains both y and x, then it's not a horizontal or vertical line — it's a sloping line. For example, $y = x + 2$ and $y = 3x - 1$ are sloping lines.

You can draw these graphs by filling in a table of values and plotting points.

Example 1

a) Complete the table to show the value of $y = x + 3$ for values of x from 0 to 5.

b) Draw the graph of $y = x + 3$ for values of x from 0 to 5.

x	0	1	2	3	4	5
y						
Coordinates						

a)

x	0	1	2	3	4	5
y	3	4	5	6	7	8
Coordinates	(0, 3)	(1, 4)	(2, 5)	(3, 6)	(4, 7)	(5, 8)

1. $y = x + 3$, so add 3 to each x-value to fill in the second row of the table.

2. Use the numbers from the first and second rows to fill in the third row.

3. Plot the coordinates from your table on a grid and join them up to draw the graph.

b)

Exercise 1

1 **a)** Copy and complete the table below to show the value of $y = x + 2$ for values of x from 0 to 5.

x	0	1	2	3	4	5
y	2	3				
Coordinates	(0, 2)					

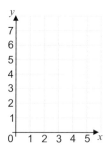

b) Copy the grid above and plot the coordinates from your table.

c) Join up the points to draw the graph of the line $y = x + 2$ for values of x from 0 to 5.

2 a) Copy and complete the table below to show the
value of $y = x - 4$ for values of x from 0 to 5.

x	0	1	2	3	4	5
y	−4					
Coordinates						

b) Copy the grid on the right and
plot the coordinates from your table.

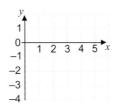

c) Join up the points to draw the graph of the line $y = x - 4$ for values of x from 0 to 5.

3 a) Copy and complete the table below to show the value of $y = 2x$
for values of x from −2 to 2.

x	−2	−1	0	1	2
y				2	
Coordinates					

b) Draw a set of axes with x-values from −5 to 5 and y-values from −10 to 10
and plot the coordinates from your table.

c) Join up the points to draw the graph of the line $y = 2x$ for values of x from −2 to 2.
Use a ruler to extend the line to show the graph of $y = 2x$ for values of x from −5 to 5.

4 For each of the following equations:

(i) copy and complete the table on the right to show
the value of y for values of x from −1 to 2,

x	−1	0	1	2
y				
Coordinates				

(ii) plot the points from your table and use these points to
draw a graph of the equation for values of x from −3 to 3.

a) $y = x + 4$ **b)** $y = x + 5$ **c)** $y = x - 1$

d) $y = x - 3$ **e)** $y = 3x$ **f)** $y = 3 - x$

g) $y = x + 9$ **h)** $y = x - 7$ **i)** $y = x + 12$

j) $y = 5 - x$ **k)** $y = -2x$ **l)** $y = -3x$

5 Draw a graph of the following equations for the given range of x-values.

a) $y = x$ for x from −4 to 4

b) $y = x - 2$ for x from 0 to 6

c) $y = x + 7$ for x from −7 to 0

d) $y = x - 6$ for x from 0 to 4

e) $y = 12x$ for x from 0 to 2

f) $y = 2 - x$ for x from 0 to 5

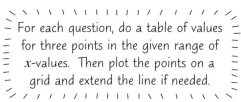

For each question, do a table of values for three points in the given range of x-values. Then plot the points on a grid and extend the line if needed.

Example 2

a) Complete the table to show the value of $y = 2x + 1$ for values of x from 0 to 3.

b) Draw the graph of $y = 2x + 1$ for values of x from 0 to 5.

x	0	1	2	3
$2x$				
$2x + 1$				
Coordinates				

a)

x	0	1	2	3
$2x$	0	2	4	6
$2x + 1$	1	3	5	7
Coordinates	(0, 1)	(1, 3)	(2, 5)	(3, 7)

1. Multiply each x-value by 2 to fill in the **second row** of the table, and then add 1 to fill in the **third row**.

2. Fill in the fourth row of the table and plot the coordinates from your table on a grid. Join up the points and extend the line to draw the graph up to $x = 5$.

b)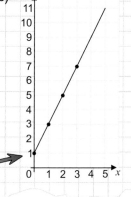

Exercise 2

1 **a)** Copy and complete the table below to show the value of $y = 2x - 1$ for values of x from 0 to 3.

x	0	1	2	3
$2x$				
$2x - 1$	−1			
Coordinates	(0, −1)			

b) Copy this grid and plot the coordinates from your table.

c) Join up the points and extend the line to draw the graph of $y = 2x - 1$ for values of x from 0 to 5.

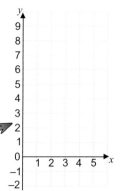

2 a) Copy and complete the table below to show the value of $y = 4 - 2x$
for values of x from −1 to 2.

x	−1	0	1	2
$2x$			2	
$4 - 2x$			2	
Coordinates				

b) Draw a set of axes with x-values from −5 to 5 and y-values from
−6 to 14 and plot the coordinates from your table.

c) Join up the points and extend the line to draw the graph of
$y = 4 - 2x$ for values of x from −5 to 5.

3 For each of the following equations:

(i) copy and complete the table on the right to
show the value of y for values of x from −1 to 2,

(ii) draw a graph of the equation for values
of x from −3 to 3.

x	−1	0	1	2
y				
Coordinates				

a) $y = 3x - 1$

b) $y = 2x + 5$

c) $y = 4x - 3$

d) $y = 6 - 2x$

e) $y = 8 - 3x$

f) $y = 1 - 2x$

4 Draw a graph of the following equations for the given range of x-values.

a) $y = 3x - 5$ for x from 0 to 4

b) $y = 7 - 5x$ for x from 0 to 2

c) $y = -2x + 8$ for x from 0 to 5

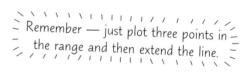
Remember — just plot three points in
the range and then extend the line.

12.4 Mixed Problems

Exercise 1

1 a) Plot the points $A(0, 3)$, $B(2, 6)$, $C(4, 3)$ and $D(2, -1)$ on a coordinate grid.

b) Join the points to draw a kite.

2 The points A and B have coordinates $A(2, 5)$ and $B(-4, 1)$.
Find the coordinates of the midpoint of the line AB.

3 Find the equation of the line which is parallel to the y-axis and passes through the point (11, −4).

4 A horizontal line is drawn on a coordinate grid. The line passes through the point (3, 7). What is the equation of the line?

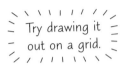
Try drawing it out on a grid.

5 Find the midpoint of the lines with the following endpoints:

    a) (0, 0) and (4, 16)
                    b) (−4, −5) and (−1, 4)

    c) (−7, 2) and (−4, −1)
                    d) (5, −2) and (2, 10)

    e) (14, −6) and (12, 0)
                    f) (2.5, −4) and (4.5, 6)

6 **a)** Write down the coordinates of each of the points A to E.

    b) Find the coordinates of the midpoint of AB.

    c) Find the coordinates of the midpoint of BC.

    d) Write down the equation of the line segment AE.

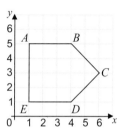

7 Draw the following lines on a coordinate grid.

    a) $x = 1$
                    b) $y = −3$

    c) $x = −1$
                   d) $y = 5$

8

Write down the sentence given by the letters with the following coordinates.

(0, 4) (8, 0) (8, 0) (0, 6) //

(4, 0) (0, 0) (2, 4) (4, 4) //

(0, 0) (6, 4) (6, 0) //

(6, 0) (8, 4) //

(4, 4) (8, 4) (4, 6) (8, 0) //

(4, 4) (0, 0) (8, 6) (4, 2) (6, 6)

These mean 'new word'.

9 Draw a coordinate grid.

    a) Plot the points $P(3, −1)$ and $Q(−1, −1)$.

    b) What is the equation of the line that passes through points P and Q?

10 a) Copy and complete the table to show the value of $y = 8 - x$ for values of x from -3 to 3.

x	-3	-2	-1	0	1	2	3
y							
Coordinates							

b) Plot the graph of $y = 8 - x$.

11 a) Copy and complete the table below to show the value of $y = 2x + 2$ for values of x from -3 to 3.

x	-3	-2	-1	0	1	2	3
$2x$							
$2x + 2$							
Coordinates							

b) Plot the graph of $y = 2x + 2$.

c) Add the line $y = 5$ to your graph.

d) Find the coordinates of the point where the two lines cross.

12 a) Plot the graph of $y = 2x - 3$ for values of x from 0 to 4.

b) Add the line $y = 2$ to your graph.

c) Use your graphs to find the value of x when $2x - 3 = 2$.

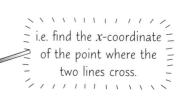

i.e. find the x-coordinate of the point where the two lines cross.

13 a) Plot the graph of $y = 1 - 4x$ for values of x from -2 to 2.

b) Find the value of x when $y = -1$.

Section 13 — Real-Life Graphs

13.1 Interpreting Real-Life Graphs

Graphs can be used to show real-life situations.

For example, you can use them to convert between different units or currencies.

Example 1

The graph shown can be used to convert between pounds (£) and euros (€).

a) Use the graph to change £350 to euros.
b) Use the graph to change €210 to pounds.

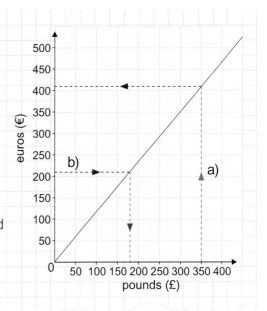

    a) Follow the grid up from £350 until you reach the line. Then follow the grid across to find the amount in euros.

    b) Follow the grid across from €210 until you reach the line. Then follow the grid down to find the amount in pounds.

        a) £350 = €410
        b) €210 = £180

Exercise 1

The graph below can be used to convert between pounds (£) and euros (€).
Use this graph to answer questions **1** to **4**.

1 Use the graph to convert the following amounts from pounds to euros.

    a) £300   **b)** £50   **c)** £250

2 Use the graph to convert the following amounts from euros to pounds.

    a) €50   **b)** €200   **c)** €400

3 A dress costs €130. How much is this in pounds?

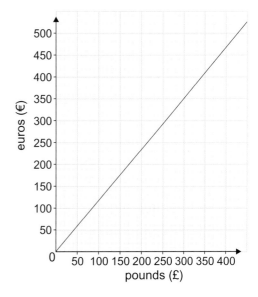

4 **a)** A TV costs £420 in the UK.
       How much is this in euros?

    b) The TV costs €480 in France.
       How much is this in pounds?

    c) Is the TV cheaper in France or the UK?

The graph below can be used to convert between pounds (£) and Canadian dollars ($).

Use this graph to answer questions **5** to **8**.

5 Use the graph to convert the following amounts from pounds to Canadian dollars.

    a) £10   **b)** £30   **c)** £44

6 Use the graph to convert the following amounts from Canadian dollars to pounds.

    a) $10   **b)** $70   **c)** $54

7 **a)** A shirt costs $60. How much is this in pounds?

    b) How much will it cost in pounds to buy two shirts?

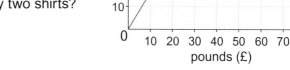

8 **a)** Convert £40 into Canadian dollars.

    b) Use your answer to **a)** to convert £80 into Canadian dollars.

The graph below shows the cost of different weights of fudge.

Use this graph to answer questions **9** to **12**.

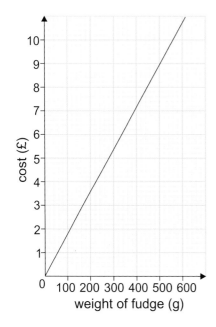

9 Use the graph to estimate the amount the shop will charge for the following weights of fudge.

    a) 100 g   **b)** 380 g   **c)** 480 g

10 Use the graph to estimate the weight of fudge that could be bought with the following amounts of money.

    a) £5   **b)** £9   **c)** £2.20

11 **a)** Find the cost of 400 g of fudge.

    b) Use your answer to **a)** to find the cost of 800 g of fudge.

12 How much fudge could you buy for £20?

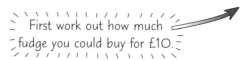

First work out how much fudge you could buy for £10.

The graph on the right can be used to convert between kilometres per hour (km/h) and miles per hour (mph).

Use this graph to answer questions **13** and **14**.

13 a) Convert 38 km/h into miles per hour.

   b) Convert 27 mph into kilometres per hour.

14 The speed limit on a road is 30 mph.

   A driver travels at 56 km/h. By how many miles per hour is the driver breaking the speed limit?

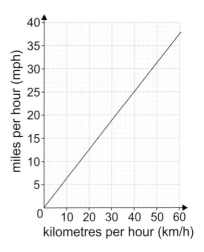

13.2   Drawing Real-Life Graphs

You sometimes need to draw graphs showing real-life situations.

To do this, you need some points to plot.

Example 1

A plumber charges customers a fee of £40, plus £30 per hour of work she does.

a)   Draw a graph to show how the cost of hiring the plumber varies with the amount of time the job takes.

b)   Use the graph to find the amount of time a job costing £190 would take.

1. A job lasting 1 hour will cost
       £40 + £30 = £70
    A job lasting 2 hours will cost
       £40 + (2 × £30) = £100
    A job lasting 3 hours will cost
       £40 + (3 × £30) = £130

2. Put these values in a table.

3. Plot the values on a sheet of graph paper and join the points to draw the graph.

4. Read off the graph in the usual way.

a)

Time (hours)	1	2	3
Cost (£)	70	100	130

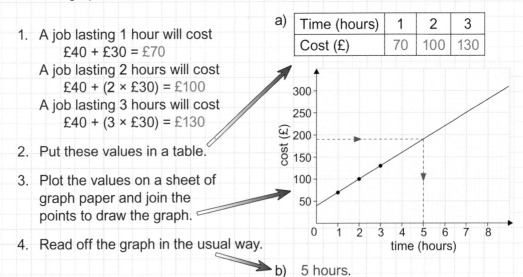

b)   5 hours.

Exercise 1

1 1 litre is approximately equal to 1.8 pints.

[T] **a)** Copy and complete the table to show the conversions between litres and pints.

Litres	1	2	3	4
Pints	1.8			

b) Copy the coordinate grid on the right, then plot the values from your table.

c) Draw a graph to show the conversion between litres and pints.

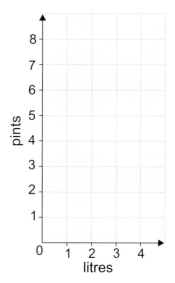

2 The cost of hiring a digger is £40 per day, plus a fixed cost of £20.

[T] **a)** Copy and complete the table to show the cost of hiring the digger for different numbers of days.

No. Days	1	2	3	4
Cost (£)	60			

b) Copy the coordinate grid below, then plot the values from your table.

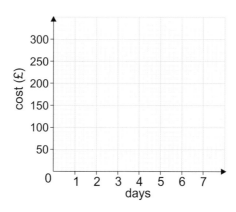

c) Draw a graph to show how the cost of hiring a digger varies with the number of days it is hired for.

d) Use your graph to find the cost of hiring a digger for 7 days.

3 The instructions for cooking different weights of chicken are as follows:
'Cook for 35 mins per kg, plus an extra 25 minutes.'

a) Copy and complete the table to show the cooking times for chickens of different weights.

Weight (kg)	1	2	3	4	5
Time (minutes)					

b) Copy the coordinate grid on the right, then plot the values from your table.

c) Draw a graph showing the cooking times for different weights of chicken.

d) A chicken cooks in 110 minutes. What is the weight of the chicken?

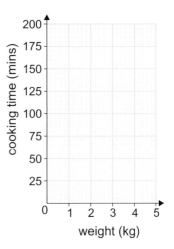

cooking time (mins)

200 · 175 · 150 · 125 · 100 · 75 · 50 · 25

0   1   2   3   4   5

weight (kg)

---

4 A delivery company charges £6 to deliver the first parcel in an order, plus £1 for every additional parcel in the order after that.

No. of parcels in delivery	1	2	3	4	5
Cost (£)					

a) Copy and complete the table above to show the delivery cost for different numbers of parcels.

b) Draw a coordinate grid on a sheet of graph paper. Plot number of parcels on the horizontal axis and cost in pounds on the vertical axis.

c) Draw a graph showing how the cost of a delivery varies with the number of parcels in the delivery.

---

5 The cost of a hotel room is £80 per night for the first 3 nights, then £50 per night for every night after that.

a) Draw a graph showing how the cost of staying at the hotel varies with the length of stay.

b) A stay at the hotel cost £440. What was the length of the stay?

Section 14 — Angles and Properties of 2D Shapes

14.1 Basic Angle Properties

Types of Angle

Right Angle

90° angles are called right angles.

Lines which meet at 90° are perpendicular.

Acute Angle

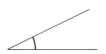

Angles between 0° and 90° are called acute angles.

Obtuse Angle

Angles between 90° and 180° are called obtuse angles.

Reflex Angle

Angles between 180° and 360° are called reflex angles.

Exercise 1

1 Which of the angles *a-e* below is **acute**?

a

b

c

d

e

> You don't need to measure the angles — just compare the shapes with the diagrams above.

2   How many **obtuse** angles are in each of these shapes?

a)

b)

c)

d)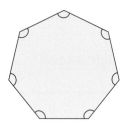

e)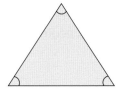

f)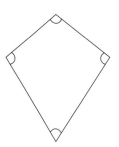

3   Name the type of each angle *a-i*.

a)

b)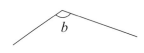

c)

d)

e)

f)

g)

h)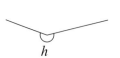

i)

Angles at a Point

Angles on a straight line add up to 180°.

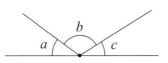

$$a + b + c = 180°$$

Angles around a point add up to 360°.

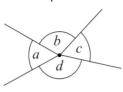

$$a + b + c + d = 360°$$

Angles within a right angle add up to 90°.

$$a + b = 90°$$

Example 1

Find the size of angle a, shown in the diagram.

1. Use the fact that angles on a straight line add up to 180° to write an equation involving a.

2. Simplify the equation.

3. Rearrange the equation to find a.

$$40° + a + 90° = 180°$$
$$130° + a = 180°$$
$$a = 180° - 130°$$
$$a = 50°$$

Example 2

Find the size of angle x, shown in the diagram.

1. Use the fact that angles around a point add up to 360° to write an equation involving x.

2. Simplify the equation.

3. Rearrange the equation to find x.

$$45° + 41° + 161° + x = 360°$$
$$247° + x = 360°$$
$$x = 360° - 247°$$
$$x = 113°$$

Exercise 2

The angles in this exercise aren't drawn to scale, so don't try to measure them.

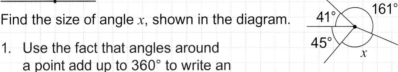

Remember — ⌐ means an angle is a right angle.

1 Find the size of each angle a-c.

a)

b)

c)

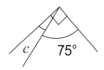

2 Find the size of each angle a-i.

a)
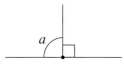

b)
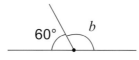

c)
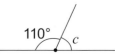

d)
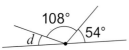

e)
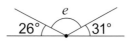

f)

g)

h)
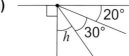

i)
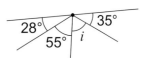

3 Find the size of each angle a-i.

a)

b)

c)

d)
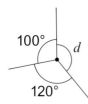

e)

f)
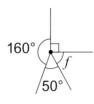

g)
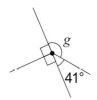

h)

i)
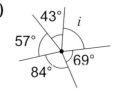

Example 3

Find the size of angle x, shown in the diagram.

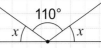

1. Write an equation involving x, as before.

$$x + 110° + x = 180°$$
$$2x + 110° = 180°$$

2. Rearrange the equation to find x.

$$2x = 180° - 110° = 70°$$
$$x = 70° \div 2 = 35°$$

Example 4

Find the value of a in the diagram shown.

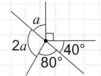

1. Write an equation involving a, as before.

$$a + 2a + 80° + 40° + 90° = 360°$$
$$3a + 210° = 360°$$

2. Rearrange the equation to find a.

$$3a = 360° - 210° = 150°$$
$$a = 150° \div 3 = 50°$$

Exercise 3

The angles in this exercise aren't drawn to scale, so don't try to measure them.

1 Find the value of each letter in the following diagrams.

a)

b)

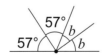

c)

d)

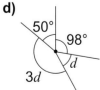

e)

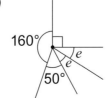

f)

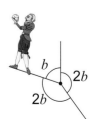

2 Find the value of x in the diagram below.

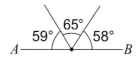

3 Is the line AB, shown below, a straight line?

Give a reason for your answer.

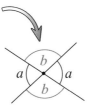

4 a) Given that $x = 40°$, find the sizes of the three angles involving x in the diagram. ⟹

b) Find the value of m.

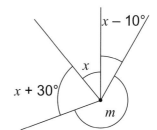

14.2 Parallel and Intersecting Lines

Opposite Angles

Intersecting lines are lines that cross or meet at a point.

At this point, opposite angles are equal.

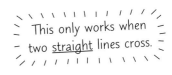

This only works when two <u>straight</u> lines cross.

Example 1

Find the size of angle x shown in the diagram.

1. The two straight lines meet at a point, so opposite angles are equal.

2. x is opposite the 160° angle, so they must be equal.

$x = 160°$

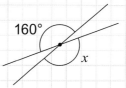

Example 2

Find the size of angles *a*, *b* and *c* shown in the diagram.

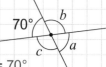

1. *a* and the 70° angle are opposite, so they are equal. $a = 70°$

2. *b* and the 70° angle are at a point on a straight line, so they add up to 180°.

    $70° + b = 180°$

    $b = 180° - 70° = 110°$

3. *c* and *b* are opposite, so they are equal. $c = b = 110°$

Exercise 1

1 Find the size of the missing angles marked by letters.

a)

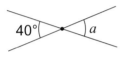

b)

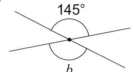

c)

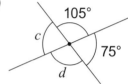

d)

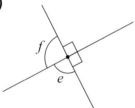

e)

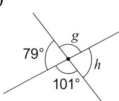

f)

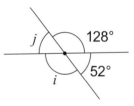

2 Find the size of the missing angles marked by letters.

a)

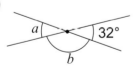

b)

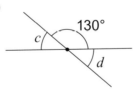

c)

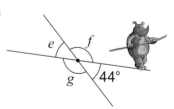

d)

e)

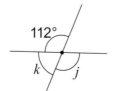

f)

3   The diagram on the right shows two triangles.
Find the missing angles marked by letters.

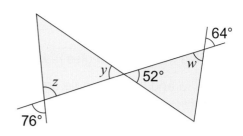

Alternate Angles

Parallel lines never meet.

Alternate angles on parallel lines are equal.

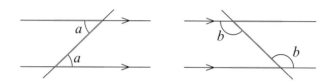

Example 3

Find the size of angle x shown.

1. The pair of arrows tell you
    that the lines are parallel.

2. Angle x and the 137° angle are
    alternate, so they must be equal.

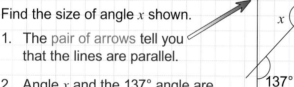

$x = 137°$

Example 4

Find the size of angles a, b and c
shown in the diagram.

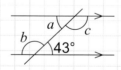

1. a and the 43° angle are alternate,
    so they are equal. $a = 43°$

2. b and the 43° angle lie on a straight line, $43° + b = 180°$
    so they add up to 180°. $b = 180° - 43° = 137°$

3. c and b are alternate, so they are equal. $c = b = 137°$

Exercise 2

1 Find the size of the missing angles marked by letters.

a)

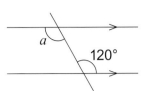

a 120°

b)

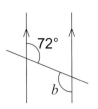

72° b

c)

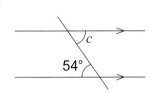

c 54°

d)

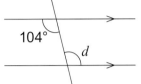

104° d

e)

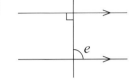

e

f)

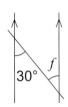

30° f

2 Find the size of the missing angles marked by letters.

a)

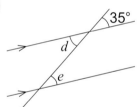

35° d e

b)

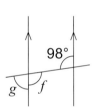

98° g f

c)

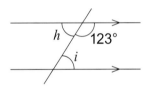

h 123° i

d)

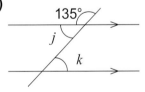

135° j k

e)

l m 140°

f)

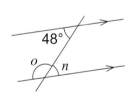

48° o n

3 The diagram on the right shows a staircase between two parallel floors of a building.

The staircase makes an angle of 42° with the ground.

a) Write down the angle that the staircase makes with the ceiling, marked x on the diagram.

b) Give a reason for your answer.

x 42°

225

4 Find the size of the missing angles marked by letters.

a)

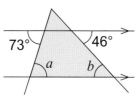

b)

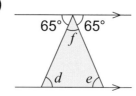

c)

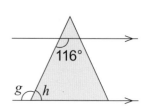

Corresponding Angles

Corresponding angles on parallel lines are equal.

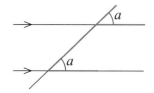
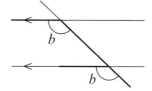

Example 5

Find the size of angle x shown in the diagram.

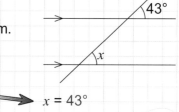

Angle x and the 43° angle are
corresponding, so they must be equal.

$x = 43°$

Example 6

Find the size of a, b and c shown in the diagram.

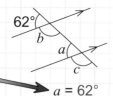

1. a and the 62° angle are corresponding,
   so they are equal.

   $a = 62°$

2. b and the 62° angle lie on a
   straight line, so they add up to 180°.

   $62° + b = 180°$

   $b = 180° - 62° = 118°$

3. c and b are corresponding, so they are equal.

   $c = b = 118°$

Exercise 3

1 Find the size of the missing angles marked by letters.

a)

b)

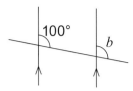

c)

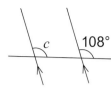

d)

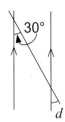

e)

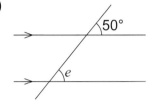

f)

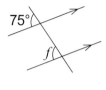

2 Find the size of the missing angles marked by letters.

a)

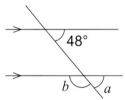

b)

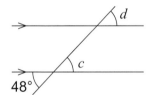

c)

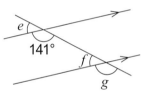

3 Find the size of the missing angles marked by letters.

a)

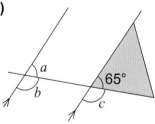

b)

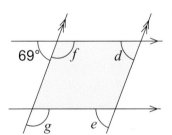

c)

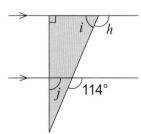

4 Two wooden posts stand vertically on sloped ground.

One post makes an angle of 99° with the slope, as shown.

Find the angle that the other post makes with the slope, labelled y on the diagram.

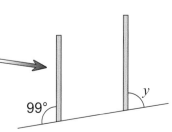

Supplementary Angles

Supplementary angles on parallel lines add up to 180°.

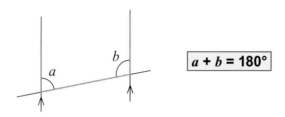

$a + b = 180°$

Example 7

Find the size of angle x shown in the diagram.

Angle x and the 45° angle are supplementary, so they must add up to 180°.

$$x + 45° = 180°$$
$$x = 135°$$

Exercise 4

1   Find the size of the missing angles marked by letters.

a)

62°

b)

30°

c)

103°

Exercise 5 — Mixed Exercise

1   Find the size of the missing angles marked by letters.

a)

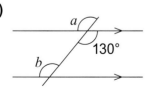

b)

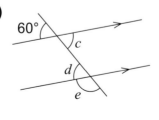

c)

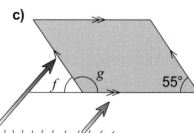

The single and double arrows tell you which pairs of lines are parallel.

228

2 Find the size of the missing angles marked by letters.

a)

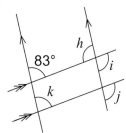

b)

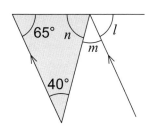

c)

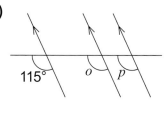

d)

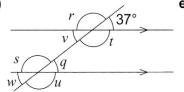

e)

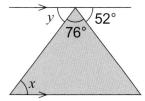

f)

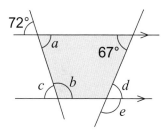

14.3   Triangles

Types of Triangle

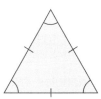

An equilateral triangle has 3 equal sides (shown by the 'tick marks'). It also has 3 equal angles.

An isosceles triangle has 2 equal sides and 2 equal angles.

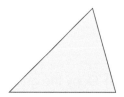

A scalene triangle has 3 sides which are all different and 3 angles which are all different.

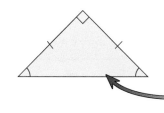

A right-angled triangle has 1 right angle.

Any right-angled triangle is also either an isosceles or a scalene triangle.

Exercise 1

1 Name each of these triangles using the definitions on the previous page.

a)

b)

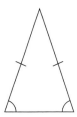

c)

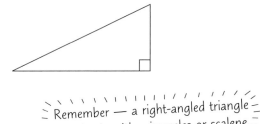

d)

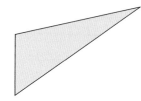

Remember — a right-angled triangle will also be either isosceles or scalene.

e)

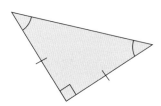

f)

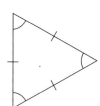

2 a) Copy the grid below, then use these coordinates to draw the triangles ABC and PQR.

    (i) $A(-2, -1)$, $B(1, 3)$, $C(4, -1)$

    (ii) $P(1, 0)$, $Q(-4, 0)$, $R(-4, 3)$

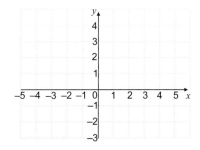

  b) Name triangles ABC and PQR using the definitions from the previous page.

Example 1

Find the size of the missing angles a and c and side length b shown on this triangle.

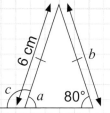

1. The triangle is isosceles, so the angle marked a must be equal to the 80° angle. $\quad\longrightarrow\quad$ $a = 80°$

2. The 'tick marks' on the diagram show that the side marked b has the same length as the 6 cm side. $\quad\longrightarrow\quad$ $b = 6$ cm

3. Use the fact that angles on a line add up to 180° to write an equation involving c. Solve the equation to find the size of c.
$\quad\longrightarrow\quad$
$a + c = 180°$
$80° + c = 180°$
$c = 180° - 80° = 100°$

Exercise 2

In questions **1 & 2**, the triangles aren't drawn accurately, so don't try to measure them.

1 Find the missing angles and side lengths labelled a-e in the triangles below.

a)

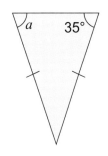

b)

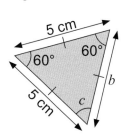

c)

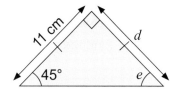

2 Find the size of the missing angle, x, in the triangle on the right.

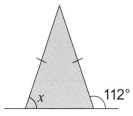

3 A farmer makes a field in the shape of an isosceles triangle using 100 m of fencing. The shortest side of the field has length 20 m, and the other two sides have equal length. Find the length, in m, of each of the other two sides of the field.

Angles in Triangles

The angles in any triangle add up to 180°.

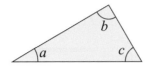

$a + b + c = 180°$

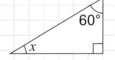

Example 2

Find the size of angle x in the triangle shown.

1. The angles in a triangle add up to 180°.
   Use this to write an equation involving x.

   $\rightarrow$ $x + 60° + 90° = 180°$

   $x + 150° = 180°$

2. Solve the equation to find x.

   $\rightarrow$ $x = 180° - 150° = 30°$

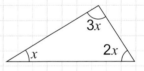

Example 3

Find the value of x in the triangle shown.

1. Write an equation involving x.

   $\rightarrow$ $x + 2x + 3x = 180°$

   $6x = 180°$

2. Solve the equation to find x.

   $\rightarrow$ $x = 180° ÷ 6 = 30°$

Exercise 3

The angles in this exercise aren't drawn to scale, so don't try to measure them.

1 Find the missing angles marked with letters.

a)

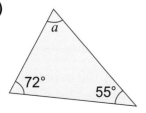

b)

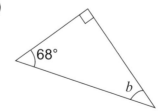

c)

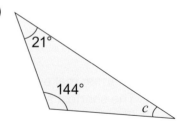

2 Find the missing angles marked with letters.

a)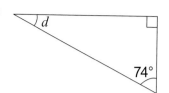

b)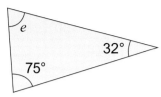

c)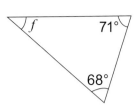

3 Find the value of the letters shown in these diagrams.

a)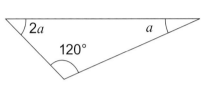

b)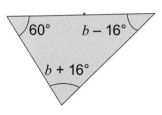

c)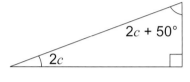

d)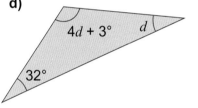

e)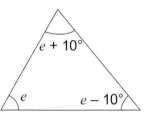

f)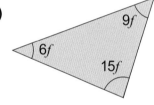

Example 4

Find the size of angles j and k in the triangle shown.

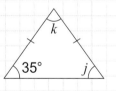

1. The triangle is isosceles, so angle j is the same size as the 35° angle.

    $j = 35°$

2. Now use the fact that angles in a triangle add up to 180° to write an equation involving k.
    Then solve your equation to find k.

    $35° + 35° + k = 180°$

    $70° + k = 180°$

    $k = 180° - 70° = 110°$

Example 5

Find the size of angle x
in the triangle shown.

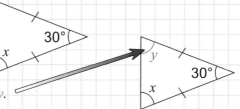

1. Call the unmarked angle y.

2. Use the fact that angles in a triangle add up
    to 180° to write an equation involving x and y.

    $x + y + 30° = 180°$

3. The triangle is isosceles, which means $x = y$.
    Rewrite the equation so it only involves x.

    $x + x + 30° = 180°$
    $2x + 30° = 180°$

4. Now solve the equation to find x.

    $2x = 180° - 30° = 150°$
    $x = 150° \div 2 = 75°$

---

4 Find the missing angles marked with letters.

a)

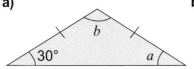

b)

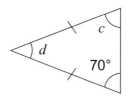

c)

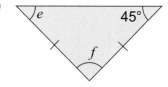

d)

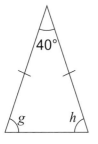

e)

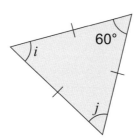

f)

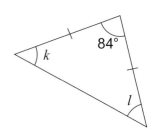

5 Find the angle marked x in each of the triangles below.

a)

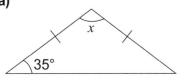

b)

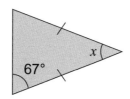

c)

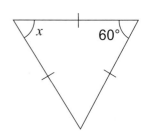

6 Find the angle marked x in each of the triangles below.

a)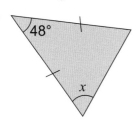

b)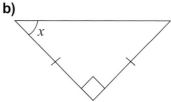

c)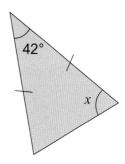

7 Find the missing angles marked with letters.

a)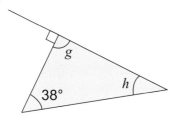

b)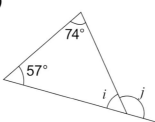

c)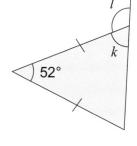

Remember the rule for angles on a straight line.

8 Find the value of x.

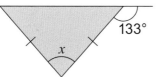

9 **a)** Find the value of x.
b) Find the value of y.

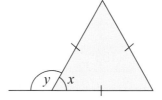

10 **a)** Find the value of x.
b) Find the value of y.
c) Find the value of z.

Hint: The angles in <u>each</u> <u>triangle</u> will add up to 180°.

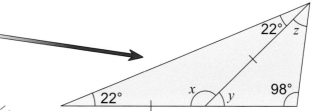

14.4 Quadrilaterals

A quadrilateral is a shape made from 4 straight sides.

The angles in a quadrilateral add up to 360°.

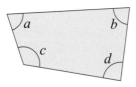

$$a + b + c + d = 360°$$

Example 1

Find the missing angle x in this quadrilateral.

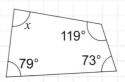

1. The angles in a quadrilateral add up to 360°.
   Use this to write an equation involving x.

2. Then solve your equation to find the value of x.

$79° + 73° + 119° + x = 360°$

$271° + x = 360°$

$x = 360° - 271° = 89°$

Exercise 1

1 Find the size of the angles marked by letters in the following quadrilaterals.
   (They're not drawn accurately, so don't try to measure them.)

a)

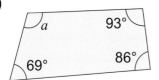

b)

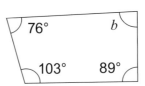

c)

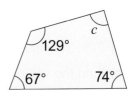

d)

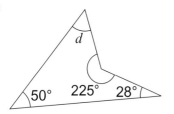

e)

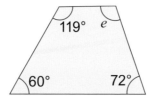

f)

Squares and Rectangles

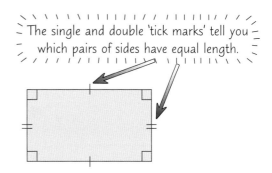

The single and double 'tick marks' tell you which pairs of sides have equal length.

A square is a quadrilateral
with 4 equal sides
and 4 angles of 90°.

A rectangle is a quadrilateral
with 4 angles of 90° and
opposite sides of the same length.

Exercise 2

1 **a)** Copy the diagram below, then add two more points to form a square.
Join the points to complete the square.

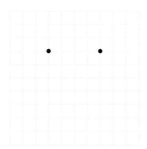

b) Copy the diagram below, then add two more points to form a rectangle.
Join the points to complete the rectangle.

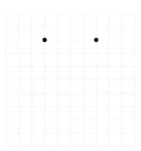

❷ A farmer has 128 m of fencing.

a) What is the side length of the largest square field he could make from his fencing?

b) The farmer builds a rectangular field using all 128 m of fencing.
One side of the field has length 24 m. Find the length of the other three sides.

Parallelograms and Rhombuses

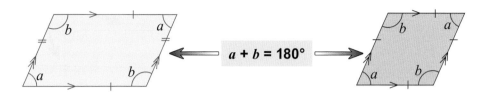

A parallelogram is a quadrilateral with
2 pairs of equal, parallel sides.
Opposite angles of a parallelogram are equal.
Neighbouring angles add up to 180°.

A rhombus is a quadrilateral with
2 pairs of parallel sides, all of the same length.
Opposite angles of a rhombus are equal.
Neighbouring angles add up to 180°.

Example 2

Find the size of the angles marked
with letters in this rhombus.

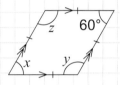

1. Opposite angles in a rhombus are equal, so... ⟶ $x = 60°$
2. Neighbouring angles in a rhombus add up to 180°. $60° + y = 180°$
    Use this fact to find angle y. $y = 180° - 60° = 120°$
3. Opposite angles in a rhombus are equal,
    so z is the same size as y. ⟶ $z = 120°$

Exercise 3

1 a) Copy the diagram on the right. Add one more point,
and join the points with straight lines to form a rhombus.

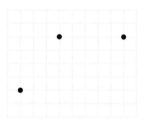

b) On a new grid, plot four points, and join them with
straight lines to form a parallelogram.

2 Calculate the size of the angles marked by letters in these quadrilaterals.
(They're not drawn accurately, so don't try to measure them.)

a)
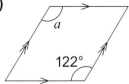

b)
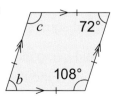

c)
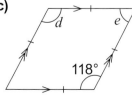

3 Calculate the size of the angles marked by letters in these quadrilaterals.
(They're not drawn accurately, so don't try to measure them.)

a)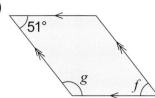

b)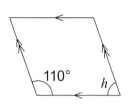

c)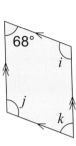

Kites

A kite is a quadrilateral with 2 pairs of equal sides and 1 pair of equal angles.

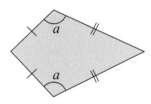

Example 3

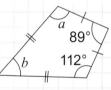

Find the size of the angles
marked with letters in this kite.

1. a and the 112° angle are equal. ⟶ $a = 112°$

2. A kite is a quadrilateral, so its angles add up to
360°. Use this to write an equation involving b.

$112° + 89° + 112° + b = 360°$
$313° + b = 360°$

3. Then solve your equation to find the value of b.

$b = 360° - 313° = 47°$

Exercise 4

1 Which letter goes in each box to complete
the sentences about this kite?

a) Angle b is the same size as angle ☐

b) The length of side PQ is the same as the length of side ☐

c) The length of side RS is the same as the length of side ☐

2 Find the size of the angles marked by letters in these kites.
(They're not drawn accurately, so don't try to measure them.)

a)

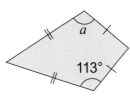

b)

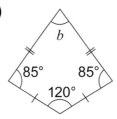

c)

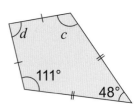

d)

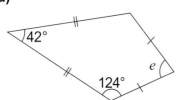

e)

f)

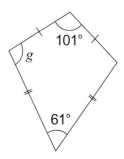

Trapeziums

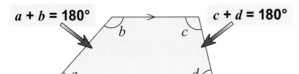

A trapezium is a quadrilateral with
1 pair of parallel sides.

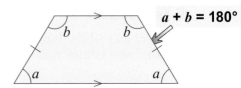

An isosceles trapezium is
a trapezium with 2 pairs of equal angles,
and 2 sides of the same length.

Example 4

Find the size of the angles marked with
letters in this isosceles trapezium.

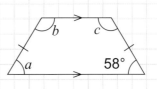

1. This is an isosceles trapezium,
    so a must equal 58°. a = 58°

2. Angle c and the 58° angle
    must add up to 180°. c + 58° = 180°
                                 c = 180° − 58° = 122°

3. This is an isosceles trapezium,
    so b must equal c. b = 122°

Exercise 5

1 Choose the correct option to complete the following sentences.

a) A trapezium is a quadrilateral with one pair of (**parallel** / **equal**) sides.

b) An isosceles trapezium has (**one pair** / **two pairs**) of equal angles.

c) An isosceles trapezium has (**one pair** / **two pairs**) of parallel sides.

d) An isosceles trapezium has (**one pair** / **two pairs**) of equal sides.

e) The angles in a trapezium add up to (**180°** / **360°**).

2 Find the size of the angles marked by letters in these trapeziums.
(They're not drawn accurately, so don't try to measure them.)

a)
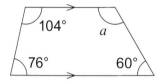

b)
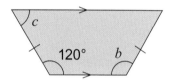

c)
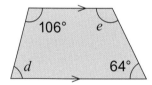

d)
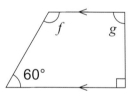

e)
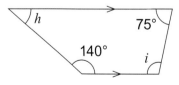

f)
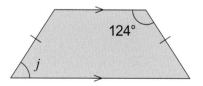

Exercise 6 — Mixed Exercise

1 Match one name from the box to each of the quadrilaterals below.

| square   kite   rectangle   trapezium   parallelogram |

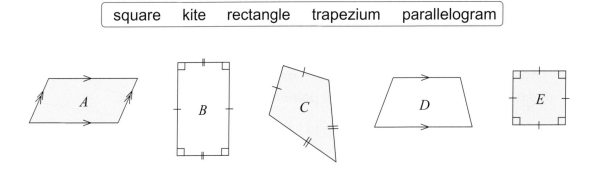

2 Write down **all** the different types of quadrilaterals which have:

a) 4 equal sides

b) 4 angles of 90°

c) 2 pairs of equal sides

d) 2 pairs of parallel sides

e) at least 1 pair of parallel sides

f) exactly 1 pair of parallel sides

3 Find the size of the angles marked by letters in these diagrams.
(They're not drawn accurately, so don't try to measure them.)

a)

b)
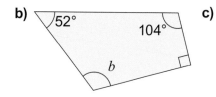

c)
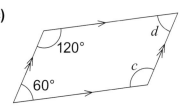

d)
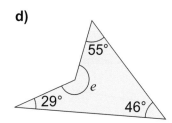

e)
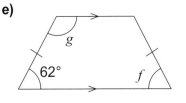

f)
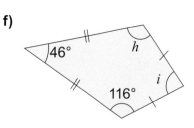

4 Find the missing angle in the quadrilaterals where the other three angles are:

a) 40°, 83°, 99°   **b)** 150°, 30°, 25°   **c)** 90°, 76°, 104°

5 Find the size of the angles marked by letters in these diagrams.
(They're not drawn accurately, so don't try to measure them.)

a)

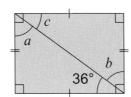

b)

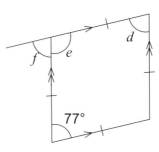

c)

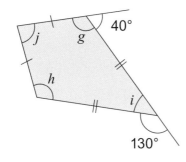

6 A parallelogram has two angles of 100°. Find the size of the other two angles.

7 An isosceles trapezium has two angles of 53°. Find the size of the other two angles.

8 Hassan is making a giant kite out of lengths of cane.
Exactly 8 m of cane is used to make the frame of the outside of the kite.

a) One of the short sides of the kite has length 1.5 m.
Find the length of the other three sides.

b) The kite has exactly one angle of 50° and exactly one angle of 90°.
Find the size of the other two angles.

14.5 Polygons and Tessellation

A polygon is a shape whose sides are all straight.

A regular polygon has sides of equal length and angles that are all equal.

Polygons have special names depending on the number of sides they have.

For example: (i) A polygon with 3 sides is a triangle.

               (ii) A polygon with 4 sides is a quadrilateral.

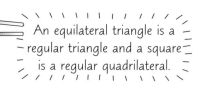

An equilateral triangle is a regular triangle and a square is a regular quadrilateral.

               (iii) A polygon with 5 sides is a pentagon.

               (iv) A polygon with 6 sides is a hexagon.

Exercise 1

1   From the box below, find the:

    a) Polygons   **b)** Pentagons

    c) Hexagons   **d)** Regular Pentagons

    e) Heptagons (7-sided polygons)   **f)** Regular Hexagons

    g) Octagons (8-sided polygons)   **h)** Regular Polygons

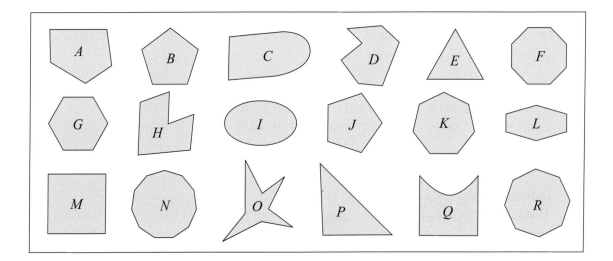

Tessellation

A tessellation is a tiling pattern where shapes fit together with no gaps or overlaps.

Some shapes don't tessellate — you get gaps or overlaps when you try and arrange them.

Example 1

a) Show how an equilateral triangle tessellates.
   You can rotate or reflect the shape any
   way you need to make them fit together
   so there are no gaps or overlaps.

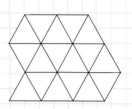

b) Does a regular octagon (8 sides) tessellate?
   If you try to tile with regular octagons,
   you'll always leave gaps, or the
   octagons will overlap.

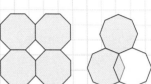

A regular octagon does not tessellate.

Exercise 2

1 By trying to make a tiling pattern, show whether or not the following shapes tessellate.

a)   **b)**    **c)**

2 For each shape below, show how the shape tessellates by
fitting together 6 copies of the shape on a grid.

a) 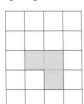   **b)** 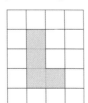   **c)**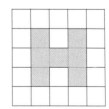

3 For each of the following, draw the shape whose corners are given by the coordinates.
⊤ Then show how the shape tessellates by fitting together 6 copies of the shape.

a) (0, 0), (2, 0), (2, 2)

b) (2, 2), (4, 2), (4, 3), (2, 4)

c) (0, 0), (4, 0), (3, 2), (1, 2)

d) (0, 0), (3, 0), (3, 1), (1, 1), (1, 3), (0, 3)

Line Symmetry

A line of symmetry is a mirror line, where you can fold a shape so that both halves match up exactly. Either side of the line of symmetry is a reflection of the other.

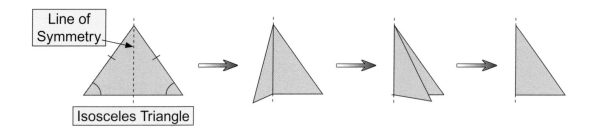

Line of Symmetry

Isosceles Triangle

Example 1

How many lines of symmetry does an equilateral triangle have?

An equilateral triangle has three mirror lines, where the shape can be folded perfectly in half.

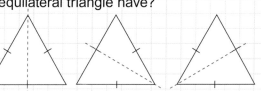

An equilateral triangle has 3 lines of symmetry.

Exercise 1

1 Copy each of the shapes below, then draw on any lines of symmetry.
  State the number of lines of symmetry you have drawn for each shape.

a)
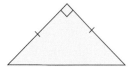

b)

c)
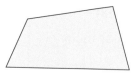

d)

e)

f)

2 Copy each of the shapes below, then draw on any lines of symmetry. State the number of lines of symmetry you have drawn for each shape.

a)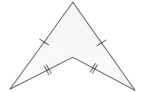

b)

c)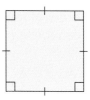

3 **a)** Copy the diagram below, then shade one more square to make a pattern with 1 line of symmetry.

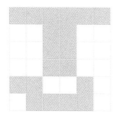

b) Copy the diagram below, then shade two more squares to make a pattern with 2 lines of symmetry.

4 Sketch each of the shapes below, then draw on any lines of symmetry. State the number of lines of symmetry you have drawn for each shape.

a) rectangle

b) rhombus

c) parallelogram

d) isosceles trapezium

e) regular pentagon

f) regular hexagon

g) regular heptagon

h) regular octagon

Look back at earlier pages to find examples of these shapes if you need to.

Rotational Symmetry

The order of rotational symmetry of a shape is the number of positions you can rotate (turn) the shape into so that it looks exactly the same.

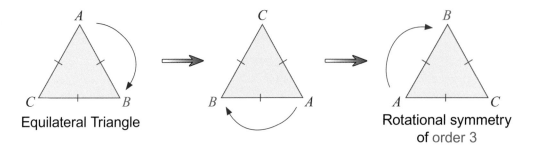

Equilateral Triangle

Rotational symmetry
of order 3

A shape that only looks the same once
every complete turn has no rotational symmetry.

Example 2

What is the order of rotational symmetry of a rhombus?

There are two positions
in which a rhombus looks
exactly the same.

A rhombus has rotational
symmetry of order 2.

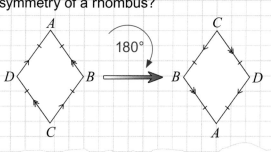

Exercise 2

1   Find the order of rotational symmetry of each shape below, where possible.

a)

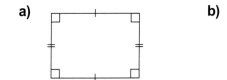

b)

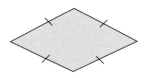

c)

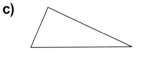

2 Find the order of rotational symmetry of each shape below, where possible.

a)

b)

c)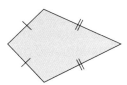

d)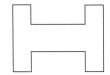

e)

f)

3 Copy the diagram on the right, then shade one more square to make a pattern with rotational symmetry of order 2.

4 Sketch each of the shapes below, then find the order of rotational symmetry where possible.

a) square

b) isosceles triangle

c) isosceles trapezium

d) regular pentagon

e) regular hexagon

f) regular octagon

Exercise 3 — Mixed Exercise

1 For each of the shapes below, find **(i)** the number of lines of symmetry

(ii) the order of rotational symmetry, where possible.

a)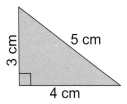

b)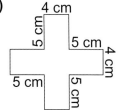

c)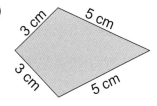

2 Copy the diagram on the right, then shade two more squares to make a pattern with 4 lines of symmetry and rotational symmetry of order 4.

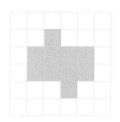

3 Decide which of the shapes below matches each of the descriptions.

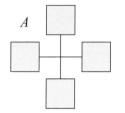 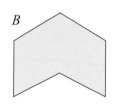 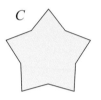 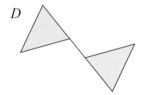

a) 1 line of symmetry, no rotational symmetry.

b) 4 lines of symmetry, rotational symmetry of order 4.

c) No lines of symmetry, rotational symmetry of order 2.

d) 5 lines of symmetry, rotational symmetry of order 5.

14.7 Angle and 2D Shape Problems

Exercise 1

1 This question is about shapes A-G below.

Which of the shapes above:

a) are polygons?　　　　　　　　　　**b)** are hexagons?

c) are pentagons?　　　　　　　　　　**d)** are quadrilaterals?

e) have at least one line of symmetry?

2 For the regular heptagon shown on the right, find:

a) the number of lines of symmetry,

b) the order of rotational symmetry.

For questions **3-6**, find the missing angles marked with letters.
(None of the diagrams are drawn accurately, so don't try to measure them.)

3 a)

162° *a*

b)

28° *b*

c)

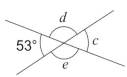

d
53° *c*
e

d)

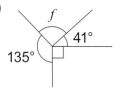

f
41°
135°

e)

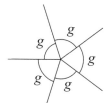

g
g *g*
g *g*

f)

h
31°

4 a)

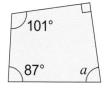

101°
87° *a*

b)

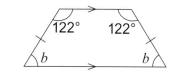

122° 122°
b *b*

c)

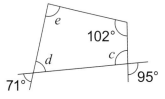

e
102°
d *c*
71° 95°

d)

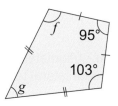

f 95°
103°
g

e)

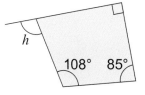

h
108° 85°

f)

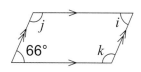

j *i*
66° *k*

5 a)

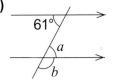

b)

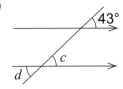

c)

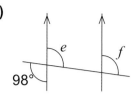

d)

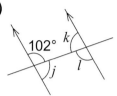

e)

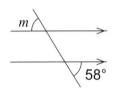

f)

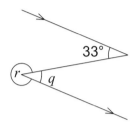

6 a)

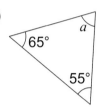

b)

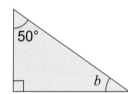

c)

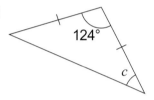

d)

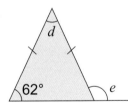

e)

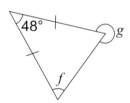

f)

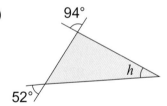

7 Draw an **irregular** quadrilateral that tessellates.
Show how your quadrilateral tessellates.

8 The diagram on the right shows a kite and a square.

a) Write down the value of a.

b) Use your answer to find the size of   **(i)**   angle b

                                  (ii)   angle c.

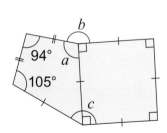

Section 15 — Units, Measuring and Estimating

15.1 Reading Scales

Scales are used to measure things.

Some marks on a scale have a number written next to them.

The marks in between are usually left blank — you have to work out what they show.

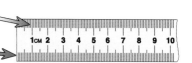

Example 1

Find the length of the pencil.

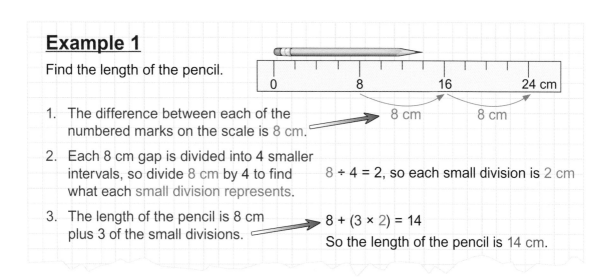

1. The difference between each of the numbered marks on the scale is 8 cm.

2. Each 8 cm gap is divided into 4 smaller intervals, so divide 8 cm by 4 to find what each small division represents.

   $8 \div 4 = 2$, so each small division is 2 cm

3. The length of the pencil is 8 cm plus 3 of the small divisions.

   $8 + (3 \times 2) = 14$

   So the length of the pencil is 14 cm.

Exercise 1

1 Measure each of these lines with a ruler. Give your answers in cm.

   a) ——————————————————————

   b) ———————————————

   c) ————————————————————————

2 Measure each of these lines with a ruler. Give your answers in mm.

   a) —   b) ——   c) ———————

   d) ——————————————————————————

   Remember:
   1 cm = 10 mm

3 Find the length of each of these bugs. Give your answers in mm.

a)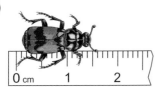

b)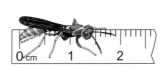

c)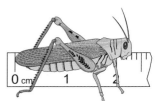

4 a) Write down the difference between each numbered unit on the ruler shown.

b) Find what each small division on the ruler represents.

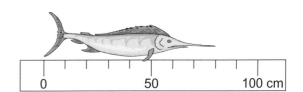

c) Find the length of the swordfish.

5 Write down the lengths shown by the arrows on the ruler. Give your answers in cm.

a)

b)

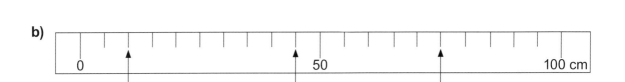

c)

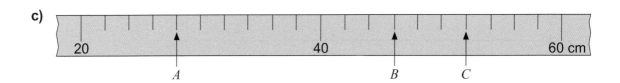

d)

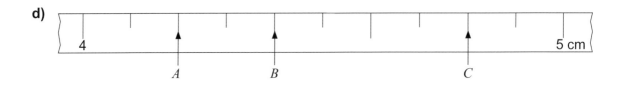

6 Write down the volume of liquid shown in each of these containers.
Give your answers using the units written on each container.

Read the scales just like when measuring lengths.

a)

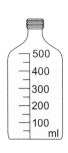

b)

c)

d)

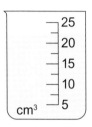

e)

f)

7 Write down the mass shown by the arrow on each of these scales.
Give your answers using the units written on each set of scales.

a)

b)

c)

d)

e)

f)

g)

h)

i)

8 Find:

    a) the height of the giraffe

    b) the height of the sunflower

    c) the mass of the banana

    d) the volume of liquid in the bottle.

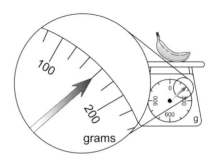

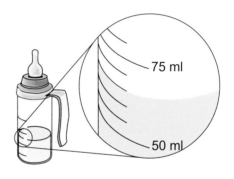

15.2   Converting Units — Length, Mass and Volume

To convert between different units, you need to know the conversion factor.
This tells you how many times bigger or smaller one unit is than the other.

When converting to a smaller unit (e.g. m to cm), multiply by the conversion factor.

When converting to a bigger unit, (e.g. cm to m), divide by the conversion factor.

Metric Units

You can convert between different metric units using these conversions:

Length:
1 cm = 10 mm
1 m = 100 cm
1 km = 1000 m

Mass:
1 kg = 1000 g
1 tonne = 1000 kg

Volume:
1 litre (l) = 1000 ml
1 ml = 1 cm^3

Example 1

a) Convert 2.5 m into cm.

1. There are 100 cm in 1 m, so the conversion factor is 100.

$$1 \text{ m} = 100 \text{ cm}$$

2. Centimetres are smaller than metres, so multiply by the conversion factor.

$$2.5 \text{ m} = (2.5 \times 100) \text{ cm}$$
$$= 250 \text{ cm}$$

b) Convert 1200 g into kg.

1. There are 1000 g in 1 kg, so the conversion factor is 1000.

$$1 \text{ kg} = 1000 \text{ g}$$

2. Kilograms are bigger than grams, so divide by the conversion factor.

$$1200 \text{ g} = (1200 \div 1000) \text{ kg}$$
$$= 1.2 \text{ kg}$$

Exercise 1

1 For each of these conversions, write down **(i)** the conversion factor, and **(ii)** whether you should multiply or divide by the conversion factor.

a) cm into mm

b) cm into m

c) km into m

d) kg into g

e) tonnes into kg

f) litres into ml

g) cm^3 into ml

h) m into km

i) kg into tonnes

For questions **2-4**, convert each measurement into the units given.

2 a) 2 cm into mm

b) 126.7 cm^3 into ml

c) 3 l into ml

d) 4 kg into g

e) 15 ml into cm^3

f) 2 km into m

g) 5.4 m into cm

h) 2.3 tonnes into kg

i) 15.3 l into ml

3 a) 50 cm into m

b) 3400 m into km

c) 40 cm into m

d) 3000 g into kg

e) 2000 ml into l

f) 500 ml into l

g) 246 kg into tonnes

h) 5430 ml into l

i) 3295 m into km

4 **a)** 2 mm into cm

b) 3.1 kg into g

c) 12.7 l into ml

d) 370 mm into cm

e) 3000 kg into tonnes

f) 123 ml into l

g) 12.6 kg into tonnes

h) 51.16 g into kg

i) 105 cm into m

5 Dermot is 176 cm tall. What is his height in metres?

6 Katy weighs 65 kg. What is her weight in grams?

7 James runs 2.2 km. How far is this in metres?

8 A car weighs 1640 kg. Work out how much the car weighs in tonnes.

9 Raj is making custard. He needs 570 ml of milk. How much milk does he need in litres?

10 Amy has a 1.2 kg box of cereal.

a) Convert 1.2 kg into grams.

b) Use your answer to part **a)** to find how many 30 g servings there are in the box.

11 **a)** Convert 5 m into cm.

b) Use your answer to part **a)** to convert 5 m into mm.

Example 2

Find the sum of 0.2 tonnes, 31.8 kg and 1700 g.
Give your answer in kg.

The question tells you which units to convert the measurements to.

1. Convert 0.2 tonnes into kilograms by multiplying by 1000.

    0.2 tonnes $= (0.2 \times 1000)$ kg
    $= 200$ kg

2. Convert 1700 g into kilograms by dividing by 1000.

    1700 g $= (1700 \div 1000)$ kg
    $= 1.7$ kg

3. Add the masses together.

    200 kg $+ 31.8$ kg $+ 1.7$ kg $= 233.5$ kg

Don't forget this amount which was already in kg.

Exercise 2

1 Copy and complete each of these calculations.

a) 3000 ml + 75 l = ⬚ l + 75 l = ⬚ l

b) 7 tonnes + 3000 kg = 7 tonnes + ⬚ tonnes = ⬚ tonnes

c) 3 kg + 500 g + 0.2 kg = 3 kg + ⬚ kg + 0.2 kg = ⬚ kg

d) 100 cm + 0.35 m + 12.6 m = 100 cm + ⬚ cm + ⬚ cm = ⬚ cm

2 A bucket contains 1200 ml of water. 2.2 l of water is added to the bucket.
How much water is there in the bucket now? Give your answer in litres.

3 Milly runs a 1500 m fun run, a 100 m sprint and a 13.2 km race.
How far does she run in total? Give your answer in kilometres.

Imperial Units

Imperial units are things like inches, feet and miles for lengths, pounds and ounces for mass, and pints and gallons for volume.

You can convert between different imperial units using these conversions:

Length:
1 foot = 12 inches
1 yard = 3 feet

Mass:
1 pound = 16 ounces
1 stone = 14 pounds

Volume:
1 gallon = 8 pints

Example 3

a) Convert 5 pounds into ounces.

   1. There are 16 ounces in 1 pound, so the conversion factor is 16.

      1 pound = 16 ounces

   2. Ounces are smaller than pounds, so multiply by the conversion factor.

      5 pounds = (5 × 16) ounces
           = 80 ounces

b) Convert 12 feet into yards.

   1. There are 3 feet in 1 yard, so the conversion factor is 3.

      1 yard = 3 feet

   2. Yards are bigger than feet, so divide by the conversion factor.

      12 feet = (12 ÷ 3) yards
           = 4 yards

Exercise 3

1 For each of these conversions, write down **(i)** the conversion factor, and **(ii)** whether you should multiply or divide by the conversion factor.

   a) inches into feet   **b)** pints into gallons   **c)** stones into pounds

   d) gallons into pints   **e)** ounces into pounds   **f)** yards into feet

For questions **2-4**, convert each measurement into the units given.

2 **a)** 2 feet into inches   **b)** 4 yards into feet   **c)** 0.5 gallons into pints

    d) 4 stone into pounds   **e)** 9 gallons into pints   **f)** 3600 yards into feet

3 **a)** 46 ounces into pounds   **b)** 56 pounds into stones   **c)** 15 feet into yards

    d) 66 inches into feet   **e)** 36 pints into gallons   **f)** 45.5 pounds into stones

4 **a)** 6 pounds into ounces   **b)** 96 pints into gallons   **c)** 144 inches into feet

    d) 17 yards into feet   **e)** 70 pounds into stone   **f)** 112 ounces into pounds

5   Charles is 6.5 feet tall. What is his height in inches?

6   A water tank holds 100 pints of water. How much is this in gallons?

Metric and Imperial Conversions

You can convert between metric and imperial units using these conversions:

Length:
1 inch ≈ 2.5 cm
1 foot ≈ 30 cm
1 yard ≈ 90 cm
1 mile ≈ 1.6 km

Mass:
1 ounce ≈ 28 g
1 pound ≈ 450 g
1 stone ≈ 6400 g
1 kg ≈ 2.2 pounds

Volume:
1 pint ≈ 0.57 litres
1 gallon ≈ 4.5 litres

The wavy equals sign: "≈" means 'approximately equal to'.

Example 4

a)   Convert 15 miles into km.

    1.   There are approximately 1.6 km in 1 mile, so the conversion factor is 1.6

                 1 mile ≈ 1.6 km

    2.   Kilometres are smaller than miles, so multiply by the conversion factor.

                 15 miles = (15 × 1.6) km
                          = 24 km

b)   Convert 126 g into ounces.

    1.   There are approximately 28 g in 1 ounce, so the conversion factor is 28

                 1 ounce ≈ 28 g

    2.   Ounces are bigger than grams, so divide by the conversion factor.

                 126 g = (126 ÷ 28) ounces
                       = 4.5 ounces

Exercise 4

1 Which is larger:

a) 1 mile or 1 km   **b)** 1 gallon or 1 litre   **c)** 1 kg or 1 ounce?

2 Convert these measurements from imperial units to metric.

a) 4 inches into cm   **b)** 12 ounces into g

c) 2 gallons into litres   **d)** 10 stone into g

e) 5 yards into cm   **f)** 25 miles into km

g) 2.7 inches into cm   **h)** 4.5 pints into litres

i) 6.9 feet into cm

3 Convert these measurements from metric units to imperial.

a) 8 km into miles   **b)** 57 litres into pints

c) 12 800 g into stones   **d)** 52 cm into feet

e) 17.5 cm into inches   **f)** 48 km into miles

g) 42 g into ounces   **h)** 7.5 kg into pounds

i) 10.4 km into miles

4 Mark is on holiday in a place where the speed limit is 90 km/h. What is this in mph?

5 **a)** Convert 18 yards into cm.

b) Use your answer to part **a)** to convert 18 yards into metres.

6 A running track is 400 m long. How many laps of the track make one mile?

15.3 Estimating Measurements

You can estimate how big something is by comparing it with something you already know the size of. E.g. the average height of a man is about 1.8 m, so something half as tall as an average man would be about 0.9 m in height.

Example 1

Estimate the height of the lamp post.

1. Write down the height of the man.

   Average height of a man = 1.8 m

2. Estimate how much taller the lamp post is than the man.

   The lamp post is roughly twice the height of the man.

3. Use this to estimate the height of the lamp post.

   So height of the lamp post ≈
   2 × 1.8 m = 3.6 m

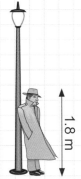

Exercise 1

1 **a) (i)** Estimate how many times taller the house is than the man.

   (ii) Estimate the height of the house.

b) (i) Estimate how many times taller the elephant is than the man.

   (ii) Estimate the height of the elephant.

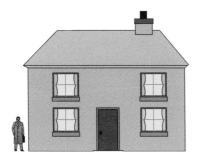

2 Estimate:

   a) the height of the bus

   b) the length of the bus

3 a) The height of the weird alien shown is 0.5 m.
Estimate the height of the rhino.

b) The height and length of the chicken shown is 30 cm. Estimate :

(i) the height of the dinosaur

(ii) the length of the dinosaur

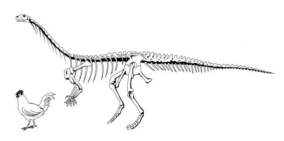

Example 2

Give sensible units for measuring the height of a room.

Compare the room to something you already know the height of.
Most rooms are taller than an average man, but not by that much.

The average height of a man is about 1.8 m, so it would be
sensible to measure the height of a room in metres.

Using cm or mm would give you a big number, and using km would
give you a very small number, so these units would be less suitable.

Exercise 2

1 Match each of the measurements below
to a suitable unit from the box.

| tonnes | kg | m | mm | km | cm | g |

a) the length of a pencil

b) the mass of a tomato

c) the height of a house

d) the length of an ant

e) the weight of a lorry

f) the weight of a baby

g) the distance from Birmingham to Manchester

2 Give sensible **metric** units for each of these measurements.

a) the height of a horse

b) the length of the M6 motorway

c) the height of a football goal

d) the length of a wasp

e) the mass of an apple

f) the length of a mobile phone

15.4 Clock Time

Times can be given in '12-hour clock' or '24-hour clock'.

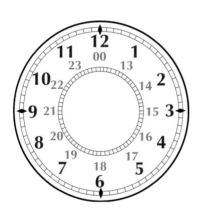

Starting at midnight, the first time round the clock runs from...	
24-hour clock	**12-hour clock**
00:00	12 midnight
to	to
11:59	11:59 am

...and the second time round runs from:	
24-hour clock	**12-hour clock**
12:00	12 noon
to	to
23:59	11:59 pm

12-hour clock times need 'am' or 'pm' to show if the time is before or after 12 noon.

After 1:00 pm, add 12 hours to the 12-hour clock time to get the 24-hour clock time (or subtract 12 hours from the 24-hour clock time and add 'pm' to get the 12-hour clock time).

Example 1

Write these 12-hour clock times as 24-hour clock times:

a) 9:45 am

This time is before 1:00 pm,
so the numbers stay the same.

24-hour clock times are always written as four digits without an 'am' or 'pm'.

9:45 am is
09:45 in 24-hour clock.

b) 9:45 pm

This time is after 1:00 pm, so add
12 hours to the 12-hour clock time.

9:45 pm is
9:45 + 12:00 = 21:45 in 24-hour clock.

Example 2

Write these 24-hour clock times as 12-hour clock times:

a) 07:17

1. This time is before 13:00, so the numbers stay the same.

2. It needs 'am' to show that it's in the morning.

07:17 is 7:17 am
in 12-hour clock.

b) 19:17

1. This time is after 13:00 so subtract 12 hours
from the 24-hour clock time.

2. It needs 'pm' to show that it's in the evening.

19:17 pm is 19:17 – 12:00
= 7:45 pm in 12-hour clock.

Exercise 1

1   Write these 12-hour clock times as 24-hour clock times:

a)   b)   c)

      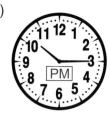

2   Write these 12-hour clock times as 24-hour clock times:

a) 8:15 am   b) 6:45 am   c) 1:05 pm

d) 7:45 pm   e) 10:00 am   f) 8:36 pm

g) 9:25 am   h) 2:05 am   i) 11:15 pm

3 Write these 24-hour clock times as 12-hour clock times:

a)

b)

c)

Plane ticket
Destination: Lapland
Departure Time: 12:25

4 Write these 24-hour clock times as 12-hour clock times:

a) 18:30 b) 06:25 c) 17:55

d) 01:50 e) 15:25 f) 12:12

g) 00:59 h) 21:54 i) 14:41

5 Write each of these times using: **(i)** 12-hour clock **(ii)** 24-hour clock

a) 9 o'clock in the evening. b) Twenty past eleven in the morning.

c) Twenty-five past four in the afternoon. d) Half past two in the afternoon.

e) Quarter past ten in the morning. f) Ten past eight in the evening.

Hours, Minutes and Seconds

There are 60 seconds in a minute and 60 minutes in an hour.

You can use these to convert between hours, minutes and seconds.

Example 3

Pretesh can run a mile in 5 minutes and 25 seconds.
What is this time in seconds?

1. First, change 5 minutes into seconds, by multiplying by 60. → 1 minute = 60 seconds, so:
5 minutes = (5 × 60) = 300 seconds

2. Then add on the remaining 25 seconds to find the total time in seconds. → 300 + 25 = 325 seconds.

Example 4

An experiment takes 135 minutes to complete.
What is this time in hours and minutes?

> Watch out — 2.25 hours is NOT 2 hours 25 minutes. Be careful when using calculators to convert times.

1. First, change 135 minutes into hours, by dividing by 60.

   1 hour = 60 minutes, so:
   135 minutes = (135 ÷ 60) = 2.25 hours

2. So, 135 minutes is **2 whole hours** plus 0.25 of an hour.

3. Find '0.25 of an hour' in minutes by multiplying by 60.

   0.25 × 60 = 15 minutes

4. Finally, put the whole hours and the minutes together to answer the question.

   So the experiment took 2 hours and 15 minutes.

Exercise 2

1 Rewrite these times in seconds:

    a) 3 minutes   **b)** 9 minutes   **c)** 17 minutes

    d) 1.5 minutes   **e)** 1 minute and 20 seconds   **f)** 2 minutes and 12 seconds

2 Rewrite these times in minutes:

    a) 3 hours   **b)** 5 hours   **c)** 6.5 hours

    d) 0.75 hours   **e)** 2 hours and 45 minutes   **f)** 4 hours and 12 minutes

3 Rewrite these times in hours and minutes:

    a) 60 minutes   **b)** 600 minutes   **c)** 270 minutes

    d) 90 minutes   **e)** 150 minutes   **f)** 267 minutes

4 Rewrite these times in minutes and seconds:

    a) 60 seconds   **b)** 180 seconds   **c)** 150 seconds

    d) 720 seconds   **e)** 129 seconds   **f)** 936 seconds

5 It takes Valerie 498 seconds to walk around the local park.
What is this time in minutes and seconds?

6 A TV program lasts 72 minutes. What is this time in:

a) seconds

b) hours and minutes?

7 **a)** Write 2 hours in minutes.

b) Use your answer to part **a)** to write 2 hours in seconds.

8 Carl's house is a 2 hour and 25 minute drive from the beach.
Carl's electric car will run for 300 minutes on a single charge.

Will Carl be able to drive from his house to the beach and back on a single charge?

9 There are 24 hours in a day. Find the number of seconds in a day.

Journey Times

Example 5

Dom set off on a trip at 9:15 am. His journey took 1 hour and 50 minutes.
What time did he arrive at his destination?

1. First add on the hours. ⟹ 9:15 am + 1 hour = 10:15 am

2. Now add on the minutes. ⟹ 10:15 am + 50 minutes = 11:05 am

So Dom arrived at 11:05 am.

Example 6

Liz left her house at 06:45 and arrived at work at 08:55.
How long did her journey to work take?

1. Split the journey into short easy stages and find the time taken for each stage:

    06:45 ――――――→ 07:00 ――――――→ 08:00 ――――――→ 08:55
         15 minutes   1 hour   55 minutes

2. Add the times for each stage together   15 minutes + 1 hour + 55 minutes
    to find the total journey time. ――――――→   = 2 hours and 10 minutes

Exercise 3

1   Find the arrival time of each journey below:

    a) Start time — 10:25 pm   **b)** Start time — 11:15 am
        Length of journey — 25 minutes   Length of journey — 1 hour 15 minutes

2   Alexandra left home for school at 8:25 am.
    Her journey took 17 minutes.

    What time did she arrive at school?

3   Mikhail leaves work at 17:35. His journey home takes 55 minutes.

    What time does he arrive home?

4   Kristen's bus departs at 07:12.
    The journey takes 1 hour and 35 minutes.

    What time will she arrive at her destination?

5   A train departs at 11:42 am and arrives at its destination 3 hours and 30 minutes later.

    What time does the train arrive?

6   Find the length of each journey below:

   a) Start time — 08:15
      End time — 08:45

   b) Start time — 12:10 am
      End time — 12:55 am

   c) Start time — 19:50
      End time — 20:40

7   Sasha walks for 10 minutes, travels on a train for 2 hours and then drives for 25 minutes.
   What is the total length of Sasha's journey?

8   Derek finished school at 3:15 pm. He arrived home at 4:02 pm.
   How long did it take him to get home?

9   A train departs at 13:10 and arrives at its destination at 16:17.
   What is the length of the journey?

10   Andy took a flight which left at 04:25 and arrived at 09:05.
   What was Andy's journey time?

11   Jeni left the house to go shopping at 11:30.
   She returned home at 15:05.

   How long was she out shopping?

12   Al arrives at his destination at 17:08 after driving for 2 hours and 45 minutes.
   What time did he leave?

Timetables

Timetables usually show times written in 24-hour clock.

Example 7

Bolney	0942	1015	1046
Sidlington	1003	1036	1107
Wenderbury	1024	1057	1128
Aylshop	1040	1113	1144

24-hour clock times are often written like this, with no ':'

a) A bus leaves Bolney at 10:46. What time does it arrive in Wenderbury?

   1. Find the row for Bolney and read across until you get to 10:46.

   2. Follow the column down until you get to the time in the row for Wenderbury.

      It arrives in Wenderbury at 11:28.

b) Ashleigh wants to be in Aylshop before 11:15. What's the latest time she can leave Bolney?

   1. Look at the row for Aylshop: there are 2 buses that arrive before 11:15.

      She can arrive in Aylshop at 10:40 or 11:13.

   2. Follow the columns up to find the time that each one leaves Bolney.

      The latest time she can leave Bolney is 10:15.

c) Lily gets the bus from Sidlington at 10:36. How long does the journey to Aylshop take?

   1. Use the timetable to find that the bus leaving Sidlington at 10:36 arrives in Aylshop at 11:13

   2. Split the journey into stages and work out how long each stage takes:

      10:36 ⟶ 11:00 ⟶ 11:13
          24 minutes   13 minutes

   3. Add the times for each stage together.

      24 minutes + 13 minutes = 37 minutes

Exercise 4

Use this bus timetable to answer questions **1 & 2**.

Acreton	—	—	0855	1330	—
Notwitch Bus Station	0540	0725	0930	1405	2015
Heatheridge	0550	0739	—	—	—
Thetfast	0625	0820	1020	1455	2100
London Wideway	0810	1015	1200	1630	2230
London Victoria	0920	1105	1250	1720	2300

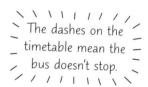

The dashes on the timetable mean the bus doesn't stop.

1 **a)** What time does the last bus for London Victoria leave Notwitch Bus Station?

    b) What time does this bus arrive at London Victoria?

    c) Give the departure and arrival times of this bus in 12-hour clock time.

2 Frank lives in Acreton.

    a) Can he get a bus on this route to Heatheridge?

    b) What is the earliest time he can arrive in Thetfast?

    c) How long does the journey from Acreton to Thetfast take on this bus route?

Use this train timetable to answer questions **3-5**.

Glasgow	0700	0745	0815	0830	0900	0915
Croy	0711	—	—	0841	0911	—
Polmont	0727	0807	—	—	—	0937
Haymarket	0750	0832	0900	0914	0943	1001
Edinburgh	0755	0837	0905	0919	0948	1006

3 Terry lives in Glasgow. He takes the 07:45 train to Edinburgh each day.

    a) What time does he arrive in Edinburgh?

    b) How long does the journey take?

    c) One day, the 07:45 train leaves Glasgow 12 minutes late.
       What time will Terry arrive in Edinburgh if the journey length is the same as usual?

4 Laura lives in Croy, a 15 minute walk from the train station.
    She is meeting a friend at 10:00 am at Edinburgh station.

    What is the latest time she can leave her house and meet her friend on time?

5 Jake works in Haymarket, a 20 minute walk from the train station.
    He starts work at 9.30 am.

    What is the latest train he can catch from Glasgow to be at work on time?

6 Which train has the shortest journey time between Glasgow and Haymarket?

Section 16 — Speed, Distance and Time

16.1 Speed, Distance, Time Calculations

Finding an Object's Speed

Speed, distance and time are connected by the formula:

$$\text{Speed} = \frac{\text{Distance}}{\text{Time}}$$

Example 1

A car travels 150 km in 3 hours.
What is the average speed of the car?

1. Write down the formula for speed.

2. Put your numbers for distance and time into the formula.

3. Give your answer with the correct units
   — the distance is in km and the time is in hours,
   so the speed will be in kilometres per hour (km/h).

$$\text{Speed} = \frac{\text{Distance}}{\text{Time}}$$

$$= \frac{150}{3} = 150 \div 3$$

$$= 50 \text{ km/h}$$

Exercise 1

1 Find the average speed in km/h of each of these journeys:

a) distance = 30 km, time = 2 hours

b) distance = 60 km, time = 3 hours

c) distance = 150 km, time = 5 hours

d) distance = 100 km, time = 2.5 hours

e) distance = 72 000 km, time = 12 hours

f) distance = 140 km, time = 4 hours

2 Andy runs 100 m in 25 seconds.
Find his average speed in metres per second (m/s).

3 Shakila cycles 30 miles in 3 hours.
Find her average speed in miles per hour (mph).

4 Find the speed of the following:

a) a car travelling 80 km in 2 hours

b) a cyclist travelling 32 km in 2 hours

c) a cheetah running 100 m in 4 seconds

d) a plane flying 1800 miles in 3 hours

e) a balloon rising 720 m in 180 seconds

f) a rocket travelling 39 000 m in 5 seconds

g) an escalator moving 15 m in 10 seconds

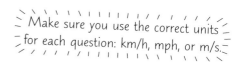
Make sure you use the correct units for each question: km/h, mph, or m/s.

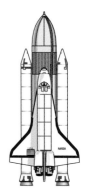

5 After lift-off, a space shuttle travelled 2040 miles in 12 minutes.

a) Convert 12 minutes to hours.

b) Find the average speed in mph of the space shuttle in the 12 minutes after lift-off.

6 Find the speed of the following in km/h.
You will need to convert the units to km and hours first.

a) a boat travelling 10 km in 120 minutes

b) a tractor driving 15 km in 30 minutes

c) a man walking 1.5 km in 15 minutes

d) a train travelling 300 000 m in 2.5 hours

e) a river flowing 2.25 km in 45 minutes

f) a dog running 240 m in 10 minutes

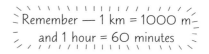
Remember — 1 km = 1000 m and 1 hour = 60 minutes

Finding Distance and Time

You can rearrange the speed formula to find distance and time:

$$\text{Distance} = \text{Speed} \times \text{Time}$$

$$\text{Time} = \frac{\text{Distance}}{\text{Speed}}$$

Example 2

A man runs for 30 minutes at an average speed of 12 km/h.
How far does he run?

1. The speed is in km/h, so convert the time into hours. This means that the distance you find will be in km.

   30 minutes = 0.5 hours

2. Use the formula for distance and put in the numbers for speed and time.

   Distance = Speed × Time

   $= 12 \times 0.5 = 6$ km.

Example 3

A train travels 60 miles at a speed of 100 mph.
How many minutes will the journey take?

1. Use the formula for time.

   $\text{Time} = \dfrac{\text{Distance}}{\text{Speed}}$

2. Put your numbers for distance and speed into the formula.

   $= \dfrac{60}{100} = 60 \div 100 = 0.6$ hours

3. Convert your answer into minutes.

   $= 0.6 \times 60$ minutes $= 36$ minutes.

Exercise 2

1   For each of the following, use the speed and time given to find the distance travelled.

   a) speed = 20 km/h, time = 2 hours

   b) speed = 25 mph, time = 2 hours

   c) speed = 10 m/s, time = 50 seconds

   d) speed = 3 km/h, time = 24 hours

2   Find the distance travelled by a bus which drives at 30 mph for 4 hours.

3 For each of the following, use the speed and distance given to find the time taken.

   a) speed = 2 km/h, distance = 4 km

   b) speed = 3 m/s, distance = 15 m

   c) speed = 15 m/s, distance = 45 m

   d) speed = 60 mph, distance = 150 miles

4 A marathon is approximately 42 km long.
How long would it take a gorilla running
at an average speed of 14 km/h to complete the marathon?

5 A flight to Spain takes 2 hours.
The plane travels at an average speed of 490 mph.

   How far does the plane travel?

6 A girl skates at an average speed of 8 mph.
How far does she skate in 15 minutes?

7 A gazelle ran for 5.6 km at 56 km/h. How long was it running for in minutes?

8 A dart is thrown with speed 15 m/s. It hits a dartboard 2.4 m away.
How long is the dart in the air?

Exercise 3 — Mixed Exercise

1 A football is passed between two players 10 m apart.
The ball travels for 2.5 seconds.

   Find the average speed of the ball in m/s.

2 A man swims one length of a pool in 50 seconds.
His speed is 0.5 m/s.

   Find the length of the pool in metres.

3 A car's average speed is 40 mph.
How long will it take the car to travel 100 miles?

4 A bobsleigh covers 1400 m in 50 seconds. Find its average speed in metres per second.

5 A tennis ball moves at an average speed of 28 m/s.
How long does it take to travel 35 m across the court?

6 A jogger ran for half an hour at an average speed of 8.1 km/h. How far did he run?

7 A leopard runs 8 miles in 15 minutes. Find the leopard's average speed in mph.

8 A tortoise walks 9 m in 3 minutes.
Find the tortoise's average speed in m/s.

9 A snail slides 0.8 m in 1 minute 40 seconds.
Find the snail's average speed in m/s.

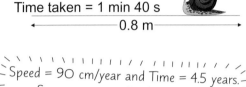

Time taken = 1 min 40 s
0.8 m

10 A tree grows at a rate of 90 cm per year.
How much does it grow in 4.5 years?

Speed = 90 cm/year and Time = 4.5 years.
So your answer should be in cm.

16.2 Distance-Time Graphs

A Distance-Time graph shows how far an object has travelled in a particular time.

The gradient of the graph gives the speed of the object — the steeper the graph, the greater the speed. A horizontal line means the object is stationary.

Example 1

Danny cycles 5 miles in 20 minutes. He stops and rests for 10 minutes, then returns home in 30 minutes. Copy the axes on the right and use them to draw a graph of Danny's journey.

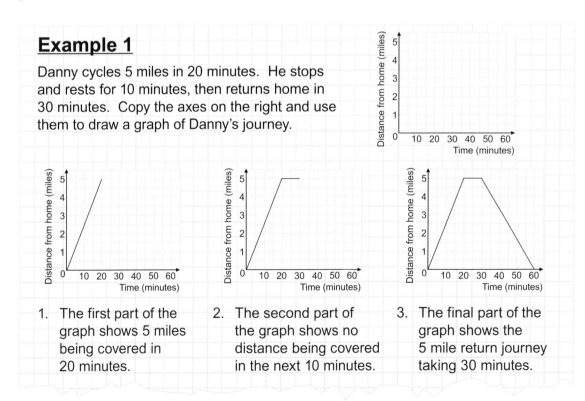

1. The first part of the graph shows 5 miles being covered in 20 minutes.

2. The second part of the graph shows no distance being covered in the next 10 minutes.

3. The final part of the graph shows the 5 mile return journey taking 30 minutes.

Exercise 1

1 Match each Distance-Time graph below to the correct description of the journey. The first one has been done for you.

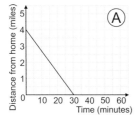 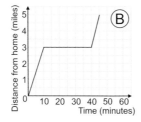 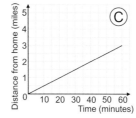 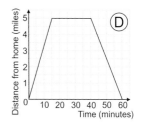

a) Amy walks 3 miles to school in 60 minutes. ⟶ Ⓒ

b) Josh starts 4 miles from home and takes 30 minutes to cycle back home. ⟶ _____

c) Curtis drives 3 miles from home in 10 minutes, is stationary for 30 minutes and then drives 2 miles further in 5 minutes. ⟶ _____

d) Lucy drives 5 miles from home in 15 minutes. She is stationary for 25 minutes and then takes 20 minutes to drive home. ⟶ _____

2 [T] Adi is a keen cyclist. Here is a description of one of her bike rides.

- Adi cycles 30 km in 2 hours.

- Then she stops and rests for half an hour.

- She then cycles a further 40 km in 2.5 hours.

Copy the coordinate grid on the right.

a) Draw the part of the graph representing the first stage of Adi's journey. This part of the graph should show 30 km being covered in 2 hours.

b) The second stage of her journey is represented by a horizontal line. Draw this part of the graph.

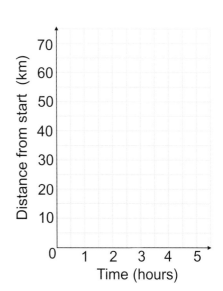

c) Draw the final part of the graph. This should show Adi taking 2.5 hours to cover another 40 km.

d) How far is Adi's final destination from her original starting point?

3 James loves to run. Here is a description of one of his runs.

- James runs 20 km in 2 hours.

- Then he stops to rest for an hour.

- He then runs back to his starting point in 2.5 hours.

Copy the coordinate grid below.

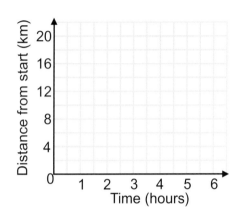

a) Draw the part of the graph representing the first stage of his run.

b) Draw the part of the graph representing his hour of rest.

c) Draw the final part of the graph.
The graph should return to a distance of 0 km at time 5.5 hours.

4 Draw a Distance-Time graph for each of these journeys:

a) Yemi drives 50 km in 1 hour, stops at a service station for half an hour, then drives a further 30 km in half an hour.

b) Sandy walks 200 m to the bus stop in 2 minutes.

She waits for 3 minutes, then travels 1 km in 3 minutes on the bus.

c) Harry walks 3 km in 45 minutes to his friend's house.

He stays there for 1 hour, then walks for 30 minutes back towards home until he gets to the park, 1 km from home.

d) Josh and Ron live 3.5 miles apart.

Josh walks 1 mile to the bus stop in 20 minutes.
He waits 10 minutes for the bus, then travels 2 miles in 5 minutes.

He gets off the bus and walks the rest of the way to Ron's house in 15 minutes.

Example 2

Bill walked from his home to his friend's house.
The Distance-Time graph shows Bill's journey.

a) How far did Bill walk?

b) How long did it take Bill to walk to his friend's house?

c) What was Bill's average speed?

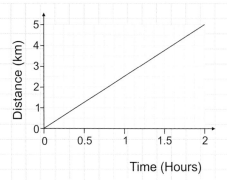

1. Read the distance and time off the graph.

   a) Distance = 5 km.

   b) Time = 2 hours.

2. Bill's speed is given by the gradient of the graph.
   Find the gradient by dividing the total distance by the total time.

   c) Speed $= \dfrac{\text{Distance}}{\text{Time}} = \dfrac{5}{2} = 2.5$ km/h

Exercise 2

1 Chay is on a cycling tour of Norfolk.
The graph below shows Chay's journey one day.

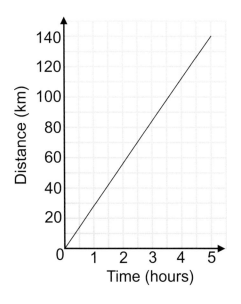

a) How far did Chay cycle that day?

b) How long did Chay ride for?

c) What was Chay's average speed?

2 The graph below shows the progress of the winner of the 10 km race at the frog-lympics.

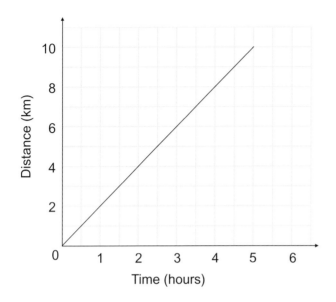

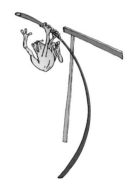

a) How long did the frog take to finish the race?

b) What was the average speed of the frog?

3 The graph below shows a family's car journey.

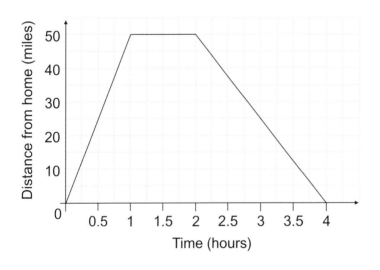

a) What was the car's average speed for the first hour?

b) What was the car's average speed on the return journey?

Section 17 — Constructions

17.1 Lines and Angles

For this topic, you'll need a ruler to measure lengths...

...and a protractor to measure angles.

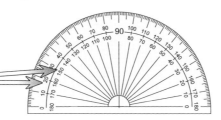

Make sure you know
how to use both scales
on your protractor.

Example 1

Measure the size of angle a.

1. Line up the 0° line of the protractor with the horizontal line. Put the protractor's cross exactly where the two lines meet.

2. Read off where the line crosses the protractor scale.

3. Use the correct scale — this is an acute angle, so use the scale showing angles less than 90°.

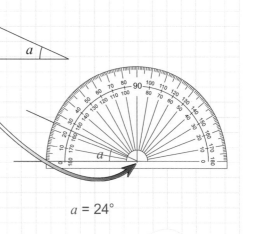

$a = 24°$

Exercise 1

1 In each diagram below, measure the size of the angle and the length of the lines. Give all lengths in mm.

a)

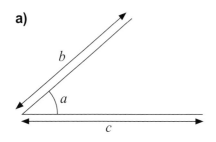

b)

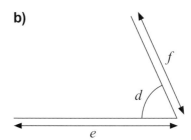

2   In each diagram below, measure the size of the angle and the length of the lines.
Give all lengths in mm.

a)

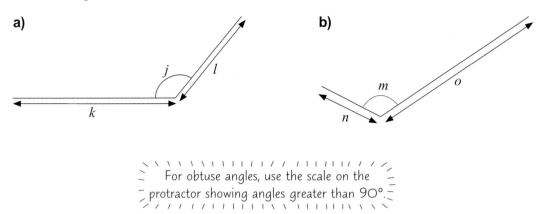

b)

For obtuse angles, use the scale on the
protractor showing angles greater than 90°.

3   Measure all the angles in the triangles below.
Make sure your answers add up to 180°.

a)

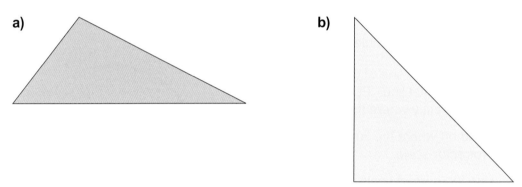

b)

4   Find the angles shown:

a)

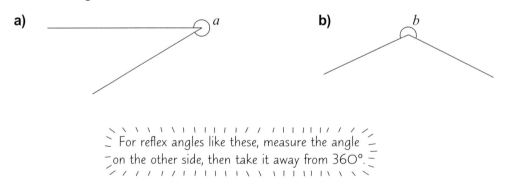

b)

For reflex angles like these, measure the angle
on the other side, then take it away from 360°.

Example 2

Draw an angle of 30°.

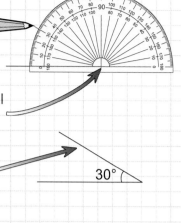

1. Start by drawing a horizontal line.

2. Put the 0° line of the protractor along the horizontal line, with the protractor's cross exactly at one end.

3. Count up the scale from 0° and put a mark at 30°.

4. Take the protractor away and use a ruler to join the mark to the end of the horizontal line.

30°

---

5 Draw angles of the following size:

a) 50°

b) 45°

c) 110°

d) 11°

e) 57°

f) 124°

6 Draw a line 6 cm long.

a) On one end of your line, draw an angle of 70°.

b) On the other end of your line, draw an angle of 30°.

7 Draw a line 8.5 cm long.

a) On one end of your line, draw an angle of 130°.

b) On the other end of your line, draw an angle of 170°.

Given 1 Side and 2 Angles

Example 1

Draw triangle ABC, where:
(i) side AB is 4 cm, (ii) angle BAC is 55°, (iii) angle ABC is 35°.

1. Draw and label the side you know the length of.

2. Use your protractor to draw the first angle.
    Angle BAC is at point A.

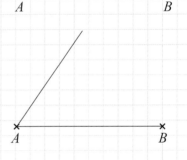

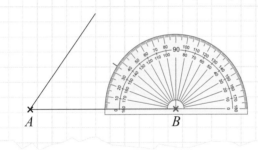

3. Draw the second angle, and complete the triangle.

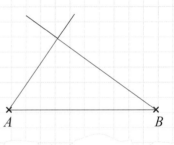

Exercise 1

1   Draw the following triangles accurately, then measure the lengths marked l.

a)
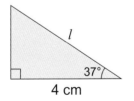

b)
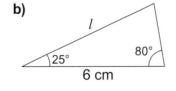

c)
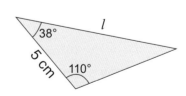

2   Draw an equilateral triangle with sides of length 4 cm.

3   a) Draw each of the triangles ABC described below.

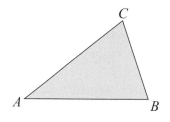

(i) AB = 4 cm, angle BAC = 55°, angle ABC = 35°.

(ii) AB = 8 cm, angle BAC = 22°, angle ABC = 107°.

(iii) AB = 6.5 cm, angle BAC = 65°, angle ABC = 30°.

(iv) AB = 7.2 cm, angle BAC = 120°, angle ABC = 28°.

b) Measure the length of side BC in each of your triangles in part **a)**.

Given 2 Sides and 1 Angle

Example 2

Draw triangle ABC, where: (i) AB is 4 cm, (ii) BC is 3 cm, (iii) angle ABC is 25°.

1. Draw and label the first side you know the length of.

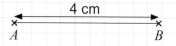

2. Use your protractor to draw the angle you know. C is 3 cm from B along this line.

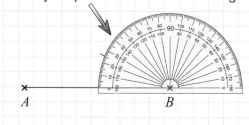

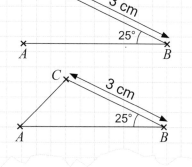

3. Complete the triangle by drawing the line AC.

Exercise 2

1   Draw the following triangles accurately, then measure the lengths marked l.

a)

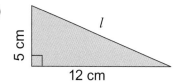

b)

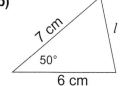

c)

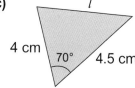

2 a) Draw each of the triangles ABC described below.

   (i) AB = 6 cm, BC = 7 cm, angle ABC = 40°.

   (ii) AB = 4 cm, BC = 3 cm, angle ABC = 110°.

   (iii) AB = 65 mm, BC = 53 mm, angle ABC = 20°.

   (iv) AB = 45 mm, BC = 45 mm, angle ABC = 45°.

   b) Measure the length of side AC in each of your triangles in part **a)**.

3 Draw an isosceles triangle with an angle of 50° between its two 5 cm long sides.

Given 3 Sides

Example 3

Draw triangle ABC, where: (i) AB is 3 cm, (ii) BC is 2.5 cm, (iii) AC is 2 cm.

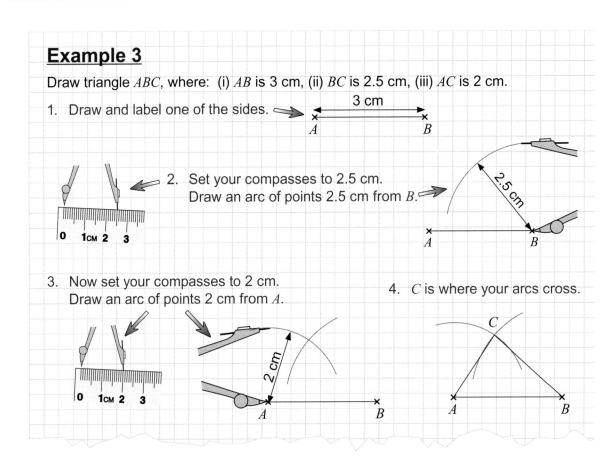

1. Draw and label one of the sides.

2. Set your compasses to 2.5 cm.
    Draw an arc of points 2.5 cm from B.

3. Now set your compasses to 2 cm.
    Draw an arc of points 2 cm from A.

4. C is where your arcs cross.

Exercise 3

1 Draw the following triangles accurately.

a)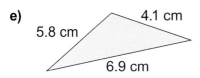

b)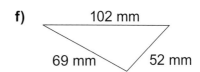

c)

40 mm 88 mm 72 mm

d)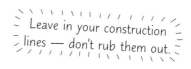

e)

5.8 cm 4.1 cm 6.9 cm

f)

102 mm 69 mm 52 mm

2 Draw each of the triangles ABC described below.

a) AB is 5 cm, BC is 6 cm, AC is 7 cm.

b) AB is 4 cm, BC is 7 cm, AC is 9 cm.

c) AB is 8 cm, BC is 8 cm, AC is 4 cm.

d) AB is 4.6 cm, BC is 5.4 cm, AC is 8.4 cm.

Leave in your construction lines — don't rub them out.

3 Draw an isosceles triangle with two sides of length 5 cm and a side of length 7 cm.

4 Without using a protractor, draw an equilateral triangle of side length 65 mm.

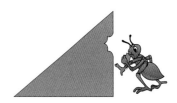

Section 18 — Bearings and Scale Drawings

18.1 Bearings

Compass Directions

A compass has 8 main directions: ⟹

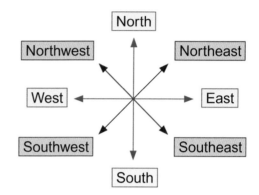

Exercise 1

1 Use your protractor and the diagram above to measure the angle between:

a) North and South

b) South and West

c) North and East

d) East and Southeast

e) Southwest and West

f) North and Southeast

2 **a)** On a square grid, start at the dot as shown and follow these directions, drawing straight lines as you go.

- East 4 squares
- Northeast through 2 squares
- West 3 squares
- North 1 square
- East 2 squares
- Northwest through 3 squares
- Southwest through 3 squares
- East 2 squares
- South 1 square
- West 3 squares
- Southeast through 2 squares

b) What shape have you drawn?

3 Look at the map below.

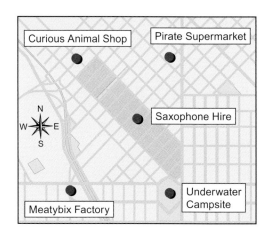

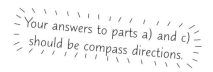

Your answers to parts a) and c) should be compass directions.

a) What direction is the Underwater Campsite from the Pirate Supermarket?

b) What is west of the Underwater Campsite?

c) What direction is the Curious Animal Shop from the Saxophone Hire?

d) What is northeast of the Meatybix Factory?

Bearings

For directions that aren't one of the eight main compass directions, you have to use bearings.

A bearing tells you the direction of one point from another.

Bearings are given as three-figure angles, measured clockwise from north.

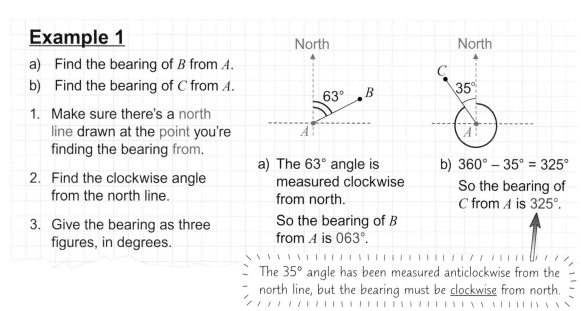

Example 1

a) Find the bearing of B from A.
b) Find the bearing of C from A.

1. Make sure there's a north line drawn at the point you're finding the bearing from.

2. Find the clockwise angle from the north line.

3. Give the bearing as three figures, in degrees.

a) The 63° angle is measured clockwise from north.

So the bearing of B from A is 063°.

b) 360° − 35° = 325°

So the bearing of C from A is 325°.

The 35° angle has been measured anticlockwise from the north line, but the bearing must be clockwise from north.

Exercise 2

1 Draw a diagram of the 8 main compass directions.
Write each of these directions as bearings.

a) East

b) Northeast

c) South

d) West

e) Southwest

f) Northwest

2 Find the bearing of B **from** A in the following.

a)
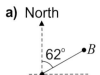

b)
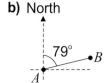

c)
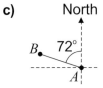

d)

e)

f)
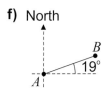

g)
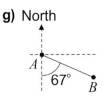

h)
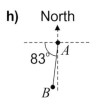

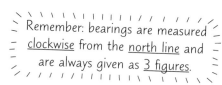

Remember: bearings are measured *clockwise* from the north line and are always given as 3 figures.

3 Find the angle θ in each of the following using the information given.

a) North

C θ D

Bearing of D from C is 111°

b) North

C θ D

Bearing of D from C is 203°

c) North

D θ C

Bearing of D from C is 285°

d)

Bearing of D from C is 243°

e)

Bearing of D from C is 135°

f) North

θ C D

Bearing of D from C is 222°

4 A ship travels in a direction which is 25° north of east. Write this as a bearing.

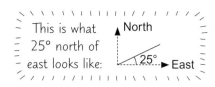

This is what 25° north of east looks like:

5 Mark a point O and draw in a north line.
Use a protractor to help you draw the points **a)** to **f)** with the following bearings from O.

a) 040°

b) 079°

c) 321°

d) 163°

e) 007°

f) 283°

6 Use a protractor to help you find the bearing of the points **a)** to **f)** from X.

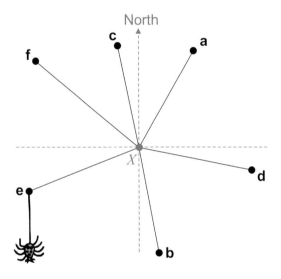

7 Leicester is 100 km south of Doncaster. King's Lynn is 100 km east of Leicester.

a) Sketch the layout of the three locations.

b) Find the bearing of King's Lynn from Leicester.

c) Draw a north line through Doncaster.
Find the bearings from Doncaster of:

(i) Leicester   **(ii)** King's Lynn

d) Draw a north line through King's Lynn.
Find the bearings from King's Lynn of:

(i) Leicester   **(ii)** Doncaster

Example 2

The bearing of X from Y is 244°. Find the bearing of Y from X.

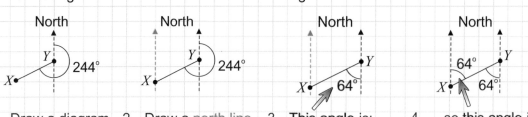

1. Draw a diagram showing what you know.

2. Draw a north line through point X.

3. This angle is:
   $244° - 180° = 64°$...

4. ...so this angle is also 64° (using alternate angles).

So the bearing of Y from X is 064°.

Exercise 3

1 The bearing of B from A is 218°.

    a) Find the size of the angle marked in red on the diagram.

    b) Use alternate angles to find another angle in the diagram the same size as the one in part **a)**.

    c) Find the bearing of A from B.

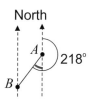

2 The bearing of D from C is 125°.

    a) Use alternate angles to find another angle of 125°.

    b) Find the bearing of C from D.

3 The bearing of F from E is 310°. Find the bearing of E from F.

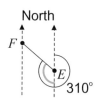

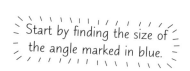

Start by finding the size of the angle marked in blue.

4 The bearing of H from G is 023°.

    a) Draw a diagram showing H and G.

    b) Find the bearing of G from H.

5 The point Q lies west of point P.

   a) Write down the bearing of Q from P.

   b) Write down the bearing of P from Q.

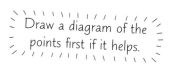
Draw a diagram of the points first if it helps.

6 The bearing of K from J is 101°. Find the bearing of J from K.

7 Find the bearing of N from M given that the bearing of M from N is:

   a) 200°   **b)** 310°   **c)** 080°

   d) 117°   **e)** 015°   **f)** 099°

8 The point Z lies southeast of the point Y.
    Find the bearing of Y from Z.

18.2 Scale Drawings

Scales with Units

Maps and plans always have a scale on them.

   E.g. A map scale of 1 cm : 100 m means that 1 cm on the map
      represents an actual distance of 100 m.

Example 1

A plan of a garden is drawn to a scale of 1 cm : 5 m.

   a) The distance between two trees
       is measured on the plan as 3 cm.
       What is the actual distance
       between the trees? ⟶ ×3 ⎧ 1 cm represents 5 m ⎫ ×3
                                    ⎩ 3 cm represents 15 m ⎭

   b) The actual distance between the garden
       shed and pond is measured as 2.5 m.
       What would the distance between the   ÷ 2 ⎧ 5 m is shown as 1 cm ⎫ ÷ 2
       shed and pond be on the plan? ⟶   ⎩ 2.5 m is shown as 0.5 cm ⎭

Exercise 1

1 A map scale is given as 2 cm : 1 km.

   a) Convert these lengths on the map to actual distances:

      (i) 4 cm   **(ii)** 6 cm

      (iii) 22 cm   **(iv)** 50 cm

      (v) 1 cm   **(vi)** 0.5 cm

   b) Convert these actual distances to lengths on the map:

      (i) 4 km   **(ii)** 8 km

      (iii) 14 km   **(iv)** 3.5 km

      (v) 5 km   **(vi)** 0.1 km

2 An atlas uses a scale of 1 cm : 100 km.
Find the actual distances represented by these lengths in the atlas:

   a) 7 cm   **b)** 11 cm

   c) 20 cm   **d)** 1.5 cm

   e) 0.5 cm   **f)** 0.75 cm

3 The scale on a map of Europe is 1 cm : 50 km.
Find the lengths used on the map to represent these actual distances:

   a) 150 km   **b)** 600 km

   c) 1000 km   **d)** 25 km

   e) 10 km   **f)** 5 km

4 The floor plan of a house is drawn to a scale of 1 cm : 2 m.
Find the actual dimensions of the rooms if they are given on the plan as:

   a) 2 cm by 3 cm

   b) 4.5 cm by 7.25 cm

   c) 3.2 cm by 1.4 cm

5 The distance from Madrid to Malaga is shown on a map as 8 cm.
The scale on the map is 1 cm : 50 km.

What is the actual distance from Madrid to Malaga?

6 The distance from Thenford to Syresham is 10 km.
This is shown on a map with a scale of 1 cm : 4 km.

a) How far apart will the villages be shown on the map?

b) The same map shows the distance from Chacombe to Badby as 1.5 cm.
What is the actual distance between these two villages?

7 You are asked to draw up the plans for a building using the scale 1 cm : 0.5 m.
Find the lengths you should draw on the plan to represent these actual distances.

a) 4 m

b) 18 m

c) 21 m

8 A map has a scale 1 cm : 0.5 km.

a) A street of length 0.75 km is to be drawn on the map.
What length will the street appear on the map?

b) What is the length of a street which has a length of 4.8 cm on the map?

9 Below is the plan for a kitchen surface.

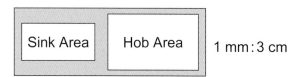

1 mm : 3 cm

Measure the lengths and widths on the plan to find the actual lengths and widths of:

a) the sink area

b) the hob area

Scales Without Units

A scale without units (e.g. 1:100) means you can use any units — but you must put the same units on both sides. For example, 1 cm:100 cm or 1 mm:100 mm.

Example 2

A map uses a scale of 1:200. What is the actual distance (in metres) between two points which are 35 cm apart on the map?

1. Write the scale down using centimetres, to match the units given in the question. ⟶ 1 cm:200 cm

2. Multiply both sides of the scale by the same number. ⟶ ×35 ⟨ 1 cm represents 200 cm ⟩ ×35
    35 cm represents 7000 cm

3. Give your answer using the correct units.   So the actual distance is 7000 cm.
    This is 7000 ÷ 100 = 70 m

Exercise 2

1 A map scale is given as 1:100.
Convert these lengths on the map to actual distances.
Leave your answers in cm.

  a) 4 cm   **b)** 7 cm   **c)** 12 cm

  d) 5.5 cm   **e)** 9.5 cm   **f)** 6.2 cm

2 A plan uses the scale 1:75.
Find the actual distances represented by these lengths from the plan.
Give your answers in cm.

  a) 4 cm   **b)** 11 cm   **c)** 5.5 cm

  d) 8.6 cm   **e)** 24.2 cm   **f)** 1.3 cm

3 Toy furniture is made using a scale of 1:40.
Find the dimensions of the actual furniture when the toys have these measurements:

  a) Height of wardrobe: 5 cm

  b) Width of bed: 3.5 cm

  c) Length of table: 3.2 cm

  d) Height of chair: 2.4 cm

4 The scale of a plan is given as 1 : 350.

    a) Convert these lengths on the plan to actual distances.
    Give your answers in metres.

        (i) 2 cm   **(ii)** 10 cm

        (iii) 6 cm   **(iv)** 5 cm

        (v) 21 cm   **(vi)** 25.5 cm

    b) Convert the following actual distances to lengths on the plan.
    Give your answers in cm.

        (i) 70 m

        (ii) 87.5 m

        (iii) 17.5 m

5 A road of length 10 km is to be drawn on a map.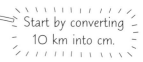
The scale of the map is 1 : 250 000.

    How long will the road be on the map? Give your answer in cm.

Start by converting
10 km into cm.

6 A model railway uses a scale of 1 : 500.
Use the actual measurements given below to find measurements for each model.
Give your answers in cm.

    a) Length of carriage: 20 m

    b) Height of coal tower: 30 m

    c) Length of footbridge: 100 m

    d) Height of signal box: 6 m

7 A map uses the scale 1 : 10 000.
Find the actual distances in metres represented by these lengths from the map.

    a) 5.4 cm

    b) 8.1 cm

    c) 13.6 cm

Scale Drawings

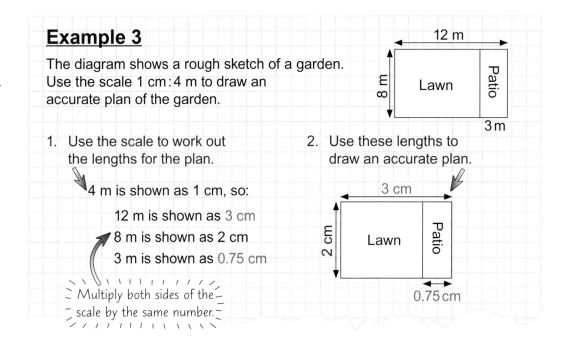

Example 3

The diagram shows a rough sketch of a garden.
Use the scale 1 cm : 4 m to draw an
accurate plan of the garden.

1. Use the scale to work out
   the lengths for the plan.

   4 m is shown as 1 cm, so:

   12 m is shown as 3 cm

   8 m is shown as 2 cm

   3 m is shown as 0.75 cm

   *Multiply both sides of the
   scale by the same number.*

2. Use these lengths to
   draw an accurate plan.

Exercise 3

1   Use the scale 1 cm : 2 m to draw accurate scale drawings of the shapes below:

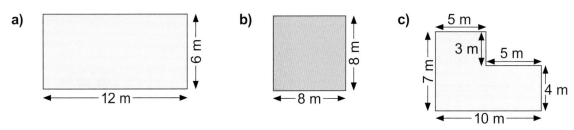

a)   12 m, 6 m

b)   8 m, 8 m

c)   5 m, 3 m, 5 m, 7 m, 4 m, 10 m

2   A sketch of the floor plan for a squash court is shown below.
Use the scale 1 cm : 0.5 m to draw an accurate plan of the court.

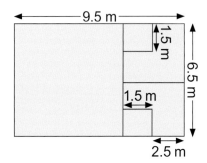

3 Brad makes a sketch of part of his kitchen, as shown on the right.

Draw an accurate plan of the kitchen using the scale 1:20.

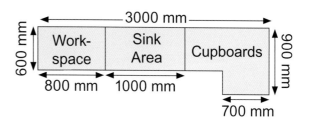

Example 1

The points P and Q are a distance of 75 km apart.
Q lies on a bearing of 055° from P.
Use the scale 1 cm:25 km to draw an accurate scale diagram of P and Q.

1. Draw a north line from P and measure the required bearing.

2. Use the scale to work out the distance between the two points:

    25 km is shown by 1 cm, so 75 km is shown by 3 cm.

3. Draw Q the correct distance and direction from P.

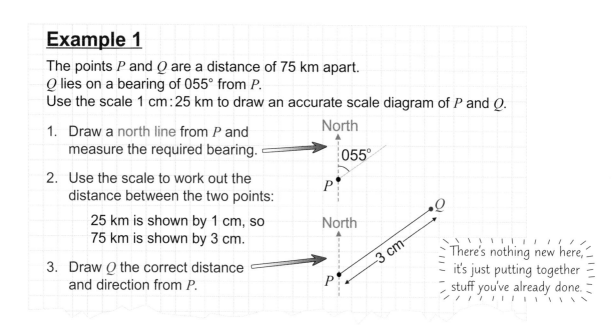

There's nothing new here, it's just putting together stuff you've already done.

Exercise 1

1 Town A is 14 km north of Town B, which is 14 km east of Town C.

Find the bearing of:

a) Town B from Town A

b) Town C from Town B

c) Town C from Town A

2 a) Find the bearing of V from U.

b) Find the bearing of U from V.

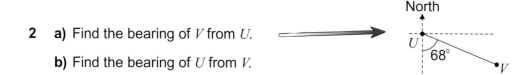

3 A rough map of part of Europe is shown below.

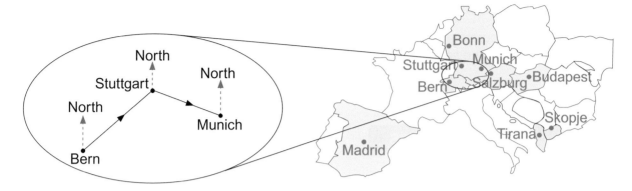

a) Part of the map has been enlarged, and drawn using a scale of 1 cm : 100 km.
Use a ruler and protractor to find the distance and bearings of these journeys:

i) Bern to Stuttgart

ii) Stuttgart to Munich

b) Skopje is 150 km from Tirana, on a bearing of 048°.
Draw an accurate scale diagram of Skopje and Tirana using the scale 1 cm : 30 km.

c) Salzburg lies 540 km from Bonn, on a bearing of 125°.
Draw an accurate scale diagram of the two locations using the scale 1 cm : 90 km.

d) A pilot flies 2000 km from Budapest to Madrid, on a bearing of 242°.
Draw an accurate scale diagram of the journey using the scale 1 cm : 200 km.

4 Below is a sketch of a park lake.

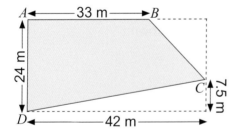

a) Draw an accurate plan of the lake using the scale 1 : 300.

b) There is a duck house at the intersection of AC and BD.
Find the actual distance from the duck house to point B.
Give your answer to 1 d.p.

5 The diagram below shows an accurate scale plan of a walk, starting and finishing at The Knott.

The scale is 1 cm : 1 km.

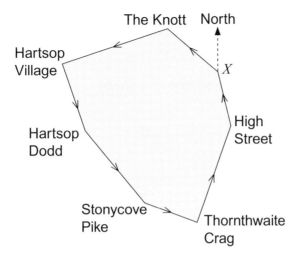

a) Measure the distances on the diagram to find:

   (i) the actual distance between Hartsop Village and The Knott,

   (ii) the total length of the walk.

Point X lies between High Street and The Knott.

b) What bearing should a walker take at X to make sure they get back to the Knott?

6 A boat sails on a bearing of 055° for 2000 m.
It then changes course and sails on a bearing of 100° for 1500 m.

a) Draw a scale diagram of the boat's journey.
Use the scale 1 cm : 500 m.

The boat returns directly to its starting point.

Use your scale diagram to find the following:

b) the direct return distance

c) the bearing of the return journey

Section 19 — Area and Perimeter

19.1 Area and Perimeter Basics

Perimeter

Perimeter is the total distance around the outside of a shape.

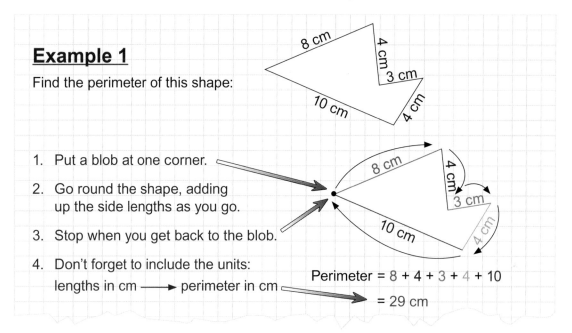

Example 1

Find the perimeter of this shape:

1. Put a blob at one corner.

2. Go round the shape, adding up the side lengths as you go.

3. Stop when you get back to the blob.

4. Don't forget to include the units:
   lengths in cm ⟶ perimeter in cm

Perimeter = 8 + 4 + 3 + 4 + 10

= 29 cm

Exercise 1

1 Find the perimeter of each shape below.

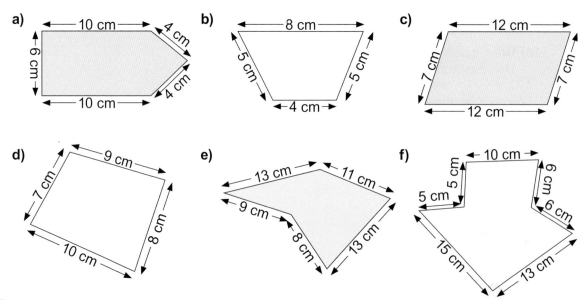

Area

Area is the total amount of space inside a shape.

Example 2

This tile has an area of 1 cm²:

Find the area of this shape made from identical tiles.

1. The shape is made from six tiles.

2. Each tile has an area of 1 cm².
   So work out the area of the shape.

3. Make sure you include the units.

1	2	3
4	5	6

Area of shape = 6 × 1
= 6 cm²

Areas have 'squared' units.
So the area of this shape is
"6 centimetres squared".

Exercise 2

1 The shapes below are made from tiles which have an area of 1 cm².
Find the area of each shape.

a)

b)

c)

d)

e)

f)

Exercise 3 — Mixed Exercise

1 The shapes below are made from square tiles which
have a side length of 1 cm and an area of 1 cm².

1 cm

Area = 1 cm²

For each shape below, find **(i)** its perimeter **(ii)** its area

a)

b)

c)

Remember — perimeter is the total
distance around the <u>outside</u> of a shape.

19.2 Squares and Rectangles

Perimeter

There are formulas for finding the perimeter of a square or a rectangle.

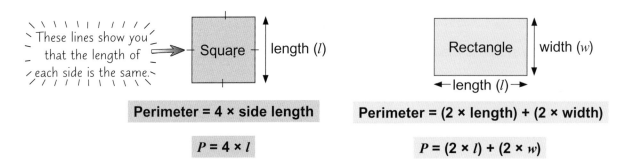

These lines show you that the length of each side is the same.

Square — length (*l*)

Perimeter = 4 × side length

$P = 4 \times l$

Rectangle — width (*w*)

←length (*l*)→

Perimeter = (2 × length) + (2 × width)

$P = (2 \times l) + (2 \times w)$

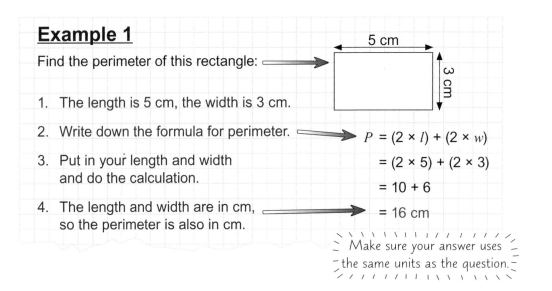

Example 1

Find the perimeter of this rectangle:

5 cm

3 cm

1. The length is 5 cm, the width is 3 cm.

2. Write down the formula for perimeter.

3. Put in your length and width and do the calculation.

4. The length and width are in cm, so the perimeter is also in cm.

$P = (2 \times l) + (2 \times w)$
$= (2 \times 5) + (2 \times 3)$
$= 10 + 6$
$= 16$ cm

Make sure your answer uses the same units as the question.

Exercise 1

1   Find the perimeter of each shape below.

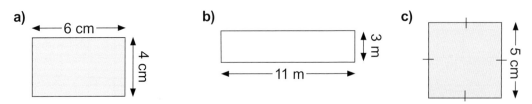

a)

←6 cm→

4 cm

b)

3 m

←11 m→

c)

5 cm

2 Find the perimeter of each shape below.

a)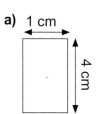
1 cm
4 cm

b)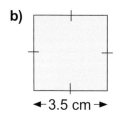
3.5 cm

c)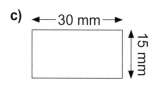
30 mm
15 mm

d)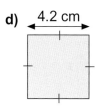
4.2 cm

e)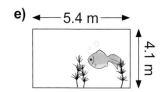
5.4 m
4.1 m

f)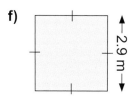
2.9 m

Area

There are also formulas for finding the area of a square or a rectangle.

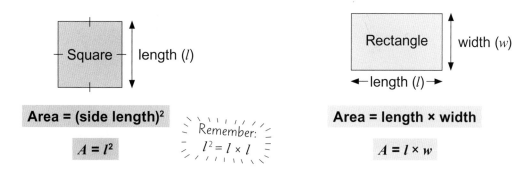

Square — length (l)

Area = (side length)²

$A = l^2$

Remember:
$l^2 = l \times l$

Rectangle — width (w) — length (l)

Area = length × width

$A = l \times w$

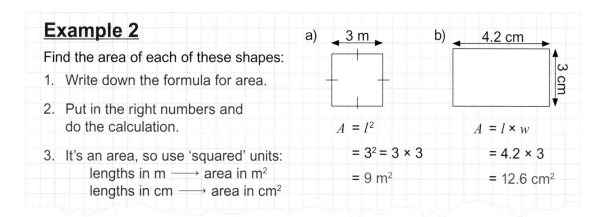

Example 2

Find the area of each of these shapes:

1. Write down the formula for area.

2. Put in the right numbers and do the calculation.

3. It's an area, so use 'squared' units:
   lengths in m ⟶ area in m²
   lengths in cm ⟶ area in cm²

a) 3 m

$A = l^2$

$= 3^2 = 3 \times 3$

$= 9 \ m^2$

b) 4.2 cm
3 cm

$A = l \times w$

$= 4.2 \times 3$

$= 12.6 \ cm^2$

Exercise 2

1 Find the area of each shape below.

a)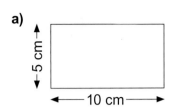

b)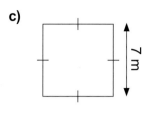

c)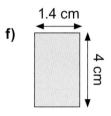

d)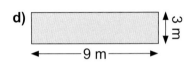

e)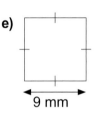

f)

1.4 cm

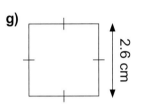

g)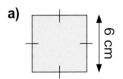

h)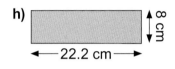

i)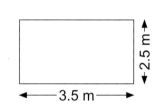

Exercise 3 — Mixed Exercise

1 For each shape described below, find: **(i)** its perimeter, **(ii)** its area.

   a) a square with sides of length 4 cm.

   b) a rectangle of width 6 m and length 8 m.

   c) a rectangle 23 mm long and 15 mm wide.

   d) a square with 17 m sides.

   e) a rectangle 22.2 m long and 4 m wide.

   f) a rectangle of length 9 mm and width 2.4 mm.

2 For each shape below, find: **(i)** its perimeter, **(ii)** its area.

a)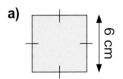

b)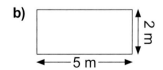

c)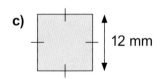

3 For each shape below, find: **(i)** its perimeter, **(ii)** its area.

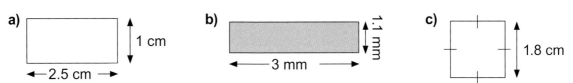

a)

1 cm

2.5 cm

b)

1.1 mm

3 mm

c)

1.8 cm

4 Barbara has a rectangular lawn 23 m long by 17 m wide.
She is going to mow the lawn and then put fencing around the outside.

a) What area will Barbara have to mow?

b) How much fencing will she need?

Composite Shapes

A composite shape is one that's made out of simpler shapes joined together.

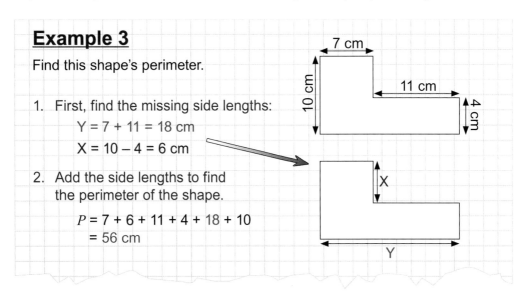

Example 3

Find this shape's perimeter.

1. First, find the missing side lengths:
   Y = 7 + 11 = 18 cm
   X = 10 − 4 = 6 cm

2. Add the side lengths to find
   the perimeter of the shape.

   P = 7 + 6 + 11 + 4 + 18 + 10
   = 56 cm

7 cm

10 cm

11 cm

4 cm

X

Y

Exercise 4

1 Find the perimeter of each shape below:

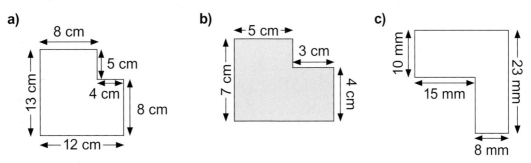

a)

8 cm

13 cm

5 cm

4 cm

8 cm

12 cm

b)

5 cm

7 cm

3 cm

4 cm

c)

10 mm

15 mm

23 mm

8 mm

Example 4

Find the area of the shape in Example 3.

1. Split the shape into rectangles A and B, and find their areas:

   Area of rectangle A = 10 × 7
   = 70 cm²

   Area of rectangle B = 11 × 4
   = 44 cm²

2. Add together the areas of A and B to find the total area of the shape.

Total area of shape = 70 + 44
= 114 cm²

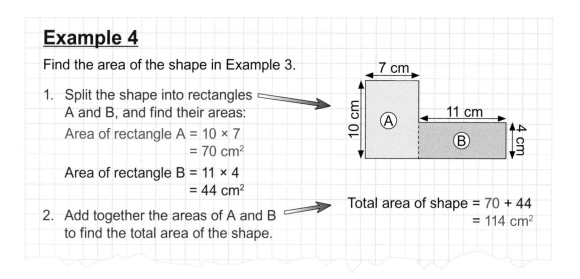

2 Find the area of each shape below.

a)

b)

c)

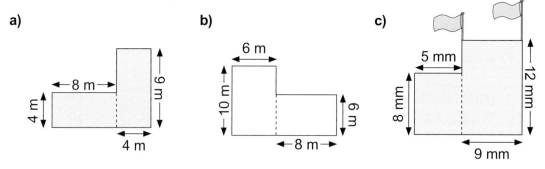

3 For each shape below, find: **(i)** its perimeter, **(ii)** its area.

a)

Remember to find any missing side lengths first.

b)

c)

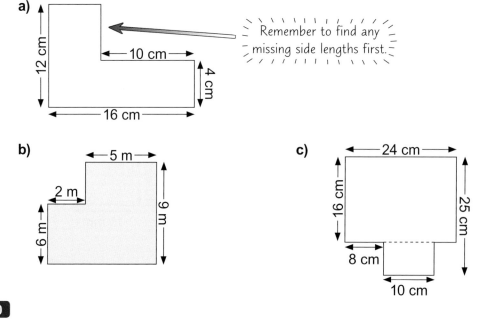

Perimeter

This is the formula for the perimeter of a triangle.

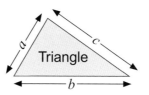

Triangle

Perimeter (P) = a + b + c

Example 1

Find the perimeter of each shape:

1. Write down the formula for perimeter.
2. Put in the values of a, b and c, then do the calculation.

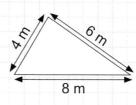

$P = a + b + c$

$= 4 + 8 + 6$

$= 18$ m

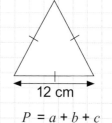

$P = a + b + c$

$= 12 + 12 + 12$

$= 36$ cm

Exercise 1

1 Find the perimeter of each triangle.

a)
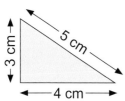

b)

c)
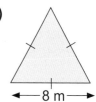

d)
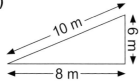

e)
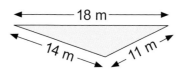

f)
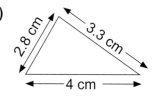

g)
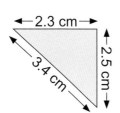

h)
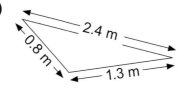

i)
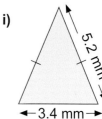

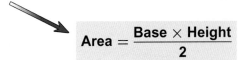

Area of Right-angled Triangles

This is the formula for the area of a triangle.

$$\text{Area} = \frac{\text{Base} \times \text{Height}}{2}$$

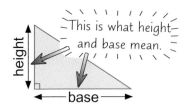

This is what height and base mean.

height

base

Example 2

What is the area of this triangle?

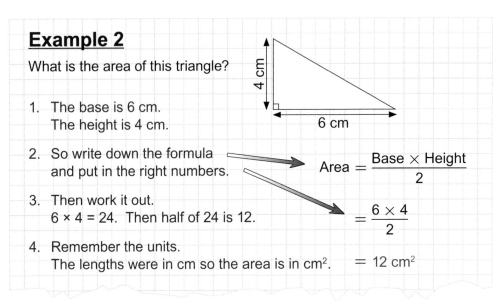

4 cm

6 cm

1. The base is 6 cm.
    The height is 4 cm.

2. So write down the formula
    and put in the right numbers.

$$\text{Area} = \frac{\text{Base} \times \text{Height}}{2}$$

3. Then work it out.
    6 × 4 = 24. Then half of 24 is 12.

$$= \frac{6 \times 4}{2}$$

4. Remember the units.
    The lengths were in cm so the area is in cm².

$$= 12 \text{ cm}^2$$

Exercise 2

1   Work out the area of each triangle.

Don't worry if your answer is a decimal.

a)

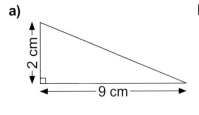

2 cm

9 cm

b)

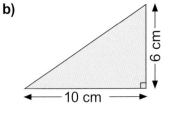

6 cm

10 cm

c)

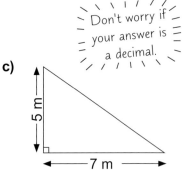

5 m

7 m

d)

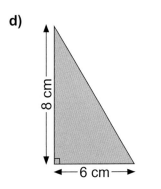

8 cm

6 cm

e)

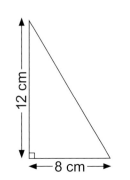

12 cm

8 cm

f)

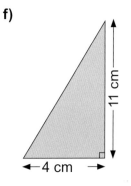

11 cm

4 cm

Example 3

What is the area of this triangle?

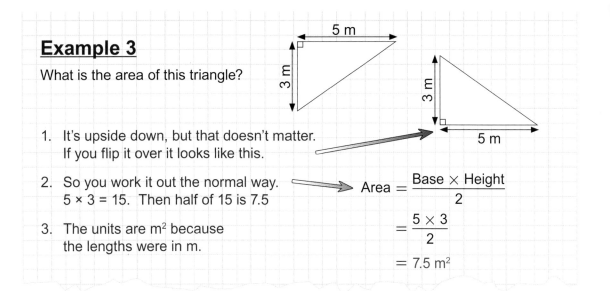

1. It's upside down, but that doesn't matter.
    If you flip it over it looks like this.

2. So you work it out the normal way.
    5 × 3 = 15. Then half of 15 is 7.5

3. The units are m² because
    the lengths were in m.

$$\text{Area} = \frac{\text{Base} \times \text{Height}}{2}$$

$$= \frac{5 \times 3}{2}$$

$$= 7.5 \text{ m}^2$$

Exercise 3

1   Work out the area of each triangle.

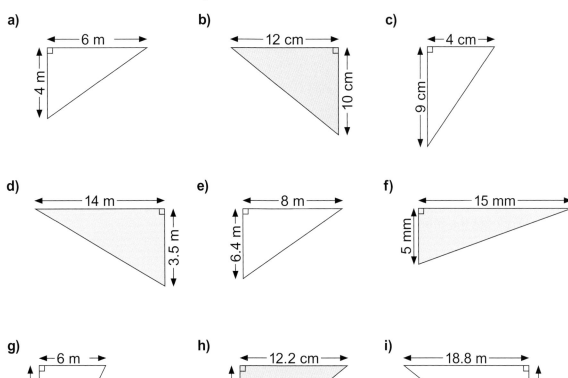

a)

6 m

4 m

b)

12 cm

10 cm

c)

4 cm

9 cm

d)

14 m

3.5 m

e)

8 m

6.4 m

f)

15 mm

5 mm

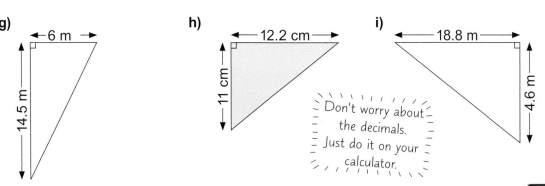

g)

6 m

14.5 m

h)

12.2 cm

11 cm

i)

18.8 m

4.6 m

Don't worry about the decimals. Just do it on your calculator.

More Area of a Triangle

The base and height of a triangle are always at right angles to each other.

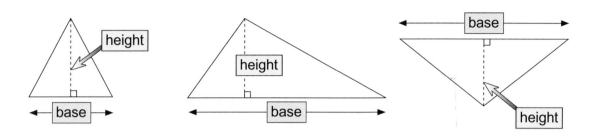

Example 4

Calculate the area of this triangle.

1. The height you need is 5 m.
   The base of the triangle is 10 m.

2. Use the same formula as always.
   10 × 5 = 50.
   Then half of 50 gives 25.

3. As ever, don't forget the units.

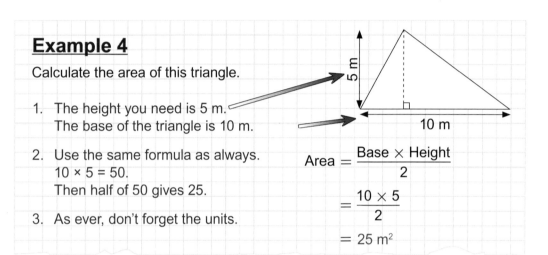

$$\text{Area} = \frac{\text{Base} \times \text{Height}}{2}$$

$$= \frac{10 \times 5}{2}$$

$$= 25 \text{ m}^2$$

Exercise 4

1   Work out the area of each triangle.

a)
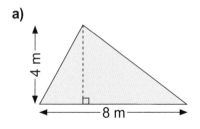

b)
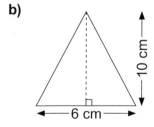

c)
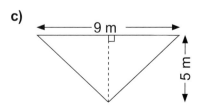

d)
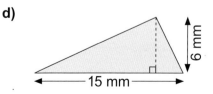

2 Work out the area of each triangle.

a)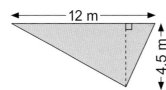

b)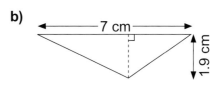

c)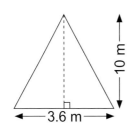

d)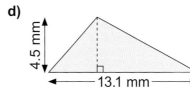

e)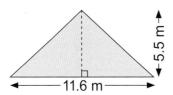

Composite Shapes

Example 5

Find the area of this shape.

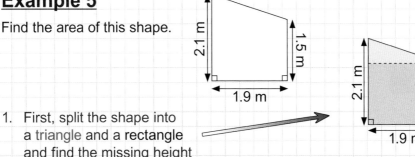

1. First, split the shape into a triangle and a rectangle and find the missing height of the triangle: 2.1 − 1.5 = 0.6 m

2. Use the formula to find the area of the triangle.

3. Now find the area of the rectangle.

4. Add together the two areas to find the area of the whole shape:

$$\text{Area of triangle} = \frac{\text{Base} \times \text{Height}}{2}$$
$$= \frac{1.9 \times 0.6}{2} = 0.57 \, \text{m}^2$$

Area of rectangle = 1.9 × 1.5
$$= 2.85 \, \text{m}^2$$

0.57 + 2.85 = 3.42 m²

Exercise 5

1 Work out the shaded area in each diagram.

a)

b)

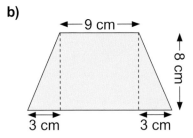

c)

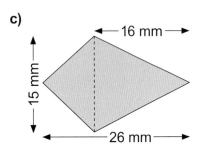

d)

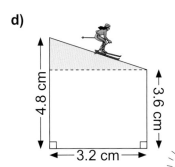

Ignore the squares
and just find the
areas of the triangles
in d), e) and f).

e)

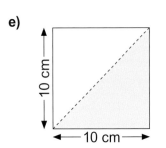

f)

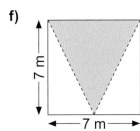

Diameter and Radius

The diameter of a circle is the length right across the circle,
going through the centre.

The radius is the length halfway across, measured from the centre.

The diameter of a circle is always twice as long as the radius:

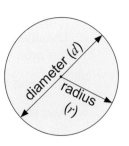

Diameter = 2 × Radius

$$d = 2 \times r$$

Example 1

Find: a) the diameter of this circle,
b) the perimeter of the square surrounding the circle.

a) diameter

The radius of the circle is 4 cm.
Use the formula to find the
diameter of the circle.

$d = 2 \times r$
$= 2 \times 4$
$= 8$ cm

b) perimeter

1. The length of each edge of the square will
be the same as the diameter of the circle.

2. So use $l = 8$ cm in the formula for the
perimeter of a square.

$P = 4 \times l$
$= 4 \times 8$
$= 32$ cm

Exercise 1

1 Find the diameter of each circle below.

a)

b)

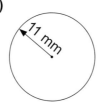

c)

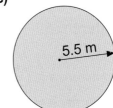

2 Find the radius of each circle below.

a)

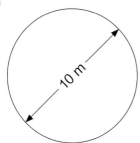

b)

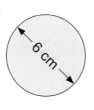

c)

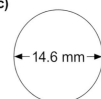

3 What is the diameter of a circle with radius 3 cm?

4 What is the radius of a circle with diameter 4 m?

5 A rectangle is drawn around two identical circles, as shown.

   a) Write down the length and width of the rectangle.

   b) What is the perimeter of the rectangle?

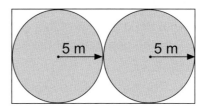

6 A square is drawn around four identical circles, as shown.

   a) Find the perimeter of the square.

   b) Find the area of the square.

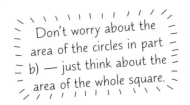

Don't worry about the area of the circles in part b) — just think about the area of the whole square.

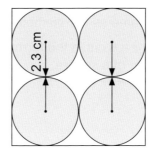

Circumference

The circumference (C) is the distance around the outside of a circle.

The circumference of a circle can be found using the formula:

Circumference = π × diameter

$$C = \pi \times d$$

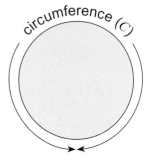

This symbol (called "pi") stands for the number 3.14159265...

Example 2

Find the circumference of the circle shown.
Give your answer to the nearest whole number.

1. Write down the diameter.

2. Use the formula $C = \pi \times d$.

3. Round your answer, and use the correct units.

Most calculators have a button for π. If yours doesn't, use the value 3.142

d = 8 cm

$C = \pi \times d$

$C = 3.142 \times 8$

$C = 25.136$

$C = 25$ cm (to nearest whole number)

Example 3

Find the circumference of a circle which has radius 6 m.
Give your answer to 1 decimal place.

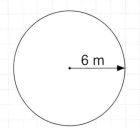

1. Use $d = 2 \times r$ to find the diameter.

$d = 2 \times r$
$d = 2 \times 6$
$d = 12$ m

2. Use the formula $C = \pi \times d$ to find the circumference.

$C = \pi \times d$
$C = 3.142 \times 12$
$C = 37.7$ m (to 1 d.p.)

Exercise 2

1 Find the circumference of each circle below.
Give your answers to the nearest whole number.

a)

6 cm

b)

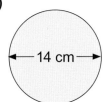

14 cm

c)

10 cm

d)

7 m

e)

5 mm

f)

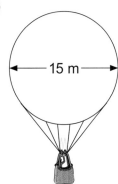

15 m

g)

2 cm

h)

9 cm

2 For each circle below, write down the diameter and then find its circumference. Give your answers to 1 decimal place.

a)

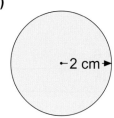

←2 cm→

b)

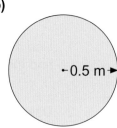

←0.5 m→

c)

2.5 cm

d)

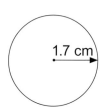

1.7 cm

e)

2.6 m

f)

1.3 mm

3 Find the circumference of the circles with the diameter (d) or radius (r) given below. Give your answers to 1 decimal place.

a) d = 4 cm

b) d = 8 mm

c) d = 9 m

d) d = 6 cm

e) r = 11 m

f) r = 22 cm

g) r = 13 m

h) r = 35 mm

i) d = 2.5 m

4 Find the circumference of a circular coin with diameter 8.3 mm. Give your answer to 1 d.p.

5 A circular field has radius 12 m. Find the circumference of the field to the nearest m.

Bits of Circles

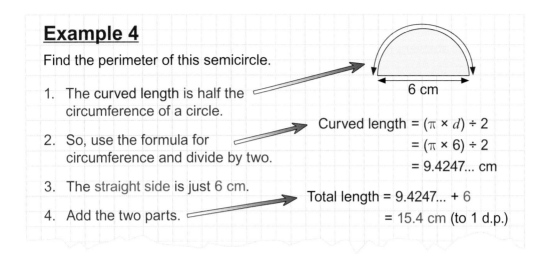

Example 4

Find the perimeter of this semicircle.

1. The curved length is half the circumference of a circle.

2. So, use the formula for circumference and divide by two.

3. The straight side is just 6 cm.

4. Add the two parts.

6 cm

Curved length = (π × d) ÷ 2
= (π × 6) ÷ 2
= 9.4247... cm

Total length = 9.4247... + 6
= 15.4 cm (to 1 d.p.)

Exercise 3

1 Find the perimeter of each shape below. Give your answers to 1 decimal place.

a)

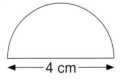

4 cm

b)

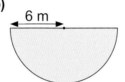

6 m

c)

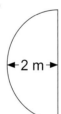

2 m

d)

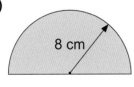

8 cm

e)

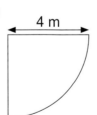

4 m

f)

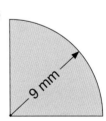

9 mm

2 A lake is in the shape of a quarter-circle. How long would a footpath around the lake be? Give your answer to the nearest m.

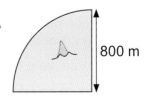

800 m

19.5 Area and Perimeter Problems

Exercise 1

Give any non-exact answers to 1 decimal place, unless told otherwise.

1 Find the area of the shapes below by splitting them into a rectangle and a triangle.

a)
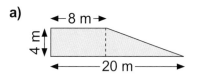

b)
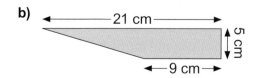

2 A circular table mat has a radius of 10 cm. What is the diameter of the mat?

3 Find the circumference of this circular cake.

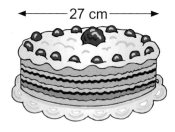

4 What is the circumference of this badge?

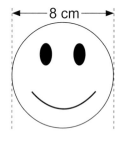

5 Find the shaded area in this shape. ⟶

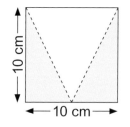

6 The police need to cordon off and then search a rectangular crime scene measuring 2.1 m by 2.8 m.

a) What area do the police need to search?

b) What is the perimeter of the crime scene?

7   A circular pond has a diameter of 84 cm.
What is the circumference of the pond to the nearest cm?

8   Find the perimeter and area of an equilateral
triangle with base 6 cm and height 5.2 cm.

9   Frank is painting the side of his shed, shown on the right.
What is the total area he needs to paint?

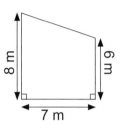

10 Which of the two shapes below has the longest perimeter?

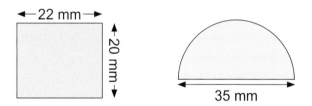

11 The rectangle below contains three circles of radius 3 cm.

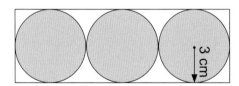

   a) Find the perimeter of the rectangle.

   b) Find the area of the rectangle.

12 A circular volcanic crater has a radius of 5.7 km.
Kate and William walked all the way around the outside. How far did they walk?

13 Find the shaded area of the shape below.

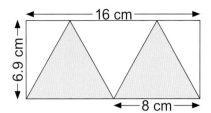

14 The shape below is made from a semicircle on top of a rectangle.
Find the perimeter of the shape.

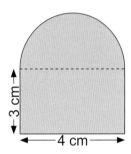

15 A rectangular garden 24 m long and 5 m wide is to be turfed.
Turf is bought in rolls that are 1 m wide and 8 m long.

   a) What is the area of the garden?

   b) What is the area of one roll of turf?

   c) How many rolls will be needed to turf the garden?

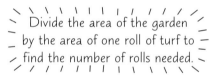

Divide the area of the garden by the area of one roll of turf to find the number of rolls needed.

16 Ali bakes the cake shown below.

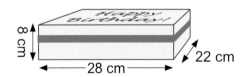

   a) What length of ribbon is needed to go around the outside of the cake?

   b) If the top and the four sides are to be iced, what area of icing will be needed?

Section 20 — 3D Shapes

20.1 Volume of Cubes and Cuboids

Volume (V) is the amount of space inside a 3D shape.

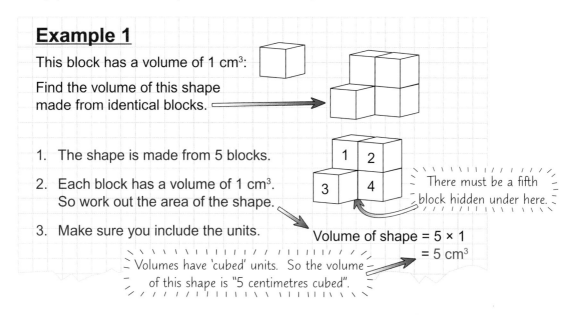

Example 1

This block has a volume of 1 cm³:

Find the volume of this shape made from identical blocks.

1. The shape is made from 5 blocks.

2. Each block has a volume of 1 cm³. So work out the area of the shape.

3. Make sure you include the units.

There must be a fifth block hidden under here.

Volume of shape = 5 × 1
= 5 cm³

Volumes have 'cubed' units. So the volume of this shape is "5 centimetres cubed".

Exercise 1

1 The following shapes are made from blocks which have a volume of **1 cm³**.
By counting blocks, find the volume of each shape.

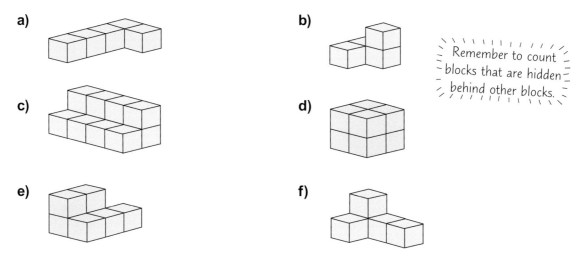

a)

b)

Remember to count blocks that are hidden behind other blocks.

c)

d)

e)

f)

2 A shape is made from eight 1 cm³ cubes.
What is the shape's volume?

3 How many 1 m³ cubes would be needed to make a shape of volume 31 m³?

The formulas for the volume of a cube and a cuboid are:

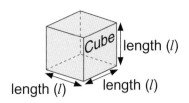

length (*l*)
length (*l*)
length (*l*)

Volume = (edge length)³

$$V = l^3$$

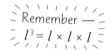

Remember —
$l^3 = l \times l \times l$

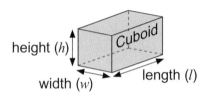

height (*h*)
width (*w*)
length (*l*)

Volume = length × width × height

$$V = l \times w \times h$$

Example 2

Find the volume of a cube with edge length 4 cm:

4 cm
4 cm   4 cm

1. Write down the formula for volume.

2. Put in the right number for the edge length and do the calculation.

$$V = l^3$$
$$= 4^3 = 4 \times 4 \times 4$$

3. It's a volume, so use 'cubed' units:
   lengths in cm ⟶ volume in cm³

$$= 64 \text{ cm}^3$$

Example 3

Find the volume of this cuboid.

3 m
2 m   5 m

1. Write down the formula for volume.

2. Put in the right numbers and do the calculation.

$$V = l \times w \times h$$
$$= 5 \times 2 \times 3$$

3. It's a volume, so use 'cubed' units:
   lengths in m ⟶ volume in m³

$$= 30 \text{ m}^3$$

Exercise 2

1 **a)** Find the volume of a cube-shaped box with edge length 3 cm.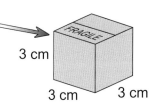

b) How many 1 cm³ cubes can be put in the box?

3 cm

3 cm   3 cm

2 How many 1 cm³ cubes can be put in a box measuring
10 cm × 10 cm × 10 cm?

3 Find the volume of each cube below.

a)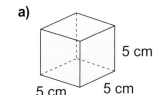

5 cm

5 cm   5 cm

b)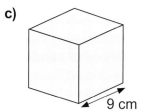

8 cm

8 cm   8 cm

c)

9 cm

4 Find the volume of each cuboid below.

a)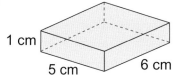

1 cm

5 cm   6 cm

b)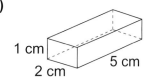

1 cm

2 cm   5 cm

```
\ \ \ \ | | | / / / /
Make sure your answer
has the correct units.
/ / / | | | \ \ \ \
```

c)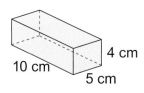

4 cm

10 cm

5 cm

d)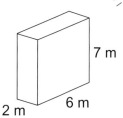

7 m

2 m   6 m

e)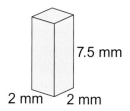

7.5 mm

2 mm   2 mm

f)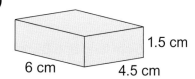

1.5 cm

6 cm   4.5 cm

5 Find the volumes of the cuboids with the following dimensions.

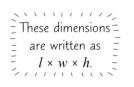
These dimensions are written as $l \times w \times h$.

a) 1 cm × 2 cm × 3 cm

b) 3 cm × 2 cm × 4 cm

c) 5 m × 2 m × 7 m

d) 20 cm × 10 cm × 8 cm

e) 2.5 cm × 3.0 cm × 4.2 cm

f) 18 m × 14 m × 3 m

g) 2 mm × 13 mm × 5 mm

h) 1.8 mm × 3.2 mm × 6 mm

Exercise 3

1 Box A measures 1 m × 3 m × 4 m. Box B measures 2 m × 2 m × 4 m. Which box has the greater volume?

2 Will 3.5 m³ of sand fit in a cuboid-shaped box with dimensions 2 m × 1.5 m × 1.5 m?

3 24 cubes with edges of length 6 cm fit exactly in a tray of depth 6 cm, as shown.

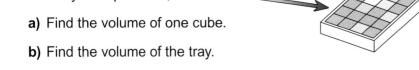

a) Find the volume of one cube.

b) Find the volume of the tray.

4 A cereal box is 9 cm long, 23 cm wide and 32 cm high. The box is half-full of cereal.

What is the volume of cereal in the box?

5 A bath is a cuboid with dimensions 1.5 m × 0.5 m × 0.6 m.

a) What is the maximum volume of water that the bath will hold?

b) Find the volume of water needed to fill the bath to a height of 0.3 m.

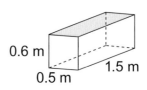
0.6 m
0.5 m
1.5 m

6 A matchbox is 5 cm long and 3 cm wide. The volume of the matchbox is 18 cm³.

What is the height of the matchbox?

Composite Shapes

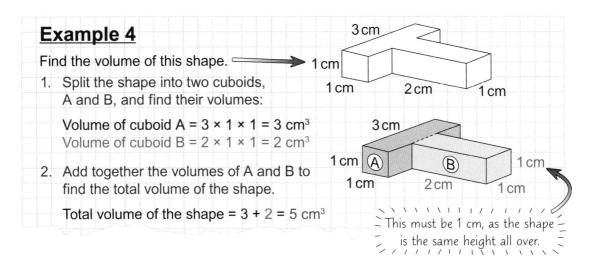

Example 4

Find the volume of this shape.

1. Split the shape into two cuboids, A and B, and find their volumes:

Volume of cuboid A = 3 × 1 × 1 = 3 cm³
Volume of cuboid B = 2 × 1 × 1 = 2 cm³

2. Add together the volumes of A and B to find the total volume of the shape.

Total volume of the shape = 3 + 2 = 5 cm³

This must be 1 cm, as the shape is the same height all over.

Exercise 4

1 Find the volume of each shape below:

a)
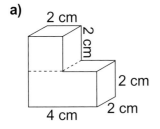

b)
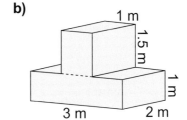

c)
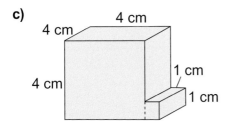

d)
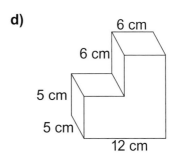

e)
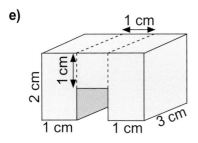

f)
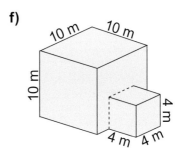

2 Find the volume of each shape below:

a)

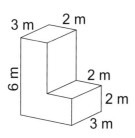

b)

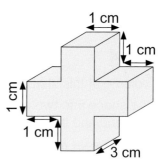

c)

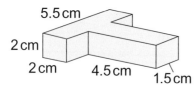

20.2 Volume of Prisms

A prism is a 3D shape which is the same shape and size all the
way through — it has a constant cross-section.

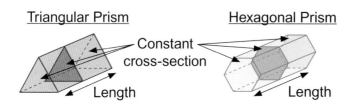

Triangular Prism   Hexagonal Prism

Constant cross-section

Length   Length

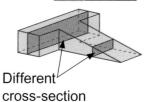

NOT a Prism

Different cross-section

Exercise 1

1 Which of the following 3D shapes are prisms?

A

B

C
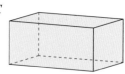

D

E

F
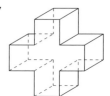

Volume of a Prism

The volume of a prism is given by the following formula:

Volume = Cross-Sectional Area × Length

Cross-Sectional Area

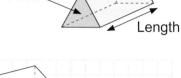

Length

Example 2

Find the volume of the triangular prism shown.

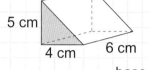

5 cm   4 cm   6 cm

1. The cross-section is a triangle, so use the formula for the area of a triangle to find the cross-sectional area.

   Cross-sectional area = $\dfrac{\text{base} \times \text{height}}{2}$

   $= \dfrac{4 \times 5}{2} = 10 \text{ cm}^2$

2. Then use the formula for the volume of a prism.

   Volume = Cross-sectional area × Length

   $= 10 \times 6 = 60 \text{ cm}^3$

3. Give your answer with the right units.

The cross-sectional area will have 'squared' units and the volume will have 'cubed' units.

Exercise 2

1 This prism has cross-sectional area 15 cm² and length 3 cm.

   What is the volume of the prism?

   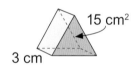

   15 cm²   3 cm

2 This prism has cross-sectional area 20 mm² and length 4.5 mm.

   What is the volume of the prism?

   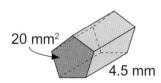

   20 mm²   4.5 mm

3 Find the volumes of the prisms with the following cross-sectional areas and lengths:

   a) area = 2 cm², length = 3 cm

   b) area = 6 cm², length = 9 cm

   c) area = 3 m², length = 6 m

   d) area = 3 cm², length = 7 cm

   e) area = 10 mm², length = 1.75 mm

   f) area = 11.5 mm², length = 9.5 mm

4 For the prism shown on the right, find:

a) the cross-sectional area

b) the volume of the prism

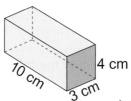

10 cm

4 cm

3 cm

5 For the prism shown on the right, find:

a) the cross-sectional area

b) the volume of the prism

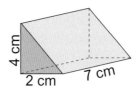

4 cm

2 cm 7 cm

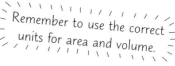

Remember to use the correct units for area and volume.

6 Find the volume of each prism below.

a)

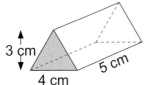

3 cm

4 cm

5 cm

b)

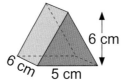

6 cm

6 cm 5 cm

c)

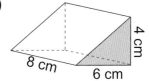

4 cm

8 cm

6 cm

7 Find the volumes of the following prisms:

a) a triangular prism of base 13 cm, vertical height 12 cm and length 8 cm

b) a triangular prism of base 4 m, vertical height 1.3 m and length 3.1 m

8 The cross-section of a prism is shown on the right.
Each grid square has side length 1 cm.

a) Find the cross-sectional area of the prism.

b) The prism has length 10 cm. Find the volume of the prism.

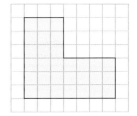

9 The following diagrams show the cross-sections of prisms of the given length.
Each grid square has side length 1 cm.   Find the volume of each prism.

a)

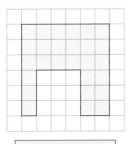

Length = 3 cm

b)

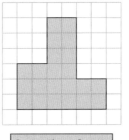

Length = 6 cm

c)

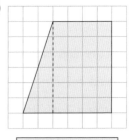

Length = 5 cm

10 For the prism shown on the right, find:

    a) the cross-sectional area

    b) the volume of the prism

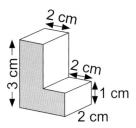

11 By first calculating their cross-sectional areas, find the volumes of the following prisms.

a)

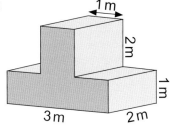

b)

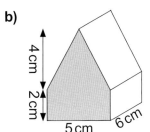

Faces, Vertices and Edges

You need to use the right names for parts of an object.

Face: one of the flat surfaces of a 3D object.

Edge: where two faces (or surfaces) meet
— edges are usually straight.

Vertex: a corner.

A cylinder has 2 circular faces...

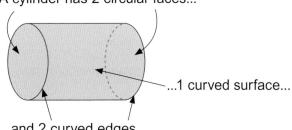

...1 curved surface...

...and 2 curved edges.

Example 1

How many faces, vertices and edges does a cube have?

1. Count the number of flat surfaces.
2. Count the number of corners.
3. Count the number of places where two faces meet.

So a cube has 6 faces, 8 vertices and 12 edges.

Exercise 1

1 Write down the number of faces, vertices and edges in the following 3D shapes.

a)

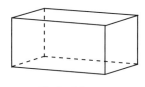

Cuboid

b)

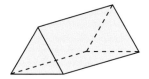

Triangular Prism

c)

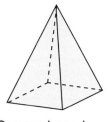

Square-based
Pyramid

d)

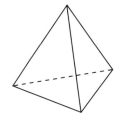

Tetrahedron

2 Name the 3D shapes described below.

a) 6 identical faces, 8 vertices and 12 edges

b) 2 parallel triangular faces, 3 rectangular faces

c) 4 triangular faces, 6 edges

d) 1 square face, 4 identical triangular faces

e) 2 circular faces, 1 curved surface and 2 curved edges

Nets

A net of a 3D object is a 2D shape that can be folded to make the 3D object.

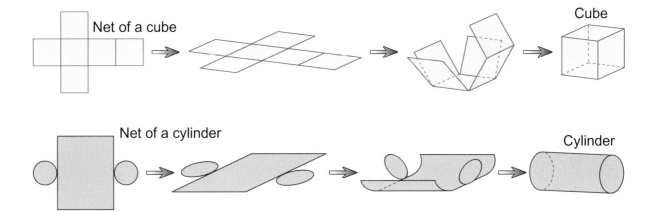

Example 2

How many a) triangles and b) rectangles are there in the net of a triangular prism?

1. Sketch a triangular prism.

2. Count the triangular faces — this will be the number of triangles in the net.

3. Count the rectangular faces — this will be the number of rectangles in the net.

So the net will have a) 2 triangles and b) 3 rectangles.

Exercise 2

1   State how many **(i)** squares and **(ii)** triangles there will be in the nets of these 3D shapes:

a) tetrahedron

b) cube

c) square-based pyramid

2   How many faces will the 3D shape with this net have?

3 Is the net on the right the net of a cube?
If not, then why not?

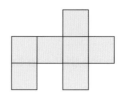

4 How many rectangles with the following
dimensions will the net of this cuboid have?

    a) 2 cm × 3 cm

    b) 2 cm × 4 cm

    c) 3 cm × 4 cm

    d) 2 cm × 2 cm

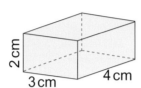

5 Name and sketch the 3D objects with the following nets.

    a)

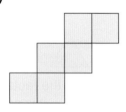

    b)

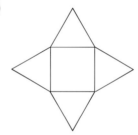

    c)

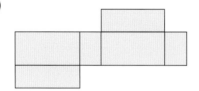

Example 3

Draw a net for a cuboid with dimensions 2 cm × 2 cm × 3 cm.
Label the net with its dimensions.

1. Sketch the
    cuboid.

2. Draw it 'unfolded' —
    there could be several
    ways of doing this.

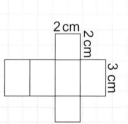

Exercise 3

1 Copy and complete the unfinished nets of the four objects shown below.

> *Count the faces of the 3D shapes to see what's missing from the nets.*

a)

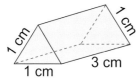

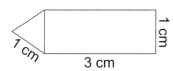

b)

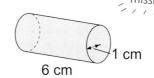

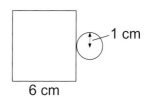

c)

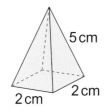

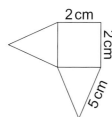

d)

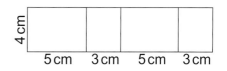

2 Draw a net of each of the following objects. Label each net with its dimensions.

a)

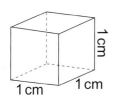

b)

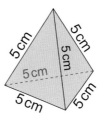

c)

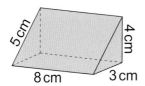

d)

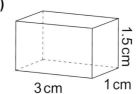

Section 21 — Transformations

21.1 Reflection

When an object is reflected in a line, its size, shape and distance from the mirror line all stay the same.

Example 1

Reflect the shape $ABCD$ in the mirror line.

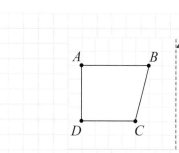

Mirror line

 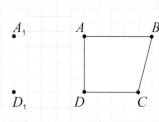 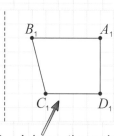

1. Reflect the points one at a time.

2. Each reflected point is the same distance from the mirror line as the original point.

3. Join up the points to show the reflected image.

Exercise 1

1   Copy the diagrams below, and complete the reflection of each shape in the mirror line.

 a)

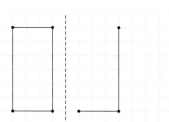

b)

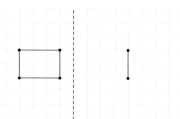

2 Copy the diagrams below, and complete the reflection of each shape in the mirror line.

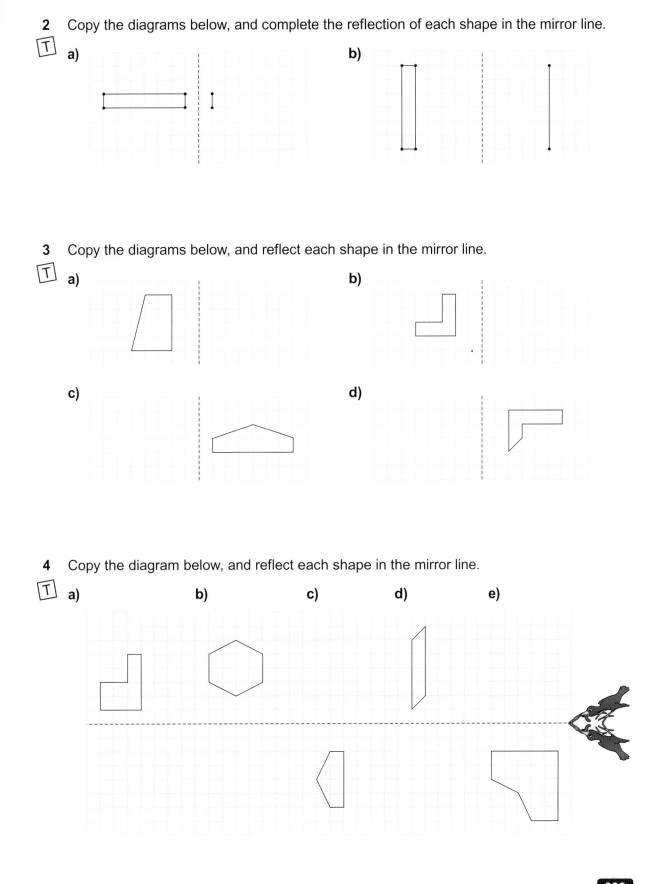

a)

b)

3 Copy the diagrams below, and reflect each shape in the mirror line.

a)

b)

c)

d)

4 Copy the diagram below, and reflect each shape in the mirror line.

a)   b)   c)   d)   e)

Example 2

a) Reflect the shape *ABCDE* in the *y*-axis.
Label the reflected points A_1, B_1, C_1, D_1 and E_1.
The first point has been done for you.

b) Write down the coordinates of the points A_1, B_1, C_1, D_1 and E_1.

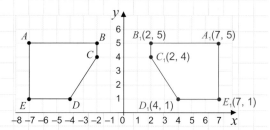

1. This time, the mirror line is the *y*-axis.

2. Reflect the shape one point at a time.

3. Write down the coordinates of each of the reflected points.

Exercise 2

1 Copy the diagrams below, and reflect each shape in the *y*-axis.

a)

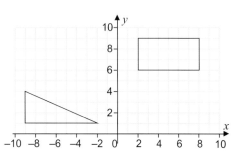

b)

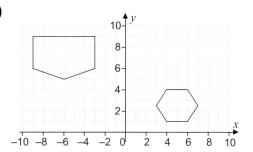

2 Copy the diagrams below, and reflect each shape in the *x*-axis.
The first one has been done for you.

a)

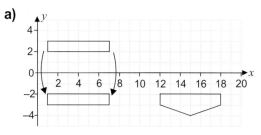

b)

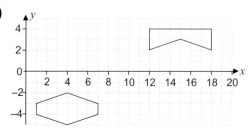

3 Copy the diagram on the right.

a) Reflect the shape in the y-axis.
Label the reflection of point A with A_1.

b) Write down the coordinates of the point A_1.

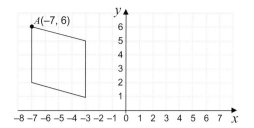

4 Copy the diagram on the right.

a) Reflect the shape in the y-axis
Label the reflected points
A_1, B_1, C_1, D_1 and E_1.

b) Write down the coordinates of
A_1, B_1, C_1, D_1 and E_1.

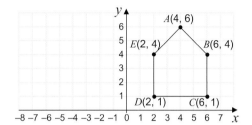

5 Copy the diagram on the right.

a) Reflect the shape in the x-axis
Label the reflected points A_1, B_1, C_1, D_1 and E_1.

b) Write down the coordinates of A_1, B_1, C_1, D_1 and E_1.

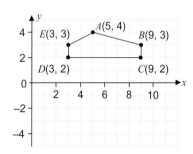

Example 3

a) Draw the line $x = 7$.

b) Reflect triangle ABC in the line $x = 7$.
Label the reflected points A_1, B_1 and C_1.

c) Write down the coordinates of the
points A_1, B_1 and C_1.

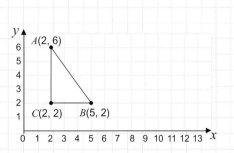

1. Draw the line $x = 7$. This is a vertical
line passing through 7 on the x-axis.

2. Reflect the shape one point at a time,
using $x = 7$ as the mirror line.

3. Write down the coordinates of each
of the reflected points.

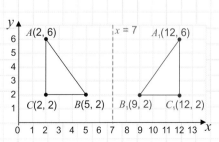

Exercise 3

1 Copy the diagram on the right.

   a) Reflect the shape in the line $x = 6$.
   Label the reflection of point A with A_1.

   b) Write down the coordinates of the point A_1.

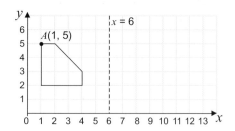

2 Copy the diagram on the right.

   a) Draw the line $x = -1$.

   b) Reflect the shape in the line $x = -1$.
   Label the reflected points A_1, B_1, C_1 and D_1.

   c) Write down the coordinates of the
   points A_1, B_1, C_1 and D_1.

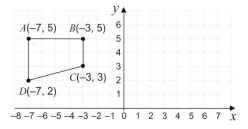

3 Copy the diagram on the right.

   a) Draw the line $y = 4$.

   b) Reflect the shapes in the line $y = 4$.

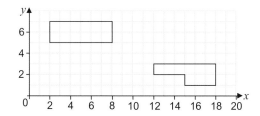

4 Copy the diagram on the right.

   a) Draw the line $y = -2$.

   b) Reflect the shape in the line $y = -2$.
   Label the reflected points A_1, B_1, C_1 and D_1.

   c) Write down the coordinates of the points A_1, B_1, C_1 and D_1.

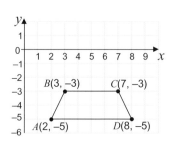

Reflection in Diagonal Mirror Lines

Example 4

Reflect the shape ABC in the mirror line $y = x$.

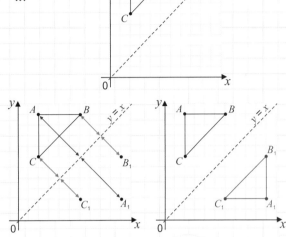

1. Reflect the points one at a time.

2. A is 4 squares diagonally from the mirror line, so A_1 should also be 4 squares diagonally from the mirror line. B and C are 2 squares diagonally from the mirror line, so B_1 and C_1 should also be 2 squares diagonally from the mirror line.

3. Join up the points to draw the reflected shape.

Exercise 4

1 Copy each diagram below, and reflect the shapes in the mirror line shown.

a)

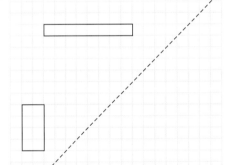

b)

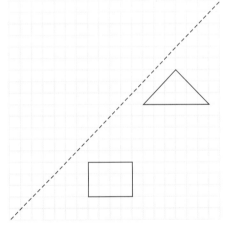

2 Copy the diagram on the right.

 a) Reflect the shape in the line $y = x$.

b) Label the reflected points A_1, B_1, C_1 and D_1.

c) Write down the coordinates of A_1, B_1, C_1 and D_1.

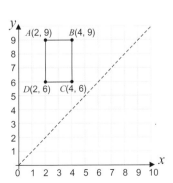

21.2 Rotation

When an object rotates about a point, its size, shape and distance from the point of rotation all stay the same.

Rotations are described using three bits of information:

1) the centre of rotation
   (the point it turns about)

2) the direction of rotation
   (clockwise or anticlockwise)

3) the angle of rotation

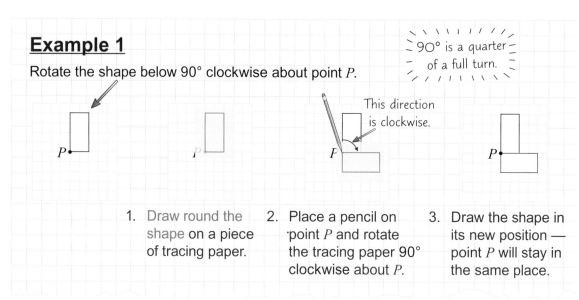

Example 1

Rotate the shape below 90° clockwise about point *P*.

90° is a quarter of a full turn.

This direction is clockwise.

1. Draw round the shape on a piece of tracing paper.

2. Place a pencil on point *P* and rotate the tracing paper 90° clockwise about *P*.

3. Draw the shape in its new position — point *P* will stay in the same place.

Exercise 1

1 Copy the diagrams below. Rotate each shape 90° clockwise about *P*.

[T] **a)**

b)

c)

d)

2 Copy the diagrams below. Rotate each shape 180° about *P*.

T **a)**   **b)**   **c)**   **d)**

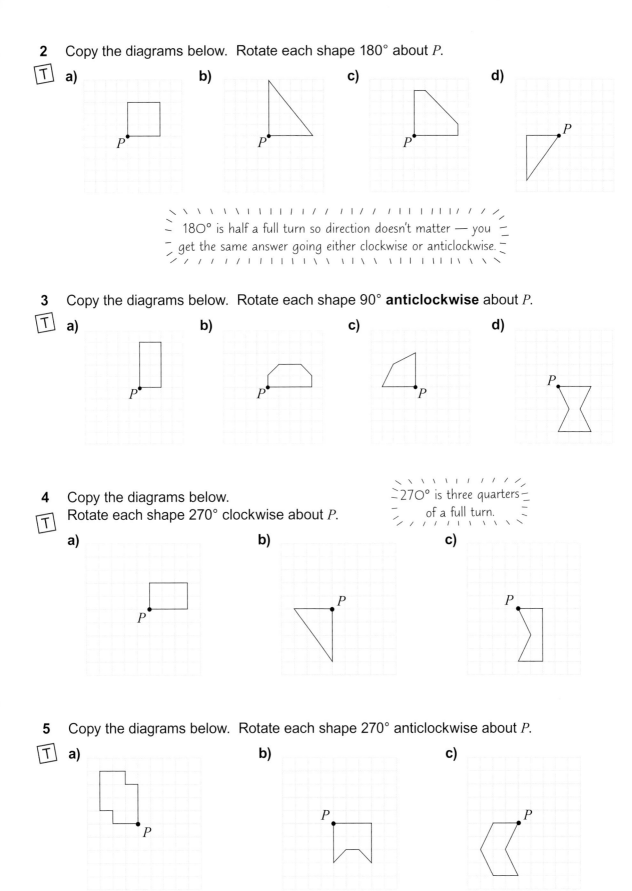

180° is half a full turn so direction doesn't matter — you get the same answer going either clockwise or anticlockwise.

3 Copy the diagrams below. Rotate each shape 90° **anticlockwise** about *P*.

T **a)**   **b)**   **c)**   **d)**

4 Copy the diagrams below.
T Rotate each shape 270° clockwise about *P*.

270° is three quarters of a full turn.

a)   **b)**   **c)**

5 Copy the diagrams below. Rotate each shape 270° anticlockwise about *P*.

T **a)**   **b)**   **c)**

Example 2

Rotate the shape below 90° clockwise about point P.

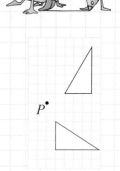

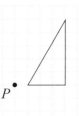

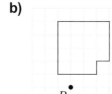

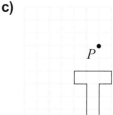

1. This time the centre of rotation is not a point on the shape.

2. Do the rotation in exactly the same way as before. The point P still doesn't move.

3. Draw the shape in its new position.

Exercise 2

1 Copy the diagrams below. Rotate each shape 90° clockwise about P.

 a)

b)

c)

2 Copy the diagrams below. Rotate each shape 90° anticlockwise about P.

 a)

b)

c)

3 Copy the diagram to the right.

 a) Rotate shape A 90° anticlockwise about P. Label the rotated shape B.

b) Rotate shape B 90° clockwise about Q. Label the rotated shape C.

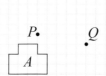

Example 3

a) Rotate triangle ABC 90° anticlockwise about the origin.
b) Label the rotated shape $A_1B_1C_1$.
c) Find the coordinates of the points A_1, B_1 and C_1.

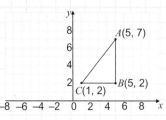

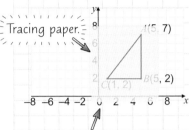

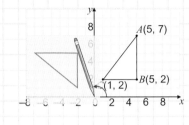

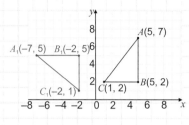

1. The origin is the point (0, 0) on the grid.

2. Rotate the shape in the usual way.

3. Write down the coordinates of A_1, B_1 and C_1.

Exercise 3

1 Copy the diagram on the right.

[T] Rotate the shape 90° clockwise about the origin.

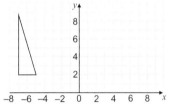

2 Copy the diagram on the right.

[T] **a)** Rotate A 90° clockwise about the origin.

b) Rotate B 270° clockwise about the origin.

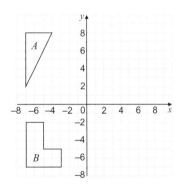

3 Copy the diagram on the right.

[T] Rotate the shape 270° anticlockwise about the point (2, 2).

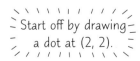

Start off by drawing a dot at (2, 2).

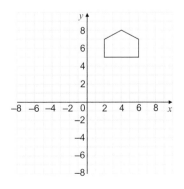

347

4 Copy the diagram on the right.

T **a)** Rotate A 90° clockwise about (1, 1).

b) Rotate B 90° anticlockwise about (1, −3).

c) Rotate C 90° clockwise about (−2, −2).

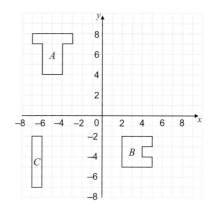

5 Copy the grid on the right.

T **a)** Rotate the shape ABC 90° anticlockwise about the origin.

b) Label the rotated shape $A_1B_1C_1$.

c) Write down the coordinates of the points A_1, B_1 and C_1.

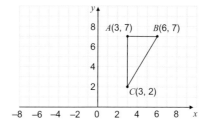

21.3 Translation

Translating an object means sliding it to somewhere else.
When an object is translated, its size and shape stay the same, but its position changes.

Example 1

Translate the shape below by 4 squares up and 3 squares right.

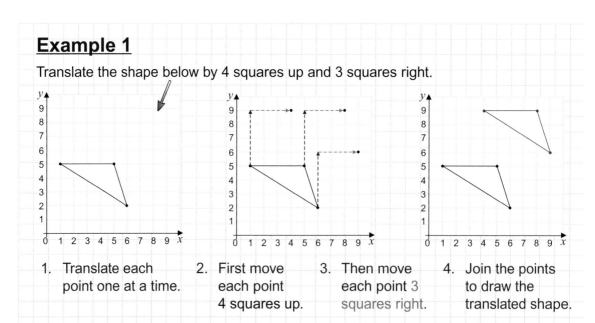

1. Translate each point one at a time.

2. First move each point 4 squares up.

3. Then move each point 3 squares right.

4. Join the points to draw the translated shape.

Exercise 1

1 Copy the diagram on the right.

 a) Translate shape A 1 square right.

b) Translate shape B 5 squares up.

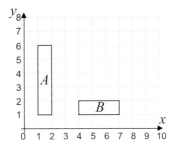

2 Copy the diagram on the right.

 a) Translate shape A 1 square down and 3 squares right.

b) Translate shape B 2 squares up and 3 squares left.

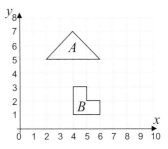

3 Copy the diagram on the right.

 a) Translate shape A 3 squares up and 3 squares right.

b) Translate shape B 2 squares down and 3 squares right.

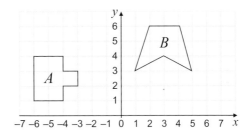

4 Copy the diagram on the right.

a) Translate shape P 1 square up and 2 squares right.

b) Translate shape Q 3 squares up and 4 squares left.

c) Translate shape R 1 square down and 4 squares right.

d) Translate shape S 3 squares down and 4 squares left.

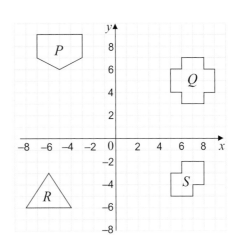

Translating Objects Using Vectors

Translations are sometimes written using vectors. For example, $\begin{pmatrix} 1 \\ 3 \end{pmatrix}$ means move 1 unit to the right and 3 units up.

Example 2

Translate the shape below by the vector $\begin{pmatrix} 5 \\ 3 \end{pmatrix}$.

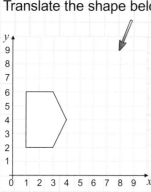

1. $\begin{pmatrix} 5 \\ 3 \end{pmatrix}$ is a translation of 5 to the right and 3 up.

2. So move the shape by this amount.

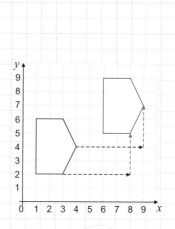

Example 3

Translate the shape below by the vector $\begin{pmatrix} -4 \\ -2 \end{pmatrix}$.

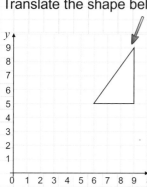

1. The negative numbers mean the object moves in the opposite direction to positive vectors.

2. So $\begin{pmatrix} -4 \\ -2 \end{pmatrix}$ is a translation of 4 to the left and 2 down.

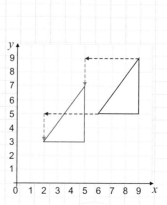

Exercise 2

1 Write down in words the translations described by these vectors:

Remember, negative numbers mean left and down.

a) $\begin{pmatrix} 1 \\ 1 \end{pmatrix}$

b) $\begin{pmatrix} 2 \\ 5 \end{pmatrix}$

c) $\begin{pmatrix} 3 \\ -1 \end{pmatrix}$

d) $\begin{pmatrix} -2 \\ 6 \end{pmatrix}$

e) $\begin{pmatrix} 0 \\ 7 \end{pmatrix}$

f) $\begin{pmatrix} -2 \\ -4 \end{pmatrix}$

2 Copy the diagram to the right.

[T] Translate the shape by the vector $\begin{pmatrix} 3 \\ 3 \end{pmatrix}$.

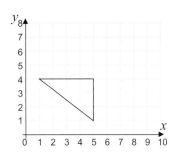

3 Make three copies of the diagram on the right.

[T] Translate shape A by the vector:

a) $\begin{pmatrix} 2 \\ 4 \end{pmatrix}$ b) $\begin{pmatrix} 3 \\ 0 \end{pmatrix}$ c) $\begin{pmatrix} 0 \\ 1 \end{pmatrix}$

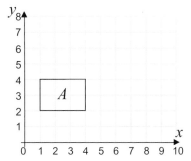

4 Make three copies of the diagram on the right.

[T] Translate shape B by the vector:

a) $\begin{pmatrix} -1 \\ -1 \end{pmatrix}$ b) $\begin{pmatrix} 0 \\ -2 \end{pmatrix}$ c) $\begin{pmatrix} -3 \\ 0 \end{pmatrix}$

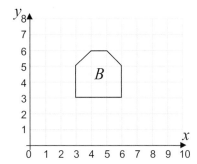

5 Make three copies of the diagram on the right.

[T] Translate shape C by the vector:

a) $\begin{pmatrix} -4 \\ -2 \end{pmatrix}$ b) $\begin{pmatrix} 2 \\ -3 \end{pmatrix}$ c) $\begin{pmatrix} -4 \\ 2 \end{pmatrix}$

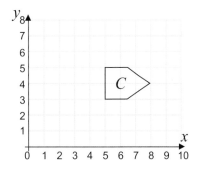

6 Copy the diagram on the right.
T Translate each shape by the vector
written next to it.

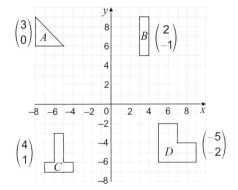

Describing Translations Using Vectors

Example 4

Describe the translation that moves
shape A onto shape B in vector form.

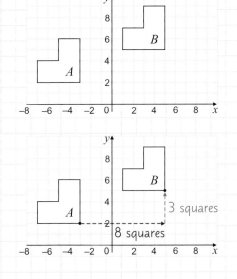

1. Pick a point on shape A and find
   the matching point on shape B.

2. Count how many squares
   horizontally ($\rightarrow$) and how many
   squares vertically ($\uparrow$) the point
   has moved.

3. Write the translation as a vector
   — remember that the horizontal
   shift goes on top.

The shape has moved 8 squares to the right and 3 squares up,
so the translation is described by the vector $\begin{pmatrix} 8 \\ 3 \end{pmatrix}$.

Exercise 3

1 Write these translations in vector form:

a) 1 to the right, 2 up

b) 1 to the right, 2 down

c) 2 to the right

d) 3 up

e) 4 to the left, 3 down

f) 5 to the left, 2 up

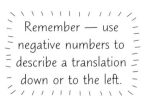

Remember — use
negative numbers to
describe a translation
down or to the left.

2 **a)** Write down in words the translation that moves shape A onto shape B.

  b) Write this translation in vector form.

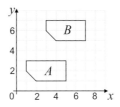

3 **a)** Write down in words the translation that moves shape B onto shape C.

  b) Write this translation in vector form.

  c) Write in vector form the translation that moves shape A onto shape B.

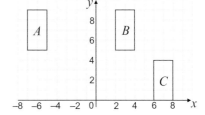

21.4   Enlargement

Scale Factors

When an object is enlarged, its shape stays the same, but its size changes.
The scale factor tells you how much the size changes.

Example 1

Enlarge the rectangle anywhere on the grid by scale factor 2.

1. Find the length and width of the shape you're enlarging.

    The rectangle has length 4 squares and width 3 squares.

2. Multiply by the scale factor to find the length and width of the enlarged shape.

    So the enlarged rectangle will have: length 4 × 2 = 8 squares and width 3 × 2 = 6 squares.

3. Draw the enlarged shape using the dimensions you've found.

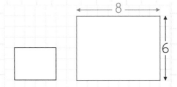

Exercise 1

1 Copy the diagrams below. Enlarge each shape by scale factor 2.

It doesn't matter where on the grid you draw the enlarged shape.

T **a)**

b)

c)

d)

2 Copy the diagrams below, then enlarge each shape by scale factor 3.

 a)

b)

c)

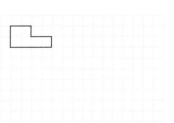

d)

3 Draw the following shapes after they have been enlarged by scale factor 5.

a) 1 cm

1 cm

b) 2 cm

1 cm

c)

3 cm

4 cm

d) 1 cm

2 cm

1 cm

2 cm

4 A square of side 3 cm is enlarged by scale factor 2.
What is the side length of the square after it has been enlarged?

5 A 5 cm × 3 cm rectangle is enlarged by scale factor 6.
What are the dimensions of the rectangle after it has been enlarged?

Centres of Enlargement

The centre of enlargement tells you where the enlargement is measured from.

Example 2

Enlarge the shape below by scale factor 2 with centre of enlargement (0, 0).

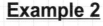

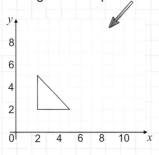

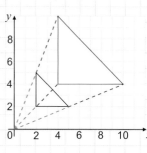

1. Draw a line from (0, 0) to each corner of the shape.

2. The scale factor is 2, so extend each line until it is 2 times as long as before.

3. Join up the ends of the lines to draw the enlarged shape.

Exercise 2

1 Copy the diagrams below.
[T] Enlarge each shape by scale factor 2 with centre of enlargement (0, 0).

a)

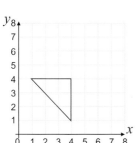

b)

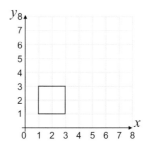

2 Copy the diagrams below.
T Enlarge each shape by scale factor 3 with centre of enlargement (0, 0).

a)

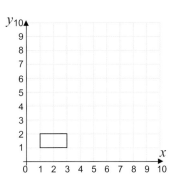

b)

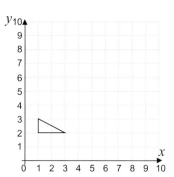

Example 3

Enlarge the shape below by scale factor 2 with centre of enlargement (−6, 8).

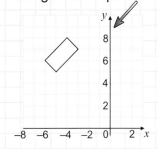

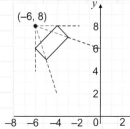

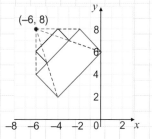

1. Mark on the point (−6, 8).   2. Enlarge the shape in the same way as before.

3 Copy the diagrams below.
T Enlarge each shape by scale factor 2 with centre of enlargement (0, 0).

a)

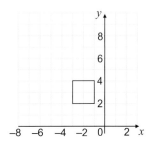

b)

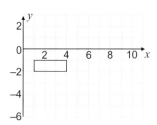

4 Copy the diagram on the right.

[T] Enlarge each shape by scale factor 3 with centre of enlargement (0, 0).

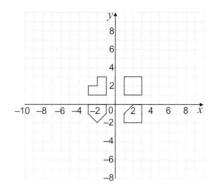

5 Copy the diagrams below.

[T] Enlarge each shape by scale factor 2 with centre of enlargement (2, 2).

a)

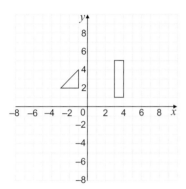

b)

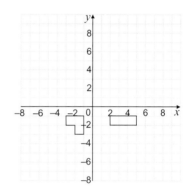

6 Copy the diagram below.

[T] **a)** Enlarge A by scale factor 2 with centre of enlargement (–8, 8).

b) Enlarge B by scale factor 2 with centre of enlargement (–8, –6).

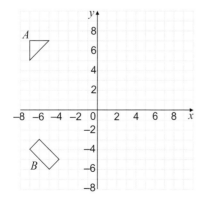

7 Copy the diagram on the right.

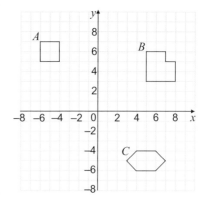

a) Enlarge A by scale factor 2 with centre of enlargement (−5, 6).

b) Enlarge B by scale factor 2 with centre of enlargement (6, 4).

c) Enlarge C by scale factor 2 with centre of enlargement (5, −5).

Here, the centre of enlargement is inside each shape. Just enlarge each shape as normal, drawing lines from the centre of enlargement through each corner.

21.5 Congruence

Two shapes are 'congruent' if they are exactly the same shape and same size. It doesn't matter if one of the shapes has been rotated (turned round) or reflected (flipped over).

Example 1

Which two of the shapes A, B and C are congruent?

1. Compare A and B — they are not congruent as they are different sizes.

2. Compare A and C — they are not congruent as they are different sizes.

3. Compare B and C — they are congruent as they are the same size and shape, just facing different directions.

   The two congruent shapes are B and C.

Exercise 1

1 Write down the letters of the congruent pairs of shapes shown in the box below. For example, A is congruent to G.

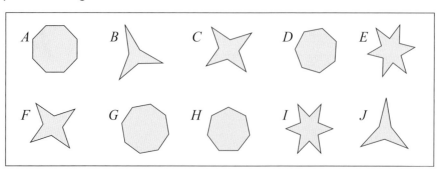

2 For each of the following, decide which shape is **not** congruent to the others.

a)

b)

c)

3 For each of the following, decide which shape is **not** congruent to the others.

a)

b)

c)

4 Write down the letters of any shapes below that are congruent to A.

A B C D E

5 Write down the letters of any shapes below that are congruent to A.

A B C D E

Remember, a reflected or rotated shape is congruent to the original shape.

6 Write down the letters of any shapes below that are congruent to A.

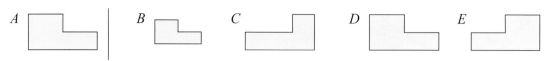

7 Write down the letters of any shapes below that are congruent to A.

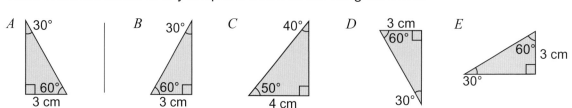

21.6 Similarity

Two shapes are 'similar' if they are exactly the same shape but different sizes.
Any enlarged shape is similar to the original shape.

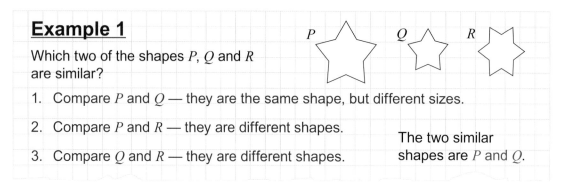

Example 1

Which two of the shapes P, Q and R
are similar?

1. Compare P and Q — they are the same shape, but different sizes.

2. Compare P and R — they are different shapes.

3. Compare Q and R — they are different shapes.

The two similar
shapes are P and Q.

Exercise 1

1 Write down the letters of the similar shapes shown in the box below.
For example, A, C and F are similar.

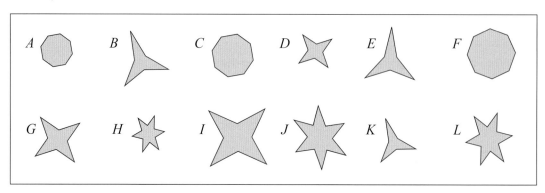

2 For each group of shapes below, decide which **two** of the shapes are similar.

a)

b)

c)

d)

e)

f)

Example 2

Are the triangles A and B similar?
Give a reason for your answer.

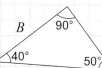

The triangles are similar because all the angles in triangle A are the same as the angles in triangle B — so it's the same shape triangle.

---

3 Decide if each of these pairs of triangles are similar.

a)

b)

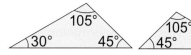

c)

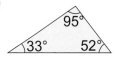

d)

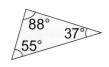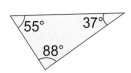

Section 22 — Collecting Data

22.1 Using Different Types of Data

The Data-Handling Cycle

The Data-Handling Cycle is used to investigate things.

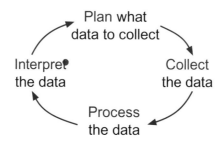

The first stage in the data-handling cycle is to decide what data you need to collect and how you're going to get it.

Primary data is data you collect yourself, e.g. by doing a survey or experiment.

Secondary data is data that has been collected by someone else.
You can get secondary data from things like newspapers or the internet.

Example 1

Marya wants to know if there's a link between area and population in 10 African countries.

a) What pieces of data does Marya need to find?

    This is the information she needs   The areas and populations of the
    to answer her question.   10 countries she's interested in.

b) Where could Marya get the data from?   E.g. she could find it on the internet.

c) Is Marya's data primary or secondary data?

    The data has been collected   It is secondary data.
    by someone else, so...

Exercise 1

In questions **1-3**, say if the data collected will be **primary** or **secondary** data.

1   James plans to interview people as they leave a supermarket to find out how often they shop there.

2   Faheem is going to use the data on election results from his local newspaper.

3   Nancy is going to time how long it takes her friends to run 100 metres.

For each investigation in questions **4-8**:

    a) Describe what data is needed and give a suitable method for collecting it.

    b) Say whether the data will be primary or secondary data.

4   Nikita wants to know what the girls in her class think about school dinners.

5   Dan wants to find the most common colour of car passing his house in a 30 minute interval.

6   Anne wants to compare the daily rainfall in London and Manchester last August.

7   Rohan wants to test his theory that the boys in his class can throw a ball further than the girls.

8   Jim wants to find out whether draws are more likely for football teams in the lower leagues.

Types of Data

Data can be qualitative or quantitative.

> Qualitative data is in the form of words — e.g. the colours of cars.

> Quantitative data is in the form of numbers, and can be either discrete or continuous.

> Discrete data can only take certain values (usually whole numbers) — e.g. the number of people in a class.

> Continuous data can take any value in a range — e.g. the time it takes to do something, or the height or weight of something.

Example 2

Decide whether these sets of data are qualitative or quantitative.
If the data is quantitative, say whether it is continuous or discrete.

a) The favourite fast food of everyone in a school.
   The data is in the form of words, so it is qualitative.

b) The number of houses on your street.
   The data is in the form of numbers, so it is quantitative.
   It can only take certain values (whole numbers), so it is discrete.

Exercise 2

1   Decide whether each of these sets of data is qualitative or quantitative.
    If the data is quantitative, say whether it is continuous or discrete.

a) The time it takes to travel to school.

b) The heights of 50 sunflowers.

c) The nationalities of your friends.

d) The time it takes people to run 100 m.

e) The number of accidents on the M1.

f) The shoe sizes of 100 people.

g) The names of garden gnomes.

h) The weights of all the potatoes in a sack.

i) The favourite colours of your teachers.

j) The number of cars in a car park.

2 Gemma thinks there is a link between the average number of chocolate bars eaten each week by pupils in her class and how fast they can run 100 metres.

a) Describe two sets of data Gemma should collect to investigate this link.

b) Describe suitable methods for collecting the data.

c) Say whether each set of data is discrete data or continuous data.

d) Say whether each set of data is primary data or secondary data.

22.2   Data-Collection Sheets and Tables

Tally Charts

Tally charts are a good way of recording the frequency of something (how often something happens).

> Remember — tally marks are arranged in groups of 5. E.g. 卌 || shows the number 7.

Example 1

A restaurant manager asks 50 customers to choose their favourite way of eating potatoes. Design a tally chart that could be used to record this data.

The table should have:

1. A column for data names, with a row for every possible answer.

2. A column with enough space to record the tallies.

3. A frequency column for adding up the tallies.

Potato Type	Tally	Frequency
Boiled		
Mashed		
Baked		
Roast		
Other		

Exercise 1

1   The chart on the right has been designed to show the colours of cars in a car park.

State **two** things that are wrong with the tally chart.

Car Colour	Frequency
Red	
Black	
Blue	
Silver	

2 Design a tally chart that could be used to record the answers to each of these questions.

    a) What is your favourite flavour of popcorn from these choices?
        • sweet   • salted   • toffee   • vindaloo   • black pudding

    b) What is your favourite sport?
        • football   • rugby   • tennis   • cricket   • badminton   • other

    c) How many times did you go to the supermarket last week?
        • 0   • 1   • 2   • 3   • more than 3

3 Design a tally chart that could be used to record the answers to each of these questions.

    a) How many brothers or sisters do you have?

    b) What mode of transport do you use to travel to work?

    c) What's your favourite type of fruit?

> Remember there has to be a place to record every possible answer.

Example 2

14 students were asked 'how many people live in your house?'
The results were: 4, 3, 2, 3, 3, 5, 4, 4, 3, 2, 2, 4, 3, 3
Record this data in a tally chart and show the frequencies.

1. Draw the table first — it should have a row for every answer given.
2. Use the results given to fill in the tally column.
3. Add up the tallies to fill in the frequency column.

Number of People	Tally	Frequency
2					3
3	ⱶⱵ		6
4						4
5			1

Exercise 2

1 24 teenagers are asked how many times they have visited the cinema in the last month.
The results are: 1, 0, 1, 3, 1, 1, 0, 0, 0, 1, 2, 0, 4, 3, 4, 2, 1, 1, 4, 1, 3, 2, 4, 0

    a) Design a tally chart to record this data.

    b) Use the data to complete the tally chart and show the frequencies.

2 A supporter records the number of goals scored by an underwater hockey team in each match they play over a 6 month period. She writes the results in a list:

    1, 0, 0, 2, 0, 3, 4, 0, 1, 1, 2, 1, 3, 0, 0, 5, 1, 2, 1, 0, 0, 1, 2, 1

Record this data in a tally chart and show the frequencies.

Tally Charts for Grouped Data

It's sometimes best to group your data — to avoid having a really long tally chart. For example, a tally chart with 100 rows would be quite difficult to use.

Each group is called a class.

Example 3

A group of students take a French test. The test is marked out of 50. Design a tally chart that could be used to record the students' scores.

1. 50 rows (for all the possible scores) would be very annoying, so group the data into a sensible number of classes. E.g. 0-10, 11-20 etc...

2. Make sure the classes cover all the possible scores, from 0 to 50.

3. Make sure the classes don't overlap — each score should only be able to go in one class.

Score	Tally	Frequency
0-10		
11-20		
21-30		
31-40		
41-50		

Exercise 3

1 The tally chart below has been designed to show the number of times people visited the cinema last year.

Number of visits	Tally	Frequency
0-10		
10-20		
20-30		
30-40		

State two things that are wrong with the tally chart.

2 The tally chart below has been designed to show the number of star jumps people can do in one minute.

Number of Star Jumps	Tally	Frequency
less than 100		
more than 100		

a) State two things that are wrong with the tally chart.

b) Design a better tally chart for recording the data.

3   A quiz has 60 questions. Bella is recording how many questions each team gets right.

   a) Is the data she is collecting discrete or continuous?

   b) Copy and complete the table below to show 6 classes that she could split the data into.

Correct Answers	0-10	11-20				

4   Joan is doing a survey to find out how many pairs of socks people own.
   Copy and complete the table below to show the classes that she could split the data into.

Pairs of Socks	0-7	8-14				36 or more

5   Alicia is doing a survey to find out the number of hot drinks people drink in one week.

   a) Copy and complete the table to show the classes that she could split the data into.

Hot Drinks	0-4	5-8				

   b) Use your answer to part **a)** to draw a tally chart that she could use to record the data.

6   A group of students take a test that is marked out of 25.
   The teacher records each pupil's mark.

   a) Write down 5 classes that the teacher could split the marks into.

   b) Design a tally chart the teacher could use to record the marks.

7   Marco asks members of the public how many text messages they sent in the last week.
   He writes the results in a list:

   0, 11, 43, 39, 26, 7, 7, 5, 1, 3, 12, 17, 19, 22, 21, 0, 4, 4, 18, 25,
   30, 10, 12, 9, 5, 8, 14, 15, 12, 0, 13, 20, 8, 0, 34, 20, 13, 25, 10, 7

   By splitting the data into suitable classes, record the data in a tally chart.

If you're investigating two different things at once, you can put the data in a two-way table.

Example 4

A survey into internet usage asks people: (i) their gender

and (ii) whether or not they use the internet.

Design a two-way table to record the results.

1. All possible answers to one question should go along the top of the table.

2. All possible answers to the other question should go down the side.

	Use internet	Don't use internet	Total
Male			
Female			
Total			

4. The totals for each row go in here.

3. The totals for each column go in here.

5. The overall total goes in here.

Exercise 4

1 A music survey asks a group of under-18s and a group of 18-and-overs whether they prefer classical, rap or rock music.

Copy and complete the two-way table designed to record the data.

			Rock	Total
Under-18				
Total				

2 Jill wants to know if there is a link between hair colour and eye colour.
She asks members of the public whether their hair is blonde, brown, black, red or 'other'.
She also asks if their eyes are blue, brown, green or 'other'.

Copy and complete the two-way table designed to record the data Jill collects.

	Blonde			Red		Total
Blue						
Other						
Total						

3 A survey asks a group of boys and a group of girls which flavour of crisps they prefer: ready salted, salt and vinegar or cheese and onion.

Design a two-way table that could be used to show the results.

4 Felicity asks a group of people whether they are left-handed or right-handed, and how they get to school — walk, cycle, bus or 'other'.

Design a two-way table that could be used to show the results.

Questionnaires

Questionnaires need to be clear and easy to answer — and the answers should give you helpful information.

Example 5

John is designing a questionnaire about public transport. He asks the question:

> *'How much do you spend on bus fares in a week?'*
>
> £1 to £3 ☐   £3 to £5 ☐   £5 to £7 ☐

a) Give one criticism of the question and write an improved question.

The question might be difficult for some people to answer if they spend different amounts each week. A better question could be: *'On average, how much do you spend on bus fares each week?'*.

b) Give two criticisms of the response section.
1. The responses don't cover all possible answers — there is no box to tick if you spend less than £1 or more than £7.

2. The responses overlap — there are two boxes that could be ticked if you spent £3 or £5.

Example 6

These questions are taken from a questionnaire on clothes shopping.
Give one criticism of each question and suggest how it could be improved.

a) | *'How much do you spend on clothes each year?'*

The question is personal — people might not want to say exactly how much they spend. It would be better to give a range of options to tick.

b) | *'Do you agree that it is important to follow the latest fashions?'*

This is a leading question — it suggests what the answer should be.
'Do you think it is important to follow the latest fashions?' would be better.

c) | *'Do you go clothes shopping a lot?'*

This question is unclear — it's not clear what 'a lot' means. It would be better to ask how many times they go clothes shopping a month, on average.

d) | *'What did you have for breakfast this morning?'*

This question is irrelevant — it has nothing to do with clothes shopping. It would be better to ask something which will give you useful information.

Exercise 5

1 Give one criticism of each of these questions.

a) How much do you weigh?

b) Do you agree that the best superhero is '*Super-Invisible-Wonder-Penguin*'?

c) Do you go to the cinema a lot?

d) How much money do you earn each month?

2 Give one criticism of the response section for each of these questions.

a) | How many pets does your family have?   1 ☐   2 ☐   3 ☐   More than 3 ☐

b) | Tick your favourite flavour of ice cream.
Vanilla ☐   Chocolate ☐   Strawberry ☐   Toffee ☐

c) | How tall are you?   150 cm or less ☐   150–180 cm ☐   180 cm or more ☐

3 Amber and Jay have designed a question about how much sport people play.

Say whose question is better, giving two reasons to explain your answer.

Amber: | How much sport do you play? |

Jay: | On average, how many times a week do you play sport? Tick one box.
None ☐   Once ☐   Twice ☐   Three ☐   More than three ☐ |

4 Write an improved version of each of these questions.

a) How many films do you watch each week?

1 ☐   2 ☐   3 ☐   4 ☐   5 ☐

b) What's your favourite type of TV programme? Tick one box.

Comedy ☐   Soap ☐   Reality ☐   Sport ☐

c) Do you agree that the gym should open a new tennis court, not a new squash court?

5 Seth has designed a questionnaire to find out about peoples' eating habits.
Give one criticism of each question and suggest how it could be improved.

1. Do you agree that it's important to eat healthily?

2. Do you eat a lot of fruit and veg?

3. On average, how much do you spend on junk food each week?

4. How many times do you go food shopping in a week?

5. What's your favourite film?

The group of people or things you're trying to find out about is called the population.

Example 1

Tim is carrying out a survey to find out if there is a difference in the favourite fast food of boys and girls in his school. What is the population for his survey?

The population is all the pupils in Tim's school.

Exercise 1

1   Say what the population is for each of these surveys.

   a) Justin wants to know the favourite colour of all the members of his family.

   b) Sally is investigating the colours of cars parked on her street.

   c) Sarosh is measuring the heights of all the flowers in his garden.

   d) Brad wants to know the shoe size of everyone in his class.

   e) Gilberto is studying the pay of workers in a local factory.

   f) Tracy is investigating how diet affects the weight of hens at a local farm.

Choosing a Fair Sample

It's often too difficult or expensive to find out about the whole population.
Instead, you can just use part of the population — this is called taking a sample.

A sample should represent the population fairly — if it doesn't, it's called biased.

To be fair, the sample should:

   1. Be big enough.

   2. Be random (everyone in the population has an equal chance of being chosen).

   3. Have the right mix of different people, so that no group of people is missed out.

Example 2

Gina wants to know what people think about a supermarket closing early on Monday evenings. She asks 20 random people outside the supermarket on Monday morning.

a) Give two reasons why her sample might be biased.

    1. Gina is only asking 20 people, which is quite a small sample, so her results might not be accurate.

    2. She is only asking people who are free to shop on Monday morning, so she's excluding people who shop at other times (including the people who are most likely to be affected by the change).

b) Say how she could improve the sample.

    1. By asking more people.

    2. By asking people on a range of different days and different times.

Exercise 2

1 Barry wants to know what people at his college think about a new film, so he asks one of his friends for their opinion.

    a) What is the population for Barry's survey?

    b) Give one reason why the sample he has used might be biased.

    c) Say how the sample could be improved.

2 In each case below, **(i)** explain why the sample might be biased,

                         (ii) say how the sample could be improved.

    a) A school cook wants to know if the pupils would like all school dinners to be vegetarian, so she asks all the members of the school's animal rights group.

    b) A librarian asks 20 people in the library on a Monday morning whether the library should close on Mondays or on Fridays.

    c) A market research company wants to find out about people's working hours. The company selects 100 home telephone numbers and calls them at 2 o'clock one afternoon.

Example 3

There are 89 people in Adam's choir. He wants to choose 20 of them to fill in a questionnaire. Explain how he could select a random sample.

1. First, he should make a list of everyone in the choir and give each person a number from 1 to 89.
2. Then he could use a calculator or computer to generate 20 random numbers between 1 and 89.
3. Finally, he can match the numbers to the people in the list to create the sample.

Exercise 3

1 A teacher wants to know what the pupils in his class think about after-school clubs. He randomly chooses five members of his class who already use after-school clubs to complete a survey.

a) What is the population for the survey?

b) Give one reason why the sample may be biased.

c) Give a better way that the teacher could select a random sample of the members of his class.

2 A dentist wants her patients to test a new type of electric toothbrush. She randomly chooses twenty of her patients who already use electric toothbrushes to test the new one.

a) What is the population for the dentist's survey?

b) Give one reason why the sample might be biased.

c) Give a better way that the dentist could select a random sample of twenty of her patients.

Section 23 — Analysing Data

23.1 Averages and Range

An average is a single number that represents a whole load of data.

The mode, median and mean are three different types of average.

The Mode

The mode is the most common number in a set of numbers.

> ### Example 1
> The number of goals scored by a footballer in his last seven games are:
>   2   0   1   1   3   0   1
> What is his modal number of goals scored?
> The mode is the most common number. $\longrightarrow$ Mode = 1

Exercise 1

1 Which number is the most common number in this list?

3	3	4	5	4	3

2 Find the mode for this list of numbers:

2	4	1	0	3	2

3 Find the mode for each of these lists of numbers:

a) 10, 11, 11, 10, 10, 12

b) 9, 8, 8, 9, 9, 7, 9

c) 9, 4, 5, 4, 7, 4, 8

d) 27, 25, 25, 26, 26, 25, 27

e) 9, 8, 9, 8, 7, 10, 6, 8

f) 1, 0, 0, 1, 0, 1, 0, 0

g) 67, 68, 70, 71, 68, 69, 67, 68, 68

h) −5, −5, −4, −4, −4, −5, 6, 6, −5

i) 5, −8, −8, 5, −7, 6, −8, 4

j) 1.3, 1.4, 1.4, 1.8, 1.3, 1.9, 1.3, 1.8, 1.9, 1.3

4   The list shows the number of sweets in ten different packets:

34, 35, 33, 34, 34, 35, 34, 32, 33, 33

What is the modal number of sweets in a packet?

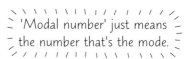
'Modal number' just means the number that's the mode.

5   The price of the same DVD in six different shops is £9, £10, £9, £10, £10 and £11. What is the modal price of the DVD?

6   The list shows the number of people in the queue at each checkout in a supermarket:

3, 2, 3, 4, 1, 3, 2, 3, 2

What is the modal number of people in a queue?

The Median

The median is the middle value in a list of numbers written in order.

Example 2

Find the median of these numbers: 5   6   4   7   2   6   1

1. First put the numbers in order. ⟶   1   2   4   5   6   6   7

2. Then find the middle number in the list.   So the median is 5.

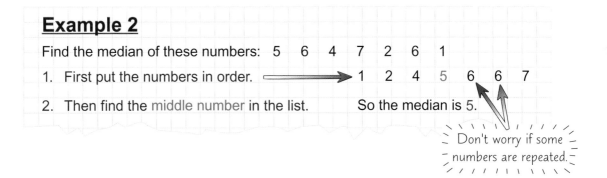

Don't worry if some numbers are repeated.

Example 3

Find the median of these numbers: 8   5   10   12   7   13

1. Put the numbers in order. ⟶   5   7   8   10   12   13

2. This time there are two middle numbers — 8 and 10.

median

$(8 + 10) \div 2 = 18 \div 2$
$= 9$

3. The median is halfway between these two numbers. Add them together and divide by 2 to find the median.

So the median is 9.

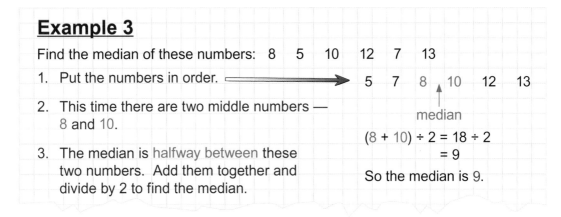

Exercise 2

1 What is the median of these numbers?

| 1 | 3 | 5 | 6 | 8 |

2 **a)** Put this list of numbers in order.

| 9 | 5 | 8 | 7 | 9 |

b) Write down the median.

3 Find the median for each of these lists of numbers:

a) 12, 11, 15, 16, 13

b) 33, 22, 34, 20, 23

c) 3, 14, 46, 11, 38

d) 8, 3, 2, 5, 7, 6, 1

e) 2, 8, 2, 5, 3, 5, 6

f) 9, 10, 8, 11, 12, 15, 16

4 **a)** Put this list of numbers in order.

| 3 | 9 | 2 | 7 | 5 | 11 |

b) Write down the middle two numbers from your list.

c) Find the median of the list of numbers.

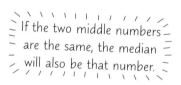

If the two middle numbers are the same, the median will also be that number.

5 Find the median for each of these lists of numbers:

a) 10, 12, 16, 8

b) 8, 6, 4, 6

c) 5, 9, 5, 6, 3, 4

d) 13, 16, 15, 11, 17, 13

e) 30, 70, 50, 40, 80, 10

f) 62, 64, 50, 58

6 These are the ages of seven workers in an office: 41, 50, 35, 33, 25, 30, 43
What is the median age?

7 The number of cups of coffee sold in a coffee shop over four days are: 88, 90, 110, 86
What is the median number of cups of coffee sold?

8 These are the ticket prices for seats at a concert: £40, £12, £28, £75, £120, £20
What is the median price of a ticket?

9 Find the median for each of these lists of numbers:

a) 3.9, 4.1, 6.6, 1.8, 3.1

b) 1.2, 6.5, 3.2, 2.6

10 **a)** Put these numbers in order, from lowest to highest.

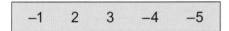

| −1 | 2 | 3 | −4 | −5 |

b) Find the median of the list of numbers.

11 Find the median for each of these lists of numbers:

a) −5, 2, −2, 3, −1   **b)** −4, −3, −6, −2, 0

c) −5, −1, −3, −3, 0, 1   **d)** −2, 1, −4, −1, 3, 4

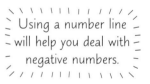
Using a number line will help you deal with negative numbers.

The Mean

You find the mean by adding all the numbers in a list together and then dividing by how many numbers there are.

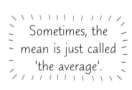
Sometimes, the mean is just called 'the average'.

Example 4

Find the mean of these numbers: 15   10   12   17

1. First add the numbers together. $15 + 10 + 12 + 17 = 54$

2. There are 4 numbers in the list, so divide by 4. $54 \div 4 = 13.5$

So the mean is 13.5.

Exercise 3

You may use a calculator for this exercise.

1 **a)** Add together the numbers in this list.

| 3 | 6 | 2 | 1 | 3 |

b) Find the mean of the five numbers.

2 Find the mean for each of these lists of numbers:

a) 2, 4, 2, 8

b) 5, 8, 6, 9

c) 10, 12, 14, 16

d) 7, 9, 8, 12

e) 21, 15, 32, 12

f) 10, 14, 13, 12, 11

g) 36, 40, 44, 39, 51

h) 91, 69, 62, 47, 81

i) 30, 30, 50, 60, 40, 30

j) 82, 67, 41, 35, 72, 63

3 Find the mean for each of these lists of numbers:

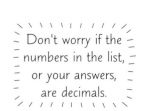

Don't worry if the numbers in the list, or your answers, are decimals.

a) 7, 5, 10, 8

b) 5, 2, 7, 4

c) 8, 9, 7, 8, 7

d) 10, 30, 42, 9, 26

e) 12, 14, 22, 9, 11, 31

f) 36, 42, 86, 39, 47, 53

g) 2, 1, 1, 1, 2, 0, 0, 2, 2, 3

h) 6.2, 3.5, 4.1, 8.2

i) 1.5, 0.6, 4.2, 2.1

j) 3.2, 0.5, 9.2, 4.4, 6.2

4 The price of the same bar of chocolate in three different shops is: 62p, 57p, 55p
What is the mean price?

5 These are the ages of the members of a family: 11, 14, 16, 38, 41
What is the mean age?

6 The weights of six apples in a pack are: 100 g, 120 g, 98 g, 105 g, 115 g, 110 g
What is the mean weight?

7   These are the daily temperatures for the first week in July:

19 °C, 20 °C, 15 °C, 16 °C, 16 °C, 18 °C, 22 °C

What is the mean daily temperature?

8   Josie goes fishing at the weekend. She writes down the lengths of the fish she catches in a list: 12 cm, 9 cm, 17 cm, 22 cm, 14 cm

a) What is the mean length of fish she catches?

b) She catches another fish of length 22 cm.
What is the new mean length of fish she catches?

9   Find the mean for each of these lists of numbers:

a) −2, −1, −5, −4

b) −6, −9, −1, −4

> Remember — adding a negative number is the same as subtracting a positive number.

c) 3, 0, −4, −7

d) −5, 9, −4, 4

The Range

The range is the difference between the highest and lowest numbers in a list.

To find the range you subtract the lowest number from the highest number.

Example 5

Find the range of these prices: £75   £94   £66   £80   £62   £77

1. It helps to put the numbers ⟶ £62   £66   £75   £77   £80   £94
    in order first.

2. Subtract the lowest number (£62)   £94 − £62 = £32
    from the highest number (£94) to
    find the range.   So the range is £32.

Exercise 4

1 Find the range of this list of numbers:

| 1 | 3 | 5 | 7 | 9 |

2 **a)** Put these numbers in order, from lowest to highest:

| 4 | 2 | 8 | 6 | 7 |

b) Find the range of the list of numbers.

3 Find the range for each of these lists of numbers:

a) 6, 8, 4, 7

b) 10, 11, 12, 10

c) 8, 9, 3, 7, 5

d) 20, 21, 30, 27, 32

e) 15, 11, 14, 11, 14, 12

f) 4, 0, 2, 4, 1, 2, 3

g) 50, 49, 19, 35, 29, 44, 38

h) 9, 10, 9, 5, 7, 9, 10, 11

4 These are the ages of five players on a team:

27, 19, 23, 26, 28

What is the range of the ages?

5 A darts player records his last six scores:

80, 60, 62, 120, 100, 45

What is the range of scores?

6 These are the daily temperatures for five holiday resorts:

29 °C, 23 °C, 25 °C, 31 °C, 26 °C

What is the range of the temperatures?

7 Find the range for each of these lists of numbers:

a) 0.1, 1.5, 3.2, 5.1

b) 3.5, 1.7, 2.6, 5.8

c) 1.7, 2.4, 1.1, 4.8, 2.2

d) 9.2, 8.9, 1.5, 0.9, 3.8

8 Find the range for each of these lists of numbers:

a) −2, −5, −1, −8

b) −3, −7, −9, −1

c) −5, 0, 2, 3

d) −2, −6, 1, 7

Exercise 5 — Mixed Exercise

1 For the list of numbers shown on the right, find:

a) the range **b)** the median

c) the mode **d)** the mean

0.5 1.2 6 0.5 7 5.3 0.5

2 Katie records the number of text messages she sends each day for six days:

26, 29, 24, 36, 15, 14

a) What is the range of the number of texts she sends?

b) Find the median number of texts she sends per day.

c) Find the mean number of texts she sends per day.

23.2 Frequency Tables

A frequency table shows the number of times things happen — a bit like tally charts.

Example 1

The frequency table shows the number of marks scored in a test by a class of pupils (none of the pupils scored less than 5).

a) How many pupils took the test?

> The frequency column shows the number of pupils who got each mark, so add up all the numbers in the frequency column to find the total.
>
> $3 + 5 + 8 + 8 + 5 + 1 = 30$

Mark	Frequency
5	3
6	5
7	8
8	8
9	5
10	1

b) How many pupils scored less than 8 marks?

> Add up the frequencies of all the pupils who scored 5, 6 or 7 marks. $3 + 5 + 8 = 16$

c) What percentage of pupils scored at least 9 marks?

> 1. Add up the frequencies of all the pupils who scored 9 or 10 marks. $\longrightarrow 5 + 1 = 6$
>
> 2. Write down the fraction of the pupils that scored at least 9. $\longrightarrow$ 6 out of 30 pupils scored at least 9
>
>   So, as a fraction: $\frac{6}{30}$
>
> 3. Find the percentage by dividing the top number by the bottom number and then multiplying by 100. $6 \div 30 = 0.2$
>
> $0.2 \times 100 = 20\%$

Exercise 1

1 Karen did a survey of the pupils in her school year.
She asked them what pets they have at home.

The frequency table on the right shows her results.

a) How many pupils have a rabbit?

b) How many pupils have a fish or a rat?

c) What is the most common pet?

Pet	Frequency
Dog	15
Cat	12
Rabbit	8
Fish	9
Rat	3
Snake	1

2 The frequency table below shows the number of people living in each house on a street.

Number of People	1	2	3	4	5
Frequency	15	22	6	12	14

a) How many houses have 5 people living in them?

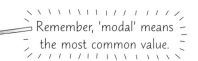
Remember, 'modal' means the most common value.

b) What is the modal number of people living in a house on this street?

c) How many more houses have 4 people living in them than 3 people living in them?

3 Ho Yin is doing a survey about shoe sizes. He asks 40 people their shoe size.
The results are shown in the frequency table below.

Shoe Size	Frequency
3	6
4	8
5	12
6	8
7	6

a) What is the most common shoe size of the people he asked?

b) How many of the people are size 4 or less?

c) How many of the people are size 5 or more?

d) What percentage of the people take size 6?

e) What percentage of the people take size 5 or 6?

Grouped Frequency Tables

Grouped data can also be put in a frequency table.

Grouped frequency tables make it easier to understand large amounts of data, but they don't show the exact data values.

Example 2

A car breakdown service records the number of calls it receives each day over a 2-month period. The results are shown in the frequency table.

Number of Calls	Frequency
0 - 50	3
51 - 100	9
101 - 150	20
151 - 200	15
201 - 250	12

a) On how many days did they get more than 150 calls?

Add together the frequencies for 151 - 200 and 201 - 250.   15 + 12 = 27

b) (i) What is the highest possible number of calls they received in one day?

The last class in the table is 201 - 250, so the highest possible number of calls is 250.

(ii) Explain why you can't know for certain if there was a day that they received this number of calls.

The data is grouped, so you don't know the exact number of calls on those 12 days — it could be anywhere in the range 201 - 250.

Exercise 2

1   The table shows the marks gained by everyone in a year group in an exam.

a) How many students are in the year group?

b) How many pupils scored 30 marks or less?

c) What percentage of pupils scored at least 31 marks?

Mark	Frequency
1 - 10	8
11 - 20	22
21 - 30	33
31 - 40	24
41 - 50	13

2   In a survey, people were asked which age group they belong to. The results are shown in the frequency table.

a) How many people took part in the survey?

b) How many of the people were aged between 21 and 50?

c) What percentage of the people were aged 41 or older?

d) Which age group had the highest number of people?

Age Group	Frequency
20 or under	9
21 - 30	19
31 - 40	24
41 - 50	17
51 or over	11

385

3   The table shows the number of peaches sold in a shop each day over 30 days.

Number of Peaches	0 - 10	11 - 20	21 - 30	31 - 40
Frequency	7	9	6	8

a) (i)   On how many days did the shop sell between 11 and 20 peaches?

(ii) What percentage of days did the shop sell between 11 and 20 peaches?

b) (i)   What is the highest possible number of peaches the shop sold on one day?

(ii) Explain why you can't know for certain if there was a day that the shop sold this number of peaches.

Finding the Mean from Frequency Tables

You can use frequency tables to find the mean of a set of data.

Example 3

Josh draws a frequency table to show the number of pets in each house on his street.

Find the mean number of pets in each house.

Pets	Frequency
0	16
1	16
2	11
3	6
4	1

1. Add an extra row and an extra column to the table.

2. In the extra column, multiply the number of pets by the frequency.

3. In the extra row, add up all the numbers in the Frequency column to find the total number of houses...

4. ...and add up all the numbers in the 'Pets × Frequency' column to find the total number of pets.

Pets	Frequency	Pets × Frequency
0	16	0 × 16 = 0
1	16	1 × 16 = 16
2	11	2 × 11 = 22
3	6	3 × 6 = 18
4	1	4 × 1 = 4
Total	16 + 16 + 11 + 6 + 1 = 50	0 + 16 + 22 + 18 + 4 = 60

5. Divide the total number of pets by the total number of houses to find the mean.

$$\text{Mean} = \frac{\text{Total number of pets}}{\text{Total number of houses}} = 60 \div 50$$

$$= 1.2 \text{ pets}$$

Exercise 3

1 The table shows the number of goals scored in all the matches in a football tournament.

Goals	Frequency	Goals × Frequency
0	4	0 × 4 = 0
1	6	1 × 6 =
2	8	2 × 8 =
3	5	
4	2	
Total		

a) Copy and complete the table.

b) Use the table to find the mean number of goals scored.

2 The table shows the number of cups of tea drunk by the people in an office one morning.

Cups	Frequency
0	8
1	4
2	5
3	8
4	6

a) Copy the table and add a 'Cups × Frequency' column and a 'Total' row.

b) Complete the table by filling in the column and row you've added.

c) Use your table to find the mean number of cups of tea drunk by the people in the office that morning.

3 The table shows the number of squirrels seen by all the families visiting a park one afternoon.

Squirrels	Frequency
1	6
2	8
3	7
4	3
5	2

Use the table to find the mean number of squirrels seen by the families that afternoon.

A two-way table shows frequencies for two things at a time.

Example 1

The two-way table shows the number of boys and girls doing each activity on an adventure weekend.

	Hiking	Sailing	Climbing	Total
Boys	10	20	15	45
Girls	8	27	12	47
Total	18	47	27	92

a) How many girls went hiking?

Find the number that's in the 'Girls' row and the 'Hiking' column.   8 girls

b) How many people went climbing?

You want the <u>total</u> number of people who went climbing, so read   27 people
off the number that's in the 'Total' row and the 'Climbing' column.

c) How many boys were there on the adventure weekend?

You want the <u>total</u> number of boys, so read off the number   45 boys
that's in the 'Boys' row and the 'Total' column.

Exercise 1

1   The two-way table below shows the favourite snacks of all the boys and girls in Year 11.

a) How many boys preferred chocolates?

b) How many girls are there in Year 11?

c) How many pupils preferred nuts in total?

d) How many pupils are in Year 11?

	Chocolate	Crisps	Nuts	Total
Boys	16	26	7	49
Girls	30	10	5	45
Total	46	36	12	94

2   The two-way table on the right shows the colours of all the vehicles in a car park.

a) How many vans are there?

b) How many vehicles are there in total?

c) How many blue bikes are there?

d) How many of the vehicles are red?

	Red	Black	Blue	White	Total
Cars	8	10	4	3	25
Vans	2	2	3	10	17
Bikes	2	1	1	2	6
Total	12	13	8	15	48

Example 2

The table shows how the boys and girls in a class travel to school.

	Walk	Bus	Car	Total
Boys	8	7	4	
Girls		5		
Total	15		7	

a) Complete the table.

The numbers in each row should add up to the number in the 'Total' column, and the numbers in each column should add up to the number in the 'Total' row.

	Walk	Bus	Car	Total
Boys	8	7	4	8 + 7 + 4 = 19
Girls	15 − 8 = 7	5	7 − 4 = 3	7 + 5 + 3 = 15
Total	15	7 + 5 = 12	7	19 + 15 = 34

The numbers in the 'Boys' row add up to give the total number of boys.

Subtract the number of boys who walk from the total number of people who walk to find the number of girls who walk.

You could also find the overall total by working out: 15 + 12 + 7 = 34.

b) What percentage of girls travel to school by car?

1. Look at the 'Girls' row. There are 15 girls altogether, and 3 of them travel by car. Write this as a fraction.

   $\frac{3}{15}$ of girls travel by car.

2. Divide the top number by the bottom number and multiply by 100.

   3 ÷ 15 = 0.2

   0.2 × 100 = 20%

Exercise 2

1   Copy and complete these two-way tables.

a)

	Walk	Bus	Total
Boys	12	6	
Girls	16	3	
Total			

b)

	Walk	Bus	Car	Total
Boys	16		4	28
Girls		4	3	18
Total	27			

389

2 The two-way table shows where all the male and female students on a language course went to study last year.

	Germany	France	Spain	Total
Male	16	7	12	
Female	18	4	16	
Total				

a) Copy the table and fill in the totals.

b) How many female students went to France?

c) How many students went to Spain in total?

d) How many female students in total went to study in Germany, France or Spain?

3 Hal wants to know if there is a link between hair colour and eye colour. He asks a group of people their eye colour and hair colour, and puts his results in a two-way table.

	Black Hair	Brown Hair	Blonde Hair	Red Hair	Total
Brown Eyes	11	17			
Green Eyes		2	1	4	11
Blue Eyes	6		12	2	40
Total	21		14	6	

a) Copy the table and fill in the missing entries.

b) How many of the people had black hair and green eyes?

c) What percentage of people with blue eyes had brown hair?

d) What percentage of all the people had blue eyes **and** blonde hair?

4 A company surveys a group of people to find out their age and whether or not they can drive. The results are put in a grouped two-way table.

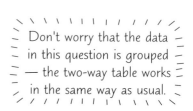

	Can Drive	Can't Drive	Total
17 - 25	24	8	
26 - 45	32	14	
46 - 60	27	5	
61 or over	25	15	
Total			

a) Copy the table and fill in the missing entries.

b) How many people aged 46 or over can't drive?

c) What percentage of the people aged 17 - 25 can drive?

d) What percentage of all the people surveyed can't drive?

> Don't worry that the data in this question is grouped — the two-way table works in the same way as usual.

Frequencies can also be shown using bar charts.
The height of each bar shows the frequency for that group.

Example 1

Nasir asked all the members of his class
to name their favourite animal.
The bar chart shows the results.

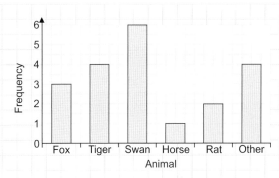

a) What was the most popular animal?

The animal with the tallest bar
in the bar chart is 'Swan'.

b) How many people are in Nasir's class?

Add together the frequencies for each animal.   3 + 4 + 6 + 1 + 2 + 4 = 20 people

c) What percentage of people said that rats were their favourite animal?

1. Look at the 'Rat' bar. 2 people out of the
   total of 20 said 'rat'. Write this as a fraction.

   $\frac{2}{20}$ of people said 'rat'

2. Divide the top number by the bottom number
   and multiply by 100.

   2 ÷ 20 = 0.1

   0.1 × 100 = 10%

Exercise 1

1   Eve asked all the members of her book group to name their favourite type of music.
    The results are shown in the bar chart below.

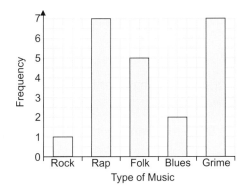

a) Which two types of music were most popular?

b) How many people like rock music the most?

c) How many more people preferred folk than blues?

d) How many people are in Eve's book group?

2 Sean counted the numbers of the different types of flower in his garden. The results are shown in the bar chart.

a) What is the modal type of flower?

b) How many lilies are in his garden?

c) How many more violas are there than roses?

d) What percentage of the flowers are violas?

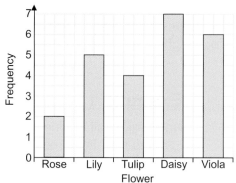

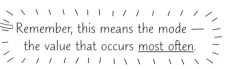

Remember, this means the mode — the value that occurs <u>most often</u>.

Example 2

Paddy asks a group of people to name their favourite shape of pasta. He puts the results in a frequency table.

Draw a bar chart to show the data.

Pasta Shape	Frequency
Penne	6
Spaghetti	5
Tagliatelle	4
Fusilli	2
Rigatoni	1

1. Draw a chart with frequency on the vertical axis and the thing being investigated on the horizontal axis.

2. Use the values from the frequency column in the table to draw bars of equal width with the correct height.

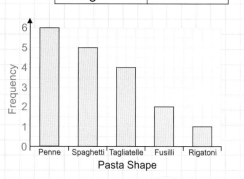

Exercise 2

1 Liz does a survey to find out how many pairs of trainers each of her friends owns. She puts the results in a frequency table, as shown.

Copy the bar chart below and use the frequency table to complete it.

Trainers	Frequency
0	2
1	4
2	5
3	3
4	1

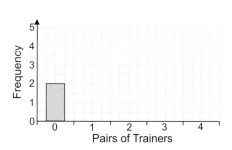

2 Jerry does a survey into where his classmates went on holiday last year.

He puts the results into the frequency table shown below.

Copy the bar chart below and use the frequency table to complete it.

Place	Frequency
Cumbria	5
Devon	2
Blackpool	7
The Wirral	1
Rest of World	3

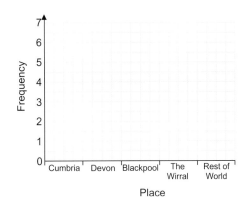

3 The frequency table shows the results of a survey into people's favourite fashion accessory.

Accessory	Frequency
Hat	8
Scarf	2
Bag	7
Bracelet	5
Necklace	4

Use the table to draw a bar chart showing the data.

4 The frequency table shows the numbers of different coloured shirts on display in a clothes shop.

Colour	Frequency
White	3
Blue	4
Pink	5
Lilac	2
Tangerine	1

Use the table to draw a bar chart showing the data.

Dual Bar Charts

A dual bar chart shows frequencies for two sets of data, so you can compare them.

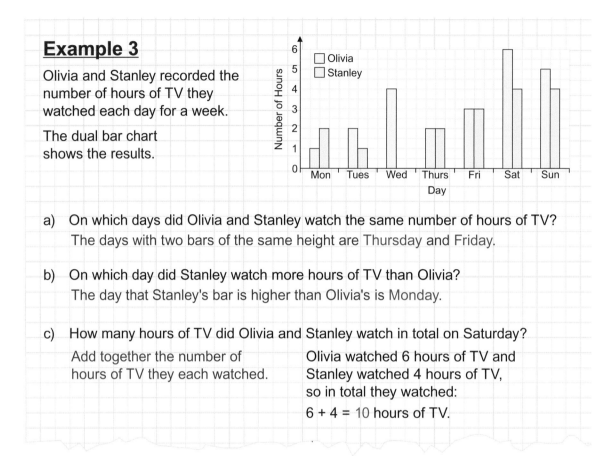

Example 3

Olivia and Stanley recorded the number of hours of TV they watched each day for a week.

The dual bar chart shows the results.

a) On which days did Olivia and Stanley watch the same number of hours of TV?
   The days with two bars of the same height are Thursday and Friday.

b) On which day did Stanley watch more hours of TV than Olivia?
   The day that Stanley's bar is higher than Olivia's is Monday.

c) How many hours of TV did Olivia and Stanley watch in total on Saturday?

   Add together the number of hours of TV they each watched.

   Olivia watched 6 hours of TV and Stanley watched 4 hours of TV, so in total they watched:
   6 + 4 = 10 hours of TV.

Exercise 3

1   The dual bar chart shows the number of fish caught by Drake and Jay on each day of a fishing trip.

   a) Who caught more fish on Sunday?

   b) How many fish did Drake catch on Friday?

   c) How many more fish did Jay catch than Drake on Saturday?

   d) Who caught more fish in total over the whole of the trip?

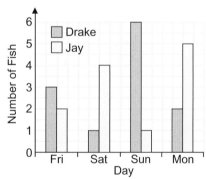

2 A teacher asks the boys and girls in his class to name their favourite season. The results are shown in the dual bar chart.

a) Which was the most popular season with the girls?

b) How many boys chose winter?

c) How many pupils chose spring?

d) Which was the least popular season overall?

e) How many pupils are in the class?

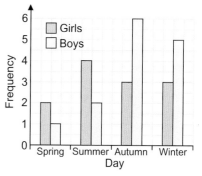

23.5 Pictograms

Pictograms show frequency using symbols or pictures instead of numbers or bars.

They always have a key to tell you what each symbol represents.

Example 1

The pictogram shows the number of pretzels eaten by a family over Christmas.

Christmas Eve	🥨 🥨 🥨 🥨
Christmas Day	🥨 🥨 🥨 🥨 🥨 🥨
Boxing Day	🥨 🥨 🥨

Key: 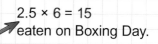 = 6 pretzels

a) How many pretzels did they eat on Christmas Eve?

 1. There are 4 symbols in the row for Christmas Eve.

 2. The key shows that each symbol represents 6 pretzels, so use this to find how many they ate.

   $4 \times 6 = 24$
   eaten on Christmas Eve.

b) What fraction of all the pretzels did they eat on Boxing Day?

 1. There are 2.5 symbols in the row for Boxing Day (🥨 is half of a symbol) and 12.5 symbols in total.

   $2.5 \times 6 = 15$
   eaten on Boxing Day.

 2. Use the key to work out how many pretzels these two numbers represent.

   $12.5 \times 6 = 75$
   eaten in total.

 3. Then write out the fraction and simplify.

   Fraction of pretzels eaten on Boxing Day $= \dfrac{15}{75} = \dfrac{1}{5}$

Exercise 1

1 The pictogram shows the number of cups of tea Didier drinks over a three-month period.

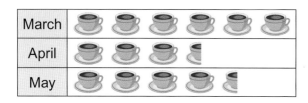

Key: = 8 cups

a) How many cups did he drink in April?

b) How many more cups did he drink in March than in May?

c) How many cups did he drink in total?

2 The local library asks a group of people how many books they have read in the last year. The results are shown in the pictogram.

Key: = 10 people

a) How many of the people read 2 books?

b) How many read 2 books or fewer?

c) How many read 4 books or more?

d) What fraction of the people asked read 2 books?

3 The pictogram on the right shows the number of hats of different colours Frank owns.

a) What is the modal hat colour?

b) How many hats does Frank own in total?

c) How many red or blue hats does he own?

d) What percentage of his hats are black?

Key: = 2 hats

4 The pictogram shows the number of letters delivered to each of the 6 houses in a street one week.

Number 1	▷
Number 2	⊠ ⤡
Number 3	⊠ ⊠ ⊠
Number 4	⊠ ⊠ ▷
Number 5	⊠
Number 6	▷

Key: | ⊠ = 4 letters |

a) How many letters were delivered to Number 4?

b) Which two houses received fewest letters during the week?

c) How many letters were delivered to the even-numbered houses?

d) How many letters in total were delivered to the 6 houses?

5 This pictogram shows the number of packets of sweets a shop sold on Saturday and Sunday.

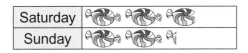

Key: 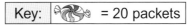 = 20 packets

Give **one** criticism of the pictogram.

Example 2

Guy asked a group of people to name their favourite meat.

  12 said beef, 8 said lamb, 4 said pork and 10 said goat.

Draw a pictogram to show this information. Use the key: 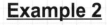 = 4 people.

1. Each symbol represents 4 people, so divide the frequency for each meat by 4 to find the number of symbols needed for that meat:

 Beef: 12 ÷ 4 = 3 symbols
 Lamb: 8 ÷ 4 = 2 symbols
 Pork: 4 ÷ 4 = 1 symbols
 Goat: 10 ÷ 4 = 2.5 symbols

Beef	🍖 🍖 🍖
Lamb	🍖 🍖
Pork	🍖
Goat	🍖 🍖 ◖

Key: 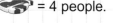 = 4 people

2. The pictogram should have a row for each meat and it must have a key.

3. Fill in the pictogram with the correct number of symbols for each meat.

Exercise 2

1 Cheryl asks a group of people to name their hobbies.
5 people said swimming, 10 people said fishing and 20 people said reading.

Copy and complete the pictogram to show this information.

Swimming	☺
Fishing	
Reading	

Key: ☺ = 5 people

2 The members of a basketball club were asked what they would like to do on a trip.
6 people said bowling, 24 people said cinema, 18 people said sailing
and 3 people said theme park.

Copy and complete the pictogram to show this information.

Bowling	🧍
Cinema	
Sailing	
Theme Park	

Key: 🧍 = 6 people

3 The frequency table shows the number of apples
sold by a grocer over four market days.

Draw a pictogram to show this information.

Represent 10 apples using the symbol:

Day	Apples
Thursday	35
Friday	50
Saturday	55
Sunday	40

4 The frequency table shows the number of letters
that were delivered to Jo's house each day one week.

a) Explain why ✉ = 3 letters would not be a suitable
key for drawing a pictogram to show this information.

b) Suggest a more suitable key.

c) Draw a pictogram to show the information
in the frequency table, using your key from **b)**.

Day	Letters
Monday	2
Tuesday	4
Wednesday	0
Thursday	6
Friday	1
Saturday	8
Sunday	0

Stem and leaf diagrams are a way of grouping and showing data.
A stem and leaf diagram always needs a key to show how to read it.

Example 1

The stem and leaf diagram shows the
number of seconds it took people to
open a jar.

```
1 | 6  8  8
2 | 0  2  4  7
3 | 1  3  9
4 | 4
```

Key:
1 | 6 means 16 seconds

a) How many people took more than 30 seconds?
1. Start by using the key to write the data as a list: 16   18   18
    The numbers to the left of the line (the 'stem')   20   22   24   27
    are the tens, and the numbers to the right ⟶   31   33   39
    (the 'leaves') are the units.   44

2. The numbers over 30 are 31, 33, 39 and 44. ⟶ So 4 people took
                                                    more than 30 seconds

b) What was the median time taken?
1. Use the list of numbers from part a).
    They are already in order, so find the middle value.
2. There are 11 numbers,
    so the median is the sixth number. ⟶ The median time is 24 seconds

c) What was the range of times?
    Subtract the smallest number from the largest number. ⟶ 44 – 16 = 28 seconds

Exercise 1

1   Write out the data from each of these stem and leaf diagrams as a list.

a)
```
5 | 1  8
6 | 3  5  7
7 | 1  3
```
Key:
5 | 1 means 51

b)
```
21 | 1  2  3  5
22 | 2  4  4
23 | 1  9
```
Key:
21 | 1 means 211

2 This stem and leaf diagram shows the ages of all the people in a library.

```
1 | 3 5
2 | 0 1 6
3 | 2 4 8
4 | 1
```

Key:
1 | 3 means 13

a) Use the diagram to make a list of the ages shown.

b) How many of the people are aged over 30?

c) How many people are in the library in total?

d) What is the age of the youngest person in the library?

3 This stem and leaf diagram shows the scores of all the teams in a quiz.

```
2 | 2
3 | 1 2 9
4 | 4 5
5 | 0 2 7
```

Key:
2 | 2 means 22

a) Use the diagram to make a list of the scores.

b) How many teams scored less than 40?

c) What was the highest score?

d) What was the range of scores?

4 The stem and leaf diagram shows the heights, in cm, of all the plants in Ken's garden.

```
1 | 2
2 | 1 4
3 | 0 7 8
4 | 8 8
5 | 3 5 6
```

Key:
1 | 2 means 12 cm

a) Use the diagram to make a list of the heights.

b) How many plants are in Ken's garden in total?

c) What is the range of heights?

d) What is the median height?

e) What is the modal height?

5 Only some of the values from the
list of data below have been added
to this stem and leaf diagram.

```
3 | 1
4 | 0  4
5 | 1  3  4
6 | 0
7 | 1
```

Key: 3 | 1 means 31

Copy and complete the stem and leaf diagram by adding the rest of the data from the box.
Use the key to help.

3̶1̶	4̶0̶	4̶4̶	5̶3̶
5̶1̶	5̶4̶	6̶0̶	7̶1̶
34	49	59	57
61	57	77	44

First, work out how to split each number
into a 'stem' and a 'leaf' and then add
them to your copy of the diagram.

23.7   Pie Charts

To work out frequencies from a pie chart, you need to know the sizes of the angles.

Example 1

A teacher carries out a survey to find out how 600 pupils
travel to school. The pie chart shows the results.

a) What is the most popular way of travelling to school?

The most popular way of travelling to school is
the one with the biggest area on the pie chart.   By bus.

b) What fraction of pupils walk to school?

  1. Find the angle that represents walking to school. → The angle for
      'Walk' is 120°

  2. Write a fraction with this angle as
      the top and 360° as the bottom,
      then simplify.   Fraction of pupils who walk = $\frac{120°}{360°} = \frac{1}{3}$

c) How many pupils travel to school by car?

  1. Find the fraction who travel by → Fraction who travel by car = $\frac{90°}{360°} = \frac{1}{4}$
      car using the angle, as before.

  2. Then multiply this fraction by $\frac{1}{4} \times 600 = (1 \times 600) ÷ 4 = 150$
      the total number of pupils.

      So 150 pupils travel by car.

Exercise 1

1 The pie chart on the right shows the results of a "Vote for your favourite pet" survey.

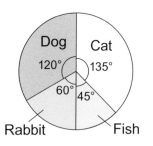

    a) What is the most popular pet?

    b) Which are more popular, fish or rabbits?

    c) What fraction of the votes were for Dog?

2 The pie chart on the right shows the proportions of people at a bus stop with different coloured hair.

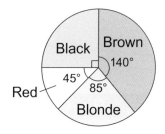

    a) What is the most common hair colour?

    b) Which hair colour is twice as common as red hair?

    c) What fraction of the people have black hair?

    d) Can you tell from the pie chart how many people at the bus stop have blonde hair? Explain your answer.

3 Jennifer asks 300 pupils in her school about their favourite pizza toppings. The pie chart on the right shows the results.

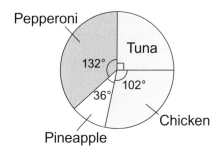

    a) Which was the most popular pizza topping?

    b) What fraction of the pupils said pineapple was their favourite pizza topping?

    c) How many pupils said pineapple was their favourite?

4 Moesha asks 280 musicians what instrument they play. The results are shown in the pie chart on the right.

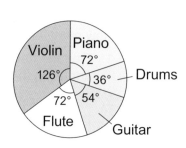

    a) What fraction of the musicians play the violin?

    b) How many of the musicians play the violin?

    c) How many of them play the flute?

5 Stan asks 200 people to name their favourite fruit.
The results are shown in the pie chart.

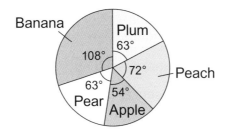

a) What fraction of people chose bananas **or** peaches as their favourite?

b) How many people chose bananas **or** peaches as their favourite?

c) How many people chose a fruit other than pear as their favourite?

Example 2

Jack asks everyone in his class their favourite colour.
The frequency table shows the results.
Draw a pie chart to show this data.

Colour	Red	Green	Blue	Pink
Frequency	12	7	5	6

1. Calculate the total frequency — this is
   the number of people in Jack's class. → Total Frequency = 12 + 7 + 5 + 6 = 30

2. Divide 360° by the total frequency
   to find the number of degrees
   needed for each person. → Each person represented by:
   $360° \div 30 = 12°$

3. Multiply each frequency by the number of degrees for each person.
   This tells you the angle you'll need in the pie chart for each colour.

Colour	Red	Green	Blue	Pink
Frequency	12	7	5	6
Angle	12 × 12° = 144°	7 × 12° = 84°	5 × 12° = 60°	6 × 12° = 72°

4. Draw the pie chart.
   The sizes of the sectors are the
   angles you've just worked out.

   Draw a start line and measure the 144° angle from this line...

   ...and so on until you get back to the start line.

   ...then measure the 84° angle from this line...

Pink 72°, 144° Red, 60° Blue, 84° Green

Exercise 2

1 Albert recorded the colours of all the cars that passed his school during one lunchtime.

The results are shown in the frequency table.

Colour	Frequency
Black	25
Silver	17
Red	8
Other	10

a) Find the total number of cars that passed his school.

b) Find how many degrees represent each car.

c) Copy and complete the table below to find the angle for each colour.

Colour	Frequency	Angle
Black	25	25 × ...... = 150°
Silver	17	17 × ...... = ...
Red	8	
Other	10	

These angles should add up to 360°.

d) Copy and complete the pie chart to show this data.

150°
Black

2 Becky asked her friends which football team they support. Their answers are shown in the table.

Team	Frequency
Wirral Whites	12
Kendal Town	9
Millom Reds	7
Fleetwood Town	17

a) Find the total number of people she asked.

b) Find how many degrees represent each person.

c) Calculate the angle for each team.

d) Draw a pie chart showing her results.

3 Clive carried out a survey to find out how many siblings (brothers and sisters) the pupils in his year group had.

He recorded his data in the table on the right.

a) Find the total frequency.

b) Calculate the angle for each number of siblings.

c) Draw a pie chart showing the data.

Siblings	Frequency
0	24
1	67
2	19
3 or more	10

4 Mina recorded the favourite flavours of crisps of pupils at her school. The table shows the results.

Draw a pie chart showing the data.

Flavour	Frequency
Ready Salted	22
Salt and Vinegar	31
Cheese and Onion	19
Prawn Cocktail	18

23.8 Line Graphs

Line graphs are useful for showing how something (e.g. temperature) changes over time.

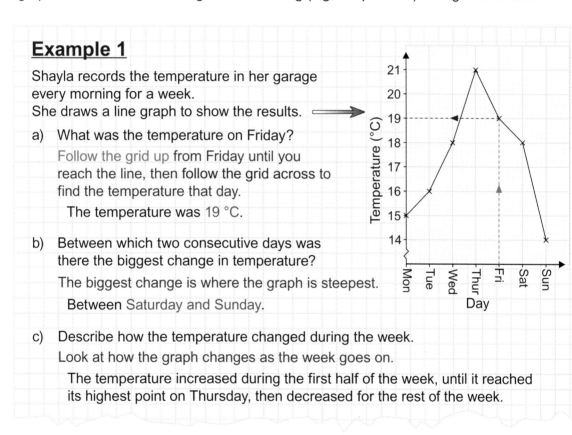

Example 1

Shayla records the temperature in her garage every morning for a week.
She draws a line graph to show the results.

a) What was the temperature on Friday?

Follow the grid up from Friday until you reach the line, then follow the grid across to find the temperature that day.

The temperature was 19 °C.

b) Between which two consecutive days was there the biggest change in temperature?

The biggest change is where the graph is steepest.

Between Saturday and Sunday.

c) Describe how the temperature changed during the week.

Look at how the graph changes as the week goes on.

The temperature increased during the first half of the week, until it reached its highest point on Thursday, then decreased for the rest of the week.

Exercise 1

1 The line graph shows the height, in mm, of a chilli plant for the first four weeks after it was planted.

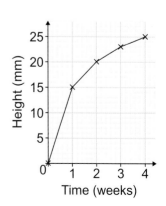

a) What was the height of the plant after 4 weeks?

b) How long did it take to reach 20 mm in height?

c) How much did its height increase between weeks 1 and 2?

d) Between which weeks did its height increase the fastest?

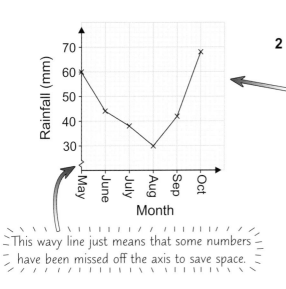

This wavy line just means that some numbers have been missed off the axis to save space.

2 Alesha measures the monthly rainfall, in mm, in her village over a six-month period.

The line graph shows the data she collects.

a) What was the rainfall in June?

b) What was the difference in rainfall between May and July?

c) Which was the wettest month?

d) What was the rainfall in the driest month?

❸ The line graph shows how the value of a car changed over time.

a) What was the value of the car when it was new?

b) How much value did the car lose during the first year?

c) How long did it take the car to fall to £3400 in value?

d) Estimate how long it took the car to halve in value.

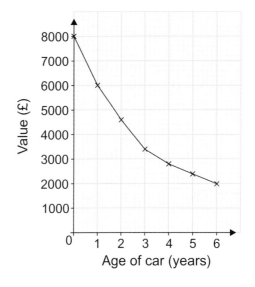

❹ The line graph shows the average number of cups of coffee ordered in a cafe per day in various months.

a) Describe how the number of cups of coffee ordered changes throughout the year.

b) Suggest a reason for this.

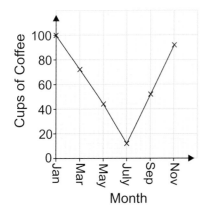

Example 2

Alec measures the temperature of a hot drink every minute for 5 minutes after it has been made. He records the data in the table shown.

Draw a line graph to show this data.

Time (minutes)	0	1	2	3	4	5
Temperature (°C)	88	74	68	62	58	56

1. Draw a grid with Time on the horizontal axis and Temperature on the vertical axis.

2. Plot the values from the table in the same way that you would plot x- and y-coordinates. (You've got Time in place of x values and Temperature in place of y values.)

3. Join up the points with straight lines.

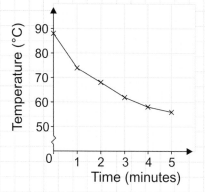

Exercise 2

1 Cassie weighs her pet hamster every month for 6 months. She records the data in the table shown.

Month	Jan	Feb	Mar	Apr	May	Jun
Weight (g)	120	132	140	146	150	154

a) Copy the grid shown below and plot the points from the table.

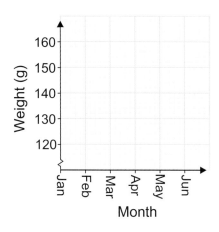

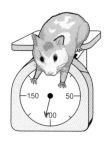

b) Join up the points to draw a line graph to represent the data.

2 The table shows the number of pupils studying history in a school each year for 6 years.

Year	2000	2001	2002	2003	2004	2005
Number	150	142	155	148	152	156

a) Copy the grid shown below and plot the points from the table.

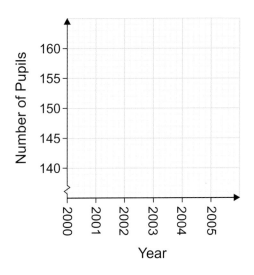

b) Join up the points to draw a line graph to represent the data.

3 The table shows the number of games won by a basketball team during each season from 1993 to 1999.

Season	1993/4	1994/5	1995/6	1996/7	1997/8	1998/9
Wins	50	58	64	72	46	42

a) Draw a grid with 'Seasons' ranging from 1993/4 to 1998/9 on the horizontal axis and 'Wins' ranging from 40 to 80 on the vertical axis.

b) Plot the points from the table on your grid.

c) Join up the points to draw a line graph to represent the data.

23.9 Scatter Graphs and Correlation

Correlation

You can use scatter graphs to show whether two things are related to each other.

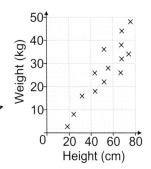

For example, this scatter graph shows some dog's heights and weights. Each point represents one dog. You can see that the taller dogs generally weigh more.

If the points on a scatter graph lie close to a straight line, the data shows correlation — the two things are related.

- A positive correlation means that as one thing increases the other thing increases too.

- A negative correlation means that as one thing increases, the other thing decreases.

If the points are all spread out, the data has no correlation — the two things aren't related.

Example 1

Does each scatter graph below show positive, negative or no correlation?

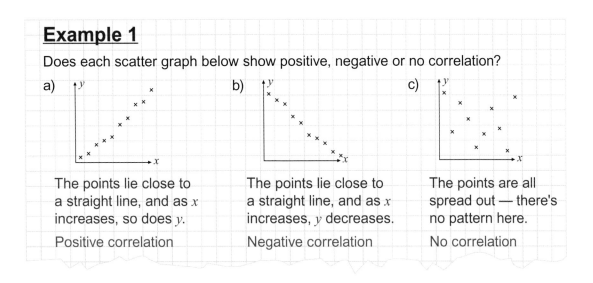

a)

The points lie close to a straight line, and as x increases, so does y.

Positive correlation

b)

The points lie close to a straight line, and as x increases, y decreases.

Negative correlation

c)

The points are all spread out — there's no pattern here.

No correlation

Exercise 1

1 Does each scatter graph below show positive, negative or no correlation?

a)

b)
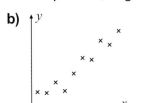

c)
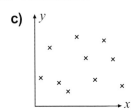

2 Are the following pairs of things likely to show positive, negative or no correlation? Explain your answers.

a) Daily rainfall and sales of umbrellas.

b) Outside temperature and sales of scarves.

c) Outside temperature and sales of bread.

d) Age of a child and his or her height.

e) Speed limit in a street and the average speed of cars as they drive down that street.

Drawing Scatter Graphs

<u>Example 2</u>

Jeremy wants to know if there is a link between a person's height and their shoe size. He measures the height and shoe size of 8 people, and records the results in the table shown.

Height (cm)	165	159	173	186	176	172	181	169
Shoe Size	6	5	8	10	8	7	9	6

Draw a scatter graph to represent the data.

1. Draw a grid with Height on the horizontal axis and Shoe Size on the vertical axis.

2. Plot the values from the table just like you would plot x- and y-coordinates.

3. Don't join up the points on a scatter graph.

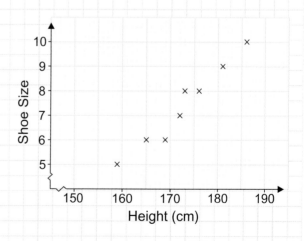

Exercise 2

1 An ice-cream van records the temperature and the number of ice creams sold
over a period of 7 days. The results are shown in the table.

Temperature (°C)	28	25	26	21	23	27	24
Ice Creams Sold	10	6	8	5	6	9	6

Copy the grid shown and plot the points from the table.
The first point has been plotted for you.

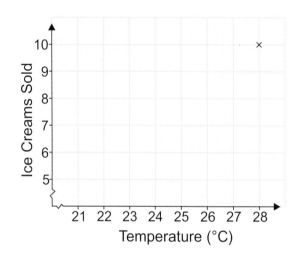

2 A group of youngsters were asked how many baby teeth they still had.
The results are shown in the table.

Age (years)	5	6	8	7	9	7	10	6
Baby Teeth	20	17	11	15	7	17	5	19

Copy the grid shown and plot the points from the table.

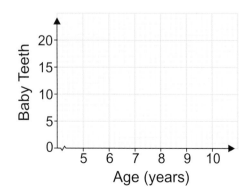

3 The table below shows the number of flags sold in a shop during the 10 days before
the start of a football tournament.

Days Before Tournament	10	9	8	7	6	5	4	3	2	1
Number of Flags Sold	12	13	15	14	15	16	15	18	18	17

a) Copy the grid shown on the right
and plot the points from the table.

b) Does the scatter graph show
positive, negative or no
correlation?

c) Explain in words what this means.

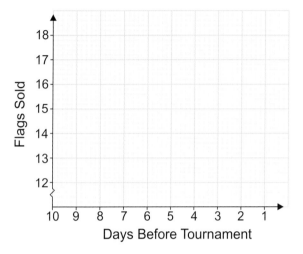

Lines of Best Fit

If a scatter graph shows correlation, then you can draw a line of best fit.
This is a straight line which lies as close as possible to as many points as possible.

Example 3

The scatter graph shows the marks scored by
pupils in a maths test and in a science test.

a) Draw a line of best fit for the data.

Draw a line that lies as close to the
group of points as possible. It doesn't
have to actually touch any of the points.

b) Jimmy scored 34 on his science test, but
missed the maths test. Use the scatter graph
to predict the score he would have achieved.

Follow the grid up from 34 on the 'Science' axis
until you reach the line of best fit, then follow the
grid across to find the mark on the 'Maths' axis.

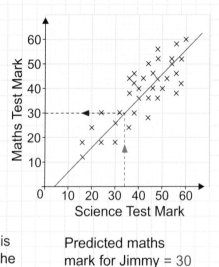

Predicted maths
mark for Jimmy = 30

Exercise 3

1 Could a line of best fit be drawn for each of these graphs?
Explain your answers.

a)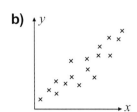

b)

c)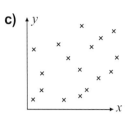

2 Decide if each of the following is a well-drawn line of best fit.
Explain your answers.

a)

b)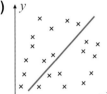

c)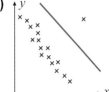

3 A Year 11 class was asked how many hours they spent doing homework and how many
hours they spent watching television last weekend.

The results are shown on the scatter graph. A line of best fit has been drawn.

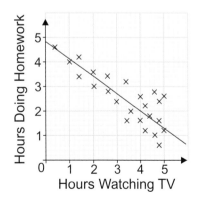

a) Describe the correlation shown by the scatter graph.

b) Josh spent 4 hours watching TV.
Use the line of best fit to estimate how long he spent doing homework.

4 The scatter graph shows the value and age of different cars of the same model.

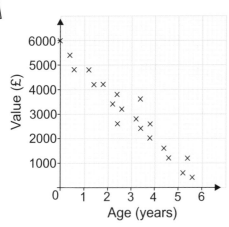

a) Copy the scatter graph and draw a line of best fit.

b) Describe the correlation shown by the graph.

c) Patti has just bought a car for £4000.
   Use your line of best fit to estimate the car's age.

d) Stuart is selling his 5-year-old car.
   Use your line of best fit to estimate the car's value.

5 A vending machine records the number of drinks sold and the temperature on different days.

Temperature (°C)	15	18	25	20	33	28	22
Drinks Sold	3	8	14	9	22	17	11

a) Copy the grid shown and plot the points from the table.

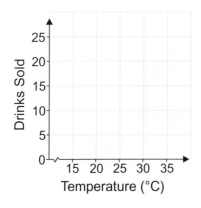

b) Draw a line of best fit for the data.

c) Use your line of best fit to estimate the number of drinks that will be sold when the temperature is 30 °C.

Section 24 — Probability

24.1 Probability — the Basics

Probability is about how likely it is that an event will happen.

The probability of an event happening is somewhere between impossible (definitely won't happen) and certain (definitely will happen).

You can put probabilities on a scale like this:

| Impossible | Unlikely | Even chance | Likely | Certain |

Example 1

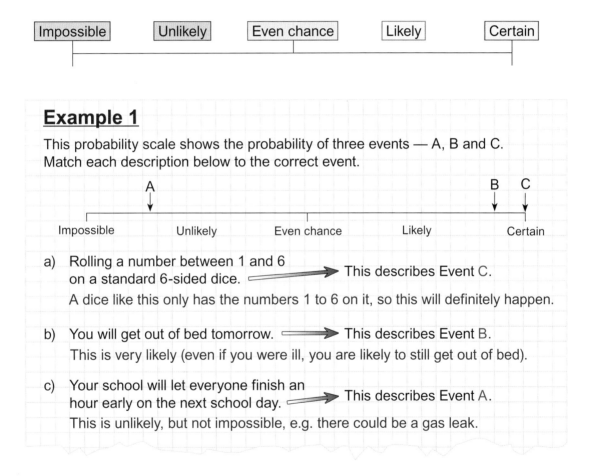

This probability scale shows the probability of three events — A, B and C. Match each description below to the correct event.

a) Rolling a number between 1 and 6 on a standard 6-sided dice. ⟹ This describes Event C.

A dice like this only has the numbers 1 to 6 on it, so this will definitely happen.

b) You will get out of bed tomorrow. ⟹ This describes Event B.

This is very likely (even if you were ill, you are likely to still get out of bed).

c) Your school will let everyone finish an hour early on the next school day. ⟹ This describes Event A.

This is unlikely, but not impossible, e.g. there could be a gas leak.

Exercise 1

1   Put the events below in order from **least to most likely**.

1. You will grow to be 10 metres tall.

2. You will have something to drink today.

3. Someone you know will win the jackpot on a lottery this week.

2 Put the events below in order from **least to most likely**.

1. You toss a fair coin, and it lands showing tails.

2. You roll a fair six-sided dice, and roll a 7.

3. The sun will rise tomorrow morning.

4. It will rain somewhere in the UK this week.

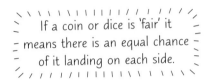
If a coin or dice is 'fair' it means there is an equal chance of it landing on each side.

3 Choose from the words: *impossible*, *unlikely*, *evens*, *likely* and *certain* to describe the probability of each event below.

'Evens' is just another way of saying 'even chance'.

a) Tossing a fair coin once and getting both heads and tails.

b) Tossing a fair coin and getting either heads or tails.

c) Spinning '6' on a spinner labelled 1, 2, 3, 4, 5, 6, 7, 8, 9.

d) Picking a red card from a shuffled pack of playing cards.

e) Rolling an even number on a fair dice.

f) Spinning 2 or more on a spinner labelled 1-4.

4 This probability scale shows the probability of three events — A, B, C and D. Match each description below to the correct event.

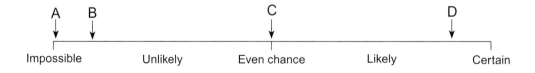

A   B   C   D

Impossible   Unlikely   Even chance   Likely   Certain

a) Everyone in your maths class will be off sick on the next school day.

b) Rolling a fair, six-sided dice and getting an odd number.

c) You have will have something to eat in the next 12 hours.

d) Rabbits will take over the world tomorrow using lasers.

5 Copy this probability scale and add arrows to show the probability of each event described below.

| Impossible | Unlikely | Even chance | Likely | Certain |

a) Rolling a fair, six-sided dice and getting a number larger than 3.

b) You spin purple on a fair spinner with one red section and two purple sections.

c) You will be older on your next birthday than you are now.

d) England will win the next 5 football World Cups.

6 One card is picked at random from eight cards numbered 1 to 8.

Copy this probability scale and add arrows to show the probability of each event described below.

| Impossible | Unlikely | Evens | Likely | Certain |

The number on the card is:

a) less than 9

b) an odd number

c) greater than 2

d) greater than or equal to 7

e) 6 or less

f) zero

7 These eight cards are placed face down on a table and one is picked at random.

P A R A L L E L

Draw a probability scale, labelled from impossible to certain, and add arrows to show the probability of picking each of the letters P, A, R, L and E.

Writing Probabilities as Numbers

All probabilities can be written as a number between 0 and 1.
An event that's impossible has probability 0 and an event that's certain has probability 1.

So, using fractions, the probability scale from before looks like this:

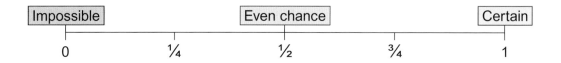

You can also write probabilities as decimals or percentages:
e.g. ½, 0.5 and 50% are all different ways of writing 'even chance'

Example 2

A fair, six-sided dice is rolled. This probability scale shows the probability of four possible events. Match each description below to the correct event.

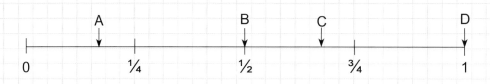

a) An even number is rolled. ⟹ This describes Event B.
    There is an equal chance of getting an even or odd number.

b) A number larger than 2 is rolled. ⟹ This describes Event C.
    Four out of six numbers are larger than 2, so this is fairly likely.

c) A number less than 7 is rolled. ⟹ This describes Event D.
    All the numbers are less than 7 so this is certain.

d) 1 is rolled. ⟹ This describes Event A.
    There's one 1 out of six numbers so this is quite unlikely.

Exercise 2

1   A card is picked at random from a shuffled pack of 52 playing cards.

This probability scale shows the probability of four possible events.
Match each description below to the correct event.

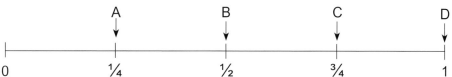

   a) Picking either a red or black card.

   b) Picking a card which is a diamond.

   c) Picking a red card.

   d) Picking a card which isn't a spade.

2   This probability scale shows the probability of four events — A, B, C and D.
Match each description below to the correct event.

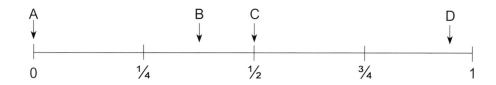

   a) The next baby born will be a girl.

   b) Rolling a six-sided dice and getting a 9.

   c) Getting blue when you roll a fair spinner with 1 blue section and 2 orange sections.

   d) Rolling a fair ten-sided dice and getting a number less than 10.

3   Draw a probability scale from 0 to 1.
Mark on the approximate probability of each event below.

   a) Rolling a fair, four-sided dice and getting a 1, 2, 3 or 4.

   b) Rolling a fair, six-sided dice and getting a 4, 5 or 6.

   c) Selecting a 7 from cards numbered 1 to 10 placed face down on a table.

4 Match each letter on this scale to the correct probability.

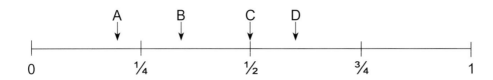

a) 0.5

b) 20%

c) $\frac{1}{3}$

d) 0.6

Remember — probabilities can be written as fractions, decimals or percentages.

24.2 Finding Probabilities

Finding Outcomes

The probability of something happening depends on the total number of possible outcomes — that's just the total number of different things that can happen.

For example, when you toss a coin, only two things can happen — landing on heads or landing on tails. So there are two possible outcomes of tossing a coin.

Example 1

A bag contains 2 red beads, 3 blue beads and 1 green bead.
One bead is picked from the bag at random.

a) List all the possible outcomes.

Each bead in the bag could be picked, so write down all the possible results.

The possible outcomes are:
red, red, blue, blue, blue, green

b) Find the total number of possible outcomes.

Just count up the possible outcomes.

There are 6 possible outcomes in total.

There are only three colours of bead, but there are six possible outcomes because there are six beads in total.

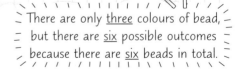

Exercise 1

1   List all the possible outcomes for:

    a) Rolling a fair 6-sided dice.

    b) Spinning the spinner shown on the right.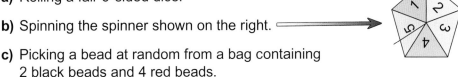

    c) Picking a bead at random from a bag containing
       2 black beads and 4 red beads.

    d) Choosing a person at random from a group of 3 boys and 5 girls.

    e) Picking a tin of soup at random from a box containing
       4 tins of tomato soup, 3 tins of chicken soup
       and 1 tin of mushroom soup.

    f) Spinning the spinner shown on the right.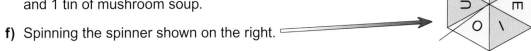

    g) Picking a button at random from a bag containing
       3 green buttons, 5 yellow buttons, 2 orange buttons and 1 red button.

2   Find the **total number** of possible outcomes in each of these situations.

    a) A six-sided dice is rolled.

    b) One day of the week is chosen at random.

    c) A ten-sided dice is rolled.

    d) A fair spinner with 8 sections is spun.

    e) One card is selected from a pack of 52.

Working out Probabilities

You can work out the probability of an event happening using this formula:

$$\text{Probability of event} = \frac{\text{number of ways event can happen}}{\text{total number of possible outcomes}}$$

You can only use this formula if each possible outcome is equally likely to happen
— e.g. throwing a fair dice or picking a ball from a bag containing only balls of the same size.

Example 2

This fair spinner is spun once. Find the probability of getting a 3.

1. Find the total number of possible outcomes. → Possible outcomes are: 1, 3, 5, 7, 8.
   So: Total number of possible outcomes = 5

2. Find the number of ways the event 'getting a 3' can happen. → There's one outcome that's a 3.
   So: Number of ways of getting a 3 = 1

3. Put the numbers into the formula:

   $$\text{Probability of getting a 3} = \frac{\text{number of ways of getting a 3}}{\text{total number of possible outcomes}} = \frac{1}{5}$$

You can use the formula because the spinner is fair — it's equally likely to land on any number.

Example 3

A bag contains 2 red beads, 3 blue beads and 1 green bead all of the same size. One bead is picked out at random. Work out the probability that the bead is red.

1. Find the total number of possible outcomes. → 2 red + 3 blue + 1 green = 6 beads
   So: Total number of possible outcomes = 6

2. Find the number of ways the event 'get red' can happen. → There are two outcomes that are red.
   So: Number of ways of getting red = 2

3. Put the numbers into the formula and simplify:

   $$\text{Probability of getting red} = \frac{\text{number of ways of getting red}}{\text{total number of possible outcomes}} = \frac{2}{6} = \frac{1}{3}$$

Again, you can use the formula because each of the 6 possible outcomes is equally likely — i.e. each bead has an equal chance of being picked.

Exercise 2

1 A fair, six-sided dice is rolled once.

a) Write down all the possible outcomes.

b) What is the total number of possible outcomes?

c) How many ways can the event "rolling a 4" happen?

d) Find the probability of rolling a 4 when a fair six-sided dice is rolled once.

2 The fair spinner shown on the right is spun once.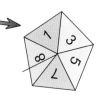

    a) What is the total number of possible outcomes?

    b) How many ways can the event
        "getting a number greater than 6" happen?

    c) Find the probability of getting a number
        greater than 6 when this spinner is spun once.

3 A bead is picked at random from a bag containing 3 black beads and 2 red beads.

    a) Work out the total number of possible outcomes.

    b) How many ways can the event "picking black" happen?

    c) Find the probability that a bead picked at
        random from the bag is black.

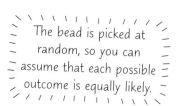

The bead is picked at random, so you can assume that each possible outcome is equally likely.

4 A person is picked at random from a group of 4 boys and 3 girls.

    a) How many ways can the event "picking a girl" happen?

    b) Find the probability that the person picked is a girl.

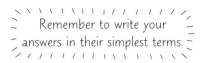

Remember to write your answers in their simplest terms.

5 A fair, six-sided dice is rolled once. For events **a)-c)** below, find:

    (i) how many ways that event can happen

    (ii) the probability of the event happening.

    a) Rolling a 5.

    b) Rolling an even number.

    c) Rolling a number less than 5.

6 A box contains 9 cupcakes. 4 of the cupcakes are lemon-flavoured
and 5 are gravy-flavoured. Find the probability that a cupcake
picked at random from the box will be lemon-flavoured.

7 A button is picked at random from a bag containing 5 blue buttons,
3 red buttons and 2 yellow buttons. Find the probability of picking a blue button.

8 In a car park there are 7 blue cars, 5 red cars, 3 grey cars and 1 green car.
One car is selected at random. Find the probability that the car is:

a) blue

b) green

c) red

9 The first letter from each day of the week is written down.
One letter is picked at random. Find the probability that the letter chosen is:

a) F

b) S

c) P

10 A fair, eight-sided dice is rolled once.
Find the probability that a number greater than 2 is rolled.

11 A standard pack of 52 playing cards is shuffled and one card is selected at random.
Find the probability of selecting:

a) a club   **b)** an ace

c) a red card   **d)** the two of hearts

12 Nine cards numbered 1 to 9 are face down on a table. One card is selected at random.
Find the probability of selecting:

a) card 4   **b)** either card 1 **or** card 2

c) an even number   **d)** a number less than 6

13 A fair spinner has 12 equal sections. 5 are yellow, 3 are green and the rest are purple.
Find the probability that the spinner lands on:

a) green   **b)** purple

c) either yellow **or** green   **d)** any colour except green ←

Find the number of ways
this event can happen.

Probability of an Event not Happening

For any event there are only two possibilities — it either happens or it doesn't happen.

So, the probability of an event happening and the probability of the same event not happening always add up to 1. This means that:

Probability an event doesn't happen = 1 – (Probability the same event *does* happen)

Example 4

The probability of Sam being late for school is 0.4.
Find the probability of him **not** being late for school.

Sam is either late → Probability Sam is not late = 1 – (Probability Sam is late)
or not late, so...
= 1 – 0.4 = 0.6

Exercise 3

1 The probability that it will rain today is 0.3.
What is the probability that it will not rain today?

2 a) The probability that Jill goes to school by bus tomorrow is 0.8.
What is the probability that she does not go by bus?

b) The probability of the bus being late is 0.1.
Find the probability of the bus not being late.

3 The probability that Clara wins a raffle prize is 25%.
Find the probability that she doesn't win a prize.

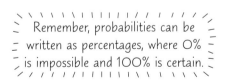

Remember, probabilities can be written as percentages, where 0% is impossible and 100% is certain.

4 The probability that it will snow in a Canadian town on a particular day is $\frac{2}{3}$.
What is the probability that it won't snow on that day?

5 In a class, the probability that a randomly selected pupil is a boy is 0.45 and the probability that the pupil has blonde hair is 0.2.

Find the probability that a randomly selected pupil:

a) is a girl

b) doesn't have blonde hair

6 If the probability that Jed doesn't finish a crossword is 0.74, what's the probability that he **does** finish it?

7 Gary and Phil have worked out that the probability that Gary beats Phil at tennis is 0.57. Find the probability that Phil beats Gary at tennis.

Exercise 4 — Mixed Exercise

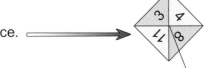

1 The fair spinner shown on the right is spun once.

a) Write down all the possible outcomes.

b) How many ways can the event "getting a number less than 8" happen?

c) Find the probability of spinning the spinner once and getting a number less than 8.

2 A bag contains pear-flavoured sweets and apple-flavoured sweets. The probability of picking a pear-flavoured sweet is 0.6.

What is the probability of picking an apple-flavoured sweet?

3 A pupil is picked randomly from a school register to receive a detention.

The probability that a boy is picked is $\frac{3}{5}$.

What is the probability a girl is picked?

4 A fair eight-sided dice is rolled. Work out the probability that the number rolled is:

a) a number in the 4 times table

b) a number not in the 4 times table

5   A fair 12-sided dice is rolled. Find the probability that the number rolled is:

   a) less than 5   **b)** 5   **c)** not 5

6   Bill and Pete are playing a board game using a fair six-sided dice.

   a) Bill needs to roll a 5 to win. What is the probability he will win on his next go?

   b) Pete needs to roll a 3 to win. What is the probability that he will **not** win on his next go?

7   A cupboard contains:

   > 5 tins of eel soup
   > 3 tins of squirrel soup
   > 2 tins of radish soup

   One tin is picked from the cupboard at random.
   Find the probability that the tin is:

   a) eel   **b)** not eel   **c)** not radish

24.3   Listing Outcomes

In some probability questions two things are happening — for example, tossing a coin and rolling a dice. It's best to start by listing all the possible outcomes.

Example 1

Two coins are flipped. List all the possible outcomes.

1. Draw a table with a separate column for each coin.

2. Write down one of the outcomes of flipping coin 1. Then fill in each possible outcome of flipping coin 2.

3. Now write down the other outcome of flipping coin 1. Again, fill in each possible outcome of flipping coin 2.

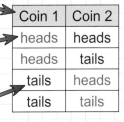

Coin 1	Coin 2
heads	heads
heads	tails
tails	heads
tails	tails

Exercise 1

1 A coin is flipped and a spinner with sections numbered 1-3 is spun.
Copy and complete the table below to list all the possible outcomes.

Coin	Spinner
heads	1
heads	
	3
tails	1
tails	2

2 One card is picked from a standard pack of playing cards and its colour is written down.
At the same time, a four-sided dice is rolled.

Copy and complete this table to list all the possible outcomes:

Card	Red	Red						Black
Dice		2		4				4

3 In Bag 1 there is one toffee and one mint sweet.
In Bag 2 there is one toffee and one sherbet sweet.
One sweet is picked from each bag.

a) Draw a table with separate columns for 'Bag 1' and 'Bag 2'.

b) Fill in your table to list all the possible outcomes of picking one sweet from each bag.

c) Count the number of rows in your table to find the total number of possible outcomes.

4 A coin is tossed and a four-sided dice is rolled.
List all the possible outcomes.

5 Rhys has two bags of beads. In Bag 1 there is one red, one blue and one green bead.
In Bag 2 there is one gold and one silver bead. He chooses one bead from each bag.

a) List all the possible outcomes.

b) What is the total number of possible outcomes?

Example 2

Two coins are flipped at the same time.
Find the probability of getting at least one head.

Coin 1	Coin 2
heads	heads
heads	tails
tails	heads
tails	tails

1. First draw a table to list all the possible outcomes.
   This is the same experiment as in Example 1, so write
   out the list of possible outcomes found there.

2. There are 4 rows in the table and
   'heads' appears in 3 of the rows, so...

   Total number of
   possible outcomes = 4

   Number of ways of getting
   at least one head = 3

3. Work out the probability using the formula:

$$\text{Probability} = \frac{\text{number of ways of getting at least one head}}{\text{total number of possible outcomes}} = \frac{3}{4}$$

Exercise 2

1 The table on the right shows all the possible outcomes
of tossing a fair coin and rolling a fair four-sided dice.

a) What is the total number of possible outcomes?

b) (i) How many ways can the event "Getting a 3" happen?

   (ii) Find the probability of getting a 3.

c) (i) How many ways can the event
      "Getting heads and a 2" happen?

   (ii) Find the probability of getting heads and a 2.

Coin	Dice
heads	1
heads	2
heads	3
heads	4
tails	1
tails	2
tails	3
tails	4

2 A spinner has three equal sections coloured blue, purple and orange.

a) List all the possible outcomes if this spinner is spun twice. ← Your table will need two columns: 'Spin 1' and 'Spin 2'.

b) Find the total number of possible outcomes.

c) How many ways can the event "getting blue at least once" happen?

d) Find the probability of spinning the spinner twice and getting blue at last once.

3 A bag contains two balls — one green and one blue.
One ball is selected at random, then replaced before a second ball is selected at random.

a) List all the possible outcomes.

b) Find the probability that the same colour ball is selected both times.

4 A burger bar offers the meal deal shown here.

Choose 1 burger and 1 drink	
Burgers	**Drinks**
Hamburger	Cola
Cheeseburger	Lemonade
Veggie burger	Coffee

a) List all the different combinations available.

Jana picks one combination at random.

b) What is the probability she chooses a cheeseburger?

c) What is the probability she chooses a veggie burger and cola?

5 The spinner shown opposite is spun twice.

a) List all the possible outcomes.

b) What is the probability of spinning 1 on both spins?

c) What is the probability of getting less than 3 on both spins?

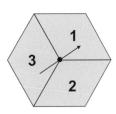

6 A fair coin is tossed three times.

a) List all the possible outcomes.

b) Work out the probability of getting:

   (i) three tails

   (ii) one head and two tails.

Using Two-Way Tables

When there are lots of outcomes, it's much easier to use a two-way table to record them all.

Example 3

Bag 1 contains 2 blue balls and 2 green balls. Bag 2 contains 3 blue balls and 1 green ball. One ball is selected from each bag. Draw a table to show all the possible outcomes.

1. Draw a table with the outcomes from Bag 1 down the side, and from Bag 2 along the top.
2. Fill in each box with the combination of colours selected.

		Bag 2			
		Blue	Blue	Blue	Green
Bag 1	Blue	B, B	B, B	B, B	B, G
	Blue	B, B	B, B	B, B	B, G
	Green	G, B	G, B	G, B	G, G
	Green	G, B	G, B	G, B	G, G

This means that the ball selected from Bag 1 was green (G) and the ball selected from Bag 2 was blue (B).

Example 4

These two spinners are spun and their scores added together.

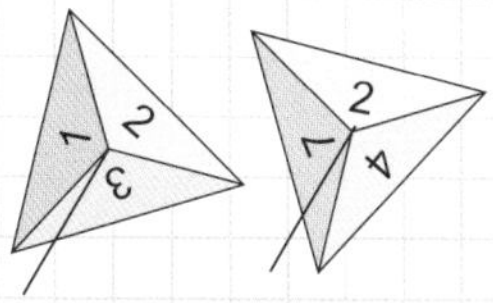

a) Draw a table to show all the possible outcomes.

1. Draw a table with the outcomes of spinning one spinner down the side, and of spinning the other spinner along the top.
2. Fill in each box by adding together the number from the left-hand column and the number from the top row.

	2	4	7
1	3	5	8
2	4	6	9
3	5	7	10

To fill in this box, add together '3' from the left-hand column and '4' from the top row: 3 + 4 = 7.

b) Find the total number of possible outcomes.

Count the number of boxes in the table.

There are 9 possible outcomes in total.

Exercise 3

1 A coin is tossed and a six-sided dice is rolled at the same time. Copy and complete the table below to show all the possible outcomes.

	1	2	3	4	5	6
Head	H1	H2				H6
Tail	T1		T3			T6

2 Bag A contains 2 green beads, 1 yellow bead and 1 blue bead.
Bag B contains 2 yellow beads and 1 blue bead. One bead is picked from each bag.

Copy and complete the table below to show all the possible outcomes.

	Green	Green	Yellow	Blue
Yellow	Y, G			Y, B
Yellow		Y, G		
Blue			B, Y	

3 The spinner shown is spun and, at the same time, a six-sided dice is rolled.
The two scores are added together.

Copy and complete the table to show all the possible outcomes.

	1	2	3	4	5	6
2	3	4				
4	5			8		10
6		8			11	
8						14

4 A spinner with 3 equal sections of red, white and blue is spun twice.

a) Copy and complete the table to show all the possible outcomes.

b) Find the total number of possible outcomes.

	Red	White	Blue
Red			
White			
Blue			

5 The two spinners shown below are spun and the scores are multiplied together.

a) Copy and complete the table on the right to show all the possible outcomes.

b) Find the total number of possible outcomes.

	3	4	5
1			
2			
3			

Example 5

The table shows all the possible outcomes of rolling two fair, four-sided dice and adding the scores.

Find the probability of scoring:

a) 5

b) 3 or less

	1	2	3	4
1	2	3	4	5
2	3	4	5	6
3	4	5	6	7
4	5	6	7	8

a) 1. There are 16 boxes in the table and '5' appears in 4 of the boxes. ⟶ Total number of possible outcomes = 16
Number of ways of getting a '5' = 4

    2. Work out the probability using the formula:

$$\text{Probability} = \frac{\text{number of ways of getting a '5'}}{\text{total number of possible outcomes}} = \frac{4}{16} = \frac{1}{4}$$

b) 1. There are 3 boxes containing a number which is '3 or less'. ⟶ Number of ways of getting '3 or less' = 3

    2. Again, use the formula:

$$\text{Probability} = \frac{\text{number of ways of getting '3 or less'}}{\text{total number of possible outcomes}} = \frac{3}{16}$$

Exercise 4

1 The two fair spinners shown below are spun.

a) Copy and complete the table to show all the possible outcomes.

	B	B	C	D
A	A, B			
A				
B				
C			C, C	

b) Find the total number of possible outcomes.

c) (i) How many ways can the event "getting B on both spinners" happen?

  (ii) Find the probability of getting B on both spinners.

d) (i) How many ways can the event "getting two different letters" happen?

  (ii) Find the probability of getting two different letters.

2 The table below shows the result of rolling two fair, four-sided dice and multiplying the scores together.

	1	2	3	4
1	1	2	3	4
2	2	4	6	8
3	3	6	9	12
4	4	8	12	16

a) Find the total number of possible outcomes.

b) (i) How many ways can the event "getting a number larger than 10" happen?

(ii) Find the probability of getting a number larger than 10.

c) (i) How many ways can the event "getting a 9" happen?

(ii) Find the probability of getting a 9.

3 Two fair, six-sided dice are rolled, and the scores added together.

a) Copy and complete the table to show all the possible totals.

	1	2	3	4	5	6
1						
2						
3						
4						
5						
6						

b) How many possible outcomes are there?

c) Find the probability of getting each of these totals:

    (i) 6   **(ii)** 12   **(iii)** 1

d) Find the probability of getting a total which is:

    (i) less than 8   **(ii)** more than 8   **(iii)** an even number

4 Bag 1 contains 4 balls: 1 blue, 2 green and 1 yellow.
Bag 2 contains 3 balls: 1 blue, 1 green and 1 yellow.
One ball is taken at random from each bag.

	B	G	G	Y
B				
G				
Y				

a) Copy and complete the table on the right
to show all the possible outcomes.

b) Find the probability of selecting:

    (i) 2 blue balls   **(ii)** 2 green balls

    (iii) 2 balls of the same colour   **(iv)** at least 1 yellow ball

5 A fair, six-sided dice is rolled and a fair coin is tossed.

a) Draw a two-way table to show all the possible outcomes.

b) Find the probability of getting:

    (i) a 3 and a head   **(ii)** a number 5 or greater and a tail

    (iii) an even number and a head

6 In a game, the two fair spinners shown on the right
are spun and the scores are added together.

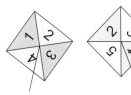

a) Draw a two-way table to show all the possible outcomes.

b) Find the probability that the total score is:

    (i) 4   **(ii)** an odd number

    (iii) a number more than 7

7 Tom rolls a fair six-sided dice and spins a spinner
with four equal sections labelled A, B, C and D.

a) Draw a two-way table to show all the possible outcomes.

b) Find the probability that Tom gets:

    (i) 6 and A   **(ii)** C and 5

    (iii) B and a number less than 3   **(iv)** an odd number and B

    (v) C and an even number   **(vi)** A or B and a number more than 4

Index

R

radius of a circle 316-317
range 381-382
ratios 107-117
  dividing in a given 118-119
  meaning of 107-108
  simplifying 109-110
  using 114-116
  writing in the form $1:n$ 112
real-life graphs 212-215
  drawing 214-215
  interpreting 212-213
reciprocals 95
rectangles 237
  area 307
  perimeter 306
reflections 338-342
reflex angles 217
rhombuses 238
right-angled triangles 229
right angles 217
roots
  cube 51
  square 50-51
rotational symmetry 248-249
rotations 344-347
rounding 36-43
  decimal places 40-41
  to estimate a calculation 42-43
  whole numbers 36-38

S

sampling 373-374
scale drawings 295-298
scale factors 353
scalene triangles 229
scales 253
  reading 253-255
  with units 295-296
  without units 298-300
scatter graphs 409-412
  correlation 409-410
  lines of best fit 412-413

secondary data 362-363
seconds 267-268
semicircles 321
sequences 191-197
  explaining the rule 191-192
  finding terms 193-194
similarity 360-361
simplifying
  expressions 151-152
  fractions 78-80
  ratios 109-110
solving
  equations 161-166
    in two steps 164
    with x on both sides 166-167
  inequalities 173-175
speed 274-275
  from a distance-time graph 281
square (of a number) 48
square roots 50-51
squares 237
  area 307
  perimeter 306
stem and leaf diagrams 399-400
straight line graphs 204-209
  horizontal lines 204
  plotting 204-209
  vertical lines 204-206
substituting into a formula 184-187
subtraction
  decimals 28-29
  fractions 85-89
  negative numbers 1-3
  whole numbers 11-12
supplementary angles 228
symmetry 246-249
  line 246-247
  rotational 248-249

T

tally charts 365-367
  for grouped data 367-368
term-to-term rules
    see sequences
tessellation 245